Around & About Herefordshire and the southern Welsh Marches

Around & About Herefordshire

and the southern Welsh Marches

by

Graham Roberts

Logaston Press

LOGASTON PRESS
Little Logaston, Logaston,
Woonton, Almeley, Herefordshire HR3 6QH

First published by Logaston Press 2004
This revised edition published by Logaston Press 2010
Copyright © Graham Roberts 2010

ISBN 978 1 904396 13 0

Set in Times and Gill Sans Serif by Logaston Press
and printed in Malta by
Gutenberg Press

*This book is dedicated to the memory of Frank Noble MBE (1926-1980),
Yorkshireman, historical geographer, teacher and WEA Tutor Organiser,
who spent many years walking throughout the Marches,
also exhaustively exploring and surveying Offa's Dyke.
Frank was the main inspiration for the National Long-distance Footpath,
opened by Lord Hunt in his home town of Knighton in July 1971.
He wrote* Offa's Dyke Path, *published by Shell in 1969, presented many papers and was
an unforgettable lecturer and speaker arising from his varied local studies.
An energetic member of the Woolhope Club, he was president in 1964*

Contents

Preface and Acknowledgements

Few places in Great Britain can match the diversity of land-form, historic association, vernacular building and scenic appeal of the once hotly disputed borderland of England and Wales which is watered by the Severn, Wye and Usk rivers and their tributaries. Any journey southwards through the geological ages commencing from the south Shropshire plains must take the rhyolitic hump of The Wrekin, the oldest known volcano and mountain in England, as the essential starting point. It serves as an introduction to ancient hill ranges some of which were formed between 650 and 1,000 million years ago in the Precambrian era. Volcanic lavas and ashes also make up the Stretton Hills which tower above the A49 opposite the flat smooth summit of the Long Mynd, of a comparable age, and close to the exposed quartzite crags of the Stiperstones further to the west. Between Much Wenlock and Craven Arms, the origins of the famous wooded escarpment of Wenlock Edge are totally different, for it developed as a tropical coral reef when the sea covered the area. Its Silurian limestone has profited quarry owners and builders for many centuries and it has become a paradise for fossil hunters, forming a rare calcareous habitat for a great range of flora and fauna. Just to the east there is a limestone ridge of quite a different origin and then in the ploughed fields signs of the red stone which underlies much of the central and southern Marches. Neighbouring Herefordshire has indeed been styled the county of the Old Red Sandstone, for it accounts for about 90% of the land surface. The Clee Hills show prominently to the east of Ludlow as two distinctive, flat-topped heights, where the sandstone is capped by coal measures and fine-grained igneous rock. To the south, the Herefordshire plain, with boundaries running clockwise from the Shropshire border to the Malvern Hills, the Forest of Dean and the Welsh mountains, hills and moorlands, offers a gentler landscape which exhibits the effects of glacial processes. From $c.70,000$ BC the last ice front ran broadly along the line from Abergavenny, Hereford, Wenlock Edge to Bridgnorth and overspread the valleys of the Wye, Lugg and Arrow to a depth of more than 600 feet before its approach to the Worcestershire border and the distinctive steep slopes of the Precambrian Malvern Hills. To the west, heights such as the Black Mountains, Long Mynd and Caer Caradoc protruded, although not the summit of Merbach Hill, at 1,045 feet above sea level, and other scattered hilltops. Retreat of the ice began in $c.10,000$ BC, and erosion of the subsequently exposed rocks led to the deposition of boulder clay, gravel and sand in the valleys.

By about 8300 BC the land was free of ice and for at least another five millennia the temperature steadily rose through what might now be termed 'global warming', reaching as much as 5° Fahrenheit above current levels. Slowly over the centuries the desolate landscape became receptive to soil-rooted plants, dwarf shrubs appeared and then came the first trees such as birch and willow. Scientific study of recovered pollens has indicated a gradual spread of hazel, pine and oak forest and it is thought that by 5500 BC much of the land below the main peaks was largely covered by oak and elm forest. So it remained for many more centuries and in course of time they were to become part of the natural raw material which has created the landscape of the region in its use for timbered buildings, fences and other structures. It has also been a source of charcoal for industrial purposes and as fuel for heating and cooking. The better quality sandstones and limestones have been used as masonry and roofing to construct churches, castles, houses and other buildings and they have also been crushed as aggregate, as well as sand and gravel, for mortar or concrete using the copious local supplies of water. Lime, sometimes in conjunction with coal, has further been used in industrial processes, as well as for agricultural and many domestic purposes. Clays have been converted into bricks, tiles, pipes and other building materials and often fired close to major projects such as the long Ledbury rail viaduct. Just to the west of Hereford, in the villages of Tyberton, Madley and Moccas, a more unusual application has produced a rare brick-built church immediately adjacent to one built of sandstone and another of post-glacial calcareous tufa, also obtained from the region, All are served by a main road which probably has been surfaced with Clee Hill dhustone or limestone from Burlingjobb near Kington.

Compared with those natural elements which were formed long ago, the impact of human activity on the border landscape did not occur until relatively recently. Old Stone Age man of about 10,000 BC was dependent on hunting on the move and as a cave dweller left few traces. All that has so far been discovered locally was at King Arthur's Cave on the Great Doward, now (although not always) some 300 feet above the River Wye near Symonds Yat. It was excavated during the 1870s and again in 1926, 1927, early 1960s and, just outside, from 1994 and different archaeological approaches propounded a long sequence of intermittent and continuous human occupation. This was revealed partly by hearths and charcoal, flint tools, and a range of animal remains which included mammoth and woolly rhinoceros, indicative of arctic climates, and black bear, beaver, hyaena and cave lion which were of a more temperate period.

As it became warmer, prehistoric hunter-gatherers began to abandon their cave dwellings to live in temporary huts in the open, until by c.4500 BC they started to adopt more settled lives, cultivating patches of ground near where they dwelt. These New Stone Age, or Neolithic, peoples developed primitive agriculture and the domestication of animals in a way which tended to avoid the lower heavily forested or swampy parts of the region. There is evidence of their existence in areas along the Usk and close to the Black Mountains, west Herefordshire and Breconshire where complicated burial rituals have left relics of chambered long barrows at Crickhowell (Gwernvale), Talgarth and Dorstone—where there are two, Arthur's Stone now ruinous but another example at Cross Lodge Farm so far appears to have been undisturbed. For more than 2,500 years these Neolithic farmers made use of implements of polished stone and flint until, in c.1800 BC, metal tools and objects came into use during a gradual emergence of the Bronze Age. Sometimes called 'The Beaker Folk' because of the distinctive and often ornate pots which archaeologists have uncovered, early Bronze Age man also adopted other customs and round burial tumuli gradually superseded the former long barrows. Numbers of these and examples of their ritual monuments may still be seen in places such as by the Portway along the spine of the Long Mynd, up the valley of the River Arrow beyond Knighton and at Ludlow racecourse, Bromfield. Harold's Stones are standing stones near Trellech in Monmouthshire of Bronze Age date and Mitchell's Fold, on the ridge of Stapeley Hill in Shropshire, is one of 900 stone circles or menhirs in the British Isles which originated before 1200 BC. But these are not the only items which mark the existence of Bronze Age man on today's landscape, for their growing use of metal for tools, redesign of the plough and development of the wheel, and a growing population, meant more intensive cultivation and a move away from somewhat bleak and unproductive upland areas towards more fruitful valleys and plains

From a cultural period which lasted for more than 1,000 years, there appear to remain some 23 barrows in Herefordshire alone and there have also been discoveries of weapons, axes, tanged and barbed arrowheads, spears and other bronze articles much further afield. Archaeologists believe that the raw material for these came from Ireland and afterwards Cornwall, Wales and the Lake District but no mention seems to have been made of use of any of the mineral resources of the Forest of Dean, whether before or since bronze began to replace copper in *c*.2000 BC. Then along the River Severn about 1,400 years later came Celtic tribes from the Rhine Valley and Western France. Their advanced experience of working with bronze and other metals, including the smelting of iron, meant that on their way northwards towards Shropshire they would hardly have missed the indications of iron and copper ores, coal and other minerals appearing before them across the tree-covered plateau above the Lower Wye Valley. Thus in around 600 BC the British Iron Age began, and it marked the ending of prehistory with the arrival early in the 1st century AD of the Romans. There had been further clearance of woodland and the creation of fields for agriculture but the principal monuments from the Iron Age are the numerous hill forts extending throughout the Welsh Marches and some of those included within the scope of this book are at Midsummer Hill and Herefordshire Camp on the Malvern Hills, Capler Camp, Symond's Yat, Little Doward, Dinedor, Aconbury, Credenhill, Croft Ambrey, Bury Ditches south of Bishop's Castle, Titterstone Clee, Caer Caradoc opposite Church Stretton and all the way back to the summit of the volcanic formed Wrekin, where this passage through the ages commenced. The fort is thought to have been the headquarters of the Celtic Cornovii tribe until the Roman invasion of Britain in AD 43 and the early establishment of a legionary fortress close by to the west at what is now Wroxeter. After some 40 years this was decommissioned when the legion moved away northwards to a new base at Chester (*Deva*) and 'civilianised' as *Viroconium Cornoviorum*, for a time the fourth largest Romano-British walled town, covering an area of 180 acres (when Roman London was just 325 acres) to become the new capital of the Cornovii. There is now relatively little left of it to see, except notably a 26ft. high wall known as 'The Old Work' alongside the exposed foundations of a public bathhouse, and throughout the Welsh Marches there is very little else above ground level to represent nearly four centuries of the Roman presence. Some camps and settlements do show up as crop marks from the air, but apart from place name clues such as Chester, Wroxeter, Kenchester and Worcester, the best indications come with the help of the road routes. Isolated lengths are still followed by present-day traffic and some will be met on these tours. The Romans had their own road map, the *Antonine Itinerary*, and the chief Roman road along the borderland passing south from Wroxeter to Caerleon was included as *Iter XII*, now also called Watling Street West. After leaving Wroxeter and passing close to Acton Burnell and then partly as the A49, this enters the Church Stretton gap and heads through Craven Arms for Leintwardine (*Bravonium*), Aymestrey, Kenchester (*Magnis*), Abergavenny (*Gobannium*) to Caerleon (*Isca*). Leading off from this principal road, others lead towards Clyro, Stretton Grandison, Weston-under-Penyard

(*Ariconium*), probably Hereford, and Monmouth (*Blestium*). Centuries of neglect occurred during the Dark Ages and continued with the Saxons, who in any case traditionally preferred river travel. And before the 18th century there were no better or worse builders of roads until the turnpike trusts were formed, with the employment of skills such as those of Thomas Telford, John Loudon McAdam and Kingsland's famed bridge-builder, John Gethin. As to any remaining Saxon buildings, during the course of these tours there are again hardly more than fragments to be seen above ground, with the great exception of St. Mary's Church, Deerhurst in Gloucestershire. Only from the Middle Ages and afterwards, and surviving in all kinds of condition, has come a wealth and variety of cathedrals, churches, abbeys, priories, castles, half-timbered and dressed masonry stately homes and other buildings of note.

The Romans were the first to introduce written history to Britain and more than 1,000 years later a description of medieval Welsh borderland geography was written in Latin in the form of a travel diary by Gerald of Wales (Giraldus Cambrensis). *The Journey through Wales* began and ended in Hereford and after 800 years some of these tours will encounter the route which he and the archbishop of Canterbury travelled. They left in March 1181 for New Radnor, then moved on to Hay, Brecon, the Black Mountains and Llanthony Abbey, Abergavenny and close to the Forest of Dean, before returning almost six weeks later along Wenlock Edge and past Bromfield Priory, Ludlow Castle and Leominster. It would have been quite hazardous and over difficult terrain without a chart. It would not be until the last 10 years of the following century that the region came to be included on any known map and this is now on display in the new library and exhibition centre at Hereford Cathedral. The Mappa Mundi was made in encyclopaedic form on a large piece of vellum (prepared calf skin) by Richard of Haldingham and Lafford as a medieval view of the world. The British Isles lie on its outermost edge—where it is just possible to pick out Hereford, Worcester, Gloucester, Shrewsbury, the rivers Wye and Severn and the Clee Hills. Not until Tudor times, when cartographers such as John Speede appeared, was there anything more useful for travellers. Since then the whole area has often been surveyed, drawn and revisited, culminating in Ordnance Survey maps such as the 1/25 000 Explorer and 1/50 000 Landranger sheets which, with many forms of Motoring Atlas, are strongly recommended for use in conjunction with this book.

As to written history, before Giraldus Cambrensis there were local references in *The Anglo Saxon Chronicle*, but in 1086 there was much more in the detailed survey results set out in Domesday Book. The works of William Langland appeared in the 14th century and during the 16th there were, for example, accounts by John Leland and William Camden and the verse of Michael Drayton. In the 17th century exceptional religious poetry was inspired in John Donne, George Herbert, Henry Vaughan and Thomas Traherne and there were travelogues from Celia Fiennes and others, most notably Daniel Defoe (1660-1731) who, in his *Tour through the Whole Island of Great Britain*, left an account of his journeys within the border regions during 1724-26. Then from the 18th century onwards the names of a great many more enthusiastic writers, poets, painters, composers, scholars and ordinary tourists joined the large bibliography of those who have found pleasure and refreshment or the inspiration for uplifting words and music in their experience of the Borderlands. Some of these are universally known and include: William Wordsworth, Elizabeth Barrett-Browning, Lord Byron, Francis Kilvert, A.E. Housman, Mary Webb, John Masefield, 'The Dymock Poets', Ivor Gurney, Edward Elgar, Ralph Vaughan Williams, Gerald Finzi, Laura Knight, John Betjeman, Nikolaus Pevsner, Arthur Mee and

George Barrow. And there are many others who have also done much to help in pointing out the right directions to follow in prospecting for places to include in this book. Many of them I have got to know as local residents, lovers of the countryside and ramblers during the past 40 years, and I am especially grateful for the help of Andy Johnson of Logaston Press who over many years has walked, motor cycled or driven over most of the borderland region, and also at Logaston for Ron Shoesmith's fund of local knowledge and experience. He has shared this many times with the Woolhope Naturalists' Field Club, which has amassed a huge treasury of studiously researched reference material, contributed by members to its *Transactions* ever since 1851. Several of them appear in the following list of those whose help I wish to acknowledge, and some of the others are represented by their books on the shelves of the ever helpful Herefordshire Reference Library in Broad Street, Hereford, or of the others consulted in six neighbouring counties.

They include: R. Baker-Gabb, Martin Beales, Arthur Bradley, Anthea Brian, Basil Butcher, James Butterworth, Christopher Catling, S.D. Coates, William Coxe, Alan Crow, John Davies, John Duncombe, Lawrence Garner, Donald Gregory, Richard Haslam, Geoffrey Hodges, Joseph Hillaby, Jenny Houston, W.H. Howse, Heather Hurley, Christopher Hussey, Simon Jenkins, Keith Kissack, E.M. Leather, Ken Lee, Alun Llewellyn, David Lloyd, F.C. Morgan, Frank Noble, Keith Parker, Pat Paterson, Oliver Rackham, Michael Raven, Paul Remfry, Charles Robinson, Trevor Rowley, John Salmon, Mike Salter, Stan Stanford, H.T. Timmins, Veronica Thackeray, Malcolm Thurlby, Jim and Muriel Tonkin, David Verey, Alfred Watkins, David Whitehead, Sid Wright, the many members of the Herefordshire Federation of Women's Institutes who contributed to *The Herefordshire Village Book* and the authors and compilers of the many town and church histories and guides which I have consulted.

Most of the photographs used in the book are my own, but I am also grateful to the following for permission to use photographs: Logaston Press pp. 1 (top), 12, 21, 22, 41, 42 (both), 43, 54 (both), 61 (top), 66 (top), 67 (top), 69, 74, 76 (all), 89 (bottom), 122 (both), 132, 136, 137, 140, 144 (both), 145 (both), 150 (top), 152 (top), 154 (bottom), 157 (both), 161, 168, 174 (middle right), 176, 193, 231, 237 (both), 238 (both), 239 (top), 275 (bottom), 283, 285, 288 (bottom); Malcolm Thurlby pp. 49, 50 (middle), 85 (lower), 103, 112, 128 (top), 149 (left), 160 (bottom right), 218; Madge Moran pp. 26 (both), 27 (top), 28, 33 (all); Pat Palmer pp. 34, 111, 113, 188 (left); John Leonard pp. 62, 233; Glyn Coppack p. 24 (top); Ben Corbett p. 159; Susie and Ivor Dunkerton p. 63 (top); Derek Evans pp. 128 (bottom), 215; George H. Hall p.129 (top); Ron Shoesmith p. 135; Alfred Watkins and Hereford City Library p. 143 (top) and Ann & John Welton p.11 (bottom). I also wish to thank Brian Byron for drawing all the maps, with the exception of those on pages 32 and 70 for which thanks are due to Stan Stanford.

Lastly this book owes much to Wendy, my wife, who whilst I have been researching, has as chauffeuse honed her driving skills between Much Wenlock and Chepstow and from the Elan Dams to Worcester, over what must amount to some 3,500 square miles of all kinds of roads, tracks and territory.

How to use this guide

There are 12 tours, varying in total length from 30 to 90 miles, that can be undertaken by vehicle in a day, and whose outline route is given on the map opposite. For each tour a more detailed map is given opposite the start of that tour. Each tour includes a description of places that can be seen from the road, together with more in-depth details of places that can be visited or explored.

At the start of each route there is a summary which indicates the total distance covered, the nature of the roads used (from A roads to narrow country lanes), the type of countryside passed through and the variety of places recommended for visits *en route*.

Everyone who uses this book will have their own particular interests and so wish to spend more or less time at the various sites suggested. As each route has more than enough to see in one day if you chose to stop at all the suggested places, it means that you may well need to omit certain suggested stops, or choose to visit them on another occasion. Therefore it is suggested that, before setting out on a particular tour, you glance through the 'boxed' information accompanying the route to decide in advance where you may wish to linger during the course of the day. In addition, many of the routes have optional 'side' trips, and you may wish to decide which of these to include in the day's exploration before venturing forth.

Each route is described as starting and ending at a market town in the area covered, and depending on where you are based you may also need to allow time to reach the start point, maybe with the aid of your vehicle's Motoring Atlas. You can, of course, also join any route part of the way along. Each tour has a succession of numbers which relate to the location on the map of the numbered 'boxed' information, hopefully meaning that this process will be easy to manage.

As a rule the book does not include specific opening times, nor recommend places to drink or eat, as such information has a way of changing over time. So it can in other respects, but the contents of this book are believed to be correct at the time of writing. To avoid disappointment the current situation can usually be checked with help from local tourist information centres.

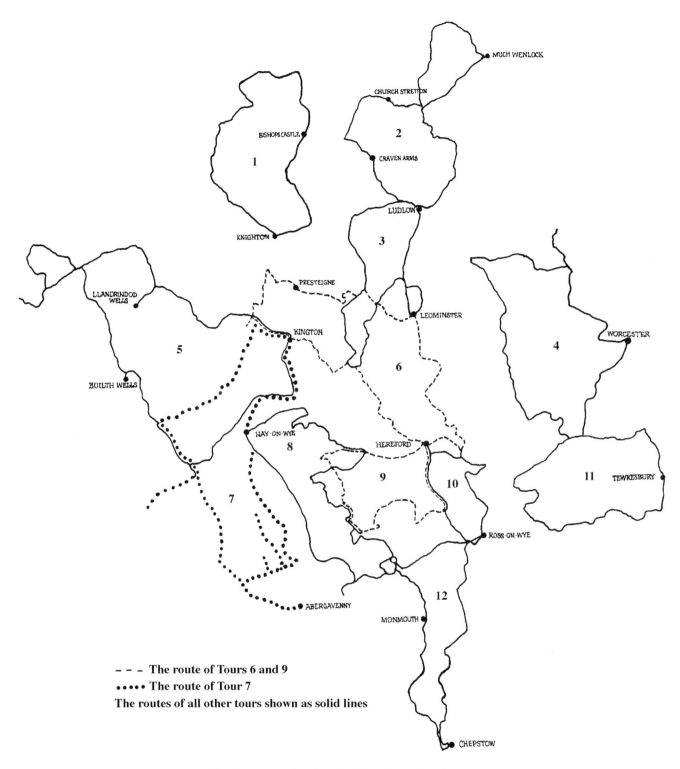

MUCH WENLOCK

CHURCH STRETTON

2

BISHOPS CASTLE

1

CRAVEN ARMS

KNIGHTON

LUDLOW

3

PRESTEIGNE

LLANDRINDOD WELLS

KINGTON

LEOMINSTER

WORCESTER

5

6

4

BUILTH WELLS

HAY·ON·WYE

HEREFORD

8

9

10

11

TEWKESBURY

7

ROSS·ON·WYE

ABERGAVENNY

12

MONMOUTH

– – – **The route of Tours 6 and 9**

•••• **The route of Tour 7**

The routes of all other tours shown as solid lines

CHEPSTOW

Outline map showing the location of each route

Knighton

The town on the Dyke, *Tref-y-clawdd* to the Welsh, Knighton is a border settlement in more senses than one. As a consequence of the Act of Union it has been at the boundary between Wales and England since 1536, but it has also been astride another frontier for much longer. This is the dyke (or *clawdd*) which King Offa is thought to have ordered to be built to define the western limit of his expanding Anglo-Saxon kingdom of Mercia, now the English Midlands, from the native British kingdom of Powys. The two invisible boundaries intersect at right angles at Panpunton Bridge, just to the west of the town—where the Heart of Wales railway enters England on the approach to Knighton station. Offa's Dyke was built at the birth of modern Britain, and was inevitably in the middle of long-running cross-border conflicts. Having been pushed even further westwards, the Welsh had been on the offensive from at least as far back as AD 784 and in 1052 launched yet another of their attacks, capturing Saxon Knighton. By the 1080s the Normans had fully taken over from the Saxons and they built a large timber and earth motte and bailey castle in the valley to the east of the town, near the River Teme. (Now known as *Bryn-y-Castell*, this can be recognised as a large mound on the playing fields behind the community centre). About 80 years later the case must have been made for a better strongpoint and so Knighton acquired a second castle. Placed up the hill above Wylcwm Brook, it was later reinforced with stone ramparts. (It is now visible from behind the fire station and just off the market square where the remains have survived

A glimpse of part of the earthworks of Knighton's second castle

in part of a private garden). The town changed hands several times during the 13th century, falling successively to Llywelyn ap Iorweth ('The Great'), the Mortimers, Llywelyn ap Gruffudd ('The Last'- see also p.116) and then the Mortimers again. The 14th century was relatively peaceful, but the 15th started badly when in 1402 Owain Glyndwr appeared, capturing and almost destroying the town.

Knighton's first church had been built within the original Saxon settlement, not long before the Conquest, and was strangely dedicated to the half-Norman King Edward the Confessor.

Looking up the High Street to the clock tower

1

Molly's Cottage, Russell Street, Knighton

The now much restored church of St. Edward occupies the same site. From the mid-17th century the town was busy as a market centre, with a considerable sheep and cattle trade, and it was on two of the principal drovers' routes between central Wales and the fattening grounds and markets in England. Then in 1865 the Central Wales Line reached Knighton, siting its station just in England across the River Teme. It quickly enlivened the local economy and the population figures, which now stand at about 3,000, and accounts for the many buildings of Victorian and Edwardian character within the town. In the sloping Market Place, one of the most glaring of these is the 1872 Clock Tower, built to a pattern then so beloved of Welsh aldermen and councillors from Hay-on-Wye through Rhayader and Machynlleth all the way to Ruthin! Another is the former bank, just opposite on Broad Street, built in 1908 with pink granite pillars and a corner turret capped with a green cupola. But there are also buildings of much greater historic and architectural virtue along and near the steep High Street and Narrows, many dating from the 17th century and even before. With a half timbered façade just by the Clock Tower, the Old House is cruck-built with some parts dating from the 15th century, while the nearby George and Dragon former coaching inn dates from 1637.

Offa's Dyke and The National Trail

The construction from *c.*784-796 of a frontier line between the estuaries of the Rivers Dee and Severn has solely been attributed to King Offa on the basis of a 9th-century reference to him by Bishop Asser as the king who 'ordered the construction of a large rampart the whole way from sea to sea between Britain and Mercia'. Yet it is difficult to think of anyone else who would then have had the power, motive or ruthless drive to mount such a colossal feat of engineering. The total distance measured along the line of Offa's Dyke is 149 miles, containing lengths of actual earthwork of some 81 miles. These vary in heights of up to 25ft., often with a 6ft. deep ditch, and pass through the wild terrain of the Welsh borderlands. It has been calculated that these works could have employed a full time labour force of 1,000 men, under the direction of Offa's field engineers and recruited either locally or from throughout the kingdom. Alternatively, local labour could have been coerced into building designated lengths, which might explain incompatibilities in the construction of some adjoining sections. It was all hand work, and depending on how this was organised it could have taken at least five years of continuous labour. Another 1,000 years would pass, until the first canals appeared, before anything else in Britain could match such an enterprise.

After approaching from the Presteigne and Kington direction, the Dyke reappears in a short stretch behind The Laurels in Penybont Road and then another below the Offa's Dyke Centre, West Street. It then continues in portions from Panpunton Hill directly to the north and runs in a north-westerly direction to reach the Clun Valley. It again disappears as the line crosses the B4368 about 2¹/₂ miles west of Clun, near Newcastle on Clun. Between these two valleys the highest point is achieved at over 1,400ft. on the plateau at Llanfair Hill. From there to Springhill Farm to the north is one of the best preserved sections of this entire earthwork. After negotiating the highest hills on its route, it crosses the Kerry Ridgeway and then descends into the countryside east of Montgomery. The lengths of dyke to the north and south of Knighton closely correspond with the line of the National Trail designated in 1955 and opened in 1971 as the Offa's Dyke Path. The years between were taken up with much discussion and negotiation with landowners, farmers and various authorities. The brunt of all this was borne and the enterprise pioneered by Knighton's historical geographer Frank Noble, to whom this book is dedicated. He was Founder of the Offa's Dyke Association, whose

The Offa's Dyke Centre

offices are in West Street, Knighton. A finger post sign there points one way to Sedbury Cliff at 80 miles away, and another to Prestatyn Beach at 97 miles. This indicates that the distance along the National Trail, which crosses the border more than 20 times, is 28 miles longer than the actual boundary line dictated by King Offa.

Offa's Dyke Centre

The Offa's Dyke Centre is thus situated near the mid-point of the Trail and is equipped to provide walkers with information on route planning and accommodation. Reasonably fit people can complete the walk in two weeks, but the Centre also provides details of shorter circular routes. It houses a Wales Tourist Board TIC, has a shop and mounts exhibition and interactive displays on subjects which include not only King Offa and his Dyke, but also the Mercians and Welsh princes, the National Trails and the flora and fauna of the Marches. The Offa's Dyke Path Management Service is based there, educational visits are available to schools and other groups, there is a meeting room for up to 40 people for hire and, in its superb setting, this fine new building is even licensed for weddings.

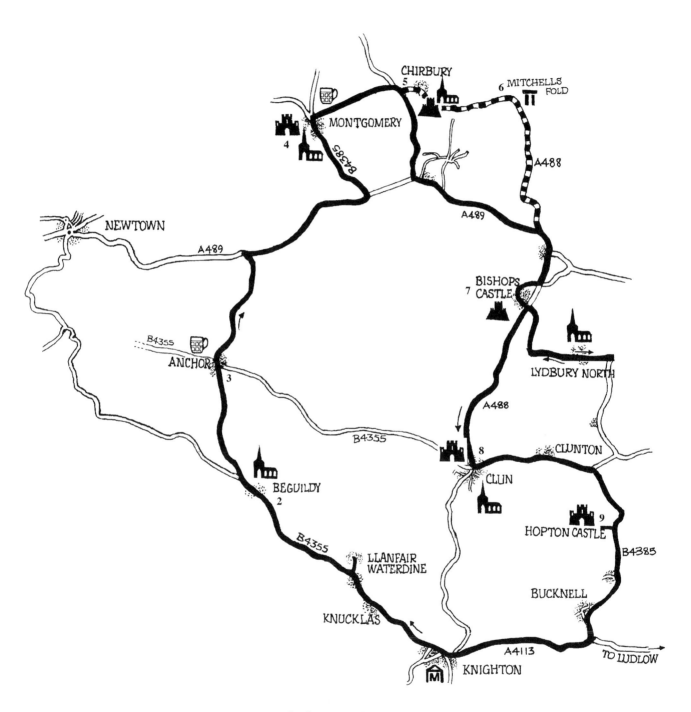

Outline map for Tour 1
The numbers 1 to 9 relate to the boxed information given within the tour

Tour 1   Where Herefordshire, Shropshire and Montgomeryshire meet

Starting at the border town of Knighton in Radnorshire (Powys), this tour winds through rolling scenery largely following B roads, with some A roads and country lanes. It takes in the remains of stone-built castles and other historic sites, including that of a terrible massacre, and characterful small border towns and villages containing old buildings of great interest and intriguingly unique churches. The total distance is about 58 miles. (OS Landranger 136, 137)

The route moves off uphill along Knighton's High Street, heading into Wales past the clock tower and turning right into the B4355 Knucklas Road just past the Offa's Dyke Centre. It then runs almost parallel with the River Teme, the National Boundary and the Heart of Wales railway, until they meet near Knucklas. Just to the north of the village on the left, and visible from the road past the Castle Inn, is the site of Knucklas Castle and a spectacular Victorian masonry viaduct.

---

1.   Knucklas, Guinevere and King Arthur

For its size, Radnorshire probably possessed more 'castles' than any other county in the UK, but none could have matched the castle at Knucklas for its awe-inspiring setting in such beautiful surroundings. On the north side of the village and shown on OS Landranger Map 137 as *Cnwclas* (meaning green mound) Castle, it is said also to have been called *Caer Gogyrfan*—Gogyrfan's castle. A tradition from the 15th century tells that Gogyrfan was a giant whose daughter, Gwenhwyfar (aka Guinevere) married King Arthur there. It would be surprising if such a commanding height was not occupied by a pre-historic hillfort, and it has certainly been established that a stone castle was begun by Ralph Mortimer and completed in 1242 by Roger, his son. Knucklas had been over-run by Llywelyn the Great in 1213 and the new castle was taken in 1262 by his grandson, Llywelyn the Last. It afterwards re-entered Mortimer hands, was besieged and taken by Owain Glyndwr in 1402 at the same time as Knighton, so that by 1828 an account in the *Hereford Journal* could only refer to some ruins. Traces of these remained until mid-Victorian times, but another local account has it that the castle's stone was 'redeployed' towards the building of a spectacular Central Wales Railway viaduct. This formed part of an extension of the service from Knighton to Llandrindod Wells, officially opened in 1865, and it still carries trains 69ft. above the Hayop valley over 13 arches,

Knucklas Viaduct

each spanning 31ft. 9ins. and supported on sturdy masonry piers between castellated end turrets. The castle has now been acquired by Knucklas people for conservation and access.

To some non-conformists Knucklas is also known as the birthplace of Vavasor Powell (1617-1670). He was one of the leading Baptists during their early days in Wales, but after serving in many Radnorshire churches he became a strong supporter of the Long Parliament, but was often in trouble because of his preachings. After the Restoration and more controversy he ended his days in London's Fleet Prison, branded as 'an injudicious zealot'. In spite of this, the Baptist Church was said to have owed him much for its strong position in the county.

The B4355 continues up the Teme valley past more hills, heading towards the distant line of Kerry Hill to reach Lloyney and Llanfair Waterdine. Both were formerly in Wales. If you wish to visit Llanfair Waterdine it is now necessary to turn right opposite the Lloyney Inn in Radnorshire and cross the border and the Teme into Shropshire, England. Then turn left to reach the village.

John Hunt of Llanfair Waterdine—A Border baron

Llanfair Waterdine is named from both languages of the border and means 'St. Mary's Church by the water'. It comprises the church, a pub, village hall and a small number of houses. It did have a post office until recently, when the postmistress retired, but the parish is sparsely populated, at a recent count containing about 49 farms and smallholdings. St. Mary's is thought to be the third church on the site and was built in 1854 by Thomas Nicholson, the Hereford diocesan architect. In using parts of previous furnishings he designed the boldly carved communion rail from a former rood screen which dated from the 15th century. The organ is a different rarity—a barrel organ from the 1840s originally at Bishop's Castle and installed in 1907. The pine pews are distinctive in that in gold lettering on the side of each is the name of a different local farm. This arrangement dates back to the era when farmers were obliged to pay a tithe to the church, and some worshippers still like to occupy their family seat. But some bear the names of farms which have long been derelict, and the village hall is also a sad illustration of the severe depopulation of many Marches parishes.

In c.1900 it was the village school with a roll of about 100 children, which by the 1930s had reduced to fewer than 60, and by the time the school was closed down in the 1950s there were just 12 pupils and one teacher. The building was sold to the villagers in the early 1960s and was grandly called Everest Hall. At over 700ft. above sea level the village is of course quite high up, yet those visiting for the first time might regard the naming as a little over the top. This is until they learn the reason, for Llanfair Waterdine was the home of John Hunt (1910-1998). In the early hours of Coronation Day on 2 June 1953, the Queen, Joy Hunt and the local people were already rejoicing well ahead of the rest of the nation after the news of the conquest of Mount Everest had been flashed to the Teme valley—for Colonel Hunt was the leader of the first successful ascent of the mountain, an expedition which had placed Edmund Hillary and Sherpa Tensing on the summit. The jubilation was but a prelude for the day of his return to the village when, by then Sir John Hunt, he was met at the parish boundary and, waving his ice axe aloft, was drawn home to Weir Cottage in a pony trap by a team of his many friends. After more than 50 years local people still remembered the official welcome outside the church and pub, the square dancing on the village green, the bonfire, fireworks and aircraft flypast, all culminating in the cutting of a huge cake the shape of Mount Everest and iced by the vicar. Little wonder that the mountain's conqueror should declare: 'This is the moment I've longed for most, the welcome of my own people, here at Llanfair Waterdine'. The village hall was named in his honour and a horse chestnut tree planted in the old school yard. After retiring from the army with the CBE and DSO as a brigadier, he did not spend all his time indulging the hobby of 'Mountain activities', as quoted in his *Who's Who* entry. He had already learnt, and spoke, Welsh and at Llanfair had taken just a month in 1953 to write *The Ascent of Everest*. He produced five more books and became involved in youth, probation, police, Parole Board, National Parks and many recreational functions, and was in 1966 created a Life Peer. There was renewed delight in the Upper Teme Valley when he chose as his territorial title that of Baron Hunt of Llanfair Waterdine, and yet again in 1979 when, in the Queen's special gift, he became one of the 24 Knights of the Most Noble Order of the Garter. At the memorial service after his death, the banner from above his stall in the choir of St. George's Chapel, Windsor was brought by the family to St. Mary's to be placed in the chancel.

Close by, planning for Everest had often taken place at the 16th-century village pub next to the church. Since drover days it was known as the Red Lion, which was common as the emblem of early Welsh rulers and adopted by some of the leading families. It has since changed name and image and has become The Waterdine.

Well signed premises in Beguildy

Tumulus to the right of the road near Beguildy

The main route continues on the B4355 to climb through scenes of increasing wildness, as steep hills crowd in on the way towards the top of the Teme Valley. Farming is important here and there are signs scattered all around the area that this has been so for many centuries. The local OS Landranger maps plot prehistoric settlements, homesteads, tumps and tumuli (or burial mounds) which date back for at least 3,000 years to the Bronze Age. North of Knighton, the lofty 12-acre fortified settlement of Caer Caradoc is typical of Iron Age preference for hill top settlements, whereas earlier Bronze Age farmers from about 1500 BC often chose valley sites and lighter sand and gravel riverside soils. Below the B4355 to the right there are instances of where they buried their dead and there is a good opportunity from a lane to the right, just beyond Dutlas, to see a tumulus at the edge of a field.

2. Bryndraenog, Beguildy and sheep

The timber hall-house of Bryndraenog signposted up a farm drive on the left, is designed on an H plan and dates from the 15th and 16th centuries. It has been described as the most complete in the Principality, with an exceptionally fine open hall 35ft. long and with immense base crucks spanning 19ft. The exterior timber frame has been shown to date from *c*.1560, but the external beauty of this private working farmhouse has been diminished by roughcast.

The house and farm overlook stunning valley scenery in the parish of Beguildy and the village is a mile further up the road, at which point it will have become evident that this is very much sheep territory. The name of the village chimes with the known truth that there are far more sheep in Radnorshire and neighbouring parts of south Shropshire than there are people, for its name is derived from the Welsh *Bugeil-dy*, which means the Shepherd's House, and being in such a hilly area was once a centre of extensive sheep rearing. Until just after the Second World War, autumn disposals of stock from the locality amounted to as many as 68,000 breeding ewes over the four September sale days at Knighton market. They attracted buyers from throughout the country, but now the lowland farmers breed their own ewes and the sale takes only a day. Those who think that sheep are just sheep will be surprised to notice the differences in local breeds, usually named after their home territory. Kerry Hills are recognised by their white faces and black markings around the nose, eyes and legs, Clun Forests have noticeably tufted wool on the tops of their heads whilst Hill Radnors have tan faces and legs. And then there are Mules, Badger-faced and Welsh Mountain sheep among many varieties roaming the hills throughout the Welsh Border counties.

Part of the rood screen at Beguildy Church

Poised high above the B4355 and the Radnorshire Arms, St. Michael's Church is in a circular raised church-yard and is mainly 15th century, furnished with a fine rood screen, with traceried panels and much elaborate carving, a Jacobean pulpit and altar table, an older font and stoup and a dugout chest which is probably older still. Apart from late Victorian restoration works, only the tower is more recent, replacing one which collapsed about 100 years ago.

The B4355 continues alongside the river towards Felindre and winds to the top of the valley, passing the source of the River Teme to the right, below Cilfaesty Hill, and of The Mule. This is also a tributary of the Severn, and the source is closer to the road near Black Gate on the descent to Dolfor and the A483 Llandrindod/Newtown road. These are veritable nursery slopes for four rivers, for on the left side of the B4355, a very short distance from the birthplace of The Mule, is that of the River Ithon. But the waters of the four will not mingle until they reach Chepstow and the Bristol Channel. For the Ithon flows towards the River Wye, as from its source beyond the extensive moorland to the south of Beguildy does the River Lugg.

Our route however leaves the B4355 just above Beguildy and crosses from Wales into England over the bridge to the right. On a ridge ahead there is a motte and bailey castle known as The Moat. Heading for Anchor, the minor road starts to climb past it on the right and upwards through Llanmadoc, adding more to the thrill of being among moors and mountains. The panoramic views over this lonely unfrequented country as one passes The Black Mountain on the right, are really breathtaking. Near Anchor, on the hillside half a mile south-west is Castell Bryn Amlwg. Little is known about this remote outpost, except that a ring-work defence was based there in *c*.1142, followed with a stone keep in the 13th century. Over the subsequent years of Welsh hostility, at one of the windiest and most isolated parts of the territory and worryingly vulnerable more than 4½ miles west of Offa's Dyke, it cannot have been the most enviable of Norman postings. And the comforts of the Anchor Inn would not have arrived for several centuries.

3.   The Anchor Inn

Following the success at Bosworth of Henry VII, himself a quarter Welsh, the Age of the Tudors brought active hostility between Welsh and English largely to an end (apart from some holiday-cottage vandalism, and graffiti denying the open welcome usually promised in song in the Welsh hillsides and dales—matched by an absence of warmth towards Channel S4C television output in Welsh from Cardiff!). The Act of Union followed under Henry VIII and the border between the

The Anchor Inn

Principality and Shropshire was set out just a few yards west of Castell Bryn Amlwg. Not far over on the English side, a customs post was installed for the collection of tolls or levies on fleeces and hides being brought across from Wales. This functioned until the introduction of tariff reform in 1825 and the establishment was afterwards converted into an inn, named by a sailor-turned-landlubber who seemingly wished to drop anchor as far away from the tang of salt air as possible. His pub quickly became popular with drovers and good provision was made in a disused quarry for the penning and feeding of their animals. Later the Shropshire novelist Mary Webb (p.38) alluded to it as 'The Inn at the World's End', and this is still as it may seem to many of today's callers. Like other such isolated pubs, it is generally open only in the evening, although possibly for longer at weekends.

The inn stands at a junction with the B4368 from Clun, which has accompanied yet another river, the Clun, towards its source in these hills. Head over to the opposite side of this road and then continue along the minor road, crossing over the Kerry Ridgeway, and prepare yourself for truly breathtaking views over the wide expanse of the Severn Valley at every yard of the way down the *c.*650ft. descent to the junction with the A489, just west of Sarn. Turn right here and carry along this trunk road until

Views along the road from the Anchor Inn

it reaches the B4385 (at an intersection with Offa's Dyke and the National Trail) on which you turn left for Montgomery, climbing the hill past the Crown Inn to turn left into Broad Street and parking opposite the Checkers Hotel.

4. Montgomery

The town acquired its English name from Roger de Montgomery through his ancestral seat at Sainte Foy de Montgomery in the Calvados department of Normandy, whilst its Welsh name and that of the pre-1974 county, *Trefaldwyn* (Baldwin's town), came from Baldwin de Boller who was one of his successors during the reign of Henry I. A kinsman of William the Conqueror, Roger was created earl of Shrewsbury and charged with

Montgomery

securing his sector of the Border. Within 10 years of 1066 he had built a motte and bailey castle at the Rhydwhyman ford just a mile north of the town with the purpose of controlling the Severn Valley route into central Wales. This is shown on the map as *Hen Domen*, the Old Mound, and, known as Old Montgomery, is generally accepted as the site of the first Norman castle. But this was not the first time for the strategic importance of the locality to be recognised. *Ffridd Faldwyn* Camp of *c*.1.2 hectares, closer to the town and still accessible, was established during the early Iron Age and, according to finds, may have been placed over an earlier Neolithic settlement. Later on, nearer the Severn and the ford, the Romans built Forden Gaer to become part of a quadrilateral of forts in the region. This is thought to have been occupied from *c*.80 and into the 4th century. Hen Domen was replaced from 1223 by a sturdy stone castle on a rocky ridge overhanging the

Montgomery Castle

Camlad valley and in 1227 the planned settlement of Montgomery below received a royal charter from Henry III. Town walls and their four gates have long since disappeared and Montgomery, its population at little more than 1,100, appears to have prospered well enough as a market centre, serving until 1974 as the traditional county capital, without really achieving its expected potential. This is rather like Bishops Castle, Clun and Knighton on this journey and Welshpool, Kington and Hay elsewhere in the Marches—in contrast with Ludlow.

Below the castle's rocky, wooded slope it remains, however, one of the best preserved small towns in mid Wales, its street layout centred on Broad Street. Many of the houses are Elizabethan, Jacobean, Queen Anne or Georgian, as discreet wall plaques testify, although The Dragon hotel, originally the Green Dragon, is outwardly Edwardian—refaced with imitation close timbering early in the 20th century. Nevertheless it probably contains some original

Looking over the town from the castle

The Town Hall

The Herbert Tomb in Montgomery Church

materials removed from the castle after its slighting by Parliament in 1649. The very steep lane beyond the hotel leads up to the castle ruins and there is an opportunity for 'a breather' part way up at what is now Castle Terrace. Built in *c*.1740, here was once Montgomeryshire's first county gaol. At one time in 1803 it was said to have held three debtors, ten felons and three lunatics, but by 1832 the count was down to just one female. Those lacking the lung or muscle power for the climb on foot can drive past the hotel on its left to reach a car park, and then it is a short almost level walk to the ruins. The effort is repaid by the hugely rewarding views laid out far below. It is easy to see how Montgomery Castle should be so impregnable, later making a highly desirable housing plot for the Herberts (see next box).

Back at the bottom of the hill, the pale red brick town hall was built in 1748 and on a rise at the opposite side of the town to the east, St. Nicholas Church is mainly 13th century. Its many furnishings and works of art include two screens, one made for the parish and facing the nave, and the other joined to it and facing the chancel. With a decorated rood loft and carved 15th-century gates, portions of this screen are believed to have come from the Augustinian priory church of Chirbury after the Dissolution of the monasteries by Henry VIII—along with choir stalls and miserere seats. Of the monuments, the most sumptuous is the canopied tomb of Richard Herbert and his family in the South

*The possible effigy of
Sir Edmund Mortimer in
Montgomery Church*

Transept. Before the Reformation the Lymore Chapel was the chantry chapel for the Herbert family and the piscina on the east wall indicates the site of the altar. One of two effigies near the tomb is of a late 15th-century member of the Herbert family, whereas the other is thought to be of Sir Edmund Mortimer (d.1409). Defeated and captured at the battle of Pilleth (p.152) in 1402, he later that year became an ally and son-in-law of his adversary, Owain Glyndwr, but after seven years he died whilst under siege at Harlech Castle.

Among the most modern items of furniture are the president's, assistant's and bishop's chairs near the altar which were designed and made in 1999 to replace others stolen from the church the previous year. This experience represents one of the reasons given for some churches (but thankfully not here) being firmly shut and locked, except during services and other events arranged for the local community. Regrettably for other enthusiastic visitors, there are not always details of access arrangements, such as the keyholders and where to find them. But fortunately the majority of clergy and churchwardens recognise the true pastoral role of their charge and at reasonable times keep it open for all comers.

In Montgomery churchyard there is a monument with a policeman's helmet, another to a goalkeeper, and the grave of John Davies, who was executed for robbery in 1821. Protesting his innocence, he vowed that no grass would grow on his grave for 100 years. This and much more of the town's long history can be learned in Arthur Street at Montgomery Civic Society's 17th-century timber-framed and brick Old Bell Museum, once a coaching inn, where the literature and exhibits may be seen at certain times, notably on Saturdays and in the summer.

The Herberts

In September 1267 at the Rhydwyman ford, or *Rhyd Chwima*, the Treaty of Montgomery was ratified by King Henry III and Llywelyn ap Gruffudd, bringing a few years of peace for Wales. It did not last and the castle resumed its military role under the Mortimers and others until hostilities finally ceased. Early in the reign of Henry VIII it came into the possession of the Herbert family, who afterwards owned it for over 400 years. A new brick house was built in the grounds but it lasted only about 30 years and was destroyed in 1649 after the Civil War. It had been the home of some of the most distinguished members of the family then headed by Richard Herbert and his wife Magdalen. Of their eight children, two of the most talented were Edward (1583-1648), who became the first Lord Herbert of Cherbury (for some unknown reason not Chirbury, his home village), and George (1593-1633). Both were among the leading writers and poets of the 17th century, but it was George Herbert, a parish priest, who became most renowned and, exceptionally, is commemorated each 27 February by a feast day in the Anglican calendar. He was one of the select group of so called metaphysical poets who employed descriptive language and elaborate imagery to inspire and appeal to the senses, and it is remarkable that two others should also spring from the middle Marches at that time. These were Henry Vaughan (1622-95) (p.173), who was greatly influenced by the Herberts, and Thomas Traherne (*c*.1636-1674) (p.162). And the appeal of the castle for poetry lovers is further strengthened through a close association with the Herbert family of John Donne (*c*.1571-1631), by origin another Welshman. He is acknowledged as the master poetical figure of them all, and those who know his work will recognise:

The Primrose, being at Montgomery Castle upon the hill, on which it is situate

whilst others with an ear for a flattering tribute to any lady 'of a certain age' will surely appreciate the 9th Elegy of *The Autumnal*. This is believed to have been addressed to Lady Magdalen:

No Spring, nor Summer beauty has such grace,
As I have seen in one Autumnal face.

Be that as it may, and despite raising numerous children, she was not so autumnal as to have lost all appetite for the state of matrimony after the death of her husband in 1596. She died as Lady Danvers about 30 years later and was buried in London, but her effigy nevertheless lies alongside that of Richard Herbert in the Lymore Chapel at Montgomery (so named after the family mansion near the town, demolished in the 1930s). They are gazed upon by youthful representations of 'colourful' Lord Herbert of Cherbury and priestly George Herbert, arcaded in pairs with their four brothers and two sisters.

After turning left from Broad Street in Montgomery this tour moves northwards down the hill in the direction of Welshpool, but quickly turns right on to the B4386 to head for Chirbury crossing the line of Offa's Dyke along the way.

5.   Chirbury

Placed at a strategic location looking west to the Berwyn Mountains, at the head of the Camlad valley, an important junction of routes and close to Offa's Dyke (and the present national boundary), the site of Chirbury must have been an obvious choice for an early border stronghold. Chirbury Castle is now just a rectangular enclosure on the left at the approach towards the A490, but some historians believe that a fortified *burh*, constructed in 915 by Saxon Aethelflaeda at *Cyrichyrig*, meaning 'church fort', equates to its location at Chirbury. An Anglo-Saxon minster church was founded early in the 10th century and later refounded and reformed as an Augustinian priory. This functioned until the Dissolution when, exceptionally like Abbey Dore, Leominster and Shrewsbury, the church was spared for parish use. This is why the massive tower and the rest of the building now seem too big for such a small village. Then, in 1733, a short incongruous and crude red brick extension was restored as a chancel to the east of the original nave and aisles. Heavy buttressing of the main body of the church may be connected with the reported lean of pillars supporting the internal Gothic arches, but it is not possible to enter any of the church interior when the entrance door combination lock is operating. Visitors may instead call at the Herbert Arms Hotel, just outside the lych gate and named after the former lord of the manor, the first Lord Herbert, succeeded now by John George Herbert, 8th earl of Powis. Alternatively the half-timbered school, still in use but built in 1675 and therefore quite late for such quality, may be reached by walking through the churchyard, and throughout this compact village there are several timber framed houses with red brick façades.

The route leaves Chirbury on the A490 leading towards Church Stoke and the A489 (on which you would turn left if not taking the side tour detailed below), but for those with an interest in prehistory and the Bronze Age, or harbouring an appetite for even more spectacular views, there is an optional detour starting a short distance from the village.

Follow the sign to the left for Priest Weston off the A490 and, once there, continue on for Whitegrit and Bishops Castle, noting the brown sign for a 'Stone Circle'. Narrow in places, the road passes the Old Miners' Arms pub to reach a broad ridge where there is another brown sign pointing to the left for the Stone Circle. A rather bumpy track covers most of the way, and then comes a short and easy walk from the carpark at the cattle grid over Stapeley Common to the site, which is in the care of English Heritage.

Afterwards, return along the track and, keeping straight on, continue downhill on the public road for a mile and a quarter through White Grit to the junction with the A488. Turn right and follow this road to the junction with the A489. Then turn right and continue on towards Bishop's Castle.

Mitchell's Fold stone circle

6. Mitchell's Fold Stone Circle

At 1,200ft. above sea level, on an exposed site with spectacular long distance views towards the highlands of central Wales, Mitchell's Fold is one of over 900 stone circles in the British Isles. The 15 stones here remain from a ring of possibly twice as many, with maybe another stone in the centre, which originated in the early Bronze Age between 2000 BC and 1200 BC. It was possibly built by a single family or small community and, with a diameter of about 90ft., it could have been a place of assembly—maybe with ritual or astronomical significance in the ceremonies of the period. The stones all came from Stapeley Hill to the north-west and the tallest is now about 6ft. high, whilst the rest are shorter and in some cases lie flat on the ground. There is another slightly smaller circle, known as the Hoarstones, about 1½ miles to the north-east, but there is now very little to see above the surface.

Back at the main route at Chirbury, after half a mile the A490 passes a lodge and the driveway leading to the late 16th-century Marrington Hall. This is regarded as one of the finest surviving half-timber houses in Shropshire, rivalling even Pitchford (p.40), but it stands back from the road and is in private occupation.

At Church Stoke, the route rejoins the A489, turns left to meet the A488 (and the Mitchell's Fold detour) and then leads towards Knighton. Continue on this road through Lydham and typical south Shropshire hill country until you reach the B4384, on which you turn right and then second right to visit Bishop's Castle, a small and atmospheric market town dating from the 12th century, with a population of just over 1,700. Park in the main street that slopes down the hill towards the church at its foot (the road on which you should have entered the town!).

Looking back up the main street to the Town Hall in Bishops Castle

7.   Bishops Castle

Soon after the Norman Conquest, most of the lands held by the English nobility were distributed by King William among his followers. One of these was Robert Losinga, a versatile scholar from Lorraine in north-western France who was consecrated 19th bishop of Hereford in 1079. He was granted parts of south-west Shropshire which included the large manor of Lydbury, and in return was expected to see to the defence of that sector of the Border against raids by the recalcitrant Welsh. So in *c.*1087 he built a motte and bailey castle on a prominence to the north-west of his territory, first known as Lydbury Castle, and during the ensuing 80 years a new town was planted down to the church at the bottom of the hill. In addition he was heavily occupied in rebuilding Hereford Cathedral after its devastation by the Welsh in 1055, and much subsequent neglect. Grandly robed as a 'Lord of the March' and a prelate of that period, he would travel about his diocese holding court, collecting tolls and taxes with a mounted retinue of at least half of his regular household of about 40, and he would also take a leading part in the conduct of State affairs in London. (By contrast, the recent 103rd bishop of Hereford also spent part of his time in the capital, and at the House of Lords championing the rural borderland and the problems of its people against neglect and indifference from town-dwelling policy makers. Looking quite unlike his predecessor of 900 years ago, he might instead have been met in the diocese riding without escort, clad in a crash helmet and leatherwear and mounted on the saddle of a Suzuki GSX-R 750 cc motor cycle).

From 1167 the timberwork of the castle was gradually replaced with stone and in 1287 there was extensive rebuilding. With the town, from then on it became known as Bishops Castle and remained habitable until the 17th century but becoming ruinous by 1700. Treated as a quarry, it was robbed of stone as a base for the hotel bowling green, which covers the site of the keep, and other elements were incorporated into houses in Market Square and Bull Street. Now there is very little left to see of what must have once been a mighty stronghold.

At the lower end of the town, the church of St. John Baptist is on the site of an earlier church. It has a low squat tower, looking Norman but possibly restored in 1662 after Civil War damage and is typical in appearance of others in this part of the Marches, such as that at Clun. Most of the present building is otherwise well designed Victorian. Between castle and church, parts of the town are

Castle Hotel, near the old castle site

built down what are called 'shuts', or passages. Leading off the public road to yards surrounded by houses and business premises, these could once be shut off for protection in emergency.

Until 1967 Bishops Castle was known as the smallest borough in England, and before 1832 was a 'rotten borough'. This was nothing to do with its character but meant that with very few voters, until the Reform Act of that year it could elect two M.P.s. Because of an insoluble tie in votes, four were actually sent to Westminster on one occasion!

The grassy site of the old castle now serves as an excellent lookout, picnic and play area at the top of the town, and just below, in the middle of the one-time outer bailey and very distinctive for such a small town, is the Castle Hotel. It started as a coaching inn in 1719 and is one of six ancient hostelries in Bishop's Castle. Famously, two of them have continued with the production of their own beers and the nearer of these is the Three Tuns on Salop Street. It has a 3-storey Victorian gravity-fed tower brewery and Grade I listed building, and this can be visited by arrangement—as can a museum of beer and brewing. The Six Bells Inn, originally a 17th-century coaching inn, is

The arms of Clive of India in the Square at Bishops Castle

in Church Street at the lower end of town. On the site of an earlier brewery, it resumed production in 1997 and has since developed nine different ales—helping to earn the inn the CAMRA (Campaign for Real Ale) West Midland Pub of the Year Award. In the Market Square and at the top of High Street, the area close to the handsome old brick town hall of 1765 is at its busiest on the main Friday market day. Just below and overhanging The Cobbles, the so called House on Crutches Museum is open between Easter and October and displays changing exhibits covering the history of the town and its surroundings. And off one of the shuts next to the Crown and Anchor inn, in what is left of a barn at the rear of 26 High Street, there is a third museum of a troubled local railway and transport history. Sadly the former 15th-century building has recently shared the misfortunes of the branch railway which, between 1865 and 1935, followed a scenic route up the Onny valley from the main line at Craven Arms. A declining population and reducing revenues quickly meant that for most of its time it was in a state of bankruptcy, and this was compounded by a catalogue of operating difficulties and other misfortunes. It was particularly hard therefore when in 2000 these persisted after a serious fire destroyed much of the museum building. It had to close for several months, but what remains is now open during weekend afternoons from Easter to October.

Clive of India

That there is a local connection with Baron Clive of India (1725-74), the British general, victor at Plassey in 1757 and statesman, is shown by his stone memorial coat of arms which was recovered from the Market Hall of 1775 when it was demolished towards the end of the 20th century. It is erected at the Old Market Square in Bull Street, and at Lydbury North there is Walcot Hall, a large Georgian brick manor house which was redesigned in 1763 for Lord Clive by Sir William Chambers. It remained in the family for 165 years, and over the course of time they planted an arboretum of 30 acres with many fine specimen trees and also set out attractive pathways. During the Napoleonic Wars, French prisoners of war extended a mile long lake, and at about the same time a free-standing ballroom was added which now enhances the appeal of the Hall as a venue for weddings, concerts and parties. The Hall, ballroom and arboretum are open for visits by the public on Open Days at advertised times doubtless known at the TIC, 29 High Street, Bishop's Castle.

The tour continues down the sloping main street but before leaving Bishops Castle, past the church and then school on the right, it is worth looking left near the crossroads with the A448 for the privately occupied Old Hall. This is a striking close-studded 16th-century black and white manor house which features prominent diagonal bracing and pronounced jettying.

There is now the chance for a small detour to see a glimpse of Walcot Hall and to visit the interesting church of Lydbury North. The main route straight to Clun turns right at the crossroads onto the A488; for the detour, take the B4385 straight ahead and after just under 3 miles the village of Lydbury North is reached where on the right, immediately before the Powis Arms inn, there is a drive to Walcot Hall. In the village a little further along, one of the two long transepts at St. Michael's Church is known as the Walcot Chapel. The other is the Plowden Chapel and is associated with the renowned Elizabethan lawyer, Edmund Plowden, whose timber-framed Hall was built a further 2 miles to the east at Plowden. The detour is completed by returning to the A488 by the same route, on which you then turn left.

The A488 first climbs past Forestry Commission woodland, and a trail leading to the Iron Age Camp of Bury Ditches, where conifers have been cleared to expose several ramparts extending over 100 yards. As the road descends towards Clun, the view to the right opens out over a broad river valley which fronts the Kerry Hills and Powys. This exposed valley at the far south-west corner of Shropshire and England, vulnerable to attack through the Welsh district of Maelienydd, just west of Offa's Dyke, would be bound to produce another castle in the Borderland chain. Sure enough, closer to the town amidst extensive earthworks on a grassy bank and above where the River Unk joins the River Clun, almost the first building on the right is the great ruined tower of Clun Castle. Continue down Castle Street, turn right in High Street, cross Clun Bridge into Church Street and make an immediate right turn to enter the riverside carpark, alongside the B4368.

8.   Quiet Clun

The river and narrow medieval saddleback five arch bridge separate the Norman castle and planned settlement from the earlier centre of Clun, around the sturdy St. George's Church at the south end of the town. Its broad buttressed tower provided refuge from attacks by the Welsh for villagers, and during the Civil War was occupied by Parliamentary soldiers, under attack by Royalists (although without the horrific consequences meted out at Hopton Castle—see below). Soon after the Conquest, the urgent need for a strong castle to control the approaches from Wales was first met with a substantial motte and two baileys joined by causeways. This was soon reinforced with a stone curtain and later a great three-storey stone tower and basement was built. This has until recently been dated towards the end of the 12th century, but there are now suggestions that it was later and nearer the 1260s or 70s. From then on Clun was in sporadic dispute between the Welsh and English until the early 15th century and peace. The castle then decayed, but now the Great Tower ruin remains tall, upright and impressive at a height of 92ft. It is owned by the duke of Norfolk, whose Fitz Alan family seat it was from the 12th to the 16th centuries, but in the care of English Heritage and with free access to its surrounds alongside the River Clun.

Clun Bridge

Clun Castle

Attempts were made by the Normans to create a town with the castle and this still shows in the grid layout of streets based on High Street, which is like a small version of Ludlow. But although this was a traditional meeting place of the English and Welsh, it was always susceptible to disputes and even battles between them and this must be one reason why there has been little growth. Since the 19th century other social and economic factors have arisen. In 1851 Clun was a busy market town with a population of around 1,200, which is equivalent to that of Bishops

St. George's church, Clun

Castle today. There were at least 14 pubs and a Temperance Hall, but at the end of the 20th century the population had reduced to just over 700. As one of the four 'quietest places under the sun' of the Shropshire jingle quoted by A.E. Housman, together with nearby Clunton, Clunbury and Clungunford, it is probably even quieter now than it was in the poet's day. Eight roads still converge on the village and it remains a shopping and social centre for a considerable area of hill country but now are just three inns—The Buffalo Head Hotel and White Horse in the Square, and the 16th-century Sun in High Street. The Town Hall of 1780 has become a museum of local items on

Tuesdays and Saturdays during the summer, but in Hospital Lane, little has changed since 1644 at the Hospital of the Holy and Undivided Trinity, the gabled almshouses and chapel first provided for 12 old men of good character and later extended to married couples.

The Forest of Clun

Clun, within a designated 'Area of Outstanding Natural Beauty', is also the 'capital' of what has been known since the Middle Ages as the Forest of Clun. It covers an area of some 17,000 acres and has some of the finest scenery of the Welsh Border, thrusting deep into the wild and lonely Kerry Hills of Montgomeryshire. But it is left with very few trees for a forest because of shipbuilding and charcoal demands during the Tudor period. In addition, wooden buildings in Shropshire and Herefordshire used up huge amounts of oak—one estimate in 1500 for a simple timber-framed farmhouse alone stated a need for 350 trees of 9ins. to 18ins. diameter. Although not to everyone's liking, modern afforestation is to an extent helping to restore a wooded character and must be having some bearing on rainwater and soil conservation. Otherwise the isolated farms and homesteads have to depend heavily on income from the Clun and Kerry sheep to which the area has given its name.

Sculpture of two former residents at Clun's almshouses

For a suggested way back to Knighton, turn left out of the carpark in Clun, then left over the bridge and turn right at the first bend onto the B4368, heading through Clunton to join the B4385 at Purslow at the Hundred House inn. This is near Clunbury and now proceed towards Hoptonheath and just after a left turn for Clungunford, there is a sign pointing right down a rather narrow road for Hopton Castle. It may require a display of courtesy and reversing skills, but in a hollow among the hills after less than a mile it reaches the hamlet of Hopton Castle, and the rewarding sight of a fine black and white former rectory.

9.   A Massacre at Hopton Castle

Visible in a field across to the left is the sturdy ruined keep of Hopton Castle itself. Like many others, it started as a castle motte in the 12th century and the rectangular great tower was probably superimposed and surrounded with wet moats during the 13th. History books do not reveal much involve-

Hopton Castle

ment in the Welsh troubles but concentrate on a black episode in 1644, during the Civil War. The castle was garrisoned by about 31 Roundheads and besieged and greatly outnumbered by a force of Cavaliers. They declined an offer of quarter and were prepared to resist to the last man, holding out for three weeks before they were overrun and captured. Because they had not quickly surrendered to an overwhelming force they were subjected to the Rules of Engagement of that time, which were observed by both sides. They were summarily executed, and accounts relate that they were tied back-to-back, slashed and drowned in the moat almost to the last man—indeed all but one. This was their commander, who presumably issued the order to resist, and Colonel Samuel More was instead taken to Hereford Castle for exchange with an equivalent Royalist prisoner, and allowed to live with his conscience! The ruins were saved from dereliction in 2008 after a few local villagers set up the Hopton Castle Preservation Trust and raised £1 million, including a lottery grant, to assume ownership and make plans for restoration and public access.

Take the direct and rather wider road past the ruins to rejoin the B4367 at Hoptonheath near the Heart of Wales railway station. This road passes through Bucknell, the next station, before turning right to join the A4113 for the way back to Knighton.

Ludlow

Seldom does the first visit to any famed historic town live up to expectations when it comes to be seen in modern guise. Ludlow, however, is different from most others in that it still receives tributes which can match 'One of the handsomest country towns in England', as it appeared in 1797 to the *Gentleman's Magazine*. 'Ludlow is one of Europe's most beautiful towns', was quoted by a much more recent publication, and in *Country Life* in 1945, architectural critic Christopher Hussey enthused: 'For sheer visual beauty coloured by .... history and substantiated in richness of architectural sequence, Ludlow stands high, perhaps first, among English towns. Others can surpass it on particular points, but few if any in this union of setting, quality and texture, each intrinsically first rate. The whole place is a national monument ....'. In 1999 the same magazine called it 'the most vibrant small town in the country' after Nikolaus Pevsner in 1958 had described Broad Street as: 'one of the most memorable streets in England'—and The Feathers Hotel at the Bull Ring as: 'that prodigy of timber framed houses'. The parish church of St. Laurence, which in 1541 Leland regarded as: 'the fayrest in all these parts', was in 1999 graded by Simon Jenkins as one of just 18 to justify a top award of 5 stars from his selection of *England's Thousand Best Churches*.

From medieval times, High Street has comprised the primary shopping axis of the town, as well as for a wide area of the Borderland. Businesses have gradually since spread into other streets, especially the upper parts of Broad Street and down Corve Street, the shop premises mostly occupied by small traders. Among them are food retailers who, by also mounting a 'Ludlow Marches Food and Drink

The keep, Ludlow Castle

Festival' every September, contribute greatly to the town's growing reputation as the food-lovers' equivalent of book-worms' Hay-on-Wye. They help to account for Ludlow's claim to be 'The Gourmet Capital of the Marches' and a draw for the new breed of 'Gastrotourists', and the shops supply its many good inns and other eating places—not least the three that have vaunted Michelin stars (a score for this small town greater than anywhere else outside London!).

Soon after the Norman Conquest, Walter de Lacy, one of the leading Marcher barons, embarked upon plans to construct a stronghold and strategic base for control of the rebellious Welshmen ranging to the west. Granted the ancient Stanton estate, he opted for a commanding clifftop above the fast-flowing River Teme in the south of his land, at the village of Dinham. But on 27 March 1085, he was killed when he fell from the battlements of his great new collegiate church at Hereford, where St. Peter's now stands. The castle keep was probably completed by his eldest son, Roger, before the end of the 11th century—but unlike the many early motte and bailey structures of earth and timber, this was built of local sandstone from the start. With it came

The castle's inner bailey, with living apartments on the left and the round chapel on the right

an immediate requirement for provisions, manpower and other services. In what is said to be a pioneering approach in complete town planning in Britain, a town was set out to a simple grid pattern to the east of the castle gate, based on a very wide spine road running along the crest of the hill. This joined the old long-distance north-south route crossing the rivers Teme and Corve—which is now recognisable as Old Street, Bull Ring and Corve Street. In accordance with common practice around the 12th century, a church was established at the opposite end of the High Street from the castle. The parish was created out of the parent ministry at Stanton Lacy to the north and its first boundaries took in the newly built town walls and the suburbs, although not the castle.

A strong border position half way between Chester and Chepstow ensured that Ludlow Castle would become an important military stronghold and it was destined to be inhabited for more than 550 years. Early in the 14th century it passed by marriage to Roger Mortimer and, when the Yorkist earldom of March merged with the crown after the accession of Edward IV in 1461, it became a royal castle (Ludlow being rewarded for its loyalty with borough status which lasted until 1967). The young princes, Edward and Richard, were sent to live there in the early 1470s, remaining until 1483 when, as King Edward V and Richard, Duke of York, they left for London, the Tower and an alleged fate at the behest of the future Richard III. In January 1501 another tragedy struck after Arthur, the 15-year-old Prince of Wales, arrived at the castle on honeymoon with his young bride, the Spanish infanta, Catherine of Aragon. By the beginning of April, aged only 16, she was a widow. Arthur's 'heart' was buried at St. Laurence's Church and his body taken to Worcester Cathedral and then, in 1509, his younger brother, by then Henry VIII, controversially married Catherine in a step which led to profound changes in English history. Their only surviving child, Mary, subsequently spent the winters of 1525 to 1528 in Ludlow before becoming the embittered 'Bloody Mary'.

In 1485 Henry VII had chosen Ludlow Castle as the seat of the Council in the Marches. Apart from short periods, this existed for more than two centuries, dominating Wales and the border counties under a Lord President. Ludlow was in effect the capital of Wales and enjoyed prosperity which can still be sensed from the quantity and quality of its half-timbered buildings, with a reminder of Welsh associations through the Harp and Feathers hotels. But in 1689 the Council was abolished, the castle soon abandoned and in ruins by the middle of the 18th century. Much restored, it is now owned by the earl of Powis.

Intense commercial and professional activity generated through the castle, augmented by a strong wool and leather industry, had consolidated the standing of Ludlow by the 15th century, at a time when many would-be towns along the borders failed, remaining little more than villages. The High Street market-place which had been laid out with pitches and stalls to the east of the castle entrance was gradually transformed with permanent buildings, and parts of its original 7 perches (35 metres) width were also taken up by infilling and other encroachments.

Overlooking Ludlow Castle, St. Laurence's Church and the town from Whitcliffe Common

To the north, near the junction with Church Street, Quality Square preserves the plan of a 16th-century town house and brickwork of the period may still be seen in the south-west corner. This is where Ludlow's wool-merchants had warehouses and in the 19th century it also contained a theatre. At the eastern end of High Street, the steep frontages of Corve Street and Old Street were developed and burgaged and by the late 12th century a grid of streets had become established between High Street and the River Teme on the sloping ground to the south. Two wide thoroughfares, Broad Street and Mill Street, were set out to be served by narrow and parallel rear access streets and everything was linked by cross lanes which are today's Bell Lane and Brand Lane, roughly half way down and extending to Old Street.

There is now so much to see, and possibly to miss, and it pays to take an early look at the literature and street maps in the Tourist Information Centre (TIC) on the corner of Castle Square and Mill Street. This, with Ludlow Museum, is in part of the old Assembly Rooms, one of the very few major Victorian buildings built within the walled town. But as well as the castle and St. Laurence's Church, there are over 500 listed buildings in Ludlow.

Entrance to the castle is through the outer bailey or ward, which was built towards the end of the 12th century over part of the early town. It is actually much larger than it first appears, for some is now separated off as a private garden, but originally all would have been used for stables, stores and workshops as well as troop exercises, tournaments and other major events. In times of warfare it also served as a place of refuge for the townspeople. On its west side the D-shaped tower was possibly built during the early 13th century and has long been known as the Mortimer Tower (although the family did not become associated with Ludlow until after the marriage of Roger Mortimer (p.61) in 1301). Its original function was as a gateway and this is thought to have lasted until the 15th century. Roger Mortimer became involved in a rebellion against Edward II in 1321 and after ending up in the Tower of London, he escaped to France after drugging his guards. A few years later he was to return in consort with Edward's queen, mounted a coup and ruled in Edward's place for three years. To celebrate his escape from the Tower he founded St. Peter's Chapel, in the outer bailey, a building that was converted during the 16th century into a courthouse.

The oldest part of the castle is the elliptical inner bailey. Probably built between 1086 and 1094, with its curtain wall 7ft. thick in places, it is dominated by the Great Tower. This has been described as 'one of the most curious Norman keeps still standing'. Entry to the inner bailey was originally through

The round chapel of St. Mary Magdalene

a late 11th-century gatehouse which formed the first phase of its construction and the rounded arch entrance and the ledge for the first drawbridge can be seen from the outer bailey. In *c.*1130 the gatehouse was raised to become a four storey tower or keep and in *c.*1190 the first entrance was blocked and the present entrance was cut through the curtain wall. A fourth phase in the 15th century saw a reduction in size of the tower and an amount of rebuilding. On the right immediately inside the inner bailey and completed in 1581 were a three storey block of offices and private rooms, referred to as The Judges' Lodgings. With its highly ornamented doorways, the Romanesque chapel of St. Mary Magdalene possesses one of only five round naves in England and was possibly influenced by the Knights Templar. Until the 16th century there were also a chancel and apse, but these were then replaced and now that version has also gone. Also in the 16th century an upper floor was formed to provide for a separate chapel for the superior classes living in the 14th-century Great Chamber Block, to which it was connected with a wooden gallery. This building was part of domestic accommodation which included the Great Hall, a service wing and further living quarters, including rooms said to have been so briefly used by Prince Arthur. To the east was the four floor 14th-century Garderobe Tower and beyond that a block including the Pendover Tower, which traditionally is said to be where 'the little Princes' lived between 1473 and 1483 before their departure for the Tower of London (p.68). These days the inner bailey provides an atmospheric setting for the Shakespeare plays which, each June/July, are produced as part of the Ludlow Festival.

Just outside the entrance to the castle, at the junction of Castle Square and Mill Street, Castle Lodge is a 16th-century building first provided for the porter, and afterwards occupied by the governor of the castle. The arched doorway is thought to be original, but much of

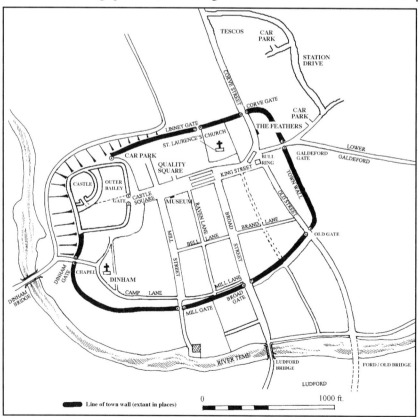

Plan of Ludlow town centre

the stonework probably dates from a rebuilding in the 1580s and the timber-framing above somewhat later. Mill Street contains many fine Georgian façades whilst the Guildhall embodies a 15th-century timber-framed aisled hall ranked as highly as that in the bishop's palace at Hereford. It was built for the Palmers' Guild, a religious institution founded in the 13th century (a palmer being a pilgrim who brought back palm leaves to show that he had visited the Holy Land) which accumulated great wealth and property enabling it to act as an early-day welfare agency for the deserving poor. The Guild played a large part in the adornment and music of St. Laurence's Church, established a school near the church and, importantly, provided for the housing and support of priests appointed to pray for members' souls. By the 16th century there were over 4,000 members—but in 1551 the Guild was dissolved. Yet its influence can still be detected throughout the town, long after the property and much of its role were taken over by the corporation. In 1768 the Guildhall was refurbished in a Gothic Revival

St. Laurence's Church

style and encased in brick and it is still much in use but better appreciated by those not loaded with guilt, for after 500 years it lives on as Ludlow Magistrates Court. Further down Mill Street a rich wool merchant's house was acquired by the Guild, where in 1527 it founded one of the oldest grammar schools in the country. This lasted until 1977 and has since become the Palmers' Hall of Ludlow College. It stands quite close to the site of Mill Gate, one of seven originally placed along the defensive walls. Here Silk Mill Lane serves as a reminder of an 18th-century riverside industry.

Back in High Street, for many years until the late 19th century there had been a market hall not far from the castle entrance but, wishing to mark Queen Victoria's Golden Jubilee in 1887, the council decided to replace it with one of the new town halls which were then all the rage. In an area rich with long-proven skills and building materials, the architect selected for this commission, came, of all places, from Twickenham. Seemingly equipped with a limited idea of Marches building vernacular and with catalogues of 'bolt on' ornamentation, he produced a £6,000 council chamber, assembly hall and ground floor covered-market. Some idea of what it looked like may still be judged in Hereford's Georgian St. Owen Street through the same man's slightly later Town Hall. Both buildings were then described in similar terms as being 'probably a little out of harmony with the surroundings'! The Ludlow building was, however, admired at the time even for its 'fiery brick and useless Elizabethan detail'. After 100 years, a short interval in Ludlow terms, it was considered to

The Guildhall

53 Broad Street, Ludlow

be unsafe, but there were still many Ludlovians who were saddened, even angry, when it was demolished in 1986. But since then the Market Place has returned for up to four days a week to some semblance of its more traditional open form and breadth. Newly repaved it becomes animated with all the bustle surrounding a busy stalls market well provided with local as well as more widely available produce. There is also a monthly Farmers Market, one of several now appearing in local market towns which offer merchandise 'grown, reared, caught, brewed, pickled, baked, smoked or processed' within a short range of the town. The main high street chains have largely by-passed Ludlow, one of its three super-markets fitting discreetly into Castle Square. East of Raven Lane, the medieval High Street has long been narrowed by infilling with shops resulting in a series of narrow lanes.

Facing down Broad Street and unusually designed in stone by William Baker from neigh-bouring Cheshire in the 1840s, the Buttercross was the first of a series of mid-18th century buildings to appear in Ludlow. Standing at its hub, it is still broadly regarded as 'an adornment to the town' and has been put to a variety of uses, upstairs from 1782 as a Blue Coat Charity School, later as a museum and now Town Council offices. In 1946, Christopher Hussey wrote: 'The excellence of the Buttercross for its position lies ... in its scale being approximately the same as the older buildings ... its parapet balls and dainty cupola echo in another key the indented Gothic skyline...'. And of Broad Street: 'There is no more beautiful street in England'. It is still largely without rival and a credit to medieval, Georgian and contemporary builders and town-plan-ners (provided that the plethora of parked cars can visually be air-brushed out). It has for a very long time been divided into 'trade' at the top end and 'gentry' towards the bottom, headed by Bodenhams, who have been outfitters for more than a century (their corner shop was assembled in the 1390s by

Broadgate, looking back into town

the Palmers' Guild from four smaller units). After De Greys tea-rooms of *c*.1570, the 300-year-old Angel Inn and other timbered buildings, lower down there are many fine and varied Georgian homes and establishments for professionals, before Broad Street has suddenly to squeeze through the Broadgate. With flanking drum towers, this dates from the late 13th century, supports a Georgian house and is the sole survivor of seven gates—the others demolished by the end of the 18th century in the cause of smoother traffic flow. A different road

The entrance to Hosyer's Almshouses

The Reader's House

improvement at this gate was performed in the 19th century by Thomas Telford, Shropshire's first county surveyor. In one of his early less spectacular schemes the steep incline for vehicles was eased by an embankment on its south (town ditch) side and a cutting excavated to the north.

Lower Broad Street widens again before reaching 15th-century Ludford Bridge. It was just built for animals and small numbers of vehicles many centuries ago and, on a slope, is still only wide enough for signal-controlled one-way traffic. There is no footway and care is needed between the refuges above the V-shaped cutwaters. White-water rapids rush towards the impressive horseshoe weir downstream, to the mill stream which once powered mills at the bottom of Old Street and at Ludford. The bridge links Ludlow with the older settlement of Ludford, St. Giles Church, picturesque almshouses and a partly timber-framed house of 1614 which used to be the Bell Inn.

Ludford House originated in Late Elizabethan or Jacobean times—its most striking feature from the road being a stone range containing four vast chimney breasts and stacks. The Overton road continues towards the new livestock market and Hereford, whilst to the right, just past the Charlton Arms pub, Whitcliffe Road heads up a slope (the 'white cliff' formed of Silurian limestone) for a classic view of the entire town, castle and much of the far countryside. Various footpaths cross Whitcliffe Common and it is then possible to re-enter Ludlow upstream across Dinham Bridge where there is much more to see. Look out for the blue flash of kingfishers among the water birds by the weir, as well as in 2009 the Michelin-starred 'restaurant with rooms'.

There is no longer a town Gate as the Dinham lane returns below the castle towards the Market Place and High Street. College Street to the north of Church Street leads to Hosyer's Almshouses, which were founded by John Hosyer (d.1463) a rich cloth merchant. They were replaced by the present building in 1758, the arms of the town incorporating the lion of the Mortimers and white roses of the House of York, placed high up on the pediment. It adjoins the Rectory at the end of the road, near the town wall and the site of Linney Gate. On the opposite side of the churchyard is the three-storey double-jettied oak and plaster porch of the Reader's House which faces the Garden of Remembrance. The house chiefly originated in the 16th century but the porch was added in 1616 by the then chaplain of the Council of the Marches. One of its most striking features for what was probably the rear of the house is the studded oak door and ornate doorway. In the 18th century, the house became the official residence of the Reader, one of the curates of the parish church. There is a plaque to A.E. Housman (1859-1936) on the outside nave north wall of the church into which his ashes have been lodged. Born in Bromsgrove in Worcestershire, he became a great classical scholar but from 1896 his name was very much identified with Shropshire through *A Shropshire Lad*, a collection of reflective poems which helped more than anything else to make the remote rural county known throughout the world. And for something quite different, formed in wrought iron, there is an upright fletcher's arrow still fixed on the roof of the North Transept, above the chapel once used by the town's arrow-makers.

The church is entered by a highly unusual 14th-century hexagonal porch and once within it pays to make for the book stall to obtain a detailed guide. It will probably be by David Lloyd, a very prolific, well-informed and readable local historian. St. Laurence's is regarded as one of the noblest parish churches in Britain and the length of 203ft. and 125ft. width across the transepts make it one of the largest. The tower rises to 135 feet and from most directions it is a greater focus of attention than the castle ruins. Apart from the font, the former Norman church has disappeared but there is evidence suggesting that rebuilding commenced in 1199, with extensions in the 13th and 14th and reconstruction in the 15th centuries. The present appearance largely dates from restoration works by George Gilbert Scott in 1859-60, but much extra attention has been required since, especially

As you explore Ludlow keep an eye out for carved brackets such as these on 14/15 Raven Lane—that to the left is 17th century, that to the right, 20th century

to the roof during the 1950s. Semblance of the church to a small cathedral extends to features such as the chancel stalls and misericords (described in a special booklet), some exceptional monuments and stained glass windows of great age which are regarded as among the best in the world. The east window dates from 1445 and tells the story of the saint to whom the church is dedicated, one of the most popular of 3rd-century Roman martyrs who was barbecued over a slow fire for not surrendering church treasures. During winter months the curfew bell rings at 8p.m. and the eight carillon bells in the tower have played a different tune nearly every day of the year since 1638 (assisted by computer from 1989 at 8am, noon, 4pm and 8pm).

King Street and the Narrows, formerly Drapers' Row, extend eastward from the Butter Cross to the Bull Ring. In the 17th century this was called 'the Beast Market' and the Tolsey or toll house was there for administration of the markets and fairs. Tolls were collected and the equivalent of today's trading standards, weights and measures and minor breaches of the law were dealt with at the Court of Pie Powder (a corruption of *pieds poudre*—'dusty-footed' travellers who required prompt attention). The name of one of the present shops preserves the link at the eastern extent of the original High Street, which had once also occupied the area extending south to Pepper Lane, Valentine's Walk and Market Street. The present shoe and chemist shops to the north were included in what was also open space 800 years ago and called 'the Shelde'—from the Latin *selda* meaning stalls. Tower Street, directly opposite, was closed to vehicular traffic in 1989 and the surface was repaved for pedestrians heading for the busy hairpin road junction at the post office store and Summerfields supermarket.

To the right, Lower Galdeford descends past the Bishop Mascall Diocesan Conference Centre, based at Thomas Nicholson's flamboyant 1855 National School, and a new police station which opened in 2002. Shortly after the school was built, the council bought land just down the road to create a new cattle, sheep and horse market. During its construction the engineer, Timothy Curley, discovered remains of the Augustine friary which had existed on part of the site between 1254 and 1538. Fine encaustic tiles, ball-flower decoration and other relics were delivered to Ludlow Museum before work proceeded. By 1900 the market had succumbed to strong competition near the railway station, and the area is now partly occupied by the Smithfield car, lorry and bus park. The road to the left at Summerfields provides for access to a public car-park and to Ludlow's Library and Museum Resources Centre. Opened in 2002 after much contention in the town, this contains natural and social history collections, provides a record of life in Shropshire through the last 500 million years and organises wide ranging educational and recreational activities for children and school groups. The museum at Castle Street will remain open. Upper Galdeford is joined from the left by Station Drive, which offers another access to the public car park, and then passes the railway station before reaching Corve Street.

For many centuries from the Middle Ages the draw of the markets, activities at the castle and proceedings of the Council in the Marches have brought in countless travellers and visitors, ranging from royalty and their many hangers-on, litigants and attorneys appearing at meetings of the Council to ordinary country folk from a few miles away. Small ale-houses, taverns and pubs proliferated and larger inns were important for travellers requiring overnight shelter for themselves and their horses. The Crown at 56/58 Broad Street was the largest, with 18 fireplaces in 1672, whilst the oldest is the Bull Hotel at 14 Bull Ring. It has been an inn since the 15th century and contains remnants of a fine medieval roof with cusped windbraces dating from *c*.1350. The long range at the rear has served as a 'medieval motel', having a style characteristic of inns of 500 years ago. The front of the hotel was destroyed by fire in 1794 and has subsequently been rebuilt in a rather bland Georgian style. It is completely outshone by the ornate timber-framed façade of the world-famous Feathers Hotel, nearly opposite at 24 Bull Ring, which was converted from a grand house to an inn in 1670. No.42 Bull Ring occupies part of a large 17th-century property which used to be the Prince Rupert Inn, and after Bull Ring enters Corve Street, there is the Michelin starred Hibiscus Restaurant at no. 17, formerly the Eagle House Restaurant and, before that in 1704, the Eagle and Child Inn. After long raging arguments about the likely effect on trade in existing independent shops, and upon the world-famous townscape, the Tesco chain eventually obtained all necessary consents for its store on the former livestock market land.

Slightly further down Corve Street, any atmosphere to compare with the miasma which once

The Merchant House

hung over the site of The former Merchant House Restaurant at No. 62 would not have favoured the award of its 21st-century Michelin star, and certainly not to a position, judged by the *Restaurant Magazine* in 2003, as the second best restaurant in Britain and 14th in the world! For this part is known as Lower Corve Street, where the pungent tannery and leather trades of Ludlow in the 16th and 17th centuries were concentrated. As a town in the centre of grazing country and served by considerable river water power, its economy was heavily based first on wool and cloth—and then on leather trades, supplying shoe-makers, saddlers and glovers (glovemaking alone employed *c*.1000 Ludlovians, producing some 670,000 gloves a year in the late 18th century).

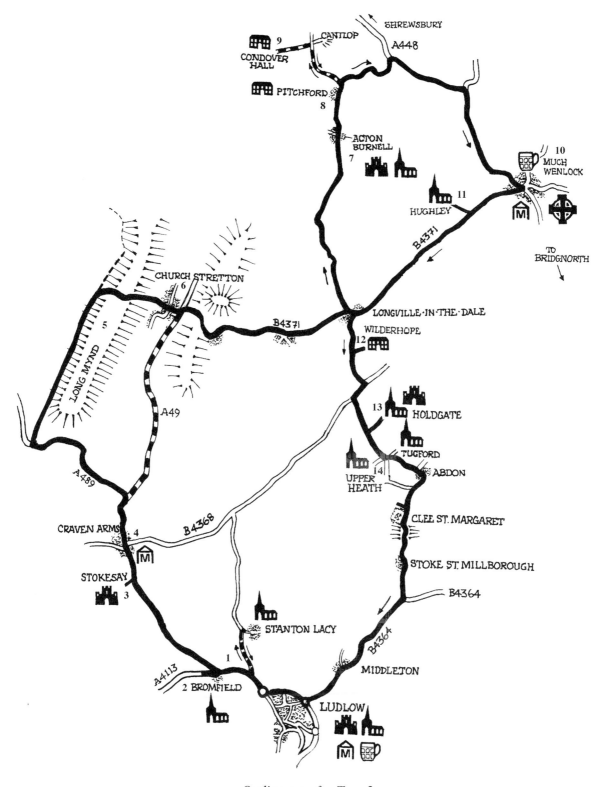

Outline map for Tour 2
The numbers 1 to 14 relate to the boxed information given within the tour

Tour 2   From Ludlow Northwards

This tour starts at Ludlow, which probably deserves a day to itself, and then moves northwards. It includes the sites of several round barrows and other prehistoric relics, the remains of Bromfield Priory with its surviving church and gatehouse and the fortified manor house of Stokesay Castle. Beyond the former railway town of Craven Arms, there is then an option of a steep climb up a mountain road to the top of the Long Mynd and then an equally steep and winding descent to Church Stretton. The route then heads eastwards to weave and roll through 'Mary Webb Country' to reach the fortified manor house and historically significant Parliament Barn ruins at Acton Burnell, and other striking Shropshire houses. Then the tour heads into Much Wenlock to see the unique atmosphere created by its architecture and the ancient priory. For the return journey, the route first ascends the ridge of Wenlock Edge, before dropping and then climbing to pass beneath Brown Clee Hill to reach a deserted village at Heath and its austere and lonely Norman chapel. Soon afterwards the journey ends back at Ludlow. The distance, without detours, is about 70 miles. (OS Landranger 126, 127, 137)

The route is on a mixture of A and B roads and narrow country lanes. It includes an optional narrow and steep ascent, crossing and descent of the Long Mynd.

Despite its appearance, Ludlow is a comparatively new town, and much younger than Stanton Lacy, the manor from which it sprang and the village for which the tour first heads. On the A49 just north of Ludlow, turn right onto the B4365, signposted for Much Wenlock, crossing over the railway and cutting across Ludlow racecourse and golf-course before reaching and taking a narrower road to the right sign-posted to Stanton Lacy. This is a village of thatched and tiled black and white cottages, the River Corve flowing by, and a cruciform St. Peter's Church. This was reconstructed in the 13th and 14th centuries but has much older Anglo-Saxon work. This can be seen at the built-up round-headed north doorway with a cross above it, the west and north walls of the Nave and those of the North Transept. Yet old as all this is, the neighbouring area between Stanton Lacy, Ludlow and Bromfield knew a high level of occupation for more than 3,000 years before the Late Saxon church even appeared.

From Stanton Lacy return to the junction with the B4365 on which you turn left, and then right onto the A49 towards Shrewsbury. After about a mile, left onto the A 4113 signposted Leintwardine/ Knighton to visit the remains of Bromfield's old priory.

Continue northwards on the A49 for about 5 miles to Stokesay, and shortly afterwards Craven Arms.

---

1.   Bromfield. The necropolis and Roman marching camp

Within Ludlow racecourse on the left-hand side of the road leading back to the A49 there are four Bronze Age round barrows among the five survivors of age-long ploughing and other disturbances which have obliterated almost 15 other barrows, whilst at Bromfield sand and gravel quarry evidence of even earlier activity has been placed by carbon-14 dating at 2560 BC. Many arte-facts were found near the excavation site, and at one part of the quarry a cemetery was uncovered containing some 130 shallow pits with a use spanning over 800 years, from between 1870 BC to 910 BC. This necropolis was succeeded nearby by pagan and then Christian Anglo-Saxon cemeteries dating from the early 7th until the 10th century AD.

A concentration of prehistoric relics and finds of later periods in the area has also included a Roman military site alongside the road between Bromfield Farm and the railway line to Shrewsbury. Aerial photographs confirm the usual rectangular shape of a marching camp with rounded corners, probably constructed for temporary overnight stops soon after the Claudian conquest of Britain in AD 43. Its date has not been established, but it could have been used in border operations from AD 47 by the legionary forces of Ostorius Scapula against resistance from Caratacus, the British leader. He was captured in Wales and taken in chains to Rome not long afterwards.

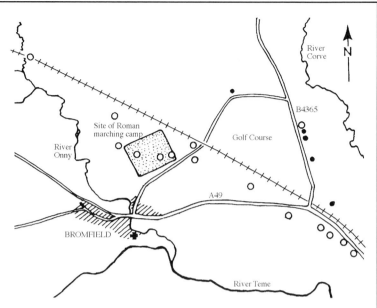

Remaining barrows are shown by black dots, those that have been ploughed out by circles

2. Bromfield Priory and Henry Hill Hickman

Bromfield is otherwise best known for its surviving medieval Augustinian priory church, sited between the rivers Teme and Onny. At the roadside, all that remains of the priory itself is a huge and very picturesque stone gatehouse with 14th-century upper storey half-timbered work, now managed as self-catering accommodation by the Landmark Trust. Within the church, one noteworthy feature is the chancel ceiling, which in the gloom of the building has been said to display 'the best example of the worst style of ecclesiastical art'! And in the churchyard there is the grave of Dr. Henry Hill Hickman (1800-1830).

The gateway to Bromfield Priory

The very year that Henry Hickman was born at nearby Halton and baptised in the 13th-century font at Bromfield, the eminent Sir Humphrey Davy suggested that nitrous oxide—laughing gas—might deaden the pain of surgical operations. Yet even his reputation failed to impress the medical or scientific world. However some 20 years later, Henry Hickman, a young member of the Royal College of Surgeons by the age of 21, was spending all his spare time as a GP searching for a way to deaden pain during surgery. He seems to have missed the great man's hint, but showed that carbon dioxide was effective at least with animals, induced into what he termed 'suspended animation' (although it would be quite out of favour now because of the risk of suffocation). But the world remained uninterested in, even hostile towards, any measure he offered to help bring oblivion to pain. Deeply disappointed and exhausted, he died aged 30 and was buried in Bromfield churchyard. Another 16 years passed before anaesthesia at last became accepted, finally to be endorsed during the birth of a prince by Queen Victoria in 1853. But only in 1913 was Hickman's role in offering the world anaesthetics acknowledged and acclaimed, and on the centenary of his death a stone was unveiled in St. Mary's Church bidding the world to 'honour a physician with the honour due unto him ...'.

Stokesay Castle Gatehouse

3. Stokesay Castle

Signposted to the left, the present buildings occupy the site of an earlier 12th-century manor and church. On the banks of the River Onny, the present 'castle' was commenced in *c*.1240, but from 1281 was developed more as a fortified manor house by Lawrence of Ludlow (d.1296), who had become rich from proceeds of the wool trade. Close to rebellious Wales, this was a risky move but he took precautions by obtaining approval to 'crenellate' or fortify his home. Welsh resistance ceased in 1282 with the capture and beheading of

Carvings on Stokesay Castle Gatehouse

Llywelyn ap Gruffudd (p.117) and a more peaceful climate encouraged the new owner to undertake considerable extensions. They included a grand Hall, solar block and South Tower with a curtain wall to surround the courtyard. The manor remained in his family for ten generations and was then in other hands until, in 1620 it was acquired by the Cravens. William, Lord Craven undertook extensive refurbishment work and, according to tree-ring analysis (dendro-dating), oak was felled in the winter of 1639/40 for the construction of a new Gatehouse.

Stokesay Castle

This still forms a wide entrance to the manor, past closely spaced timber-framed rooms on a stone plinth and beneath an overhanging upper storey and attic gable with decorative 'lozenges' between the timbers. Having crossed over the moat to enter the courtyard through the gatehouse, it is important not to miss the superb wood carvings, which range from Neptune-like figures, dragons, angels and dolphins to representations of Adam and Eve with the serpent and forbidden fruit. The level of craftsmanship has been compared with that achieved slightly earlier around the south porch doorway of the Reader's House at Ludlow and it is reckoned to uphold standards set in stone by the Herefordshire School (p.226) in the 12th century. Once Lawrence of Ludlow had completed his ambitious and costly building programme at the end of the 13th century he was able to live in the style to which he aspired and it requires little imagination to picture him, his family and the whole household seated at long tables in the splendid Hall in the usual manner of the Middle Ages. It is likely that the family would eat at a raised high table across the 31ft. width of the hall at one end, warmed during the winter by a fire below a smoke hole in a roof supported by great crucks, while the others sat at long tables down the 52ft. length. There were private rooms for the lord and his family in the solar range south of the Hall, access to the lord's private room being by an outer stairway. It is panelled with oak from floor to ceiling and has a splendid chimney piece with a mass of ornate carving.

The buildings, although not the church, survived the worst excesses of the Civil War, but after the early 18th century they suffered from neglect and misuse until rescued in 1869 by John Hallcroft, a Worcester industrialist and MP. Eventually acquired by English Heritage in 1992, Stokesay, is now open all year as one of the very few fortified manors of its period and is described as 'one of the most charming survivals of medieval England'. And whilst there, anyone who has seen Thomas Telford's epic Menai Suspension Bridge on his busy A5 route to Holyhead might care to compare it here with his early cast-iron bridge over the River Onny.

4.   Craven Arms—'The Junction'

The Craven family was probably the most famous of later owners of the estate, and the coat of arms of Lord Craven, en-nobled in 1627, was used for the name of the local inn. The present Craven Arms is thought to have been built shortly before 1808 at the expense of a later Lord Craven. It duly gave its name to the hamlet and railway station, subsequently called 'The Junction' by Mary Webb, the

Shropshire poet and poetic novelist (p.38). The LNWR service towards Hereford opened in 1852 and soon Craven Arms became the junction of lines from Builth and Knighton, Ludlow and Shrewsbury, Much Wenlock and Ironbridge and Bishops Castle. Although not as large as Swindon or Crewe, it expanded as a busy railway town, with a large goods yard and shunting depot and a centre for large stock auctions. Now Craven Arms is just an unmanned halt, serving the Marches Line from the north-west, through Shrewsbury and Hereford, to the south-west, and The Heart of Wales Line.

Originally called the Central Wales Line, from 1868 this linked the industrial north to the south Wales coalfields and ironworks and was of crucial importance during both World Wars. It was also a lifeline for the scattered communities of the Shropshire hills and the mountains of mid-Wales and for some it still provides the only means of transport. Downgraded from 1964 to light railway status with no goods traffic, it has been marked down for complete closure at least twice. The word is that an unassailable case had been presented to the Wilson Cabinet, but was reversed when George Thomas MP, the Welsh Secretary (later Speaker and from 1983 Viscount Tonypandy), pointed out that the line ran through a number of marginal constituencies. Money for increased grants was miraculously found and there have since been drives to attract more passengers.

Although few people visit Craven Arms expecting to view great buildings, it is ideally situated on both road and rail systems as a centre for tourism. After Shrewsbury and Church Stretton, 'Sprinter' carriages calling on their 120 mile journey to Swansea also stop at Knighton, Knucklas, Llangunllo, Llandrindod Wells, Builth Road, Cilmeri and other intermediate halts within the rolling and tree clad borderland covered by tours in this book.

As a gateway to the Shropshire hills, the town now has the Secret Hills Discovery Centre (beneath an amazing grass roof made from 1,000 sq. metres of turf weighing over 70 tonnes). As well as 25 acres of meadow walks and woodland wanders in the Onny Meadows, it offers informative exhibition displays and the latest hands-on and computer interactive displays, even a simulated hot-air balloon ride over the Clee Hills, Long Mynd and Stiperstones.

Continue on the A49 through Craven Arms soon after which a decision has to be made as to which route to take. It is possible either to continue direct to Church Stretton along the A49, or reach the town in quite a different way by turning left onto the A489, signposted for Welshpool and Newtown, about a mile north of Craven Arms, onto a route that takes in some amazing countryside up and over the Long Mynd, but on narrow roads, some with sharp drops to their side.

If you decide to go the direct route then you now need to go to page 37 and the entry for Church Stretton. Otherwise, having turned left onto the A489, pass beneath the railway line and follow the River Onny for about 4 miles and take the narrow road to the right signposted to Asterton (if you reach the village of Plowden you have gone just too far). In Asterton turn sharp right up the flank of the hills. In rising 1,000ft. over a relatively short distance it is very steep in places and great care is needed in keeping to the road. The route follows the pre-historic Port Way, which runs along the crest of the Long Mynd for some 8 miles. The Saxon name meant an important track between trading centres and as evidence of much earlier occupation and use it passes about 24 Bronze Age barrows. More recently this route has been travelled by cattle drovers, whereas the Romans opted for the valley floor for their Watling Street West road from *Viroconium* (Wroxeter) to *Bravonium* (Leintwardine), as have subsequent road and railway engineers.

The western slopes, past Myndtown down in a knoll, are steep and smooth, whereas the eastern side is divided by numerous precipitous valleys, 'hollows', 'batches' and 'gutters', partially clad with fern and gorse. The road passes the Midland Gliding Club and, further on, reaches a parking place not far from Pole Bank. At 516m. (1,693ft.), it is the highest point of The Long Mynd and the views are outstanding.

5. Blue remembered hills

Although Worcestershire poet A.E. Housman earnestly wished that his ashes be buried at Ludlow (p.27), during his lifetime he seems to have spent little time in Shropshire, although he 'had a sentimental feeling for it because its hills were on our western horizon'. Certainly the very first line of his poem, *The Shropshire Lad*, refers to what later he calls 'the high-reared head of Clee', whilst some of his most popular verse is about Wenlock Edge and the Wrekin. An Iron Age hillfort existed on Titterstone Clee Hill where coal was once extracted from the highest measures exploited in the British Isles, and the hard, skid-

The Long Mynd

resistant volcanic basalt (locally called dhustone) has been quarried to surface countless miles of roads. More recently the 'golf ball' radar station near the top has been a prominent feature of the national air traffic control system.

Almost due north, The Wrekin, known to Mary Webb as Mount Gilbert, rises between Telford and Shrewsbury and is also shaped from lava and ash from England's oldest known volcano of some 650 million years ago. It is regarded as the oldest mountain in England and it is said that 15 counties can be seen from the top. Wenlock Edge was however a tropical coral reef and its limestone makes it famous for flower-rich woodland and pastures, where at least nine orchid species have been found. Parallel with the A4368/4378, it runs diagonally between Craven Arms and Much Wenlock and is flanked by Ape Dale and Corve Dale. It overlooks typical south Shropshire countryside as far as the Stiperstones to the north-west.

On the opposite side of the valley, the hog-back Stretton Hills are another old volcanic range running to the east of the A49, extending from Ragleth Hill, opposite Little Stretton, Caer Caradoc Hill, Hazler and Hope Bowdler facing Church Stretton, and The Lawley, opposite the north end of the Long Mynd. At 1506ft. the highest and finest of these is Caer Caradoc (fort of Caratacus), which it is quite permissible to imagine as the legendary chieftain's stronghold until he was finally defeated by the Romans in AD 50. A Celtic hill fort, with double defences, and some caves near the summit add support for such a theory, but it is just one of a number of contenders for the site of Caratacus's last battle.

The Long Mynd (to rhyme with 'sinned' and Welsh for 'mountain') is on the western side of the A49 and it has been described as 'a broad-backed lofty ridge; true moorland running north and south for many miles and throwing out high precipitous spurs into the vale (1,000 feet) below'. Further to the west is the stark white quartzite ridge of the Stiperstones, a National Nature Reserve with a rich fund of folklore and literary connections rising above a carpet of heather, whinberry and cowberry. Here are the secrets of Lion Rock and the Devil's Chair.

As the Port Way continues north-eastwards, our route instead turns to the right signposted to Church Stretton to make a rather hair-raising drop of another 1,000ft. to the town itself. As the road levels out at the start of the town an immediate left turn, and then another, lead to the very popular Carding Mill Valley and a National Trust information centre and café. Here there are topographical models, walking trails and NT ranger-guided walks for all levels of ability wishing to take on the winding gorge. These can be followed to the summit ridge along routes variously called Mott's Road, Jack Mytton Way and Marches Way, or to the left through Light Spout Hollow past the waterfall there. Alternatively carry on ahead into Church Stretton.

6.   Church Stretton, 'Little Switzerland'

Thomas Brassey's 50-mile Shrewsbury to Hereford railway opened as far as Ludlow in 1852, but its effect upon Church Stretton was quite different from that at Craven Arms. With hills and mountains all around and fine views in every direction, the tiny market town gradually started to attract 'the discerning visitor' for holidays. All enjoyed the almost Alpine feel, whilst retired colonels, diplomats and memsahibs could reminisce over far more distant hills in the Punjab. From 1885, a housing fashion developed for them, what Pevsner called 'neo-half-timbering', and in 1900 The Hydropathic Establishment ('Hydro')

View over Church Stretton from the Long Mynd

opened as a spa. This could only offer local spring water, any spa water coming from Llandrindod Wells via the Central Wales railway. It was almost too late by then, and the Hydro afterwards became the Long Mynd Hotel, its name blazoned in huge letters across the valley. Now at the heart of the Shropshire Hills Area of Outstanding Natural Beauty, the town and its surroundings have become home for the highest proportion of retired people in Shropshire. And it remains a fashionable resort with a special appeal for walkers enjoying the neighbouring hills. The golf course laid out on the Long Mynd challenges the claim of Kington to be the highest in England, and as having the finest views, whilst the town below upholds its market tradition with a varied range of shops and services. Although there are interesting 16th- and 17th-century buildings, mostly in the High Street, the architecture largely dates from the end of the 19th century, with the outstanding exception of the parish church of St. Laurence. Still in Hereford diocese, and dedicated to the same saint as at Ludlow, the nave is Norman with a north doorway, above which there is an uncompromisingly immodest Celtic sheela-na-gig 'fertility figure' (cf Kilpeck, p.225, and Holdgate and Tugford below). The rest of the building work followed from the 13th-century Early English period until the 19th century. All Saints' Church at Little Stretton, along the old main road and just to the south, is quite different. Timber-framed, it was only built in 1903 and, with Brockhampton, Herefordshire (p.237), is a rarity as one of the country's few thatched churches. There are also much older timber framed houses—the *c*.1600 Manor House, the Tan House and Malt House. Older still was Brockhurst Castle, where a Roman fort was replaced by a moated Saxon *burh* and then a Norman stronghold. The surviving earthworks are now gradually disappearing. Not far beyond, the old cottages of Minton (in Domesday, *Munetune*—township by the mountain) are tucked below the eastern slopes of the Long Mynd around a small green and near a Norman, possibly Saxon, motte.

The Strettons derive their names from the Roman road or street, which here is now superseded by the A49. The tour crosses the A49 at traffic lights to join the B4371 and goes through Hope Bowdler to enter the area south of Shrewsbury and the River Severn sometimes known to literary tourists as Mary Webb Country.

Mary Webb – Shropshire's inspired author

It is a sad coincidence that the two best-known poets and writers about Shropshire should have been such melancholy people. But whereas classical scholar Alfred Housman seemed so often to be obsessed with death, gallows and graves for his work, Mary Webb (1881-1927) vividly brought to life the legends, geography and natural history of the county. She was Salopian, through and through, born at Leighton just to the south of 'fire-formed Wrekin' and brought up until she was 15 at The Grange, Much Wenlock. In 1912 she married Henry Webb (a nephew of Captain Matthew Webb, who in 1875 was the first person to swim the English Channel) at Meole Brace parish church and they spent their honeymoon near Church Stretton, which in one of her novels she would call Shepwardine. After a period of absence they returned to Pontesbury and then lived in a cottage on the slopes of the Stiperstones. Not well off, at one time Mary regularly walked the nine miles to Shrewsbury to sell garden flowers and fruit at the market, and they both suffered from ill health. By the time she was 21 Mary had developed Graves' Disease, an auto-immune disorder distinguished by an overactive and enlarged thyroid gland which produced an embarrassing effect on her looks. As if this was not enough to make her reclusive and melancholy, her work did not really sell, allegedly found unreadable by all but a limited literary following. She only received any tangible encouragement just two years before her premature death with the award of a prize for *Precious Bane*, the best fictional work of poetry or prose of English life by a relatively unknown author of that year. And it was sadly but five months after she died when her name finally became established, after Stanley Baldwin, the Prime Minister, praised her work at a literary event—making her a bestseller almost overnight.

Take the B4371 for Much Wenlock, which runs alongside Wenlock Edge. Our route soon heads north, turning left at Longville in the Dale, first following the signs for Plaish, Chatwell and Acton Burnell along a succession of narrow country lanes. The first sign for Acton Burnell is 4½ miles from the village and the road reaches a sign 1¼ miles away at a signpost for Langley Chapel to the right. Now in the custody of English Heritage and not always open, the chapel is thought to have been rebuilt in 1601, maybe using earlier elements, and is mainly noted for its furniture and fragments of plaster roof. Not unusually the better class box pews for farmers' families are placed in front of ancient benches for the labouring classes and there is a musicians' pew at the rear.

Continuing in the direction of Acton Burnell at the junction, there is a sign at the village entrance pointing to the right for the castle and the car park which is in front of the church. The footpath to the castle is at the far end of the car park.

---

7. Acton Burnell and an important place in the history of Parliament

From the Saxon for the homestead or village by the oak tree, Acton is a common place name and to distinguish it from other places it has often been given an added family name. Acton Pigott, Acton Round and Acton Scott are all in Shropshire, not far away, and the Burnell family probably contributed their name in the 12th century. Robert Burnell (d.1292) is the only member to create more than a local impression, but in more ways than one he went a long way towards making up for all the others. He was said to be an excellent and capable administrator and became private chaplain and a great friend of the future Edward I. As king, Edward saw that Burnell was made Chancellor of England and also elected Bishop of Bath and Wells, but a further attempt at what might be termed medieval 'cronyism' failed after the king sought to have him elected as Archbishop of Canterbury. Perhaps it was partly because his high public renown could not over-ride a reputation for private immorality. Robert Burnell's chapel and great hall still exist at Wells, although the latter has long been a ruin, but it was in 1283 at Acton Burnell where Burnell entertained the king and where one of the first Parliaments was attended by both the Commons and Lords. Just east of the ruined 'castle' there are still two tall gables of a huge building which was 157ft. long and 40ft. wide and nicknamed the Parliament Barn, where they are thought to have met. Royal Assent was given there to an Act for the regulation of trade which has since become known as The Statute of Acton Burnell. The picturesque red

Acton Burnell Castle

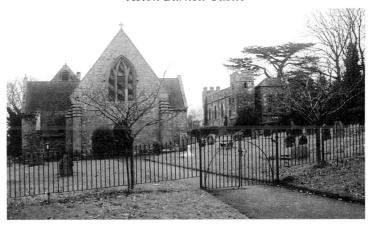

Acton Burnell Church, and Castle to the right

Acton Burnell Castle, more accurately one of the oldest fortified houses in England, was subsequently built for Robert Burnell in 1284 and he also became responsible for the nearby St. Mary's Church. Most of its architecture is original apart from the small Victorian tower. The *c.*1280 font and a late Elizabethan tomb are among fine features which furnish the church, now esteemed as 'a beautiful example of building style towards the end of the 13th century'. The Park, Shadwell Lake and Black Dick's Lake are close by, and to the south of Acton Burnell Hall which is now a private international college of further education.

Just to the north of the village are two of Shropshire's finest and most famous inhabited old houses. One is a spectacular creation in half-timbering and the other was built of creamy pink sandstone and is now regarded as arguably the grandest Elizabethan house in the county. To see the first, leave Acton Burnell on the road signposted for Pitchford. At the far end of Acton Burnell parish, Pitchford Hall is ¼ mile north of the village of Pitchford.

To reach Condover Hall there is a north westerly detour of just over 2 miles through the rolling country by Cound Brook. Follow the road towards Cantlop and turn left there for Condover.

8. Pitchford Hall

Pitchford Hall

Like many other great houses in the county, such as Stokesay, Pitchford Hall was built from the profits of the wool trade. Adam Ottley was a Shrewsbury merchant and his house must have been built some time before his death in 1578. Creating a 'zebra' effect, the timber framing makes lavish use of close studding and diagonal chevron and lozenge bracing, the expense involved a sure sign of the owner's affluence. Nikolaus Pevsner approved, observing also that the house combined its considerable size with an undeniable homeliness. It is widely regarded as one of the finest timber-framed country mansions in Shropshire and is enhanced by ornate brick chimney stacks of a star-shaped section typical of its period. St. Michael's Church, a small aisle-less Norman building, is in the park just to the north and is much older than the house. Its greatest treasure is a decorative tomb shaped from a single block of oak. It bears a cross-legged effigy more than 7 feet long in chain mail and surcoat and identified by its heraldry as commemorating Sir John de Pitchford (d.1285). It is an acknowledged rarity among just about 100 others in Britain which have been fashioned from wood. The house is private but it may be seen from the churchyard or from the south lodge gates on the Acton Burnell road.

9. Condover Hall

Condover Hall

Among habitable great Elizabethan stone-built houses, Condover Hall is also a rarity but it was built not for a wealthy wool merchant but a lawyer, who doubtless could just as easily afford it. The great misfortune of Thomas Owen, however, was that he died in 1598 before his house was finished. But although he would not now recognise the interior, he would surely approve of the wide creamy-pink sandstone frontage, with its gables and chimney stacks, and its present use as a RNIB school for the blind. The nearby church of St. Mary and St. Andrew is of a similar sandstone and much rebuilt. It is known for the hammerbeams and collar beams of the nave roof and for an exceptional collection of monuments.

The route next heads for the A458 Much Wenlock road by returning to the junction just north of Pitchford and then following the direction sign for Cross Houses, 3 miles away. Often in sight of the wooded peak of The Wrekin, this is a winding road which is signed for Upper Cound and Cressage. Keep following signs to Cressage and then turn right onto the A458 to head through Cressage for Much Wenlock. (The hamlet of Cressage is named from the Old English 'Christ's Oak', which is thought to refer to a prominent tree where the Gospel was preached. In the mid-Saxon period this practice often provided the location for the parish church and it is considered significant that an ancient church there was dedicated to the Celtic Saint Sampson).

10.   Much Wenlock

The Guildhall to the left and Holy Trinity Church to the right

Mary Webb could remember Much Wenlock from the happy days of her childhood as 'a very Rip Van Winkle of a borough ... that had fallen asleep somewhere in the Middle Ages'. Situated as it was near the edge of the Shropshire coalfield, this had been a close thing, for the impact of the late 18th-century Industrial Revolution had only just missed her early rustic idyll. Nearby Coalbrookdale, Ironbridge, Madeley, Coalport and Broseley, blessed with coal, limestone, iron ore, timber and river transport resources, had been transformed into the most industrialised places on earth at the very epicentre of the movement.

Although the town has suffered from periods of decline due to local commercial competition, and lost its borough status in 1966, it has retained much medieval character which is rich with picturesque and historic timber, brick and stone buildings. A former Victorian market hall houses the Museum and TIC, where in addition to finding *A Town Trail and Brief History* and other useful literature it is also possible to learn about the local GP and physical education pioneer, Dr. William Penny Brookes. In 1850 he inspired the modern Olympic movement by founding the Much Wenlock Olympic Games and these

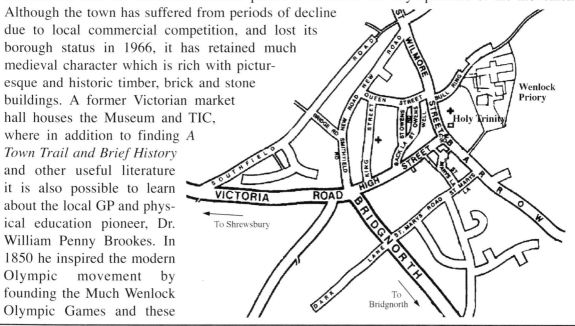

41

are still held every summer. In *c*.1853, Dr. Brookes bought Ashfield Hall, a pre-Reformation house built of stone and timber framing in the High Street. Its Tudor-style chimney stacks, fine panelling and a labelled cheese room are among its special distinguishing features and it is one of a number of fine buildings in what was formerly called Spittle Street. Barclays Bank at 15 High Street occupies a 17th-century box-framed building and at the rear is a base-cruck and crown post unit dating from 1407-8. Originating from about the same time and extended in at least five subsequent building phases is Raynald's Mansion, a most spectacular timber-framed building and,

The Guildhall from the street side, with Holy Trinity beyond

nearly opposite, the street frontage of the Talbot Hotel. In comparison it is quite dull, but inside it reveals a timber-framed structure and the roof timbers are thought to date from the second half of the 15th century. The malthouse at the rear is where they used to brew their own beer and it has survived since 1762. High Street meets Barrow Street and Wilmore Street at the Square, which is dominated by the Guildhall, built over an open market place in *c*.1540. The open ground floor still serves as a market place and the rooms upstairs are in full use for meetings. Wilmore Street passes Holy Trinity Church to reach Brookhouse Farm which, close to the centre near other premises at 50 Sheinton Street, serves as a reminder of the role of agriculture in the past fortunes of Wenlock, the former name of the town.

The way to the extensive remains of the 11th- to 15th-century priory buildings, and a car park, is signposted to the north of the church. Of just two Cluniac ruins left in England, the priory was built of pale limestone quarried at Wenlock Edge, on the site of a convent founded shortly after 680 by the Anglo-Saxon King Merewalh, when the place was called *Wimnicas* or *Wininicas*. His daughter, Milburga (Milburge/Milburh), succeeded as its second abbess in 687, ruling over a double house of monks and nuns and during 30 years of service was famous for her miracles and became recognised as a saint after her death. This was replaced by Earl Leofric *c*.1040 and parts of the west front and of the south transept of the priory are still standing at a height of up to 70ft. The roofless 12th-century chapter

Streetscape in Much Wenlock

42

The Prior's House

house is entered through three decorated Norman arches which lead to rich carving on the south wall in the form of interlaced false-arcading. This is where the main business of the monastery was conducted, and where a chapter of the Rule of St. Benedict was ritually read each day—hence its name. This rite was evidently not sufficient to guarantee obedience from the monks and, to correct their easy living, a list of Injunctions and Exhortations was issued in 1521. The more mentionable reminded them of the rules of continuous silence, avoidance of women, no late drinking, regular attendance at church—without dozing off, no dogs or hunting and payment only for ministering at funerals. Not exempt, the prior was discouraged from indulging in luxurious and extravagant living and running a large household and what this meant could be judged from the splendour of the surviving Prior's House, according to recent scientific timber analysis dating from 1425 and now in private occupation. Much of the lavish design and detail is said to reflect the ambitions of John Stafford, prior at the time, and accounts for its wide reputation as an early 15th-century architectural gem. The adjacent priory infirmary on the south side, started in the 12th century, also still stands and there is much more to see within the peaceful and beautiful ruins in helping to visualise the life of the community between the early 11th century and the Dissolution. The cloister is now host to strange Victorian topiary.

Wenlock Priory is now in the care of English Heritage and there are charges for admission, which include car-parking, and also for a well illustrated and informative guidebook and audio aids which provide a full description of the priory and its colourful history.

Wenlock Priory: left to right: three tiered interlacing decoration in the Chapter House; carvings of saints on the lavatorium; site of St. Michael's Chapel

This tour now returns towards Ludlow, starting with a short westward return along the A458 Cressage and Shrewsbury road and then turning left onto the B4371, soon reaching a line of limestone quarries to a magical drive on Wenlock Edge. There is a short detour to Hughley to see the church (see box), by turning right after 2¹/₂ miles on the road signposted to Hughley at a junction near a car park.

Continuing along the B4371, after a fine easterly view of Easthope in Hope Dale, the road descends towards Longville in the Dale, met earlier, but this time the route turns left onto a country lane signposted to Wilderhope Manor, climbing uphill crossing the Jack Mytton Way and Shropshire Way long-distance paths. These both pass Wilderhope Manor, further signposted to the left and which is reached along a National Trust access drive. It is now a youth hostel, so the exterior can be readily viewed.

---

11.   On Wenlock Edge and Hughley

Its beauties and unrivalled views have long been a source of great inspiration, not least for poets and musicians such as A.E. Housman and Ralph Vaughan Williams. And once it even served as an escape route, when the Royalist Major Thomas Smallwood of Wilderhope Manor was under hot pursuit by Roundheads. 'Major's Leap' is shown on the OS Landranger Map just to the north of the first road junction, as the place where he made his horse jump the cliff—and survived to celebrate the Restoration, sadly without his less fortunate steed.

Hughley was adopted by Housman for *A Shropshire Lad* poem entitled *Hughley Steeple*:

> The vane on Hughley steeple
> Veers bright, a far-known sign,
> And there lie Hughley people,
> And there lie friends of mine.

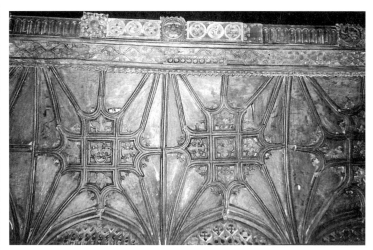

The Rood Screen at Hughley

Nit-pickers have long grumbled that the 13th-century St. John Baptist Church does not boast a steeple, whereas defenders of artists' licence retort that the poet was not in the business of producing a tour guide! In fact he admitted that he had an entirely different church and place in mind, but used Hughley 'for the sake of euphony'—in order to create a pleasing sound. The hands of his clock 'which strikes the hour' were for many years stuck at 4 o'clock and despite all efforts, new positions have made no difference, making Hughley 'a place where time stands still'! The church is nevertheless well worth a visit for its rood screen, carved with grapes, flowers and birds by local craftsmen in the 15th century and thought by Pevsner to be perhaps the finest in the county. There is a *c.*1600 timber framed Old Hall in the village which is also worthy of notice now that repairs have been completed.

12.   Wilderhope Manor

Wilderhope Manor

This was the seat of the Smallwoods and was built in 1586 in what has been termed a rather stark, spartan style. Mary Webb referred to it in her novel *Gone to Earth* as Undern Hall—'a strange sinister house crouched under a hill like a toad', but it is specially renowned for an original spiral staircase and decorated plaster ceilings. It really was lost to the world for many years until rescued from dereliction by John Cadbury for the National Trust. Leased to the Youth Hostels Association, on two major hiking trails and close to a working farm, the atmosphere there now is far from sinister or gloomy and it is open to the public from April to the end of September each Wednesday and Saturday afternoon.

After returning along the drive from Wilderhope Manor, turn left to drop to a junction with the B4368, on which you turn right. After half a mile turn left at Broadstone onto a country lane signed to Abdon. After about 1¼ miles, there is a T junction at which you take the left arm, signposted to Holdgate. After visiting the hamlet, return to the T junction and continue straight ahead for Tugford and then start a climb of nearly 300ft. to Abdon another 3 miles further on, where the road bends to the right towards Clee St. Margaret.

13.   Holdgate, Tugford, Abdon and deserted medieval villages

At the narrowest part of Corve Dale, Holdgate was once of significant military importance. It had a motte fortification which was mentioned with the manor in the Domesday Book, and then came a stone castle which was rebuilt in *c*.1280, it is thought, by Robert Burnell who was building his own 'castle' near the time. A semi-circular tower and other elements survive at Holdgate, at the rear of the present 16th-century farmhouse.

Holdgate Castle remains

Holy Trinity Church is Norman and fine work has been executed at the south doorway and, strikingly with deep and elaborate carving to the rounded bowl font. Like further examples of the period at Tugford, it is akin to that of the Herefordshire School of Romanesque Sculpture, whose work in the 12th century extended to south Shropshire. And, intriguingly, out of just 18 throughout England, it has one of Shropshire's four grotesque sheela-na-gig 'fertility symbols' (cf Church Stretton and two at Tugford). Just to the rear of the farm at Holdgate there is the site of a deserted medieval village, one of several in the vicinity of Brown Clee Hill. Holdgate is one of 35 shrunken or deserted settlements identified in Corve Dale by the Shropshire landscape archaeologist Trevor Rowley, and some 2,000 have been recorded across England, chiefly in the Midlands and the east. At Holdgate there are earthwork signs of former buildings and roadways as well as vestiges of medieval ridge and furrow cultivation. Many reasons have been given for there being so many instances like this in Corve Dale, not least being that of the spread and virulence of the Black Death in 1348-9. Failed harvests and climate changes, which were particularly severe in the 14th century have also been cited, for much of the ground here can be poor and difficult to farm, especially at higher levels. Enclosed pastoral farming, which replaced the former arable open field system, has also played a part in what has usually led to gradual depopulation and departure of subsistence marginal communities (just as, far more recently, Border farmers and smallholders have been giving up and leaving the land for not dissimilar reasons).

Not all abandoned settlements are still as plain to see as they are at Abdon, a small hamlet very much on marginal land, about 800ft. high on the west side of Brown Clee Hill. Old records and recent archaeology have revealed much about the distinct house platforms, hollow ways indicating former streets and lanes, and ridge and furrow patterns at the village edge. St. Margaret's Church is up a hill some way from the present community and much closer to the 1.3 ha. of ancient earthworks in a sloping field to the east. Evidence of a long fluctuation of population is supported by a longhouse site excavated near the church which was thought to predate 1300. Following 14th-century abandonment of the village, another house on the site appears to have been occupied in the 16th century, at a time when mining and quarrying on Brown Clee Hill were reaching a peak. Repopulation continued for several years, but by the end of the 18th century the village was once more in decline and eventually the present settlement developed further to the south-west.

Just over a mile beyond Tugford there is a small crossroads and it is well worth making the small detour to the right to see Heath Chapel. Here there is another well defined medieval village, and in a field to the right there is what has been described as a 'perfect example of a primitive Norman parish church'. Services are still held in the chapel, and details of these and of means of entry are available at Bitterley Rectory, near Ludlow (01584 890239).

14.   Heath Chapel

The chapel is pure Norman, built roughly in 1150 and not afterwards messed with apart from the addition of one small window by the pulpit. This was apparently to help a 17th-century parson to read his sermon notes because the existing round arched window openings were so small. As it is a chapel of ease within the parish of Stoke St. Milborough it has no dedication to a saint and it was intended to provide for the ease and convenience of parishioners living some distance away from the parish church. Whilst they could be baptised in the Norman tub-shaped font they could not marry or be buried at Heath, although there is now a graveyard close by. For such a relatively expensive stone chapel to be built here suggests that at the time there was a community of sufficient numbers and means to support it from working the low-yielding land, which is over 800ft. above sea level. But this was not to last beyond the 15th century, and no further funds could be afforded for improvements or 'restoration' schemes—apart from some insensitive routine work early in the 20th century. So now the original tiny chapel survives intact, whilst close by there are just mounds, hollows, ridges and furrows in the field to show where once there were houses, roads and busy farming activity.

With no tower or belfry, the double cell chapel has a single round arch doorway where the Norman mason has applied elaborate carved ornamentation, whilst equal craftsmanship has extended to details such as the crescent-shaped ironwork on the old oak door. Signs of medieval wall paintings show beneath the flaking whitewash and the pulpit, box pews and other furnishings seem mostly to have been made or improvised during Tudor or Georgian times.

Heath Chapel

Looking down to the long 'ford' in Clee St. Margaret

Returning to the crossroads, turn to the right for Clee St. Margaret, one of the two principal villages of 'The Clee'. At the road junction in the village, the direct route to Ludlow appears to be by water, for the Clee brook runs down the full width of the road, which continues out of sight round the corner—but the brook then drops down sharply to the left and the rest of the 7 miles journey continues in the dry! About 400ft. higher up the hillside behind the village and about half a mile walk to the east on a spur of Brown Clee common, is Nordybank Camp. Of the four Iron Age hillforts on Brown Clee and Titterstone Clee, it is the only one to have escaped quarrying damage.

Continuing southwards, the road reaches Stoke St. Milborough, the other principal village of the Clee and the centre of an extensive parish. The views here are magnificent, and of the many brooks issuing from the hillside, St. Milburga's Well near the parish church concerns the grand-daughter of King Penda of Mercia and abbess of the small nunnery at Wenlock. The legend goes that she escaped 'a grave peril' at the spot—and that the spring was first revealed by a blow from her horse's hoof.

About a mile further on, the road joins the B4364 on which you turn right and at Middleton it crosses the line of the dismantled railway, which until 1952 ran from the main line near Ludlow through Bitterley to the quarry faces and crushing plant, high up on Titterstone Clee Hill. Part of the way up, the line changed to 1¼ miles of a very steep, self-acting (whereby the filled and therefore heavier down load in descending pulls an empty wagon back up the slope) 3ft. gauge for the final incline near the settlement now shown as Titterstone. During quarrying in Victorian times there were two rows of terraced houses at this spot, with an idyllic view, and there had at one time also been a lunatic asylum close by. This had locally been associated with the notorious London asylum of St. Mary of Bethlehem, colloquially known as Bedlam. And so for a time this Shropshire hamlet also acquired the same name.

Beyond Middleton the road soon joins the A4117, on which you turn right and return to Ludlow.

Leominster — and Wool

*The lion carving on the west doorway of
Leominster Priory*

The first thing to know about Leominster, is that it is pronounced 'Lemster'. Other recorded names started with *Leofminstre* in the Domesday Survey and this was soon followed in a charter of 1123 with Leominstre. Queen Mary Tudor's important 1533 Charter of Incorporation recites the name Leompister, alias Lempster, and Loveminster also appeared at one stage. There can therefore be little doubt that the name has to do with the monastery, or minster, which existed there from very early days. The origin of the prefix is not so certain. The Welsh Border is just 14 miles away, and one school insists that it derives from an Old Welsh word meaning stream — there are many watercourses encircling the town, notably the Lugg, Pinsley, Kenwater and Arrow. Another opinion recalls a Mercian king named The Lion and the legend of his founding of a Saxon church in the 7th-century. Two lions' heads are certainly among the intricate carving to be found at the west door of the Norman nave of the church. This book however favours a link with Lady Godiva (p.234), forever remembered along with 'Peeping Tom' of Coventry, as well as with her husband Leofric the powerful earl of Mercia. A close friend of Edward the Confessor, he was the founder of Wenlock Priory (p.42), and also built a minster here early in the 10th century. By 1086 the town was entered in the Domesday Book as Leofminstre.

Leofric's nunnery was far from being the first religious community, for it is thought that the earliest could have been founded as long ago as the 6th century by St. David. Certainly a church was established in 598 by the Saxon ruler, Merewald, and there have been leading places of worship at Leominster ever since. These often suffered attacks from the neighbouring Welsh, who named the town *Llanllieni*, meaning the 'church of nuns', and in 1055 they eventually seized the town but were expelled by King Harold. Leofric's attempt to re-establish a monastery of Benedictine nuns during the early 11th century seemingly failed, for by mid-century it is intriguingly said to have been 'dissolved for its Sins'. This could be connected with an occasion quoted by local historians from *The Anglo Saxon Chronicle* for 1046. Eorl Swein (brother of the future King Harold), returning home through the town from successful operations against the Welsh, is said to have over-availed himself of nunnery hospitality and 'had fetched to him the abbess of Leominster, Edgiva, and kept her while it pleased him, then let her go home'. (Apparently he too went home, returned to his unit in France for four years).

Another century was to pass before a new Benedictine priory was established, after Henry I had granted the manor of Leominster to Reading Abbey in 1123. A priory, this time of monks, was subject to the abbot of Reading and the nave of their new church was consecrated in 1130. It still serves as the parish church for Leominster, but in 1269 its south aisle was replaced by a new nave for the local parishioners. Then in 1320, a third extension was added to form the south nave, although it is generally regarded as more of a wide aisle. Its west and four superb south windows are profuse with carved ballflower decoration, a particular Herefordshire feature. As a further sign of the prosperity of the town, as well as the devotion of its people in applying profits from the woollen trade towards the enlargement and adornment of their church, a 45ft. high window of

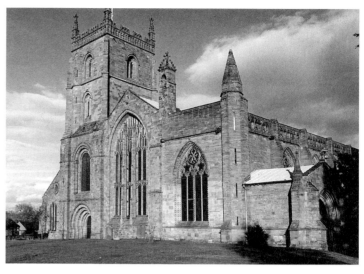

West front of Leominster Priory Church

eight lights was inserted at the west of the central nave. The west tower above the Norman nave was also raised to its present height. Below, the intricate sandstone carving around the 12th-century west

*Carvings on the outer capitals
of the priory's west doorway*

doorway belongs to the Herefordshire School of Romanesque Sculpture, the capitals shaped with figures which include The Green Man (p.235), a pre-Christian fertility spirit represented in different ways without any qualms at several churches met on these tours. Details of the spacious re-erected 13th-century south porch, and much more, are given in the literature available at the church.

Treatment for a common scold

Because of a serious fire in 1699, there are not many internal furnishings at Leominster but there is a mobile ducking stool in the north aisle. To many, a church not practising the baptism rite of total immersion may seem to be a peculiar home for such an instrument. However it has been there

since 1895, when it was transferred from the Corporation gaol after often being wheeled around the town in the 'Ancient and Universal punishment of Common Scolds, and for butchers, bakers, brewers, apothecaries and all who gave short measure or vended adulterated articles of food'. The last recorded use of such a device anywhere in England was at Leominster in 1809, when Jenny Pipes, alias Jane Curran,

The ducking stool in Leominster Priory Church

was ducked in one of the local streams. Now that fewer scolds are left, maybe it ought to be placed at the disposal of the Trading Standards Department?

Dissolution

Despite a stormy history, which had seen Leominster reduced to ruins by the murderous William de Braose during the reign of King John, misfortunes during the baronial wars, and in 1402 the usual wanton destructiveness of Owain Glyndwr, by the late 15th century the town had regained its strength. There were guilds of mercers, tailors, drapers, dyers and glovers and all was governed from the priory. With the parent abbey at Reading it too was in a good state, until England broke away from the Church of Rome. Henry VIII became head of the new Church of England and seized upon the opportunity to close, or 'dissolve', all monasteries and claim their lands and possessions. This was the first large enforced exchange of property ownership since the Norman Conquest and the fate of John Glover, the prior, is not known, but at Reading the abbot was hanged outside the gates of his abbey. By 1539, much of the priory, including the central tower, was scheduled for demolition, but the parishioners stood out for their parish church and they erected the wall which now closes the building at its eastern end. The effect of dissolution upon the economy of the town was shattering, for it could not fall back on the business which could be obtained from castle residents at towns such as Hereford and Ludlow. For Leominster never had a castle—but what it did have, however, was its wool.

Lemster Ore

Although much is still heard about the quality of Hereford cattle, from very early days Leominster had been equally notable for the wool obtained from one of the oldest breeds of English sheep, the docile and hardy Ryeland. The breed has been recorded as far back as 1343 and the delicate texture inspired many poets from at least the days of John Skelton (?1460-1529). Michael Drayton (1563-1631) wrote:

> Where lives the man so dull on Britain's furthest shore
> To whom did never sound the name of Lemster ore
> That with the silkworm's web for smallness doth compare?

A Ryeland sheep

Robert Herrick (1591-1674) described 'a bank of moss more soft than the finest Lemster ore', whilst Izaak Walton (1593-1683) found that 'certain fields near Leominster are observed to make the sheep that graze upon them more fat than the next, and also to bear finer wool'. It even figured in plays by Ben Jonson (1572-1637). Up to the 17th century Leominster boasted the best wool market in England, while Herefordshire vaunted its six 'W's, Wool heading the list, followed by Water, Wood, Wheat, Wine (apple cider) and, last but not least, Women! Still excelling in both flesh and wool, the placid Ryeland is a good forager and is considered to be ideal for smallholders, lending itself to organic farming as a sheep that does well on good grass alone.

After the Dissolution

Despite hostilities which did not completely ease until Union between Wales and England in 1536, Leominster Priory and the community formed around it prospered well enough during the later Middle Ages under the jurisdiction of the prior, acting as the chief citizen of the town. With the Dissolution, the manor belonging to the priory and its appendages were transferred to the Crown, its courts abolished and until 1553 the local government of the townspeople transferred to the Lord Marchers. Yet as well as the church, there still remain some of the buildings and activities which surrounded it. Signs point to the sites of the early monastery, medieval church remains and the 13th century stone-built Priory House. This is the last remnant of the priory, its reredorter receiving special mention from Leominster Civic Trust in its helpful *Leominster Town Walk* leaflet. A facility which enjoys many other names, the reredorter was known to the monks as 'a house of easement' or the 'necessarium'. Those now in use by the present residents are better known as 'the loos' and no longer draughtily installed over the cleansing waters of the babbling Pinsley Brook, for they have been diverted. The priory building has had many uses since 1539 and in 1837 it was sold to the Poor Law Guardians for £745 and was incorporated into the Leominster Institution to be adapted as a workhouse. It has since served as an old peoples' home and a Youth Hostel. The priory grange, which had doubtless been the home farm for many of the community's Ryelands, has also been put to many uses—once as a rubbish tip. In 1855 it was rented from the lessees and transformed into a recreation ground and gardens and now The Grange is Leominster's most popular open-air amenity.

Of all the buildings in Leominster, none could ever compete with the splendour of the Market Hall, or Buttercross, which was built at the top of Broad Street by John Abel in 1633. (He was later to be dubbed 'The King's Carpenter' by Charles I for services rendered during the siege of Hereford in 1645). Like the market-hall and guild-hall at Hereford, erected late in the previous century, and the many showy town halls of the Victorian era much later, it was designed to impress the world with how important and prosperous Leominster and its merchant guilds really were. It was 46ft. long and 25ft. wide, the two storeys were supported on 12 Ionic oak pillars and the open ground floor served as a market for butter and eggs. The upper floor and dormer rooms were for local government headquarters and then later adapted to other public purposes. Every accessible portion of the timber framing was carved with a profusion of inscriptions, monsters, lions and even busts of men and bare-bosomed women. Expense seemed to be no obstacle and the building must have been the pride and joy of the townspeople, until it started getting in the way of the traffic. And in 1853 the (then horse-drawn) traffic won, and the building was put up for auction. It went for just £95 (perhaps about £5/6,000 today) and was sold on to John

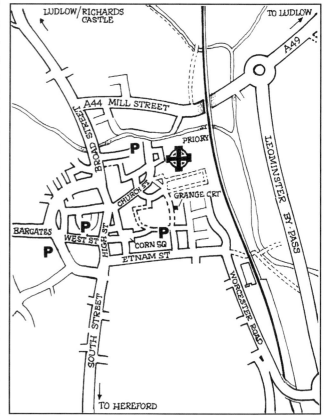

Map of central Leominster

Grange Court

Arkwright (grandson of the inventor of the Spinning Jenny). It was re-assembled for use as a private house at the east side of the The Grange until 1937, when it was almost sold for trans-shipment to the USA. But instead the local council bought it for their use as offices and it has remained with successor councils ever since, while new plans for its restoration and use were launched in 2008.

Just outside the former main gateway of the priory precinct, and nearly opposite a huge house fittingly called The Gatehouse, the Forbury Chapel dates from 1284. It was presented by John Peckham, archbishop of Canterbury, in recognition of hospitality afforded by the community and is dedicated to St. Thomas Becket of Canterbury. A plain building with a good east window, it has been classified as a Scheduled Ancient Monument but has not always been so highly regarded, experiencing neglect and many unworthy uses such as offices and auction rooms, as well as being the local theatre. Now, however, it has been sympathetically restored with the aid of grants and is open for meetings and other appropriate uses and functions. It is next door to The Forbury, a Grade 2* listed building dating from the 17th century which serves as a nursing home. Church Street contains many other elegant buildings in a range of architectural styles, many of them Georgian (*c*.1714-1830). Others are much older than they appear, for timber structures have been partially removed during the past 250 years to be replaced by more 'fashionable' façades. It is now no longer possible to identify the place 'at the top of Church Street' where, in 1402, Owain Glyndwr is said by some to have confined his captive, (and future ally and son-in-law) Sir Edmund Mortimer, after the rout and slaughter of his English forces at the Battle of Pilleth that June (p.52).

The story of Leominster's development, revealed in the different phases of the priory church, its precincts and in Church Street, is built into the shape of other buildings and the streets of the town centre. The wool market was buoyant for some 600 years until the 18th century and this shows from evidence of considerable rebuilding during the 17th century in the area south of Church Street, such as in Cordwainers' Lane, Ironmongers' Row and Corn Square, displaying their medieval character with narrow gables, projecting upper floors and carved timbers. Corn Square was the centre of the corn trade, served from *c*.1600 by the Three Horseshoes Inn at the entrance to School Lane. On the opposite side, the half-timbered shop is thought to date from the 15th century and there the two flanking premises form part of a wide range of ages and building styles in School Lane, passing through the Victorian era up to the present day. At the southern end, Etnam Street is much wider after modernisation with many 18th century buildings, some again covering earlier structures. There are several buildings of special interest, including the Chequers Inn of *c*.1600 and the White Lion, said to date from the early 16th century. The Baptist Church and manse date from the 18th century and Leominster Museum is housed in the former Victorian Railwaymen's Mission Hall. Etnam Street forms part of the A44 Worcester to Aberystwyth road and at the west end joins South Street at Dutton House. Seemingly this building is Victorian Gothic, but structurally and in other respects dates from the 16th century. The High Street is another part of the narrow medieval street grid which contains an assortment of timber-framed buildings and, at no.2 there is the birthplace of painter John Scarlett Davis (1804-

Drapers' Lane and Cordwainers' Lane, Leominster

1845). He was noted especially for his large-scale pictures of public building interiors. Then just past this house the scene abruptly widens out at the junction with Church Street, where Broad Street was modernised during Georgian times like Etnam Street. The Market Hall used to be here. The many surviving grand red houses in the street are a further sign of the prosperity at the time and particular attention is drawn by the Civic Trust to Lion House, where the recumbent form of a lion is poised on the parapet. This was once a coaching inn, the archway leading to a stableyard at the rear. There, on the left, is a Regency (1811-1820) assembly room with a recently restored and very fine interior.

In reward for its support of Mary Tudor against Lady Jane Grey after the death of Edward VI in 1553, the town was granted a Charter of Incorporation that year by the new Queen Mary. This placed local government in the hands of a select council of town worthies and Leominster continued to prosper until the 18th century. But then, because of the relative isolation and poor communications which it suffered with Hereford and other Border towns, it started to lose way against competition with towns which were better placed to benefit from the Industrial Revolution. The local wool trade and associated leather, glove-making and hat industries could not compete with the textiles and other products coming from the mill towns of the north-west, Yorkshire and elsewhere. An initiative was commenced in 1796 for a canal which would link Kington through Leominster to Birmingham, but little progress was made. Attempts were started to make more use of the River Lugg as a waterway. At least nine locks were built as far as the confluence with the Wye at Mordiford and there are still signs along the river of where clearances at road bridges were increased to allow the passage of barges. But this approach was not very successful and although cargoes of timber, cider, malt, hops, wool and corn were probably conveyed by teams of 'bow hauliers', the only firm and oft quoted information concerns the recasting of the priory bells, which were conveyed to Chepstow and back on the Lugg and Wye in 1756. The Shrewsbury and Hereford Joint Railway was sanctioned by Parliament in 1846 and it arrived at Leominster in 1853, just as the Market Hall was about to be moved. A branch was opened to Kington in 1857 and was then extended to Presteigne and New Radnor in 1875 while, after long delays, a rail link with Bromyard and Worcester was finally completed in 1897. Until they closed in 1955 and 1964, these branch lines helped considerably in bolstering Leominster's position as a commercial, social and main service centre for large parts of north Herefordshire and central Wales. But in recent years, decline in the rural economy resulting from market upheavals, and new factors such as subsidy removal, has accelerated the fall in traditional agricultural employment within these areas and this in turn has had its effect on the economy of Leominster. Official planning studies produced in 2002 indicated that the town contained one of the two main areas of poverty and deprivation in Herefordshire. To help offset this, the modern industrial estate on the Hereford Road is likely to be extended by a further 16.6 hectares after further roads have been built. Although there were deep worries about the effect of a large new supermarket at Baron's Cross, the town centre remains bustling and buoyant, its independent shops reinforced by the weekly Friday stalls market in Corn Square, a wealth of antique shops, fine art salerooms which attract buyers from home and abroad and a good sprinkling of tourist visitors. With potentially significant effect for Leominster, in January 2004, after 157 years trading from headquarters in Hereford since 1846, a leading firm of auctioneers and valuers which operates in the Marches and much further afield, moved to a new head office. Now employing many of its 140 full and part-time staff at Easters Court near the western end of the Leominster by-pass, Brightwells will conduct its nationally renowned fine arts and, up to now exclusive four-by-four motor vehicle businesses, as well as car and commercial vehicle, livestock, horse and pony, agricultural professional services and land sales, auctions, machinery and liquidation and other related operations from under one roof at its new premises.

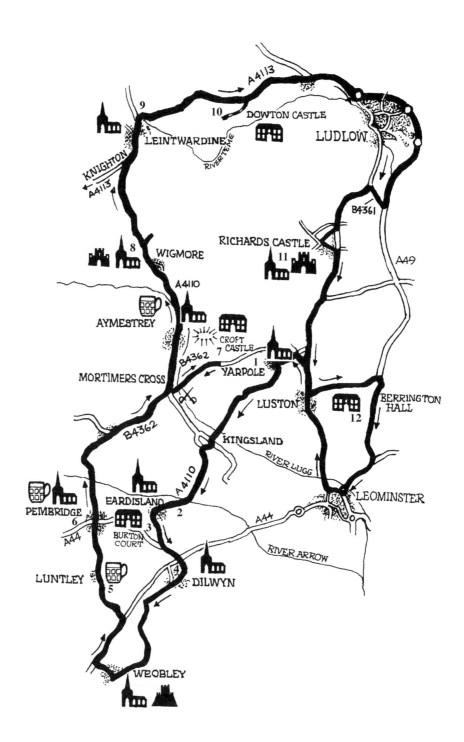

Outline map for Tour 3
The numbers 1 to 12 relate to the boxed information given within the tour

Tour 3   Timber-framed Buildings and Villages near Leominster

This tour takes in many of the villages and hamlets boasting a large number of timber-framed buildings that feature in the Black and White Village Trail which ranges for 40 miles through north-west Herefordshire, including Luston, Yarpole, Dilwyn, Weobley and Pembridge. There are also three of Herefordshire's peculiar detached bell-towers—places of refuge for villagers in years gone by, a brick-built dovecot that can be visited and a timber-framed one that can only be seen from the outside. Also a small country mansion, a scattering of churches, Dunkertons Cider company, two National Trust properties (Croft Castle and Berrington Hall), a Wars of the Roses battle site, Wigmore Castle and the castle at Richard's Castle. Without detours the distance is about 62 miles. (OS Landranger 137, 149)

On a mixture of A roads and country lanes.

Timber-framed buildings

Comparisons of the amount of woodland existing within Herefordshire and Shropshire between the Domesday Survey of 1086 and government department returns at the end of the 19th century (before modern commercial afforestation and orcharding were introduced), showed an almost unchanging coverage of about 8%. But there was a large difference in the composition of tree varieties, especially in the acreage of the common oak. Lonely survivors are still scattered over the two counties, and there is a traditional private oak park at Moccas, but once they were so prolific that they were known locally as 'the weed of Herefordshire'. It was far more useful than most weeds, for from very early days until well into the 17th century it supplied the main framework for the domestic building industry as well as other constructional and practical needs. Leominster was just one of many towns and villages, as well as farmsteads, which were largely built with oak timber during the Middle Ages (broadly AD 1000 to the 15th century) and afterwards.

Unsurprisingly, oak has long been the natural building material used for many of the region's houses. With an average life of 250 years, trees have been felled at between 25 and 100 years of age—using some 350 for a normal-sized farmhouse. Conservationist minded medieval carpenters selected just the smallest trees which they needed for their task, the majority being less than 9ins. in diameter. These would be squared with a broad axe, or adze, leaving rounded corners and some of the softwood and bark. In modern times this has been important in establishing the age of buildings through dendrochronology (dating through tree-ring analysis). Making comparisons with firmly dated local reference timbers, it is now possible to establish to within a few years and sometimes precisely the felling date of an oak tree. From this the date of building can be determined, for the timber would have been promptly used in its 'green', unseasoned state, otherwise, even if today's tools had been available, it would soon have become rock hard and difficult to saw and cut for joints. This building practice meant that a timber-framed house inevitably warped and twisted during the early years of its life, accounting for the numerous 'characterful' shapes now to be seen.

There are two basic types of construction—the cruck frame and the box frame.

The cruck, or crutch, frame is by far the older method, thought to date back to the Ancient Britons. It was widely adopted using pairs of huge incurving timbers, cut from a single large tree. These rose from a sill at ground level and met at the ridge of the roof. Some forms stopped at a collar beam level, where a separate roof structure continued to the apex. Examples may still be seen in gable ends, such as at the rear of the Red Lion inn at Weobley (p.158) whilst others, sometimes four or five crucks in the same building, are encased in plaster or otherwise out of view.

The box frame method is now far more common, dating mostly from late medieval and Tudor periods. It comprises horizontal and vertical timbers which are sometimes reinforced for rigidity with braces and struts. The timber structure is set on a footing of impervious damp proof material, such as slate, often on a low stone or brick wall. A horizontal oak sill, or plate, is placed on this footing into which strong posts, or studs, are mortised as the vertical members, and to which horizontal timbers are tenoned. As wall plates these support the lower ends of the roof rafters and might also be linked as cross rails to the back or front of a house. In two or three storey houses, those at floor level are known as bressumers and carry the upper floor joists. Where an upper storey projects over those below, the overhang is described as a jetty.

The timber panels tend to be square shaped and in some instances where owners wished their affluence and social standing to be reflected, oak being rather costly, they added further vertical timbers as 'close studding', or they specified decorative plain or lozenge motifs and additional chevron bracing. The world famous Feathers Hotel at the Bull Ring, Ludlow, is an outstanding example of this form of indulgence and so are Hereford's Old House of 1621, with its moulded bressumers, carved barge boards, pendants and scrolled brackets, and the Grange House at Leominster. Within the panels, vertical staves were fitted into grooves in the framework and wattles of underwood hazel, elm, sallow or oak laths interwoven horizontally then plastered on both sides with a recipe which might contain clay or dung, reinforced with straw or reeds, horse or goat hair, coarse grit or lime depending on the locality. A final protective coat of lime plaster on the outside completed the process and the whole surface was treated with a lime wash every few years. In the late 16th century, wattle and daub panelling was often replaced by bricks and the extra weight sometimes contributed a new 'character' to the building. The practice of treating the framework with a black water-proofing compound was a 19th-century development, for oak needs no protection and allowed to weather it takes on an attractive silvery look. This is well illustrated at The Ley near Weobley, and some 'restorers' seek to remove the black paint to arrive back at a similar 'authentic' effect and erase the 'magpie' look of their houses!

By the late 17th century, timber-framed buildings started to become unfashionable and stone and brick gained favour. Also forests had become depleted after much timber had been used in shipbuilding, iron smelting and mining, added to which there was a heavy demand for oak bark. Because of its high tannin content, only this would do for the curing of leather.

The tour starts by heading northwards along Bridge Street, and continues straight ahead at the mini-roundabout on the B4361, signposted Richard's Castle, leading through pleasant hill country to Luston, about 3 miles to the north. Set back from the road on the right opposite the small Methodist chapel, the striking Tudor House was placed as Jacobean by Pevsner, who warmed to the cusped concave-sided lozenges below the gable. The Balance Inn is next door and before a return to open countryside, there is a variety of half-timbered and other venerable houses along the straight road as far as Townend House. The next objective is Yarpole, for which take the second signposted left turning along an unclassified road and within sight of the 'high reared head of Clee', far across to the right in Shropshire.

When you reach a crossroads with the B4362 turn left and the road enters the village alongside a brook which is spanned at intervals by small flat bridges to the characterful houses on the left, among them the medieval stone gatehouse of a former manor house. Its subsequent history is thought to have included use as a gaol, illicit Quakers' meeting house and, more recently, a bakehouse. Turn right into a road with a variety of Tudor houses and cottages. On land which has contained a church since the 13th century, the first large building on the right is St. Leonards, now also venue of the 'community shop'.

---

1.   St. Leonard's—Britain's 10th oldest surviving timber building

 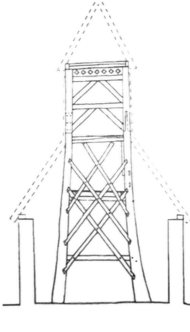

The present church building is in the Decorated style of English Gothic architecture, meaning that it mostly dates from between *c.*1290 to *c.*1350. The crown post roof is most striking, but there is another distinguishing feature. The towers of fewer than 50 churches in Britain are not contained within the main body of their church, of which Herefordshire has seven and this tour will include three. The reason was often to provide villagers with a place of refuge. Yarpole's tower is 40ft.

Yarpole's church tower—and an outline of its construction

high, supported by four huge corner oaks of between 25 and 30ins. diameter. These have been ring-dated to when they were acorns in 1004, which means that they were already mature at the time of the Norman Conquest, and over 200 years old when they were cut for the belfry. Massive internal scissor bracing and other supports were felled during the winter of 1195-6 and there is every reason to accept the claim that this is the 10th oldest surviving timber structure in Britain. Probably the entrance door of the stone base of the tower and its hinges are original. The weather-boarded bell stage and the projecting ledges of the roof, topped by a spire, create something of an eastern pagoda look, rather like the bell tower at Pembridge further along the route, but smaller and plainer.

For many years, the aged condition of the tower made it unsafe to ring the three bells, but after repairs and refurbishment of the frame they started to ring out again each Sunday from 1997.

Return to the junction and turn right towards Kingsland. The road continues on past Bicton and soon arrives at Kingsland at the junction with the B4360. Our route crosses over the B road, but if you wish to see more of the village, turn left to find many of its half-timbered buildings, and you turn off this road to the right to park by the church. The main features, including the earthwork remains of a castle, the mysterious Volka Chapel and the part Kingsland played in the Wars of the Roses, commemorated by the monument at the north western end are described at pp.148-9.

Once across the B road our route soon meets the A4110 on which you turn left. Soon reached on the right it passes the modern timber-framed premises of Kingsland Sawmills Ltd. who, as Border Oak, are perpetuating a long-standing local housebuilding tradition and some of their work is in evidence at our next call. The road crosses the Pinsley Brook, which flows on to Leominster, and at Lawton Cross you turn right on the continuation of the B4529 to Eardisland and are soon close to the River Arrow on the left.

2. Eardisland, 'An uncommonly pretty village'

Eardisland

Each year, Herefordshire calendars rarely miss including a picture of this village of half-timbered and stone-built cottages along the banks of the Arrow. A photogenic mill pond has been created there by damming the river downstream and this is crossed by a bridge next to which a millstream flows from under the Georgian Old Mill House. Close by there is a very unusual 17th-century red-brick dovecote associated with the timber-framed manor house and its Queen Anne additions, which are just to the west. There are over 900 nesting alcoves in the upper storey and now it all belongs to the people of the village who have transformed the downstairs room into a heritage and tourist information centre and, more recently, a convenience store to serve local needs after a lapse of 10 years without a village shop. Bridge House on the opposite side of the bridge was once the Old Schoolhouse, where a chilling reminder of the 'Good old days' is represented by a village whip-ping post, complete with manacles. North of the river on the Leominster road, Staick House was once a yeoman's hall and then a mote house or council chamber and dates back to the 14th century, but it has a 17th-century wing and lozenge-framing in the gable.

The Church of St. Mary the Virgin dates from the end of the 12th century but it was heavily renewed in Victorian times. Unlike some others elsewhere, it aims to be open all day and every day, and this policy is reinforced with a regular major photographic exhibition. There is a tree-clad castle mound of some 72ft. diameter and about 16ft. high just to

Eardisland's dovecote 'museum'

the north, rising above a wet moat which is fed from the Arrow. On the other side of the river, a low flat circular and ditched mound is known as Monks' Court, but its origins are one more mystery. Church Lane leads to St. Mary's churchyard between the Cross Inn and the White Swan and there are a tea room, gift shop and sitting-out gardens near the lych gate.

Continue on the B road through Eardisland and at the first road junction just beyond the edge of the village, turn left in the direction of Burton Court. (Open during afternoons from Spring Bank Holiday to the end of September). After about half a mile the entrance drive is signposted to the right.

3. Burton Court

At first sight the building appears to date from the late 18th century, except for the front which is in a neo-Tudor style, devised by Clough Williams Ellis (of Portmerion Italianate village fame) just before the First World War. The surprise comes inside—a 14th-century hall reaching to a fine roof, where the future Henry V is said to have been based in 1402 during operations against Owain Glyndwr.

Burton Court

With other rooms in the house, it is now used to display a collection of European and Oriental costumes. Ship models, a model fairground, a collection of natural history specimens and a working model railway are also on hand. Should all this not appeal, there will be the opportunity to consider buying a book on local cookery, or perhaps railway history, by the joint owner, Helen J. Simpson, or in season engage in 'picking your own' from her soft fruit fields outside.

The country road continues south to its junction with the A44, on which you turn left for a short distance to reach a junction with the A4112, where you turn right. After about 1 mile, and in a dip in the road, turn left into Dilwyn.

4. Dilwyn

The village green is arguably the main distinguishing feature of the village, for nowadays it is quite rare, and faced by most of Dilwyn's oldest half-timbered houses. About 20 of them are cottages converted from farm buildings which date back over 300 years. Just to their west, and utterly different, the stone-built Great House, with its fine wrought iron gates mounted on tall piers, is early Georgian and was also connected with farming,

Dilwyn

61

for this whole community can trace its history back to the time when its many farms were named in the Domesday Book. Five of these in the parish still survive with their names unchanged after over 900 years, but many others have been absorbed into larger units. The very impressive St. Mary's Church seems to dominate the village from a mound to the north of the green. It provides a challenge for any keen 'church crawler' to disentangle, for it has passed through many changes since Norman times. It comprises an intermixture of Early English (roughly 13th century), late Decorated (c.1290-1350) to Perpendicular (until c.1530)

Dilwyn Church

architectural styles and retains many fine furnishings. New villagers have arrived in recent years and they are mostly housed in cul de sacs leading from the green heart of Dilwyn. They are well situated therefore to share in the hospitality of the Crown Inn, modestly set back on its eastern flank.

In the village, the route turns left past the pub and follows the signs for Weobley, involving a right turn as you leave the village and a sharp right turn after a mile and then some twists and bends before reaching The Throne at the corner of the Hereford road in Weobley. Continue straight on past The Unicorn on your right and then turn right into the village centre. For a tour of Weobley see p.158. Follow the road round to the left at the bottom of the main street, and then turn right onto the B4230 at the T junction ahead. Follow this to its junction with the A4112, where you turn right and follow this road towards Leominster for about 1³/₄ miles until it reaches a minor road to the left signposted for Luntley, Pembridge and a brown sign for Dunkerton's Cider. Turn left and pause after about 2 miles to look at a black and white gabled dovecot, said to have 500 nesting holes at Luntley, and Luntley Court, a Jacobean manor house of outstanding charm close to the road in a setting of similarly attractive outbuildings.

Dunkertons Cider Mill and Cider House Restaurant appear on the right in another half mile further on towards Pembridge, favoured with immense farmland views.

The tour continues on the minor road into Pembridge and to pause awhile, turn right at the junction with the A44 and after a couple of hundred yards a car park is signposted off to the left.

5. Cidermaking and Dunkertons

Most of the orchards seen throughout Herefordshire produce apples which are not suitable for normal eating and each Autumn they are sent to Hereford for the large scale production of cider. However the fruit from around Luntley is used for a 21st-century version of the drink which was once produced by many farmers in part payment of their labourers at haymaking and harvest times. Some men were capable of accommodating two gallons a day, but not the sweet and fizzy product now available at supermarkets. When waterborne diseases such as typhoid and cholera were endemic, their rough, strong drink also served as a life-saver, for its acidity killed off the germs. The farmers gathered the apples from their own orchards and used their experience in blending the varieties to produce a good result.

Dunkertons' Cider House Restaurant

Over 80 varieties of cider apple, containing varying degrees of acid and tannin, are still grown and Dunkertons have a number of these, each recognised by ancient names such as Foxwhelp, Brown Snout, Yarlington Mill, Strawberry Norman, Tremletts Bitter, Frequin and Roi de Pomme. Their art of cider making comes in blending the different types of these apples when, after separate fermentation, the juices are added to the 1,200 gallon vats at the farm. Akin to single malt whiskys in Scotland, Dunkertons also produce ciders from three single apple varieties: Breakwells Seedling, Court Royal, and Kingston Black which is considered to be the greatest of all cider apples and is now quite rare. And for something really special there are their Organic Premium Cider and Black Fox ciders.

All the ciders are naturally still and, depending on the summer weather, can have an alcohol content of up to 8%. They are available on draught or in bottles at Luntley and throughout the region in dry, medium dry, medium sweet and sweet forms or in the 400-year-old timber-framed Cider House Restaurant that is open during certain holiday weekends.

6. Pride of Pembridge

Butter Market and New Inn, Pembridge

With a population of hardly 900, Pembridge cannot rank as a town, and yet nearly 800 years ago it had become a borough, with privileges in 1240 confirmed by royal charter for highly significant market and fair rights. However these failed to bring expected benefits and growth so Pembridge gradually went into decline to become another Marches 'failed borough', rather like Richard's Castle to be visited later, and Huntington to the west. One effect was that the people of the parish could no longer afford to improve their houses, or build new ones, but had to make do with what they had. This has resulted in the 'old world charm' and heritage appeal of places such as Pembridge (and it now also prevents today's wealthier owners from doing too much of what they want with their homes, because of 'listed building' and planning restrictions!)

Alongside West Street (A44)

The markets and May hiring fairs are no longer held, and only the huge church of cathedral-like proportions remains to reflect the former importance of the place. The half-timbered houses date from the 14th to the 19th century but not all of them are black and white, for some of the brick noggin panels are coloured in light shades of red and pink. It is also noticeable that first floor overhangs were much in favour here and at Ye Olde Steppes (a rectory from 1777, and now part of a general store) the barge-boards are carved with dragons, fruit and flowers. Other features of particular interest are exterior cruck-trusses on the east wall of the 14th-century building at the far end of West Street and at Bridge Cottages down near the River Arrow.

The Red Lion separates the old rectory from the other features forming a group around the Market Place. The Market House dates from the early 16th century, and of its eight wooden pillars one stands on the base of an even older market cross. It is opposite the half-timbered New Inn, with its gabled cross wings and projecting upper storey and only 'new' in Pembridge terms, for it was built in 1311 after the former inn burned down. The main supporting oak pillars of the detached bell tower, visible up the steps from the Market Square leading to St. Mary's Church, are nearly 200 years older. They have been ring-dated to 1115, but even they are a century 'younger' than their counterparts at Yarpole! This tower is larger than that at Yarpole, requiring eight immense oak pillars, braced horizon-tally and scissor fashion. It is usually possible to explore the inside of the base and see this impressive timber structure within the thick stone walls, loopholed from when the tower was the village stronghold. Dating from the 14th century, the base is an octagon 45ft. in diameter of four long and four short sides, roofed in stone below a vertical weatherboarded bell stage with a clock and a truncated pyramid roof. It is all crowned with a third, smaller boarded stage with a little shingled spire. The peal of five bells is hung in an old oak frame and there is also a small sanctus bell. As the local people say of the 'Pride of Pembridge', there is no other campanile in England exactly like it.

St. Mary's church was built upon the site of a Norman church and traces of this still remain. In 1349, not long after work started, the Black Death struck and decimation of the labour force meant that there was a long delay before it was finished. It is now a spacious building with a fine interior and artistic range of Jacobean and other fittings.

The detached bell tower, Pembridge

Heading out of Pembridge down Bridge Street, on the left is one of the two 17th-century black-and-white almshouse terraces which are still in use in the village. And in complete contrast, note the gargantuan brick built rectory of 1852 on the right, just before reaching the bridge across the River Arrow.

Continue along this road, past Clearbrook, a decorative early 17th-century half-timbered house with elaborate chimneys on the right, and after about ³/₄ mile, turn right at the crossroads for Shobdon. There could well be low-flying light aircraft or hang gliders, because a turning to the right at the entrance to the village, gives access to Herefordshire's only airfield. When you reach the B4362 just past the turning to the airfield, turn right towards Mortimer's Cross, passing the Bateman Arms on the right, and an entrance to the famous Strawberry Hill Gothic Church of St. John the Evangelist on the left (p.149).

The crossroads junction with the A4410 at Mortimer's Cross is close to the scene of the action which in 1461 resulted in the proclamation and crowning of the Yorkist Edward Mortimer as King Edward IV (p.148). The battle of Mortimer's Cross was fought on land belonging to the Croft family, their destiny for centuries linked with that of their powerful neighbours, the Mortimers of Wigmore.

The tour turns left here, but if you want to find out more about the Crofts, their ancestral home is Croft Castle, 2 miles further along the B4362 beyond Lucton and is in the care of the National Trust—so you may wish to make a detour. If so, cross over at the crossroads and drive for some 2¹/₄ miles, well passing Croft Castle, for the entrance drive doubles back. Opposite a turning to Yarpole on the crest of a small rise in the road, Croft Castle is signposted to the left, and you turn left again immediately to follow the drive to a car park. To rejoin the route you can complete the recommended one way system and drop straight back down to the B road, on which you turn right to Mortimer's Cross, and right again at the crossroads onto the A4110.

7.   Croft Castle and Croft Ambrey

Croft Castle

Bernard de Croft is named in Domesday Book in 1086 as holding Croft and he is generally regarded as the ancestor of the family which subsequently remained in possession until 1746. During this time, in different walks of life, they played leading parts in the conduct of affairs in the county, and of the nation. Outstanding were the adventurous Croft who, in 1265, joined in the hazardous enterprise of delivering Prince Edward from imprisonment at Hereford, and the pious and brave Herbert Croft who, during the impact of turbulent mid-17th century events upon the Church and State was between 1644 and 1691 successively dean and bishop of Hereford.

After 1746, the estate passed to Richard Knight, the celebrated ironmaster of Downton (p.71) and thence, through marriage, to Thomas Johnes of Hafod in Cardiganshire, and afterwards to others. The Crofts returned in 1923, but by the 1950s death duties and other problems called for a rescue exercise which also involved the Ministry of Works and the National Trust, which now holds the freehold of the 1,329 acres estate. Members of the family continue to live at the castle, whilst part of the castle, gardens, tearoom and church are open to the public from the end of March until early November. Several public footpaths cross the grounds.

The four round corner towers and ancient walls of the castle date from the 14th or 15th centuries and inside there are a fine Georgian Gothic staircase and rooms and galleries which contain a wealth

Croft Ambrey

of interesting furniture and family portraits. Outside there are borders and interesting shrubs, and one of the finest restored walled gardens in Herefordshire, whilst stretching for half a mile, a line of Spanish chestnuts forms just one of the great avenues of trees which create the main glories of Croft.

Long before the appearance of the Crofts, Iron Age families had lived for some six centuries on the ridge to the north of the present and previous castles. Painstaking excavations in the mid-20th century have shown that Croft Ambrey was occupied from about 550 BC until AD50, after the Roman Conquest.

Now the eight acre village site is grass-grown, with many trees, but on a clear day it is reckoned that the climb through the woods could be rewarded with a view of 14 counties, including much of Wales.

Once on the A4110 you soon reach Aymestrey church on the right. The building was reputedly used by the Yorkists for stabling horses and equipment prior to the Battle of Mortimer's Cross, and after this experience it is gratifying that early in the 16th century it should be graced with its tall and beautiful rood and parclose screen. Soon after that was added, a longhouse was being built on the opposite side of the road, close to the bridge across the River Lugg. This was a once common form of agricultural dwelling, found especially in Wales, where the farming family lived at one end and their livestock in a byre at the other. It is now the Riverside Inn and Restaurant.

Rood screen in Aymestrey Church

The A4110 at this point follows the course of the Roman road, diverging slightly at Yatton as both approach Wigmore, now a quiet village set below superb woodland in hills at the extreme north-western corner of Herefordshire. It is also a place for indulging the imagination, in a time-warp extending back over 1,000 years. A Roman fort, close to Watling Street and near Bury Farm is the first hard evidence of a settlement here. Then in 921, Edward the Elder, son of Alfred the Great, established the Anglo-Saxon *Wicingamere*, which means 'unstable moor', and some historians believe that the first Norman castle was built on

Cottages in Aymestrey

the site of a formidable stronghold, erected there by his sister, Ethelfleda. It became a defence against the 11th-century invaders under the leadership of Edric the Wild, Lord of Wigmore. Then the Normans arrived.

In order to visit the village, church and castle ruins, it is necessary to leave the A4410 by turning right at the Old Oak inn. Just past the Compasses Hotel there is a further sign pointing at the village hall and public car park, next to the High School and County Primary School entrance. There are several timber-framed buildings on the way to the church, and by the centenary village green, just across the A4110, is one of

The Riverside Inn in Aymestrey

several informative interpretation boards. There is a fairly stiff climb up the huddled village, thought to have been set out on a grid-iron plan parallel to the ridge on which the church stands. A footpath leads past Green Hill Farm to meet the first sight of the castle ruins. Some of the slopes within are quite steep, but the steps have been safeguarded with non-slip surfaces and are equipped with strong handrails. The views from the various levels are well worth the effort of getting to them.

8.   Wigmore and the House of Mortimer

Soon after the Norman Conquest, William fitz Osbern, earl of Hereford, was charged by King William with securing the border with Wales from Ludlow to Chepstow. This involved the siting or strengthening of castles at strategic points along the border including Ewyas Harold, Hereford, Clifford and Wigmore. As one of the chief outposts in the central Marches, fitz Osbern's original castle is likely to have been a modest enclosure, built just west of the church at Green Hill: only in the late 12th century was a massive stone castle commenced

Wigmore Castle gateway, showing the level of fallen masonry

on wider land further to the west. In 1075, a number of manors in Herefordshire and Shropshire had been bestowed on Ralph Mortimer and he made Wigmore the head of these, where he built his great hall and held court. For the next four centuries his acquisitive and opportunistic heirs were to dominate the central Marches, extending their lands and control from Cleobury and Leintwardine in the east, far into the central uplands of Wales. There were always strong, often evil, personalities in the Mortimer family to play a leading part in English and Welsh affairs during the Middle Ages. During the early 14th century, Roger Mortimer stood out as probably the most notorious. The fourth to bear the same name on the family tree, he was responsible for deposing King Edward II—possibly even conspiring in his murder, conducted an affair with the queen, Isabella, assumed for himself the title

Outline shape of Wigmore Castle

of earl of March and, for a period at the end of the 1320s, exercised near-regal powers with little resistance. But it came to an end in 1330 when he was tried by his peers for 'treasons, felonies and misdeeds made against ... the king' and several other crimes, was found guilty and hanged like a common criminal at Tyburn. Yet despite this damaging episode, for much of the 15th century the family were legitimate heirs to the English throne. Finally, in 1461, although by then only through the remaining female side, Edward, earl of March became King Edward IV, the first sovereign of the House of York. This followed his victory over the House of Lancaster at the Battle of Mortimer's Cross, and apart from one short interval he reigned until his death in 1483, whereupon his 12-year-old son succeeded as King Edward V. He ruled—in name only—for just three months between leaving the Yorkist stronghold of nearby Ludlow Castle, with his brother, Richard, duke of York, and their disappearance, presumably murdered, in the Tower of London. Their uncle, the brother of Edward IV, was crowned in his stead as King Richard III. He was killed at the Battle of Bosworth in 1485, after just two years, and the crown was removed from his helmet to be placed on the head of Henry Tudor. As King Henry VII he speedily married Elizabeth, sister of 'the princes in the Tower' and daughter of Edward Mortimer, so uniting the lines of Lancaster and York, ending the Wars of the Roses and introducing the Tudor House of the double

Herringbone masonry at Wigmore Church

rose. From then on, the House of Mortimer faded from the royal scene—and the heyday of Wigmore Castle was over.

As it had evolved, the borough established by fitz Osbern in the 11th century advanced to become almost a small market town. It had long been close to the main Roman trade route which serviced the Marches and for more than a century before the arrival of the Normans had been a major trading centre. The Mortimer castle garrison required provisions and services from the village trades-people and artisans, and under close military protection the chartered markets and fairs ensured a monopoly of trade from the surrounding area, as well as a good share of the revenues and tolls. For almost 800 years Wigmore retained its borough status, furnished with its open market hall and first floor meeting room which stood until *c.*1848 on the Pavement in the triangular market place in front of the Old Oak inn.

The massive St. James' Church was built on top of an earlier Saxon building. Founded by the Mortimers, the oldest part is its nave and worth more than a cursory glance is a fine example of 11th-century herringbone masonry on the outside of the north wall. Much of the remainder of this Grade I listed building, including the chancel, south aisle and west tower, followed on in the 14th century and much restoration work was subsequently carried out by the Victorians. At the start of the 21st century it is evident that much more needs to be done to keep it safe and in working order.

In 1179, Hugh Mortimer founded an abbey for Augustinian canons at Adforton, just to the north. It was soon demolished by the Welsh and then rebuilt, only to be destroyed again in the 1530s at the Dissolution, the last resting place of many generations of Mortimers.

The castle became a royal property of Edward IV, and he paid occasional visits, but eventually it passed into private hands and in 1643 was slighted to prevent its use by Royalists during the Civil War. It became privately owned, by Mr. John C. Gaunt, but from 1995 the ruins were stabilised and conserved and the natural habitat protected by English Heritage. Full of romantic interest, it is now freely open to the public, who are reminded that it is classed as a Scheduled Ancient Monument, a Special Wildlife Site, a Site of Interest for Nature Conservation and a Regionally Important Geological Site. Added to all this, much of the village is designated as a Conservation Area!

So now St. James's is the only, rather fragile, survivor of three main components of the active times when the little town bustled with trade and was accustomed to the presence of crowned heads, steel-clad nobles, knightly warriors, high clergy, men-at-arms and retinues of courtiers and liveried retainers. After these departed, Wigmore was not able to adjust and prosper solely as a local market centre and it steadily lapsed into decline, emphasised in 1930 when Wigmore Rural District ceased as a local authority, and in 1971 when its magistrates court was closed.

There is far less left to see of Wigmore Abbey, and in order to appreciate its setting it is necessary to return to the car and drive back to the A4110, turning right at the Old Oak inn to head for 1¼ miles towards Adforton. Just before Adforton Hill turn right down a single track road, signposted Burrington and Downton, and the site of the abbey is about ¼ mile further down on the right. The ruins of the outer gatehouse are visible from the road and so are other masonry remains forming part of the private farm.

Some oak stalls, choir benches and miserere seats are the only furnishings of the abbey which are thought to have survived the Dissolution in 1538 and these were removed to the chancel of the church of St. Mary Magdalene at nearby Leintwardine. Since 1976 it has been part of the parish of Wigmore Abbey, but there have been links for much longer. Each year, on the festival of the Blessed Virgin Mary, the abbot used to preach his annual sermon there in the company of his community of monks and members of the Mortimer family.

It is likely that they processed to and from Leintwardine, close to the Roman road which joins the abbey grounds and the village, and the same route may still be taken along a single track road today. This option continues on past the farm as far as the next crossroads, and then turns left for Leintwardine, taking in the striking half-timbered Paytoe Hall on the right of the junction. The other way is to return from the abbey site to the A4110 and then turn right for Leintwardine. Between these two routes after about a mile is Brandon Camp, a Roman temporary marching camp which

The gateway to Wigmore Abbey

69

was one of a number in the Marches set up by Ostorius Scapula during the 1st century AD. About a century later, the Romans chose the rising ground on the opposite side of the River Teme as the site for a base to form part of a borderland chain extending along Watling Street West from today's Caerleon, through Abergavenny, Kenchester and Wroxeter to Chester.

The A 4110 joins the A4113 which crosses over the Teme by an old packhorse bridge and enters

The bridge over the Teme into Leintwardine

Leintwardine. The most interesting route through the village, is to turn right immediately over the bridge, and then first left up Watling Street. In due course you'll rejoin the A4113, turning right to head for Bromfield, the A49 and Ludlow. And with many twists and turns the River Teme heads in a similar direction, rushing lustily through Downton Gorge and below Downton Castle in a succession of rapids and pools. It is difficult to believe that this picturesque wooded country was once occupied by smoking furnaces of the iron industry.

Plan of Leintwardine showing how the layout of the Roman fort relates to the village as seen today

9. Leintwardine / *Bravonium*

Unlike the town of *Magnis* (Kenchester), near Hereford 19 miles to the south, which was a stone-walled small town, *Bravonium* was a 4.5 hectares fort surrounded by a timber-laced rampart and ditch, thought to hold a cohort of 500 men. It is considered likely that it served as a supply depot for the central Marches and, like *Magnis*, had four entrances—with Watling Street West passing through the north and south and the *Via Principalis* running from the west to the east gateways. A parallel north-south road ran just beyond the east ditch line. To the south, a bathhouse was placed within an annexe rampart between the fort and the River Teme—close to today's Mill Lane and behind the present post office and Lion Hotel. The fortress remained in service until the late 4th century and it might then have easily disappeared. But probably because of the attractions of the site, the Saxons overcame their customary superstition, which they followed at *Magnis*, about adopting a Roman site and built their settlement there. This became Leintwardine, which means 'the enclosure of the River Lent' (an old name for the River Clun, which enters the Teme just above the old packhorse bridge). They were followed in due course by the Normans, who inherited the problems created by the recalcitrant Welsh. St. Mary Magdalene church dates from the 12th century and its sturdy 13th-century tower was, like many others in the Marches, accordingly built partly as a refuge for the villagers. There is no sign of the former Saxon church on the site, but beneath the chancel is the eastern rampart of the Roman fort and this explains why its floor level, and that of the Mortimer Chapel, is about four feet higher than that of the nave, which is within the settlement enclosure.

As an optional detour from the A4113, turn right just over a mile from Leintwardine and follow the signposts for Downton on the Rock, passing close to St. Giles' Church on the left after entering the driveway to Downton Castle, and the carpark.

10.   The Knights of Downton Castle

Forge Bridge, Bringewood, over the River Teme below Downton Castle

Downton Castle is not like most of the castles met on these tours for it was built between 1773 and 1778 as a castellated mansion for one of the early iron masters. In those days the essential combination of an abundant supply of wood for charcoal and a fast-flowing river made it worth the expense of bringing the ore on horse- or mule-back from Staffordshire to this part of Herefordshire. The charcoal-fuelled blast furnaces were at Bringewood and the site of the forge and the very fine Forge Bridge are still shown on OS Landranger Map 137. The high annual level of iron production which was achieved would quickly have exhausted the existing woodland supplies without coppicing, a management technique possible with most natural broadleaf trees. After they are felled, new growth commences from the 'stools' and this enables the trees to be grown as a sustainable crop over a cycle of up to 20 years. The power from the rapid flowing Teme at that point was of course convincingly sustainable.

Richard Knight of Madeley (1659-1745) and his family first lived at Bringewood Hall but they then moved upstream to Downton. The property was duly inherited by Richard Payne Knight and he may actually have designed the present imposing pile of towers and battlements himself, and would certainly have practised his widely renowned skills in landscape gardening. In 1861, a new church was built in the grounds at the expense of a descendent, A.J. Rouse-Boughton-Knight, and this was dedicated to St. Giles, just as the ruined church in the village had been. In the Early English style, New St. Giles stands back from the public road and entrance to the car park down the approach drive is permitted and rewarded with a fine vista of the park. The castle is no longer the seat of the Knights and the annual Open Day at daffodil time has ceased, but access to parts of the estate and to a view of the outside of the building, may still be gained from signed footpaths.

After returning to the A4113, turn right for Bromfield (p.31), joining the A49 at a T junction to head for Ludlow (p.21). (To pass through the town, bear left to join B4361 at the end of the by-pass. This road passes through the centre, up Corve Street to the traffic signals and then down Old Street towards the river and Ludford Bridge. Turn left to cross the River Teme and after a mile, turn right at Overton). To avoid the town centre, travel along the by-pass, crossing two roundabouts and about two miles further on, turn sharp right onto the B4361 signposted for Ludlow and Richard's Castle, and after a mile make a left turn at Overton.

The B4361 continues to Batchcott, and the first of two churches which serve Richard's Castle. All Saints is in Shropshire and was built towards the end of the Victorian era. Turn right at this point, leaving the church on the left, and continue along a narrow road to the next crossroads, entering Herefordshire. Turn right here for the car park serving St. Bartholomew's Church, and the ruins of the castle just to the west.

---

11.   Richard's Castle and St. Bartholomew's Church

The castle is one of only three or four constructed of stone in Britain which predate the Norman Conquest, in this case by about 16 years. The original motte and bailey castle was built during the reign of Edward the Confessor and a large octagonal tower, 50 feet in diameter and with a 20 feet thick wall, was erected on top of the motte in the 12th century. A curtain wall was added early in the 13th century and

Richard's Castle Church and tower

subsequently altered and augmented by a large square residential tower, semi-circular mural towers and other features. The entire settlement may then have been enclosed by a stone wall, according to excavations and researches by Dr. Thompson in 1962-4. The church placed within its defences as a place of worship for the population of the Norman borough was probably founded by Richard fitz Scrob, from whom both castle and village derive their name. The earliest part of the present church is the 12th-century north wall of the nave and the rest was mostly built in the 14th century. One important exception was the detached bell tower, the third to be seen on this tour. This dates from the latter half of the 13th century and its position and openings probably relate to those of the castle to the west and to their mutual defence. Towards the end of the 20th century the church had come to the end of its working life and in 1986 the Redundant Churches Fund and English Heritage commissioned a condition survey of its fabric. Three phases of extensive repairs followed and early in 2001 St. Bartholomew's came under the care of The Churches Conservation Trust, joining some 325 other churches of outstanding historic, architectural or archaeological importance, no longer needed for regular worship. All the Trust's churches remain consecrated and, as at Richard's Castle, they are used for occasional services and other events. In addition, as there is no churchyard at All Saints, funeral services there are often followed by burial at St. Bartholomew's.

The problem of redundant churches

Apart from St. Bartholomew's Church at Richard's Castle, other Herefordshire churches cared for by the Trust are: Holme Lacy, St. Cuthbert; Llanrothal, St. John the Baptist; Michaelchurch, St. Michael; Moreton Jeffries Church; Stretford, St. Cosmas & St. Damian; Wormsley, St. Mary; Yatton Chapel and Yazor, St. Mary the Virgin. These form a small proportion of the 417 Anglican churches currently in use in the Hereford diocese which originate from nearly every age since before the arrival of the Normans until the 20th century. Many are listed as of special architectural and historic interest, are usually in attractive settings and form a decided part of the national heritage. Several, such as St. Bartholomew's, Richard's Castle, have distinctive features which place them among the most treasured churches in all Britain. They are of interest not only to students of ecclesiastical architecture, history or local landscape but also to the general public and a growing number of enthusiastic tourists. But the upkeep of a great many of them has become a serious challenge for a greatly reduced number of parish clergy and their diminished congregations. In some instances it has become necessary to combine ten or even more parishes and their churches into groups and these might serve a scattered population of scarcely more than 1,000 people—and far fewer regular worshippers. Not very long ago, before the onset of acute reductions in agricultural employment and associated changes in rural society and for previous centuries, these often large churches would be filled and sustained by far greater numbers of church-goers. But nowadays as one parish priest at Worfield in Shropshire has put it: 'Serious choices will have to be made if clergy are not to be so involved in fundraising and administration that there is little room for mission and ministry'. Another, faced with the daunting task of raising £47,000 for repairs to the church tower at Leintwardine, in accepting that churches: 'hold our human story and the sense of ownership which the villages have for their churches, which makes them, like the village pub, shop and school one of the signs of community—often nowadays the last sign', also added 'Christianity is not an architectural appreciation society'. And after the money is raised, she wrote 'the building will still be uncomfortable, without the most basic facility and totally unsuitable for most of our purposes'.

Not surprisingly therefore there is increasing talk of some closures, perhaps 'mothballing' or alternative uses. Some churches in the diocese have already been turned into houses, offices or public meeting rooms and, in one exceptional case, as a place of worship combined with a café (p.136). Added to all this there is now an increasing problem of theft of donation money, furnishings, and even slates off the roof in one recent case, as well as mindless vandalism. This creates an argument for churches to be locked for most of the time, except during services and parish events, but unfortunately it results in a denial of their immemorial pastoral role.

From the car park head down through the village and turn right on to the B4361 when you reach it. The route continues past the Maidenhead inn west of Orleton and then turn left (in essence heading straight ahead) so as to stay on the B4361, heading for Leominster. As soon as you reach Luston, turn left on to Eye Lane, signposted Eye and Moreton, and cross over the railway main line, just before reaching Eye Manor and the church of St. Peter and St. Paul.

Eye Manor was bought in 1673 by 'Captain' Ferdinado Gorges, who made a fortune out of sugar and slaves, earning himself the title 'King of the Black Market'. The present Manor House was finished in 1680 but its panelled interior and glorious plaster ceilings must have taken longer to complete. The Great Parlour, Staircase Hall, Writing Room, bedrooms and other parts of the interior and their splendid furnishings are no longer open to visitors, but a good view of the pink brick face of the house may be seen across the lawn from the church access drive.

After passing through Moreton, the road reaches the entrance to Berrington Hall on the right.

12. Berrington Hall, and the sacrifices of the Cawleys

Known as Beriton in 1236, the estate was bought from the ancient Herefordshire Cornewall family in 1775 by Thomas Harley (1730-1804), a banker and government contractor. His fortune came from supplying pay and clothing to the British Army during the War of American Independence and he became Lord Mayor of London at the age of 37. Between 1778 and 1781 he employed the fashionable Whig architect, Henry Holland junr., to design his new house. Holland

Berrington Hall and parkland as seen from the A49

had eminent assistance in siting the building and designing the parkland from his father-in-law, Lancelot 'Capability' Brown. His setting gave an illusion of wide pastureland, punctuated by carefully placed trees, belts of woodland and a 14-acre lake and 4-acre artificial island. Natural features of the surrounding countryside were skilfully incorporated to provide views of the distant hills, extending as far as the Black Mountains, Brecon Beacons and Radnor Forest.

Holland's house exhibits a plain neo-classical exterior, whereas the interior is lavishly enriched with painted ceilings and a masterpiece staircase hall with a cantilevered staircase rising to a central dome. The many rooms and halls contain a wide variety of furnishings, notably a collection of French Regency furniture and there are numerous portraits and paintings of present and previous families on the walls. Others are great battle pictures recalling the renown of Admiral Lord Rodney, hero of the Battle of the Saints of 1782, whose son married Anne, the daughter of Thomas Harley. The Rodney family occupied Berrington Hall until 1901, when the 7th Lord Rodney sold the estate to Frederick Cawley, M.P., who became the 1st Lord Cawley in 1918. He is portrayed in a 1908 photograph in one of the rooms in a hunting group outside the Hall portico with his four sons. Three of these were killed during the Great War and, at the age of 24, Captain John Cawley, a son of the only survivor, was killed in Tunisia in 1943 during the Second World War.

The house was built from stone quarried on the estate at Shuttocks Hill but this is very soft and decays rapidly where exposed and between 1966 and 1970 extensive restorations were undertaken, using a more durable sandstone from Hollington, near Uttoxeter (a source previously used for the 1904 Oldrid Scott west front of Hereford Cathedral). By then the House, Park and Berrington Pool had been surrendered to the Treasury in part payment of estate duty and all were transferred to the National Trust. A fully detailed park survey was carried out in the 1980s and after much work, which has included the planting of many young trees to replace the mature oaks, it all looks much as 'Capability' Brown would have seen it over 200 years ago. The Gardens and Grounds, a Park Walk and the House are open to the public at times and prices which are shown on National Trust brochures.

To return to Leominster, rejoin the road from Luston, turn right for Ashton and then right on the A49 soon to catch a last glimpse of the Park, Hall and Pool over on the right of the road.

Bromyard — 'Enclosure where broom grows'

Set in a hollow and bordered by the River Frome, the town is home to many fine 17th-century buildings but much of it dates from the 18th, although subsequent changes have led to a pronounced sprawl into the surrounding countryside. The central street pattern has been almost unchanged for over 700 years and until the 1950s, Bromyard's population, long wavering at around 1,650, made it the smallest of Herefordshire's market towns. However by the end of the century the count had more than doubled to just over 4,000, placing Kington at the bottom position with just 2,250, whilst the numbers are now at around 4,600 and 3,300 respectively. Along with Leominster, both towns are on the A44 Worcester to Aberystwyth trunk road, which has been diverted from the centre of the two with a bypass. Bromyard's turn came first in 1967 and followed a much earlier relief measure in 1835 when New Road, at a daunting gradient of 1:11 against the preferred (certainly by the horses) slope of 1:30, was introduced to augment Old Road, the main road to Leominster. Like Kington, Bromyard also lost its railway at this time when the Worcester-Bromyard railway was closed in 1964 after only 87 years service, the loss-making line to Leominster having already preceded it in 1952.

Spelt as *Bromgeard*, a Saxon word meaning broom enclosure, the first recorded evidence of the town is in an Anglo-Saxon charter of 840, in a grant by Cuthwulf, bishop of Hereford between c.838 and c.866. This concerned property associated with a minster or large church and by c.975 it was suggested that, after Hereford and Leominster, Bromyard was the third most important ecclesiastical centre of the county. By 1086 it appeared in Domesday Book as *Bromgerbe*—where as well as villagers and smallholders, two priests, a chaplain and three of the bishop's men-at-arms are registered as tenants of the bishop of Hereford, to whose predecessors the extensive manor of Bromyard had belonged before 1066. Called the Bishop's Palace, vestiges of the manor house, court house and dungeon remained until c.1790, sited close to what was then a large ecclesiastical precinct. Today this area is occupied in part by the now closed churchyard of St. Peter's, whilst former houses, dovehouses and other buildings have long been superseded. The subsequent buildings have in turn been replaced or re-appropriated.

There is no trace of the Saxon church, except that the carved figure of St. Peter and a consecration cross above the south doorway are thought by experts to come from the earlier building and certain stonework in the north and south walls of the chancel also suggest a Saxon origin. The present building dates from the last quarter of the 12th century and the original chancel, north and south transepts and nave have since been augmented with side aisles, and exten-

St. Peter's Church, Bromyard

The range of Norman doorways into St. Peter's Church, Bromyard, that on the left, the south door, with the figure of St. Peter and the consecration cross above

sive modifications have produced many internal changes in form and use down the centuries. Addition of the 13th-century aisles meant that the Norman doorways, one in the north aisle and the larger south doorway, were moved from their original positions and set in the new walls, whilst the Norman font has more recently been restored to its proper position at the west end of the church. Rather exceptionally, the register extends as far back as 1538 and one curiosity from 1670 which may be seen in the church is the metal Bromyard Bushall Measure, standing on four short feet and with two handles. Viewed from the outside, the central tower has a circular stair turret with a castellated top, which is another unusual feature of St. Peter's. Also there is surprisingly no evidence of any lych gate (or corpse gate), but the original Schallenge (which is a Herefordshire or West Country term for it), now leading from Cruxwell Street and Old Road to the church, provides a clue as to its possible former position.

Before exploring the rest of the town it is worth first the TIC at the Bromyard Centre, Cruxwell Street. The old market square was once the site of a High or Market Cross and, until 1844, an open Market House standing in front of the Hop Pole inn. This housed the town stocks and whipping post and there was an enclosed room above where the 10 gallon Bromyard Bushall Measure, engraved with the name of John Baynham (the presumed toll-gatherer), and other weights and measures were likely to be kept. During the 19th century, nearby Broad Street was the site of the butter and live poultry markets and also where a room at the Falcon Hotel was provided for the sale of dairy produce and dressed poultry on market and fair days. Hay and corn were sold there, Frog Lane up the High Street to Cruxwell Street was the cattle market and, not surprisingly, the sheep market took place in Sheep Street, now called Old Road, but formerly Cruxwell Street. High Street, Broad Street, Rowberry Street and the Market Square embrace one of the oldest parts of the town. A distinguishing feature of this core area is the narrowness and depth of many of the buildings which have been built at right angles to the main shopping streets. This arises from the medieval process which created long burgage plots which were subject to rents applied by the lord of the manor. Their modest width was placed parallel with the street—as can also be seen in many other ancient towns met on these tours, such as Hereford and Kington. The appearance of much of the centre dates from the 18th century, and in many cases a

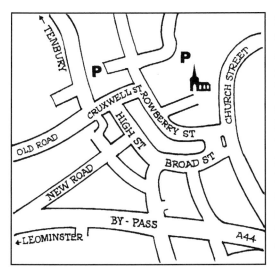

Map of central Bromyard

new Georgian brick front was added to an older building that had been built with oak, which until the late 17th century was the most commonly used building material in Bromyard. There are good examples at the White Horse in Cruxwell Street and at houses on the south side of the market square and in Broad Street. A close look here and in High Street will also reveal how some houses were increased in height in order to produce more headroom on the top floor. The Bay Horse inn appears to have been raised twice at the west end and another clear example exists at the Falcon Hotel, where a complete storey has been added by 18th-century carpenters, whose workmanship and budget were clearly not up to those of their predecessors. As old photographs of the early 1900s show, this frontage, like others, was once masked not by brickwork, but by a complete coat of stucco. The Falcon dates from 1535 and used to be an important coaching inn, serving the Royal Mail and passengers on the London to Aberystwyth coaches, and it still retains the ample courtyard at the rear as its car park.

One of the finest timber-framed and close-studded houses in Bromyard is now rather isolated from the others on Tower Hill, just on the opposite side of the A44 by-pass. Called Tower Hill House, it dates from 1630 and is said to have been lived in by the Baynham family (see John Baynham above) and reputed also to have been one of many places where Charles I stayed the night during 1645. Again it is quite obvious that additions have been made above the upper storey, possibly in the late 17th century, after which the original roof and gable timbers were replaced.

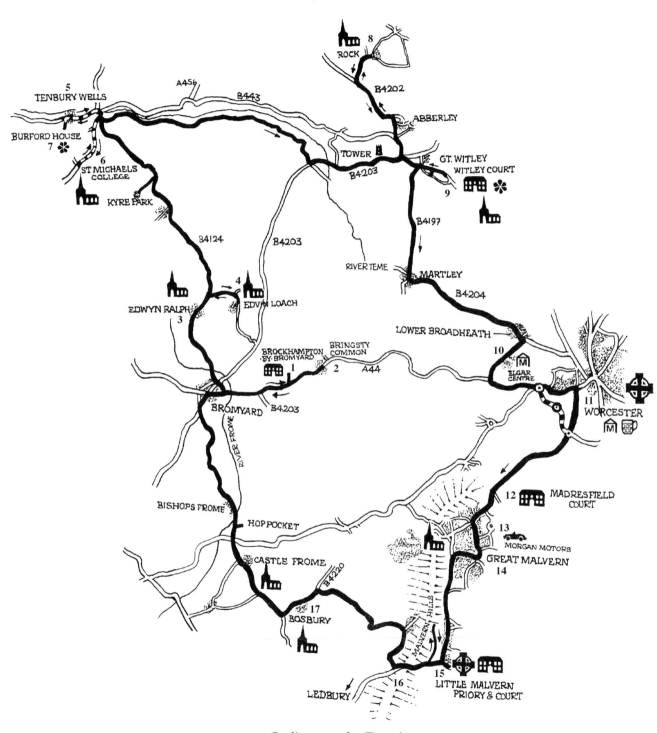

Outline map for Tour 4
The numbers 1 to 17 relate to the boxed information given within the tour

Tour 4   Bromyard to Worcester and Back

The tour includes a number of small villages with their mixture of churches, gardens open to the public, moated manor houses, the ruins of a palatial house at Great Witley Court, the birthplace of and museum to Sir Edward Elgar and much besides, along with the Malverns and Great Malvern itself. Much of the route is through rolling hill country with some fine views. There is also the opportunity to visit Worcester.

The route is mainly on a mixture of A and B roads, but with some minor roads too. Excluding the potential detours the distance is approximately 65 miles. (OS Landranger 138, 149 and 150)

Sights in the vicinity of Bromyard

Bromyard Downs, Brockhampton Manor and Bringsty Common, nearby attractions popular among Bromyardians and visitors alike, are situated between 2 and 3 miles beyond the by-pass along the A44 towards Worcester. Bromyard Downs are reached off to the left near the top of the climb up the A44, signposted along an unclassified road. The Downs are some 350 acres of unenclosed bracken and grass spread out below Warren Wood. The walks and open spaces provide extensive views, not only over the town but far out towards the Clee Hills, Wales and the Malverns.

Back on the A44, a few hundred yards driving beneath a leafy tunnel leads to a drive to the left signposted into the Brockhampton Estate.

Again, further along the A44, Bringsty Common is reached as the road initially levels out after dropping from the Bromyard Downs.

---

1.   Brockhampton-by-Bromyard

The word Brockhampton derives from Old English and means 'farmstead by the brook', of which there must have been many in country areas. It is perhaps surprising therefore that there are not more such place names. As it is, there is just one similar settlement in Herefordshire and to avoid confusion this is often called Brockhampton-by-Ross (for which see p.237).

Brockhampton-by-Bromyard Manor

The 1,700 acre Brockhampton Estate comprises some 1,000 acres of farmland and 700 acres of mixed woodland and the first part of the drive leads through trees to reach the chapel, designed for the estate in a pretty neo-Perpendicular style in 1799. It is close to the 7 bay red brick Brockhampton House, which was built during the mid-18th century, subsequently restored and remodelled and out of bounds in private occupation. The estate car park, information centre, tea room and shop are in between and at the beginning of a long, winding drive of about a mile, down to what arguably ranks as Herefordshire's most picturesque timber house, lying deep in a wooded valley surrounded by damson orchards close to a farmyard and carpark. It is moated, once completely, and apart from serving as a fish-pond could also safeguard stock in times of trouble. Today access is through Lower Brockhampton's famous half-timbered gatehouse, which was probably built to display the owners' status in *c*.1530-40, perhaps even earlier in the 1480s. The house is a south-facing two bay open Hall with a large contemporary east wing and architectural evidence indicates that it was built between 1380 and 1400. The Great Hall was the main living room and provides a good illustration of the use of a base cruck which, jointed to a collar beam, makes the hall both wider and higher than it could have been with full height crucks (see also p.58). The two storey east wing contained the Buttery, service and store rooms and a subsequent 17th century Parlour on the ground floor and above was the Great Chamber. The oldest building of the group was the small Norman chapel to the west of the house, probably dating from *c*.1180. It is now a ruin, open to the elements, but the gabled east wall still stands to its original height, showing the new window inserted soon after completion of the house in around 1400, with which the stone font is thought to be contemporary.

Part of the remains of the old chapel

The estate has been managed by the National Trust since 1946, and as well as providing for paid entry to the house and to the tearooms on Wednesday and Sunday afternoons between early April and the beginning of November, and on Bank Holiday Monday afternoons during the same period, free admission to a selection of parkland and woodland walks ranging from one and a half to four and a half miles is offered from dawn to dusk throughout the year.

2. Bringsty Common

Another much appreciated public open space lies a short distance further to the east from the entrance to Lower Brockhampton and one special attraction there has been called The Garden at The Bannut. Its entrance appears on the right hand side of the A44 and the display comprises two and a half acres of formal and informal gardens, some planted to colour themes. There is a path, planted mainly with rhododendrons, azaleas, pieris, magnolias etc., and beyond there is a further collection of interesting trees and shrubs, heathers, clematis and other varieties—leading back to tea-rooms and a plant sales area. The Garden is open some afternoons (mainly weekends) from about the end of March until the end of September.

A convenient starting point for the main tour is at the Tenbury Road car park at the rear of Bromyard Leisure Centre near the small 150 seat Conquest Theatre. Turn right at the exit to join the B4214 and head for Edwyn Ralph, about 1¹/₂ miles along the road, and before the village is reached, a sign points right to Edwyn Ralph church.

3. Edwyn Ralph

The present chancel and nave of St. Michael and All Angels date from *c*.1170, the tower is early 13th century and the porch and vestry were added during the 19th. Just to the west there is a moated platform with traces of a fortified mound and nearby a hollow which is thought to be where a pond provided fish for monks of a one time religious community. These, with church records, are indications that here was the centre of the former village prior to decimation of its population during the Black Death at the end of the 1340s. The earliest instance of the parish having the suffix Rauf or Ralph came at about this time, although there is also an earlier connection from a Pipe Roll of 1175-6 with one Radulfus de Yedefen. The first part of the name, however, still seems far from settled. It was Edevant in the 11th century, Yedefont in the 14th and had become Edwin in the 16th century. And there are still different spellings in the 21st century, even within the church, and they are plotted on OS Landranger map 149.

Return to the B4214 and about half a mile beyond the long resited village of Edwyn Ralph there is a right-pointing sign to Edvin Loach. The views from the road thus far have surely been fine enough, and there is much more to come, but none of it can surpass the vista from Edvin Loach. There is no sign of hamlet or settlement, simply two churches, and the thoroughly worthwhile detour amounts to about a mile and a half along a signposted narrow road, with passing spaces, ending with a fairly rough track to the gate at about 500 ft. above sea level. The sweeping scene far across to the Malverns in the south-east, round to the Shropshire Clee Hills in the north, is truly stunning even from the car park, and it becomes inspirational from within the churchyard.

4. Edvin Loach

For those with an appetite for the past, there is also still enough of the ruined 11th-century Saxon Church to appreciate the character of its sandstone rubble and tufa masonry. Underpinning the Romanesque work, much herringbone masonry remains in the lower part of the north wall and is thought possibly to have been carried out by Saxons under Norman direction. According to a postcard print in the new church, in *c*.1860 the roof was still present and there was far more to see when Sir George Gilbert Scott was completing his Early English-style handiwork at St. Mary's.

The old and new churches at Edvin Loach

Continuing along the B4214, near the 7 miles signpost for Tenbury Wells, and where there is a good view of Clee Hill directly ahead, the route passes from Herefordshire to Worcestershire between Collington and Stoke Bliss. Some 3 miles further on again there is a brown sign pointing left to Kyre Park Gardens and Toy City. The 29 acre garden and shrubbery was planned and laid out from 1754 by Lancelot 'Capability' Brown and is now being restored, featuring lakes, waterfalls, a tithe barn well over 350 years old and a very old dovecot. They are open to the public at certain times. The route continues to Tenbury Wells where you join the A4112 on which you turn right. At this junction is the black and white Pembroke House inn, which over the years has acquired a pronounced backwards lean from its masonry foundation.

The main car parks are signed to the right from Teme Street, further down the road.

Pembroke House Inn

Spa, Tenbury Wells

Tenbury Wells Market House

5. Tenbury Wells

The historic role of Tenbury has been as market centre for a large rural hinterland formed from parts of three counties which meet close to a major river crossing in the Teme Valley. This would first have been a ford, quite possibly protected by a castle on the site of Castle Tump—which can still be seen on the north side of the river, (from Old English and Celtic derivations, Tenbury means 'Fort on the Teme'). A charter to hold a market every Tuesday, and an annual fair, was granted in 1249 and Roger de Clifford, the owner of the rights, built the first bridge and divided Teme Street into burgage plots to let to shopkeepers and traders as part of the financial arrangement. Today, the river is crossed by the much later Telford bridge, though it retains part of the earlier medieval structure, but a canal and a railway service have come and gone. One of Tenbury's distinctive buildings is the Round Market House, designed by James Cranston in the triangular Market Square in 1811 and looking and functioning rather as it must have done then. There is still a sprinkling of attractive 17th-century half-timbered pubs and houses, and some of impressive 18th-century brick.

Walking from the car parks it is impossible to miss the newly restored and rather gaudy Spa or Pump Room at the rear of the Crown Hotel, sometimes described as 'Chinese Gothic', or 'something out of Disneyland'. Largely prefabricated, it was based by James Cranston on greenhouse designs, with the glass replaced by wrought iron sheets, and installed in 1862 some 20 years after a curative mineral well was discovered by the Kyre Brook. The 'Wells' was later added to the name of the town to attract those who might wish to 'take the waters' and it enjoyed modest popularity for some 50 years, sometimes attracting calling passengers on the London to North Wales coaches. But despite many attempts to make it pay, it was all rather too late and could never emulate Malvern, Llandrindod or other fashionable watering places or the facilities which they could offer, becoming like Church Stretton and Llandegley a 'failed Spa'. They all went out of fashion soon after the First World War and Tenbury has now reverted chiefly to an agricultural role, with its added name for annual Christmas mistletoe and holly sales, and also as a useful base for walkers and other tourists.

On leaving Tenbury Wells it is worth considering a couple of detours. The first is to head back up the A4112, passing the Pembroke House Inn on the left, and carrying on up the hill and across the common at the top for a couple of miles in total till you reach St. Michael's College on the left at the far end of the common. Turn left into the drive beyond the church to the car park. Even when closed the chapel's exterior is worth seeing. (You will need to head back into Tenbury once you have completed the detour).

The second is a three-quarters of a mile detour to see the National Collection of Clematis held in Burford House Gardens. To do this, first cross the Teme bridge into Shropshire and turn left to follow the A456 westwards, turning left as prompted by the Burford House sign and then left again down the drive leading to a right hand entrance to the car park. (You will need to head back into Tenbury once you have completed the detour).

To follow the main tour, read on from overleaf.

6.   St. Michael's College

Two miles towards Leominster on the A4112, past the Fountain inn on the right and at the far end of Oldwood Common, there is what someone has likened to a French cathedral. But for well over 100 years the sounds from within were quintessentially English, equalling the standards of the nation's finest cathedral and collegiate choirs. St. Michael's College was built as a preparatory school at the expense of Sir Frederick Ouseley, a rich priest and baronet, precentor of Hereford Cathedral and professor of music at Oxford. Dedicated with ideals promising 'a course of training and to form a model for the daily choral services in these realms' on its patronal day at Michaelmas, 1856, it has since provided a firm first rung on the ladder of musical education for a great many boys. These include Dr. G.R. Sinclair, a renowned late 19th- / early 20th-century director of music at Hereford Cathedral (pp.133 & 137) and a more recent holder of similar posts at Worcester Cathedral, St. George's Chapel, Windsor and St. John's College, Cambridge. As at St. Mary's, Tenbury Wells, the architect was Henry Woodyer, and those who know his work will recognise a passion for steep roofs and arches. A 14th-century style is carried through to the college chapel, to which it is connected with a wooden cloister linked with one of stone. The college library of 8,000 books ranked among the most important music collections in Europe and America and included unique copies of works by Byrd, Purcell and Blow—as well as the copy of *Messiah* used in Dublin by Handel at his first performance. The core of the library has been placed on loan at Hereford cathedral Library. Sadly, adverse economic conditions during the 1980s led to closure of the school in 1985 and it was then empty for five years. But now the boys' familiar bright red uniform blazers have been replaced around the College by more varied apparel, worn by secondary level pupils of an international independent boarding school. St. Michael's Chapel is no longer directly linked with the College, except in the churchyard by the Founder's grave and those of former Fellows and pupils, but it continues to serve the local congregation in one of a group of parishes, and the superb acoustic of Ouseley's building and his Father Willis organ still feature in special music events.

7. Burford House Gardens

This is far more than the usual garden centre, as will be appreciated from the first sight of Burford House. Built in 1726 on the site of Scrobs Castle and associated with the Mortimers of Ludlow and Wigmore, after 1304 it was held by the Cornwall family for 400 years and there are monuments to many of them in the nearby church. The estate passed through several hands before the house and c.11 acres became the property of John, Richard and Michael Treasure in 1954. Since then the gardens have been carefully landscaped with meandering borders, lawns and a bridge and with over 2,000 kinds of plants, as well as the 300 varieties of clematis. The National Collection, of what is often reckoned to be the second most popular flower after the rose, is made up of around 500 varieties of clematis and these are held in the Gardens, the maze and the nursery. The Burford Garden Company, the successor to Treasures thinks that during the summer there may be as many as 80 in flower at any one time. The gardens are open most of the year and also sells Treasure's clematis, roses, shrubs, tree, herbaceous plants and much more.

The main tour moves on from Tenbury by first following the B4204 Kyrewood road, turning left from the swimming pool long-term car park and taking to the country road at the first junction to the left, signposted for Eastham and Lower Rochford. This is the start of a drive down the Teme valley through a landscape of great charm and beauty, created by the river, fields, orchards, hopyards and kilns (as hopfields and oasthouses are called hereabouts), densely treed hills and unobtrusive villages. It would not do to rush, even if this were possible along the narrow road as it weaves and rolls past Rochford and its 12th-century church and Victorian letterbox, Eastham, Orleton and Stanford-on-Teme. The road is never far from the river, and for miles is also within sight of a tall and prominent tower which any mobile phone engineer could only dream about. This is in the grounds of the Abberley Hall, which is now a school for junior boarders and day-boys and girls at the approach to Abberley. Built in 1883, the tower is 161ft. high, has 20 bells tuned to play 42 melodies and is visible for many miles. It is said not only to have been a son's memorial to his father, but also, according to local wags, something to impress his noble neighbour at Witley Court (below), where it can also clearly be seen, becoming known as Jones's Folly.

At Stanford-on-Teme the route rejoins the B4203 from Bromyard on which you turn left and head for its junction with the A443, south of Abberley. For anyone with a special interest in the work of the Herefordshire School of Romanesque Sculpture and one of its founding masons, (p.226) there is an unmissable diversion at this junction to the imposing 12th-century church of St. Peter's at Rock, which lies just to the south of Wyre Forest. The church key may be borrowed from a nearby house.

To make this detour, turn left and follow the A443 for a short distance. Soon afterwards, branch off to the right on the B4202, noting the brown sign pointing right to the ruined Norman church in the charming hillside village, and continue past the Bell inn, Pensax, Snead Common for just over 2 miles, before turning right at the sometimes overgrown sign for Rock. You will then need to retrace your steps to the B4202 and thence the A443, on which you turn left.

8. St. Peters Church, Rock

High up on a hill, St. Peter's is another landmark which it is not possible to miss. As the largest Norman church in Worcestershire it has another special distinction in the high quality of decorative skill applied to some of its stonework. This was carved by a founder master of the Herefordshire School of Romanesque Sculptors and experts have established that the same hand was respon-

Rock Church and details of the font

sible for the much applauded sculptural decoration at Shobdon and Aston in west Herefordshire. Now flaking after more than 800 years of exposure, his work at Rock to the elaborate north doorway is applied to an enriched arch of three orders, each with a different motive. It serves as a preparation for the sight of the detail of the three orders of decoration of the impressively tall and wide chancel arch within. The elaborate carvings on the capitals are partly allegorical, in accordance with the taste of the Cluniac monks, and partly Celtic fantasy, and it is interesting to learn that they were originally semi-circular but have flattened as a result of settlement. The massive bowl of the font, carved with flowers and leaves in a chain of medallions, is thought to be contemporary with surviving Romanesque parts of the church which have been identified at the south-west corner and north and east walls of the nave and in two bays of the north wall of the chancel. Separated from the chancel and nave by a glass screen, the Lady chapel of *c.*1510 was once occupied by a priest who was endowed to serve as a schoolmaster and for more than 200 years until 1806 the village children attended there for his classes. Some of their elders must also have required lessons at times but the triple stocks, last used in 1860, and the whipping post with manacles, dating from 1773, were eventually removed from the lane just outside and since 1965 they have been kept safe at the west end of the nave.

The main route continues on the A443 past the Georgian red brick Hundred House inn to Great Witley. This village is said to have been created when the local estate owner persuaded his tenants to move about a mile so that their former houses could be flattened out of sight. This was to avoid spoiling the views from his new mansion, and what a mansion it became! Some idea can still be gained by following the directions from the main road down the minor road signposted in brown to the right, the first sign to Witley Church and the next to Witley Court (English Heritage/ admission charge) and Church (no charge, but donations welcomed). There is a large car park at the entrance and visitor centre.

9.   Witley Court, an astonishing fountain and baroque extravaganza
The modern history of Witley Court began when in 1655 Thomas Foley, a prosperous ironmaster, bought the estate with the red brick Court, dating from *c.*1600. It remained in his family until 1838, by which time his descendents had added many extensions and had also built the adjacent baroque

The ruins of Witley Court and the fountain in action

parish church. Everything was then sold to W.H. Humble, a coal-mining magnate and later to become the first earl of Dudley, and the vast ruined shell seen today owes much to the huge amount of money he lavished on the building—and to a disastrous fire on a September evening in 1937. The new owner did not stint on the garden, and at one time it occupied 40 gardeners who were included on a payroll which included 25 park gamekeepers among a total staff complement of more than 100. The stately home assumed a palatial scale of magnificence which could hardly be contemplated even by the most profligate of today's screen, soccer or pop icons, but 17 years after a change of ownership to an aspiring Kidderminster carpet magnate, the 1937 fire destroyed much of the structure and its sumptuous furnishings. What was left was gradually sold for salvage, broken up or vandalised and not until 1972 did hope revive for the future of the property,

when it was acquired by the Department of Environment. Since then, restoration and conservation works have extended to the gardens, where English Heritage has aimed to reproduce a high proportion of the 1853 work of W.A. Nesfield (1794-1881), a leading landscape designer. Grass and weeds have now been skimmed off to original green and path levels, gardens are being re-created to echo original Victorian patterns, using varieties of plants of the time (but only employing 3 gardeners and not 40!) and matching new stonework for steps and balustrades has been brought in from Portland. Most excitingly, the Perseus and Andromeda fountain, reputed to be the largest in Europe, has been meticulously repaired and restored to use, employing not the original 40-horse-power steam engine and beam pumping engine, but 10 electronically controlled pumps. These fire the fountain's 120 jets, hidden among giant shells, sea nymphs, dolphins and a huge serpent, and the 90ft. high main jet for 15 minute periods each day at times notified at the Visitor Centre, where informative guide-books are available to complement useful portable audio-commentaries.

The Church of St. Michael and All Angels is a Grade I listed building attached to the west of the ruined Court, but it is the responsibility of the parochial church council and the local community and not English Heritage. Consecrated in 1735 to replace the former 13th-century parish church, from the outside it appears to be rather a plain, rectangular building and for the first 12 years there cannot have been anything remarkable about the interior. But no-one entering it for the first time today can really be prepared for what they face, and there can be nothing else quite like it anywhere in Britain, or nearer than the baroque churches of southern Germany or Italy. Until 1747, however, much of the

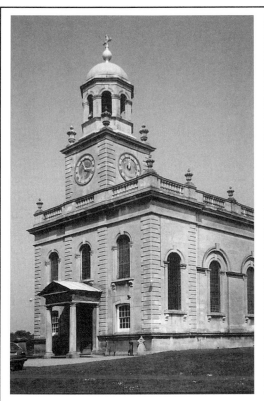

Witley Parish Church

same interior decoration graced the chapel of another great stately home, at Cannons in Edgeware, Middlesex, the palace of a financially ruined Duke of Chandos. At an auction of his effects, the second Lord Foley bought many of the decorative chapel fittings, including stained glass and enamel painted windows, gilded stucco mouldings and plaster work, ceiling paintings on canvas by the Venetian artist, Antonio Bellici (1654-1726), and the organ case of the instrument used by G.F. Handel (1685-1759) during his term as music director at Cannons (when he composed his familiar Chandos anthems). All purchases were gingerly transported to Great Witley and built into the church, the windows arguably becoming the greatest of the glories. The organ was enlarged and rebuilt by Nicholsons of Worcester in 1858, to a specification by Sir Frederick Ouseley of St. Michael's, Tenbury (p.83) and in 1861, under the competent direction of architect, Samuel Daukes, the 1st earl of Dudley undertook extensive and sympathetic refurbishment of the fittings and refaced the exterior with ashlar to match his additions to Witley Court. Further enhancements followed in the early 20th century and the church did not suffer any fire damage in 1937, but subsequently began to deteriorate until 1962, when the parishioners took action to prevent further decay and the fruits of their dedicated and continuing work are there to be seen.

To continue the tour, turn left out of the entrance drive and left again further on, returning to the A443 before quickly making another left turn onto the B4197, signposted for Martley. Once in the village, turn left again to join the B4204 for Worcester and follow the signs to Lower Broadheath, turning right just before the Bell inn. The unclassified road passes the Dewdrop inn on its right and just after common land on the left the route follows the brown sign pointing left to the Elgar Birthplace Museum on Crown East Lane. Entrance to the car park is just past the Plough inn.

10. Edward Elgar and his Birthplace Museum

Elgar's birthplace at Broadheath

Edward William Elgar (1857-1934) was born at Broadheath, the fourth child of William and Anne Elgar. After serving a musical apprenticeship, his father had established a music business in Worcester and from 1843 became piano-tuner for the instruments at Witley Court (above) during the tenancy of Queen Adelaide, widow of William IV. His resulting royal warrant led to many other commissions and he joined in musical life as pianist and church organist and was a violinist in the Worcester Three Choirs Festival orchestra. He was to be followed in all these activities, and very much more, by his son Edward—the only member of his family of seven to be born within sight of the Malvern Hills at the Firs, Broadheath. When Edward was only two years old, the Elgars returned to live in Worcester but he retained a deep affection for his birthplace and when, three years before his death, a baronetcy was added to his many honours he took the title of Sir Edward Elgar of Broadheath. He also expressed the wish that the small country cottage should be set up as a museum of his life and music and this was fulfilled by the Elgar Birthplace Trust, established by his daughter, Carice, and friends. Some time afterwards a £1 million appeal was controversially launched to build a visitor centre and study library at the birthplace, and although some Elgar admirers felt that such a large development would overshadow the humble cottage it went ahead and the Elgar Centre opened in 2000. The resulting increase in display space and facilities allows the intriguing life story of the man whose familiar face has appeared on the £20 note to be followed and the unique Museum collection is set out to show the composer's musical development and his role in English musical renaissance as he progressed from obscurity to fame. His desk in the cottage has been laid out as it was when he was composing and elsewhere a varied events programme includes special exhibitions, talks, concerts, choral workshops, musical weekends and children's holiday activities. Admission is free to Elgar Society members, but there is otherwise a scale of charges which covers on-site car parking.

Upon leaving the museum, turn left alongside the Plough inn and continue along the road as far as the A44 junction where, turning left again, Worcester is shown to be 2 miles further on. If you want to go into the city, turn left at the first roundabout. The route passes through St. John's and after turning left at the large signal-controlled roundabout, it heads for the riverside and crosses the bridge making an obligatory left turn along North Parade and North Quay. These lead to a selection of council car parks and the nearest for a long stay, with 238 spaces, is at Croft Road, served by Grandstand Road, at the first turning to the left. Most of the others in the city centre have short-stay tariffs and there are large privately controlled spaces at the CrownGate Shopping Centre and Lychgate multi-storey car parks.

If you want to pass by Worcester, then go straight over the first two roundabouts on the by pass, and then turn right at the third, signposted for Malvern. Now you need to go to the first full paragraph on p.95.

11.   Worcester. 'The Faithful City'

Worcester stands alongside the River Severn towards the centre of its county on land which has been populated for more than 2,000 years. Iron Age settlers were followed by the Romans, who may have called the place *Vertis*, but it could not be compared in size with the major settlement, or *colonia*, at Gloucester (*Glevum*) or even the walled town of Droitwich (*Salinae*) to the north-east. A turbulent history produced marauding Anglo-Saxons, Danes and Welsh and a castle was built in 1069, only to be in ruins by the 14th century and soon to disappear. Terrible damage was done during the Civil War up to 1651 when Worcester became the stage for its final battle, and although it came safely through both 20th-century World Wars, it soon afterwards suffered as much from insensitive developers and architects as many cities which had been bombed. In what became widely known as 'The Rape of Worcester', the intrinsic character of much of the city centre was lost with the wholesale destruction of many of its historic buildings. These made way for unattractive replacements: even the handsome Guildhall of 1721 in High Street was threatened, but public outcry came to the rescue and this is now a useful starting point for a walking tour around the city centre. The building has an ornate Queen Anne front, designed by a Worcester pupil of Christopher Wren and later restored by George Gilbert Scott.

Caricature of Cromwell's head nailed on Worcester's Guildhall

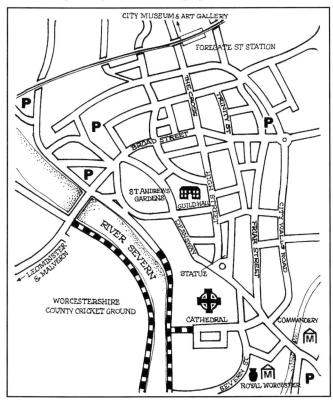

Map of central Worcester

Worcester Cathedral

Statue to Elgar in High Street,
near the cathedral

The carved statues of the two Stuart kings on either side of the doorway, and a grotesque caricature of Cromwell, his head nailed by the ears above it, leave no doubt as to where the loyalty of the city lay, for the citizens supported Charles I and II and chose the motto carved on the building: 'May the Faithful City Flourish'. The Assembly Room on the top floor is worth the climb, not just to see the splendid ceiling and Italianate-style decor, the Reynolds portrait of George III and other interesting items, but perhaps also to partake of refreshments and meals in such a grand setting, sometimes to the rarity of a piano accompaniment. High Street has been the main shopping thoroughfare for centuries, but by the 1960s the combination of local traffic and that of the A38 through route had produced nightmare conditions. New roads and re-routing came by 1980 and this allowed the street to become pedestrianised. As in other historic towns in the area many of its half-timbered buildings were given brick façades during the 18th century, whilst in more recent times the independent traders have largely given way to the chain stores to be found everywhere in towns of this size. There are links with the extensive CrownGate Shopping Centre and the street market in Angel Place, and within the Centre is the Countess of Huntingdon Hall. This was previously one of the finest of many Nonconformist chapels provided during the 18th century by the concerned benefactress to combat a widespread lack of religious faith. It too came close to demolition, but public objection and a great deal of expense instead resulted in what is now a fine, galleried concert hall, coupled with a home for the Elgar Music School and other amenities. Encouraged by the progress made, after closure of the Swan Theatre at the Moors in 2003, Hall personnel and others started to develop ideas for taking it over for re-opening and they have since been achieved.

The Tourist Information Centre is housed at the side of the Guildhall. Outside it, a right turn along High Street leads towards the cathedral, passing Fish Street and the Farrier's Arms in one of the partly surviving historic streets, and then to the statue of Sir Edward Elgar. This is not far from 10 High Street, since lost to the Lychgate Centre, now the Cathedral Plaza Centre, where the Elgar family moved to rooms above Elgar Brothers' shop in 1866 after a brief stay at 1 Edgar Street. It is not far either from where Elgar often stood as a conductor of cathedral concerts, or the memorial window, designed to a theme inspired by his oratorio *The Dream of Gerontius*.

Within Worcester Cathedral, the crypt is the earliest surviving building in the city, dating from 1084 and a relic from the days of Wulstan, the only Saxon bishop not replaced after 1066 by a Norman. Reached by a staircase leading down from the dean's chapel, it is the largest crypt in England and second oldest, and a forest of plain stone pillars supports a simple vault. Above it is the quire, and before the high altar the tomb of King John (1166-1216), whose body was brought to the cathedral in accordance with his last wishes. He lies with his head on a pillow supported by two bishops, thought by some to be Worcester's saintly Wulstan and Oswald whom he regarded as patrons. The king's figure is said to be the earliest royal effigy in England, the Purbeck marble slab dating from *c*.1240 to serve as the lid of his stone coffin, whereas the lower part of the tomb was produced in the 15th century. It is very unusual to find the tomb of a sovereign so far from his capital, but at Worcester there are also other royal remains. Arthur, Prince of Wales (1486-1502), heir of Henry VII and elder brother of Henry VIII, married Catherine of Aragon when he was just 15 and died five months later at Ludlow. His heart was buried there and his body brought to Worcester on St. George's Day in 1502 and, with great ceremony, placed in a plain tomb to the south of the high altar. It is now within an elegant lierne-vaulted chantry of richly carved white stone, regarded as an almost perfect example of Tudor art in its slender grace and wealth of

King John's tomb, Worcester Cathedral

ornament. The entrance steps from the chancel have been well worn down over the centuries and, standing beside the tomb, countless pilgrims during the next five centuries must have mused over what would have become of the kingdom if its occupant had lived on to become King Arthur and Henry, his younger brother, a Roman Catholic archbishop—as his father had intended!

Standing by King John's tomb and looking west to the handsome west window, far beyond the chancel screen and east, past the high altar and its elaborate marble reredos to the Lady chapel, it is possible to appreciate with some awe the full 400ft. length and 70ft. height of the building. Furnishing of the cathedral interior has taken numerous forms, especially since the Reformation of the church instigated by Henry VIII and consolidated by his son, Edward VI (1537-1553). As the first Protestant monarch of England, he enthusiastically saw to the destruction of statues, other furnishings and stained glass, and what remained was further broken up and pillaged by Parliamentary troops during the Civil War. Repair works slowly proceeded during the ensuing centuries but by the middle of the 19th the entire building was in a parlous state. Much of what is to be seen today, both inside and out, was undertaken between 1854 and 1875 and although not everyone is now likely to approve of the Victorians' restoration approaches, there would have been very little left had they not acted when they did. As it was, the view from the nave was unblocked by removal of the organ and stone screen from the chancel entrance, revealing a remodelled east end, designed to conform with the Early English style of the Lady chapel by A.E. Perkins, the cathedral architect. At the west end a new window, depicting aspects of the Creation story, was inserted in 1875 to replace a former indifferent one marking a visit by George III and his queen to the Three Choirs Festival. The floors were repaved, most of the walls and the tower re-cased in new stone and the nave pulpit, choir screen, bishop's throne, reredos and roof paintings were all part of an extensive restoration and renewal programme. In addition ancient fittings and furnishings were either removed or repositioned, retaining many monuments and effigies of varying interest and appeal, to which was later added the tomb of the first earl of Dudley (1818-85), creator of Witley Court (see above), who had paid for much of the work. A new 20-year restoration programme began in 1988 and it will eventually provide an opportunity for future generations to comment on Elizabethan handiwork! During 2003, some of these skills were being applied at the Norman chapter house dating from *c*.1120, which is approached through the elaborate 15th-century Prior's door on the south nave aisle. Entered from the east cloister, this was unusually built not as a polygon but on a circular plan, with a ribbed vault springing from a central pillar. Until the Reformation it was for nearly 600 years the meeting place for the monks of the community, where they would conduct monastery business and be read a daily chapter of the Rule of St. Benedict—hence the title of the room. When the builders have finished, the present dean and chapter will return there, also to conduct the business affairs of the cathedral, but to the accompaniment of prayer and not readings from St. Benedict. The cloisters were completed during the 14th century and, with the church, chapter house, dormitory and refectory or dining room were where the monks spent their lives until the monastery was dissolved in 1540. There is a way out to College Green, which is largely lined with buildings of the King's School and where, since the Reformation, the monks' refectory has been used by the school and is now known as College Hall. The ruins near the archway to the left of the exit were once part of the guest house where visitors to the monastery were lodged under the care of the Hospitaller. Called the Guesten Hall, it was built in 1320 but by 1862 the building was considered to be unsafe and all but the east wall was taken down. The gateway leading out to Severn Street has become known as the Edgar Tower and was the fortified main entrance to the monastery, built in c.1350. Severn Street leads to the river and after a short distance reaches the entrance to The Dyson Perrins Museum.

Lea and Perrins

Sauce addicts might wonder here whether there is any connection with the firm of Lea and Perrins, manufacturers of Worcestershire Sauce. Crucially it was in the person of C.W. Dyson Perrins (1864-1958), whose grandfather, W.H. Perrins, ran a chemist's shop at 68 Broad Street early in the 19th century in partnership with J.W. Lea. Legend has it that one day in 1835, a nobleman who had been out East, filling offices such as Governor of Bengal, called in with a recipe which he had been given in India and asked the chemists to make it up for him. They also made some for themselves and allowed it to mature, finding that it had become 'most delectable'. They went into production in the back of the shop, but from 1837 the sauce has been produced commercially, basically to the secret original recipe and process. C.W. Dyson Perrins was taken into partnership with the firm of Lea and Perrins in 1894 and, known as Dyson, accumulated great wealth which he devoted to several philanthropic causes. He also indulged his passion for Worcester Porcelain and built up a priceless collection. He became deeply involved with the factory, became a director and, in 1902, chairman, and helped to keep the company afloat in hard times with loans and advances, until it entered the hands of a receiver. It was shut down briefly in 1929 and then resumed trading under the receiver until 1934, when Dyson Perrins bought the company outright. During his involvement he had injected capital by buying the contents of the company's museum of porcelain and after he died, aged 94, his widow donated money to enable his entire collection to be put on fitting display. It was an obvious move to name it The Dyson Perrins Museum. Due to him, this operates as a charitable trust, quite separately from Royal Worcester Ltd., and it illustrates the history of Worcester Porcelain from 1751 to the present day in a most striking manner (due in no small way no doubt to the work of Henry Sandon, familiar to BBC Antiques Roadshow devotees, who was the curator for many years).

Meanwhile, its recipe still secret to all but two or three people, The Original and Genuine Worcestershire Sauce continues to be made at the factory in Midland Road, and since 1837 is thought to have found its way to every part of the globe, still retailed in old round medicine-style bottles as it had been at the rear of the Broad Street chemist shop. One can only wonder what would have transpired if the unknown nobleman had not called with his recipe at Broad Street back in 1835! There would have been no dash of sauce with the tomato juice, Dyson Perrins could probably not have afforded to indulge such a passion for collecting Worcester porcelain and who knows what would have become of Royal Worcester without him? And without the sauce and Royal porcelain, it is not too fanciful to conclude that Worcester's claim to fame might well have had to depend on its cricketing and Elgar connections!

Worcester Porcelain

The first Worcester Porcelain factory was founded in 1751 under the leadership of Dr. John Wall, MD, (1708-1774), an eminent local physician and

Entrance to the Dyson Perrins Museum

co-founder of Worcester Royal Infirmary. With William Davis, an apothecary, he perfected the recipe for soft paste porcelain, giving his name to the factory's early wares. This was the 'Dr. Wall Period' between 1751 and 1774, when the porcelain quickly built up a reputation for excellence. After many changes in fortune and ownership, in 2008 the company went into administration. Some buildings have been demolished and the sites of others have been redeveloped into a range of attractive housing units.

The city centre

As well as four 18th-century churches, there are still other buildings of age and beauty left in parts of the city centre and the first to be met after turning right out of Worcester Porcelain's factory gates are the fine Georgian houses of Edgar Street. To visit a much older group, turn right at the end into Sidbury and on the opposite side of the road and just across the Worcester-Birmingham canal bridge is The Commandery. It is on a site just outside St. Peter's Gate which was once occupied by a hospital founded by St. Wulfstan in 1085. It gained its puzzling title because from the late 13th century, the masters of the hospital called themselves preceptors or commanders. The present canal-side half-timbered buildings date from *c.*1500 and the main attractions are the Great Hall and its magnificent open roof, the surviving wall paintings and the fine Elizabethan oak staircase leading to the upper rooms. During the Battle of Worcester it became the base of Charles II and now there are opportunities to relive the days of Cavaliers and Roundheads and view a major exhibition telling the story of those turbulent times. The gardens allow for a restful break, perhaps with a picnic, and there is also scope for a short walk to Fort Royal Gardens for more distant and splendid views. There is the opportunity here to see the earthworks constructed by Worcester's Royalist defenders after the site had earlier been used by Cromwell's forces to pound that part of the city.

There are not many other half-timbered buildings left to see in the city centre, and most are to be found scattered along Friar Street and New Street. They can be reached by returning up Sidbury, crossing over the City Walls Road dual carriageway and then taking the first right hand turn. There is the Tudor House from the mid-16th century on the west side, opposite Laslett Almshouses, and next comes The Greyfriars, which is regarded as one of the finest timber-framed houses in the county. Just after the Second World War, amazingly it too came close to demolition but was rescued and it is now owned by The National Trust. It was built in 1480, next to a Franciscan friary, and was originally a merchant's house and it has now been restored and refurbished. Character has been added to the panelled rooms with interesting textiles and furnishings and through an archway outside there is a most attractive garden. The 3-storey Old Pheasant inn dates from *c*.1580 and after being a private house it boasted a bowling green at the rear, there was accommodation for 80 horses and it became a principal cock-fighting centre until the 'sport' was made illegal in 1850. King Charles' House was built at about the same time and obtained its name after being a refuge for Charles II before he escaped from his enemies following the Battle of Worcester at a time in 1651 when, according to an ancient account, 'the streets were foul with carnage and the vast cathedral was used as a loose box'. He vanished through the northern city gate and after many adventures, Charles reached the coast and France, creating on the way the legend of the Royal Oak near Boscobel, still remembered on his birthday in May as Oak-Apple Day. The building is now a restaurant, whereas not far away, at the junction of The Trinity with Trinity Street, Queen Elizabeth House is a small two-gable timber-framed building with an overhanging storey and the centre for Worcestershire Racial Equality Council. During Queen Elizabeth's week-long stay there in 1574, she is said to have addressed her subjects from the gallery. This now overlooks a slightly different part of the street, for to allow for a new traffic scheme the entire house was moved—to where it now contrasts violently with awful Elizabethan architecture of a later reign. New Street ends at the Cornmarket, and Mealcheapen Street enters from the left. The 17th-century Rayned Deer inn has been converted into Reindeer Court, another of Worcester's quite new shopping centres. Here it is possible to browse in a relaxed atmosphere among specialist shops and restaurants whilst on the way to links with New Street, The Shambles—and quickly back to High Street and the Guildhall.

Greyfriars, Friar's Street

Old Pheasant Inn

From Worcester, the route returns across the River Severn to join New Road, which is familiar to cricket enthusiasts as the address of Worcestershire C.C.C. Worcester Cathedral is a familiar backdrop to the east and it has been the home ground of renowned players such as Graveney, D'Oliveira, Headley, Botham, Imran Khan, Hick and McGrath (of the Australian variety)—and the venue for many enjoyable, exciting days of first class cricket. Turn first left at the roundabout and take the A449 for Great Malvern. Just after a mile, and across one more roundabout, the road reaches Powick Bridge across the River Teme. After flowing for many miles from its source in Wales it is about to merge with the River Severn. In 1651, the final battle of the Civil War took place close by at Red Hill and Perry Wood. Take the second exit at the roundabout reached across the bridge and continue towards Malvern.

The main 'tour' route and Worcester 'diversion' have now rejoined. About a mile from the roundabout there is a sign pointing left for Madresfield, dominated from the 14th century by Madresfield Court, seat of the Lygons and subsequent earls of Beauchamp. Only take this road if you want to make your own detour, for the house is rarely open to the public. They were renowned as great supporters of all forms of arts, crafts and design in Herefordshire and Worcestershire, a role now taken up by the Elmley Foundation.

---

12.   Madresfield Court and an enigma

Madresfield Court is a privately occupied moated house which, after many changes during the Victorian era, still retains Tudor elements. Mostly of brick, it stands in 60 acres of formal gardens and parkland which contain rare species of mature trees, majestic avenues, rock gardens, a maze and many other attractions. Visits between April and August may be made by appointment at the Estate Office and an annual National Gardens Scheme charity event towards the end of October exhibits autumn colours at their best. Madresfield is said to have been where Evelyn Waugh wrote *Brideshead Revisited* and, as at a great many local places, there is also a strong Elgar connection. Among his close Worcestershire friends was Lady Mary Lygon, a pioneer of the musical festival movement and heavily involved with the Madresfield music festivals. After prolonged speculation since 1899, and despite other theories, a legend firmly persists that Variation XIII of his *Enigma Variation*s, headed * * * concerns Lady Mary as 'One of the Friends Pictured Within'. This was his opus 36 composition, and for some special reason the initials L.M.L. were replaced in the published score with asterisks.

Malvern is made up of townships which have become collectively known as The Malverns. Extending down the eastern side of the Malvern Hills they are Malvern Link, Great Malvern, Malvern Wells and Little Malvern. North Malvern leads to West Malvern, which faces Herefordshire on the far side of North Hill. The name means 'bare hill' and comes from Celtic words relating to the modern Welsh: *moel* - 'bare', and *bryn* - 'hill'. In Domesday Book it was *Malferna*. At Malvern Link, the second word originates in the Old English *llinc* - 'ledge' or 'terrace' and relates to the modern English golf 'link'.

Malvern Link is also the title of the official magazine of the Morgan Motor Company Limited and the factory is reached by turning left into Pickersleigh Road. This is at the first major traffic signal controlled road junction to be met at Malvern Link.

---

13.   Morgan Motors

The son of the vicar of Stoke Lacy, Herefordshire, H.F.S. Morgan (1884-1959), founder of Morgan Motor Company Limited, was born shortly before the first car appeared on a British road. An imported Benz three-wheeler, its speed was restricted to 4 mph until 1896 and a man had to walk in front with a red flag. There were still only about 20 cars in the UK by that year but Morgan took an early interest in mechanics, attended an engineering college and served an apprenticeship with the Great Western Railway. He left in 1906 to open a garage and bus service in Malvern Link and was also encouraged to undertake experimental work in the better equipped workshops of Malvern College.

A 2litre 4-seater Morgan Plus 4

The company's own very first production model of the Plus 8 (recently rebadged 1) alongside new cars awaiting delivery

With parental assistance he began to develop a light three-wheeled single-seater car with a tubular chassis and Peugeot engine and in 1910 exhibited it at the Olympia Motor Show. It attracted much interest and 30 orders were placed, but he quickly realised that a two-seater would have even greater appeal and when he produced a model at the 1911 Show he was overwhelmed with orders. Attempts to interest a larger manufacturer failed and thus Morgan Motor Company was formed. (It is unlikely that it would have survived to become the world's oldest independent car manufacturer until now had any of his approaches succeeded). The company moved to the present factory site in 1923, and because of stiff competition from the Austin 7 and other mass-produced small and cheap cars, it introduced a 4-wheeler in 1936 and from 1950 concentrated on four- rather than three-wheelers. So emerged the Morgan 4/4 (meaning 4 wheels and 4 cylinders), and in 1968 it was joined by the Plus 8, powered by an 8-cylinder 3.5 litre Rover engine.

During the late 1990s, a TV documentary produced a retired icon of modern British business—Sir John Harvey Jones—to comment upon manufacturing and assembly methods at the company, and to suggest ways in which it could expand production of the cars evocative of the 1930s and 1940s and reduce a long waiting list. The more he saw, the more he gasped and as he departed he warned of a bleak future in the absence of radical changes at the Pickersleigh Road factory. By then, Morgan Cars had passed down to Peter (d.2003), son of the founder, and Charles the grandson, and they remained resolute in their wish to maintain their independence, unique character, work ethic and quality of build. Nevertheless, continuing attention to new technology and work practices has brought in new systems, a state-of-the art paint shop facility and other significant developments which have drastically reduced production bottlenecks. And after 35 years, developments in engine technology have meant that the Morgan Plus 8 ceased production in 2004. In 2002, a special commemorative edition of 80 of these and 4/4 Le Mans '62 models sold out within just 72 hours of going on sale. So much for the bleak future! To follow on, hand made to order the open two-seater Aero 8 was the world's first all aluminium coach-built car. Capable of 160 mph, with a BMW 4.4-litre V8 engine generating 325 bhp, it came a long way from the pioneering Peugeot-powered 76 hp three-wheeler of 1910.

There is a visitors' car park and the reception office is just inside the gate with information about models, specifications, visiting arrangements and other data. There are two enthusiasts' Car Clubs, and rare also is the chance to talk over individual ordering requirements directly with the boss.

To continue towards Great Malvern, turn left out of the main gate and continue along Pickersleigh Road as far as the roundabout at Barnards Green. The Science Park is signposted to the left but for the town centre take the fourth exit for Barnards Green Road. This continues into Church Street and there are signs for car parks for both sides of the road before reaching the congested main shopping street.

14.   The Malverns

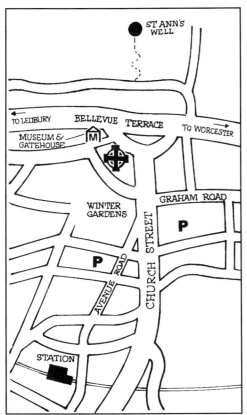

Map of Great Malvern

Malvern Priory Gatehouse

The history of Malvern first began with the foundation of a priory, a cell of Westminster Abbey, beyond the River Severn within the 8,000 acres of wood, scrub and marshland of Malvern Chase. The remote site was chosen beneath the Malvern Hills in order to satisfy the desire of the Benedictine community for solitude to allow quiet contemplation and prayer, commencing it is thought in *c*.1085. This is likely to have prompted the beginning of Malvern as a settlement outside the monastery precincts, where one vital asset shared by monks and villagers was a copious supply of fresh spring water, streaming down from what would become known as St. Anne's Well. But after some 400 years, the priory was in need of drastic repair and the high standard of work performed by the monks in the 15th century, and the outcome of the Dissolution of the monasteries which unexpectedly followed shortly after, largely account for what there is to see today. For after the monks were forced to depart, the local villagers were allowed to purchase their disused church to serve parish needs. For £20, paid in two instalments, they acquired the main priory church, belfry, chancel, aisles and chapels. After this outlay, there was to be little money available for future repairs, let alone for the work of restorers, and so the 'Popish' medieval glass, floor and roof tiles and some of the monks' misericord tip-up seats survived to become rare treasures of the church today. Because of its origins, it is wide and spacious inside and the early Norman arcades stand out within what is otherwise predominantly a Perpendicular church. As a late example of medieval glass, the Magnificat Window of the north transept, presented by Henry VII, dates from *c.*1501 and is the largest of this period to survive in Britain. The west window of nine lights came rather earlier, probably between 1474 and 1485, and it is thought to be the gift of Richard, Duke of Gloucester, the future Richard III, and his wife Anne.

Apart from the church, the only other surviving priory building is the gatehouse into the former monastic estate. Constructed probably in place of an earlier entrance in *c.*1480-1500, this has since had many uses. It has been said that Henry VII stayed at The Guesten Hall nearby (demolished in 1841) during his visits to Malvern, and it certainly housed the office of architect Troyte Griffith, the subject of *Troyte*, Elgar's *Enigma Variation VII*. Malvern Museum is now open there during the summer months with exhibits covering most aspects of local history and geology. The adjacent Abbey Hotel occupies the sites of the former cloisters, living quarters, Guesten Hall, prior's lodging, infirmary and gardens, and below

Malvern Priory Church

to the east, Priory Park once was part of the monastic lands and, fed by a spring, the present boating lake, Swan Pool, was the monks' fish pond.

Malvern Water

Some time after the first discovery of the waters of Malvern Wells, the enterprising Dr. John Wall (see above), who practised in the town for 18 years, published a treatise in 1756 extolling their special properties. The modern history of Malvern can be said to have commenced from then, but unlike the waters of most other Spas, the Malvern water was prized for its exceptional purity and lack of minerals and foul taste. This produced at the time an oft-quoted couplet: 'The Malvern Water says Dr. John Wall is famous for containing nothing at all'. Its source is still a mystery but it issues from numerous springs and by the late 18th century several firms had started to bottle it. It was being sold on the streets of London at one shilling (5p.) a bottle and it has been said more recently that Queen Elizabeth II takes Malvern Water whenever she travels abroad. Within a short time after Dr. Wall's analysis, people were flocking to the town to drink or be treated with it. New houses, hotels, boarding houses, a library, post office, baths, a

One of the many springs in Great Malvern

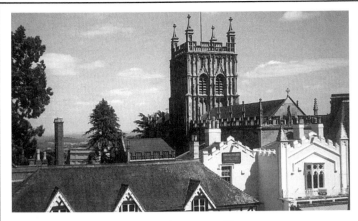

Great Malvern roofline

pump room and other establishments sprang up at Great Malvern and in 1842 so did Drs. Wilson and Gully, two extrovert physicians of a rather different stamp to Dr. Wall. They introduced hydrotherapeutic (Water Cure) treatments which they had learned about in Austria, and from then on well-to-do people with stomach disorders, ulcers, gout,

Decorative ironwork at Great Malvern Station

aching bones and other real or imagined maladies placed themselves at their mercy. The 'patients' not only drank gallons of the special water but were given constant baths in it, wrapped up in wet cold sheets first thing every morning and exposed to douches and jets coming from all directions. Afterwards they could be sent on strenuous hikes on the hills to seek out further health-giving springs. For them it was all rather grim, but for the local economy the revenue brought great cheer and between 1845 and the 1860s the small village expanded into an affluent town, receiving a further boost when the railway arrived. Designed by the local architect, E.W. Elmslie, Great Malvern Station was opened by the Worcester and Hereford Railway in 1863 and the Company and the successor Great Western Railway briefed the same man to design the grand Imperial Hotel nearby. For the comfort of guests arriving by rail it connected from the down platform with a covered way, nicknamed 'the worm', it offered every kind of bath and among its many luxuries was incandescent gas lighting, the first such installation in the world. At the station a special waiting room was built for the personal use of the autocratic Lady Emily Foley of Stoke Edith and this is still there and now open to everyone as Lady Foley's Tearoom. Arson in 1987 damaged the station, but British Rail and English Heritage quickly set about renovation and went to great lengths to redecorate the ornate Victorian columns supporting the platform canopies and their capitals of brightly coloured wrought iron foliage and much other

Elgar statue in Great Malvern

fine detail in order to produce some idea of what it all used to look like. As a spa town, Malvern did not produce grand Parades and Crescents like Bath and Cheltenham, and there appeared instead large buildings of a wide variety of national architectural styles and periods. The houses were well planned and spaced out amidst generous landscaping along Abbey, Priory, College, Wells Roads and other nearby thoroughfares. Much involved prior to the introduction of local government in 1867, the Foleys, not least Lady Emily (d.1900), exercised manorial rights as major landowners in requiring demanding building and layout standards for many of the houses, hotels and water cure establishments—as well as regulating the course, levels and design of the railway line and station.

For the pleasure and recreation of those then sought after as 'the right sort of visitors', Priory Park was expensively landscaped as promenade gardens, and today the paths, greenswards, boating lake, bandstand, rare and unusual trees and shrubs exist as a legacy of those extraordinary times, joined now by a modern Splash Leisure Pool and Complex on Priory Road.

After little more than 20 years the hydrotherapy craze ebbed, Dr. Wilson died in 1867, Dr. Gully retired in 1872 and moved away and later there was an outbreak of typhoid in 1905 which led to bankruptcy at one of their surviving establishments. The days of Hydrotherapy were over, but by then the beauty of the area and its equable climate were encouraging some genteel visitors to settle in Malvern. It became recognised as a desirable retirement place for ex-colonial administrators, service officers and others like them and efforts were made to provide further amenities, and to encourage more people to come. Resembling a miniature Crystal Palace, the Winter Gardens was built in Grange Road in 1884 and also opened into Priory Park, and after further additions and alterations the annual Malvern Drama Festival was established there in 1929, premiering plays by George Bernard Shaw and J.B. Priestley, followed soon by the music of Sir Edward Elgar. The main disturbance to peace and quiet was chiefly from the sound of blasting in the hills above, but ended as the Malvern Hills Conservators gradually acquired and shut the quarries. All the enterprises helped to sustain the town after the decline of the hydrotherapy industry, but compared with its heydays Malvern was just treading water. The Imperial Hotel closed in 1919 and luckily was taken over by Malvern Girls' College. Malvern College for Boys had expanded since 1862 and the appeal of the Malverns was attracting an exceptional number of other independent schools and colleges, some of which have settled in former water cure establishments.

Malvern Girls' College,
formerly the GWR Imperial Hotel

Dr. Roget's *Thesaurus*

One physician who went to live in Malvern in the 19th century, and who is buried there, was untypically not famed for water cures, yet his name has been known for over 150 years throughout the world. After taking his degree at Edinburgh, Dr. Peter Mark Roget (1779-1869) followed with a spectacular career in medicine, became secretary of the Royal Society, a professor of physiology and writer of scientific treatises. During all this time he also built up a manuscript of words and ideas, synonyms and their opposites, as an aid to improving his writing and speeches. Finally, after 50 years and at the age of 71, he published in 1852 his *Thesaurus of English Words and Phrases*. Before he died at West Malvern 17 years later, it had run to nearly 30 editions and has since been regularly updated by members of his family, and then others. By the 150th anniversary edition of 2002, over 30 million copies had been sold world-wide, many to the later generations of avid crossword-solvers.

The waters recede

Dr. Gully's establishment at Neubie House and Holyrood House in Wells Road eventually became the Tudor Spa and then Tudor Hotel and it has only very recently closed. Next to the still elegant Georgian Mount Pleasant Hotel, from 1876 Lloyds Bank took over the Crown Hotel site, where Dr. Wilson first set up practise in Belle Vue Terrace, the early 19th-century Royal Library became Barclays Bank, and just beyond, on the Worcester Road, rooms of the historic family-owned Foley Arms Hotel continue to look out on panoramic views over the Severn Valley, as they first did in 1810. Many large houses have been divided into smaller units, one of the most extensive conversions being at Dr. Wilson's mid-19th-century purpose-built Hydropathic Establishment at Abbey Road. It became The Malvern Hydro in 1915 and the County Hotel in 1930, was occupied by military personnel during the war and from 1983 gradually divided into 44 apartments and maisonettes as Park View Apartments. But immediately beforehand, from 1951, it was named Parkview Hostel and housed up to 150 scientific officers and students working at the Telecommunications Research Establishment.

Malvern's major contribution to the war effort

Exactly 100 years after the arrival of Drs. Wilson and Gully, the Telecommunications Research Establishment made its home at Malvern Boys' College, which was transferred to Harrow for the duration of the war. As the school's commemorative clock records: 'Here civilian and Service personnel worked together to further the cause of the Allied Nations by the development of Radar'.

As war clouds gathered and Nazi bomber fleets formed during the 1930s, there was increasing alarm that the only available warning of approaching aircraft was the sound of their engines. As flying speeds increased, this was completely inadequate for defence and alternative systems were urgently needed to provide the RAF with sufficient warning of approaching attacks. Thoughts turned to the possibility of radio detection and location and in 1935 Robert Watson-Watt, in charge of the Radio Research Laboratory, Slough, was able to demonstrate to military experts and politicians that it could be done. A secret research programme was promptly launched and this was the origin of what became the Royal Signals and Radar Establishment (RSRE) at Malvern College in 1942. The early radar work of civilian and Service personnel led to critical research for navigational and bomb-aiming systems for Bomber Command, detection devices crucial in winning the decisive Battle of the Atlantic, ground radar systems for D Day, improved gun-laying radars to counter the V-weapons and other devices which made a major contribution towards the war effort. Since called the Defence Research Agency, and now puzzlingly dubbed QinetiQ, the organization has more recently worked on lasers, infra-red research, fixed and mobile communication networks, satellite communications, guided weapons and missile detectors and has been awarded more than a dozen Queen's Awards for Advanced Technology. Its continuing presence at St. Andrew's Road has revitalised the local economy, and this is further bolstered by a growing influx of visitors. These include patrons of the new Malvern Theatres Complex at Grange Road and the many thousands who attend the wide choice of events at the Three Counties Showground at Malvern Wells.

To continue the tour, from whichever car park you've used, turn to continue heading uphill through Great Malvern, cross the traffic lights at the lower end of the shopping street, then turn left past buildings and post office on the left and left again at the top to join the A449 heading towards Ledbury. After about 2 miles, devoted trackers of the Elgar Trail visit the composer's grave at St. Wulstan's RC Church, Little Malvern, just below the road on the left. After the not quite continuous ribbon development of buildings on both sides of the road, turn left onto the A4104 signposted for Upton-on-Severn for an intriguing very short detour to Little Malvern Priory. Just a few yards further along the priory is reached on the right, and there is a car park on the left hand side of the road. The priory is in the most idyllic setting and has been used as a place of worship since the first half of the 12th century.

Little Malvern Court.
The priory is just to the right of the picture

15. Little Malvern Priory and Court

The priory was one of the smaller Benedictine monasteries, a cell of the abbey at Worcester, and in the same way it was also sited far from human habitation beneath the bare hill, beyond the vast wilderness of Malvern Chase. It had been allowed to become a monastic slum by the 15th century and the neglectful monks spent two years under correction at Gloucester Abbey while the church and domestic buildings were being restored. The priory was dissolved in 1534-35 and only the choir, crossing tower and small south transept escaped demolition. These now comprise the parish church, a Grade I listed building, and there is much to occupy the senses in its timeless atmosphere, perhaps when sitting in the monks' stalls, admiring the 15th-century tiled floor, marvelling at a bell dating back to the 14th century or viewing the remains of the Norman nave arcade. The adjacent restored domestic buildings form part of Little Malvern Court and this incorporates the medieval house now known as the Priors Hall.

To resume the tour, turn right from the car park and go back to rejoin the A449, turning left to begin a winding climb up the eastern flank of the hill to reach Wynds Point, and one of the largest car parks located among the Malvern Hills, as well as the Malvern Hills Hotel. Both are close to the border between Herefordshire and Worcestershire and lie just below British Camp, the ancient Iron Age (*c.*800BC-AD43) hill fort, which is also known as the Herefordshire Beacon. Use the car park if you want to venture onto the hills.

16. The Malvern Hills
Adjacent to Midsummer Hill Camp to the south, British Camp was one of the strongest hill forts in Britain and commanded what was once an important pass through the hills. Originally it covered about 9 acres, but at some stage was extended to the north and south and for a long period is thought

to have been occupied by some 2,000 Celt villagers in houses of wood and daub. Then after 1066 the summit was adopted by the Normans for a ringwork fortification, known as The Citadel. But if this now seems a long time ago, the Malvern Hills were formed an incomparable 650/1,000 million years ago, during the pre-Cambrian period—making the granite rocks the oldest in England and Wales. The hills also yield fossils which come mostly from the Silurian Age (*c*.539 million—*c*.409 million years

Walking towards the Worcestershire Beacon

ago), when the sea covered the area. The highest point at 1395ft. is The Worcestershire Beacon, one of some 20 distinct, named hills running north to south. Rising sharply from the Worcestershire plain, they combine to form a roughly 9 mile inverted V-shaped ridge as a very distinctive landmark which can be seen from many miles away, and from which ten or more counties can be seen on clear days. (From the Worcestershire Beacon in 1588: 'Twelve fair counties saw the blaze from Malvern's lonely height' wrote Macaulay in *The Armada*). The entire length is open for the pleasure and recreation of the public (and its dogs off the lead, as long as they behave), and all have the freedom of some 100 miles of footpaths and bridleways which are managed by the Malvern Hills Conservators of elected and nominated members. Many people have been inspired by the hills. Some 600 years ago William Langland (?1330-?1400) is thought to have composed his allegorical poem: *The Vision of William concerning Piers the Plowman* as a unique description of a medieval peasant's life, 'ae on a May morwenyng on Malverne hulles'. These same hills attracted Jenny Lind, 'The Swedish Nightingale' (1820-1887), one of the greatest singers of the 19th century, and four years before her death she bought a house at Wynds Point and lived there every summer until she died (when she was buried at Great Malvern). And everyone who saw Ken Russell's notable TV film about Edward Elgar will surely be aware, with many others, of how the Malvern Hills inspired some of the greatest of English musical works.

Looking towards British Camp

Access to the hills may be gained from many places, the most popular at Great Malvern being via St. Ann's Road and 95 steps up to St. Ann's Well and café. The Conservators have placed convenient car parks in several places, including those off Jubilee Drive, starting alongside the side of the Malvern Hills Hotel, and have recently opened 'easier access paths' for those who cannot manage a gradient greater than 1:12. And in the town, and all around the hills,

103

there are over 80 springs, spouts, fountains and holy wells of pure and refreshing Malvern water where, at some, it is possible to avoid the expense of otherwise paying almost £1 per bottle.

On clear days the range of the views from higher levels has been put at 10,000 sq. miles and there is usually no difficulty in picking out the Cotswolds, parts of the Severn and Avon valleys, Evesham, the Shropshire Hills, the Forest of Dean and mountains of Wales. Atop British Camp it is possible to make out to the north-west many of Herefordshire's knolls and valleys on the return route to Bromyard.

Turn left to leave the car park to continue on the A449 towards Ledbury, About 300 yards along and to the right there is a path leading to Pewtriss Well, one of many to be found around the Malvern Hills. The spring water from this one is piped down the hill to Colwall and the Schweppes bottling works. Roughly opposite there used to be another well, and also a coach house once used as a studio by Dame Laura Knight, RA, in the 1930s. Continue down the A449 on Chances Pitch (a pitch is a short steep bank), and just before the bottom turn right on the B4218, signposted for Colwall and Coddington Vineyard. The B road passes the Yew Tree inn, Colwall Green and the Malvern Water Bottling Factory, where Schweppes is now part of Coca-Cola Enterprises Ltd. and enjoying royal patronage. Turn left on the road signposted for Colwall, reached just before the Ballards Old Court Nursery Gardens on the left, which holds, and in the early Autumn displays, the National Collection of Michaelmas Daisies.

Pass through Colwall Stone to Colwall and then follow the signs for Bosbury staying on the 'main' minor road, with the western flanks of the Malvern Hills showing clearly to the right. The Coddington Vineyard is indicated by brown signs and is open at some times of the year. Turn left onto the B4220 just before you enter Bosbury, in gently rolling fruit- and hop-growing country still within sight of the Malvern Hills.

17. Bosbury

Much of the main village street is built upon a single side only and the Bell inn is one of a number of fine black and white houses appearing on the left. Built opposite Holy Trinity church, it was first mentioned as an inn in 1870, when there are said to have been five inns in the village. However it once comprised two houses which dated from the 15th century, owned by the bishops of Hereford. The red stone church across the road is much older, for it was founded in the 1180s on the site of an earlier

Bosbury

church, and its architecture is transitional between Norman and Early English. The font is of *c*.1200 and other objects of interest inside are the rood screen, pulpit, reader's desk, other fine carved woodwork and two elaborate monuments to the local Harford family. The unbuttressed bell tower is one of seven in Herefordshire which are detached from the main building—in this case by about 80ft. Looking very solid, it measures 29ft. square and 48ft. high, is pierced only with lancets, and has a ring of six ancient bells. The bishops of Hereford had a palace or manor to the north of the churchyard and the site is now occupied by Old Court Farm, where the old stone gatehouse still survives. According to a local account, 27 May used to be known as Royal Oak Apple Day, when everyone in the village wore oak leaves or oak apples to commemorate the escape of King Charles II from the Roundheads (see above).

Bosbury is one of Herefordshire's most important hop-growing centres, with six farms in the parish involved until recently. Because of a need for rich soil, abundant water and efficient drainage, hopyards have concentrated in some of the county's river valleys, notably that of the Frome.

The font at Castle Frome

Continue on the B4220 through Bosbury and shortly after leaving the village, turn right onto the B4214. This soon reaches Castle Frome, so named because of the *c.*late-11th-century timber castle which can still be recognised by the surviving *c.*14ft. high motte in thick woodland high above the Norman church of St. Michael.

For many 'church-crawlers' the chief reason for a visit would be to see the old red sandstone font. It was carved by a Master craftsman of the Herefordshire School of Romanesque Sculpture and is only matched in quality by the font at Eardisley and the south doorway decoration at Kilpeck (p.225). Canon Frome is in a valley sign-posted to the south-west, and so named because the canons of Llanthony administered it. (Priors Frome, associated with the Hereford priory, is near the confluence with the River Lugg). Next along the way comes the A4103 junction for Fromes Hill, which rises immediately to the right via steep Locks Hill. At the start of the Motor Car Age, just about 100 years ago, the Hereford Automobile Club organised a Hill Climb there. According to a local account, ten cars entered to see which could climb the hill in the fastest time. Not all reached the top, but on 17 June 1905, Mr. R.J. Hopkins of Canon Frome in a 20 hp Wolseley took three minutes five seconds from a standing start to win the coveted silver cup.

A short distance further along the B4214, at New House Farm, Bishops Frome (where the bishops of Hereford had an estate on the Frome), the tour meets with the Bromyard Hop Trail which starts in Bromyard.

Hops and bitter beer

Kent is not the only hop-producing area of England, as some people may think. In 1998, Herefordshire grew almost as many, and with Worcestershire farmed 1,287ha—then over half the UK total area, exceeding that of all Kent, Sussex, Surrey, Oxfordshire and Hampshire. The modern hop has been developed from a wild plant used long ago as a medicinal herb to treat liver disease and general digestive complaints. Related distantly to the cannabis plant, only its female flowers bear the hop cones required in the brewing process. The essential substance is lupulin, its resins and oils in the burrs conferring bitterness, flavour and preservative properties. There are 14 varieties of hop and the quality and character of any beer is as much a function of which one is used as the water, yeast and malted barley. Traditionally the perennial plants are grown with the support of strings (always winding

---

upwards clockwise), wires and poles to a height of at least 16ft., sending their roots down to a depth of some 12ft. It requires heavy capital investment and, before the days of modern mechanical harvesting, involved an annual expense for stringing and training (or 'twiddling') the bines and picking the crop by hand. This often provided for the annual countryside paid holiday of working-class families from the Midlands, South Wales and London and tended to dictate where hops should be grown. During the heyday of the hop-picking era in the 1920s, the population of Bishops Frome is said to have risen from about 700 to as many as 5,000. The hops are ready for picking in September, and after careful sorting to separate the valuable cones from leaves and stem, drying takes place in a kiln (or oast house in the south). This is the distinctive round building with a conical rooftop and wooden cowl where the moisture content of the cones is reduced from about 80% to 10% before the product is packed into pockets, or bales, for despatch to the breweries. In 1977 an alternative 'hedgerow' growing system was mooted, involving 6ft. fences instead of the traditional 16ft. tall structures and a pioneer at Claston Farm, Dormington, near Hereford, has since cropped 65 tonnes from 43ha so grown, and 110 tonnes from 53ha of his tall hops.

But the art of hop growing has recently ended at Claston after more than 260 years, the hopyards have been cleared and the land used for potatoes and beef rearing. And at Bishops Frome another hop growing dynasty has diversified and part of the hop kilns have become the Hop Pocket Craft Centre, Restaurant and Shopping Village. Much of the change is because of falling beer sales and cheap hops from abroad: only some 30 hop farms are left in the country, growing mostly for real ale breweries.

In order to check on the hop content of locally available beers or ales, it is also possible to travel a short distance further along the B4214, crossing over the River Frome, to the Chase or 17th-century Green Dragon public houses. They stand almost next to one another and are two of six left in the parish from the days when there were many more hop farms and thirsty casual labour forces. Bishops Frome also produces its own wines. These can be found by driving a further mile or so towards Bromyard and then turning right at the brown sign for the Frome Valley Vineyard at Paunton. Eight or nine varieties are grown among 4,000 vines on the banks of the River Frome, there is a tasting room and the opportunity to buy any of the seven main wines currently produced. It tends to be open during the afternoons (except Monday and Tuesday) from around Easter till the Autumn.

Afterwards, rejoin the B4214, turn right and following the adjacent River Frome upstream, return to Bromyard.

Kington—Royal Town

About two miles from the Welsh border and straggling for over a mile along the Arrow valley, Kington might not even have been in England at all had it not been for Harold Godwineson, earl of Hereford (as well as of Wessex). Acting in 1063 for King Edward the Confessor, he took forceful measures to overcome potential Welsh claims to the area. It could be from this time that its earlier name *Chingtune* arose, derived from Old English words meaning 'royal manor, or town'. This was as the town was recorded in the Domesday Book in 1086. There are, however, suggestions of an earlier royal connection to account for its present name, favouring King Offa. It is his dyke which runs just to the east of the town (this is not the waymarked Offa's Dyke Path—which passes right through the centre of Kington).

Harold became king in 1066 and after his death at Hastings later that year, the Normans erected a series of castles from which to control the country, including some 90 in Herefordshire. The castle guarding the Gilwern valley at Kington was probably one of them, and this tour and book will encounter many others. With a population of about 2,300, and one of five market towns in Herefordshire, Kington occupied land around its castle to the west of the present limits. Castle Hill, the lane leading off Church Road to the south of the church at Castle Hill House, leads to a tree-topped knoll which is assumed to be the site of the late, short-lived 11th-century castle. This is thought to have been abandoned towards the end of the 12th century, replaced as the seat of the barony at Huntington. The sturdy tower of the church was built with 6ft. thick walls in *c.*1200 and was originally detached and

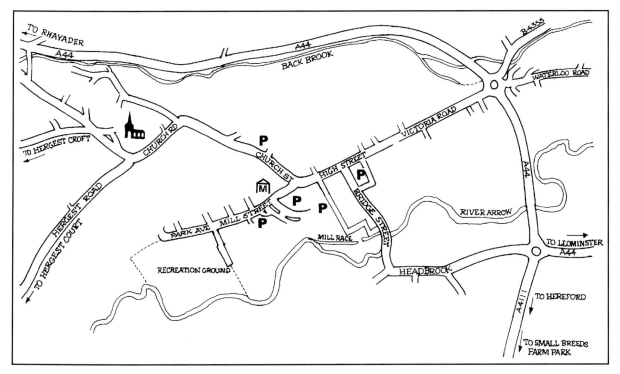

Map of Kington

Kington Church

The tomb of Thomas and Ellen Vaughan in Kington Church

unbuttressed. Like others within the turbulent Welsh borderland, such as at Presteigne and Bronllys, it served when necessary as a defensive stronghold. The present chancel followed early in the next century and the nave and the remainder of the church dates from the 14th century onwards. Inside it contains a Norman font bowl (which is near a covered 17th-century immersion pit 'for the Ministration of Baptism to such as are of Riper Years') and the 15th-century alabaster altar tomb of Thomas Vaughan of Hergest Court and his wife, Ellen the Terrible.

The town spread onto level ground as early as the 13th century, to be sometimes known as 'Kington in the fields'. There is a characteristic grid pattern of streets and passages and the lord of the manor allocated strips of land as the narrow burgage plots where the medieval Kingtonians built their timber-framed houses. These were usually placed sideways on to the road because the plots were so narrow, and in subsequent centuries the street frontages came to be faced with stuccoed rubble or were rebuilt in stone or brick. In 1632 a grammar school was founded by Lady Hawkins, second wife of Sir John Hawkins, sailor, adventurer and slave-trader, and just a little of John Abel's building may still be seen at the present Lady Hawkins School in Church Street. At the road junction at the bottom of the hill is the liverish red brick Market Hall, designed by F.R. Kempson. Adorned by a later clock tower, it is unfortunately prominent on a corner site, once occupied by the Kings Head pub. Even as early as 1885 it was described by the *Hereford Times* as 'the foolish Market House Scheme for Kington'. It does, however, have the advantage of being near the public conveniences and award-winning Kington Museum in Mill Street, and the Primary School. All occupy a former field at the rear of the King's Head, provided for customers' ponies and horses whilst they went about their business in town. The motor age version, the main car park, is on the opposite side of Mill Street close to the TIC and the Recreation Ground is further along the road.

Kington has long been an important market centre at the north-western gateway from Wales and in the early 19th century the town's economy was supposedly helped by the improved state of the turnpike roads—and the revenues collected at the River Arrow bridge tollhouse. Kington had been a natural assembly point for drovers who, however, subsequently sought to avoid the new tolls. During the 1830s more violent resistance produced attacks on the gates by Rebecca rioters. Today the livestock market is busy with a considerable 'throughput' of sheep every Thursday.

Open to guest players, Kington Golf Club's 18 hole course is on National Trust land at Bradnor Hill and at 1,284ft. it is the highest in England and Wales. In clear weather the panoramic views extend across seven counties, taking in the Black Mountains, Radnor Forest, Brecon Beacons, Clee Hill, the Long Mynd,

Kington Market Hall

the Malverns and May Hill. It is one of the few places where walkers can actually look down on ground-attack training aircraft, and they should also watch for low-flying golf-balls.

The Offa's Dyke Path passes close to the church, and just beyond it joins Ridgebourne Road and reaches an entrance to Ridgebourne, a 17th-century farmhouse rebuilt by Edmund Cheese, one of the founders in 1808 of the Kington and Radnorshire Bank. He could hardly have dreamt that, nearly two centuries later, it would become part of the Hong Kong and Shanghai Bank. Next comes Hergest Croft, (pronounced Hargist—with a hard 'g'), built in 1896. Since then, three generations of the same Banks family have developed a very special garden in four distinct areas extending over 50 acres. There is a Kitchen Garden with spring and double herbaceous borders, the Edwardian House garden, an Azalea Garden and Maple Grove—with birches and maples that form part of the National Collections held at Hergest Croft and, half a mile away in a secluded valley, Park Wood and many giant rhododendrons and exotic trees within an ancient oak wood. Closed during the winter months, there are otherwise definite times, days and months of opening, obtainable from local TICs. The customary gift shop and plant sales area adjoins a tea room which has recently gained a Flavours of Herefordshire award.

If you have the time, the thigh muscles and clothing to allow for sudden changes in weather, your enjoyment will be further enhanced by walking onwards up Offa's Dyke Path towards the summit of Hergest Ridge. This is the old drove road, and on the way up there are, surprisingly, traces of an ancient racecourse. This was built in 1825 to replace an even older one on Bradnor Hill, where races on foot had pre-dated horse-racing. The hugely popular and socially important annual horse races lasted until 1846, with occasional revivals. Round to the right is The Whetstone, a boulder which is the subject of local legends about being a plague market place, but also with an ability to move around. Certainly it has moved some distance in its time, for to the geologist it is one of a number of glacial 'erratics', left by melting ice some 10-12,000 years ago. Nearby you may also wonder how monkey puzzle trees from Chile have arrived at such a place—but also gasp at the panorama opening up across the Radnor hills to one side and Herefordshire on the other. There are few better places to get your highs than this!

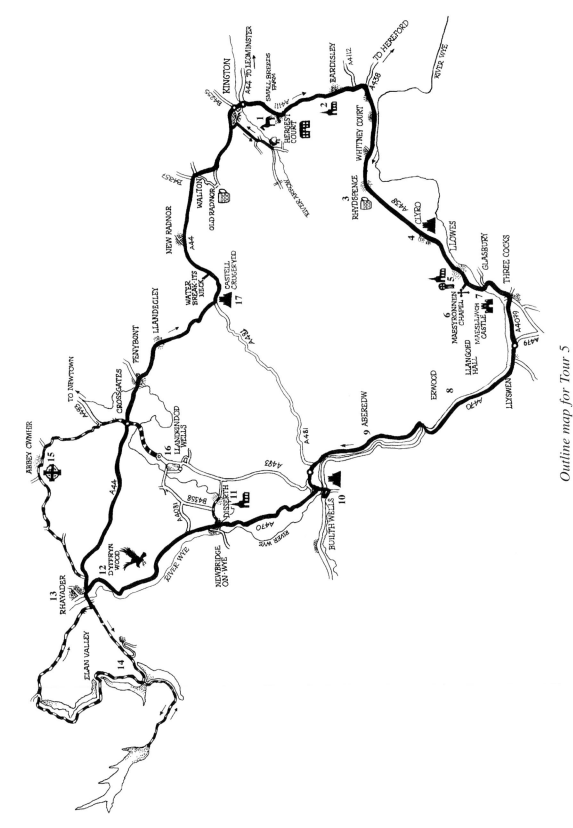

Outline map for Tour 5

The numbers 1 to 17 relate to the boxed information given within the tour

Tour 5   Into Central Wales and the Wye and Elan Valleys

This tour is largely scenic, with market towns, some churches and a ruined abbey scattered along the route. It climbs away from the valley of the River Arrow at Kington and drops to the upper Wye valley about 13 miles above Hereford, closely follows the course of the river, which is often within sight, and at Rhydspence crosses the Welsh border. After Glasbury it begins to climb towards Builth Wells, passing through a gorge, and then continues to Rhayader. After crossing the town's river bridge, the route leaves the Wye, the road narrowing as it shadows the River Elan to the Elan Dams. Each dam is visited before the return to Rhayader is made via the old mountain road. The return route to Kington can involve an optional detour to Abbey Cwmhir, and thence to Crossgates. Here there is another opportunity for a rewarding diversion, this time to Llandrindod Wells. Without the added distances, the total tour amounts to about 90 miles. (OS Landranger 148, 160 and 161)

Mainly on A roads, with narrow country lanes if you follow the detour to Abbey Cwmhir.

Just below Kington church a minor road signposted Brilley, Huntington and Hergest heads for a mile to reach Hergest Court, 15th-century home of the Vaughan family and reported to be haunted by the ghost of a black bloodhound and by 'Black Vaughan'. The *Red Book of Hergest* was discovered there, the basis of the book of Welsh mythology known as *The Mabinogion*. Now a private farmhouse, surviving portions of the much larger half-timbered house may be seen from the road. Across the Arrow there is a small motte known as Castle

Hergest Court

Twts, derived from the Anglo-Saxon name for a look-out. There are further border defences at the remote township of Huntington, to where the barony moved after Kington's castle was abandoned. A 30ft. high motte and oval bailey, together with an outer bailey, may be found to the north of the church of St. Thomas of Canterbury and, not far to the east, Turret Castle in Hell Wood, a late 11th-century motte and bailey. Just below that there is another motte, and another, Turret Tump, at Middle Hengoed and yet another, a 10ft. high mound just to the south again.

The main tour heads south from the southern roundabout on the Kington by-pass, up the hill on the A4111 towards Hereford. In about 2 miles a brown direction sign points right to the Small Breeds Farm Park and Owl Centre at Kingswood.

---

1. Animal Farm

This place can be great fun for all ages; it is certainly very 'child friendly'. It looks back on Bradnor Hill and Hergest Ridge and is attractively laid out for a variety of unfamiliar animals, including Kune Kune pigs, various breeds of goat, Dexter cattle, Soay sheep, Alpacas, miniature horses and donkeys. There are many unusual breeds of poultry and a pet animal house. The Owl Centre provides a rare opportunity to see all the British owls and many other species.

Not far from this junction, the A4111 reaches the crest of the hill to provide a panoramic view over the Wye Valley to the Black Mountains to the right, and over the Hereford plain to the left.

The next village reached is Eardisley, one of the villages on the Black and White Village Trail. At the Tram Inn you can turn right for Woodseaves for the ancient Great Oak. This is estimated to be over 800 years old, appears on local maps of 1650 and is said to be probably the only surviving tree from the forest recorded in the Domesday Book. It is about a mile down the road.

Tram Square was probably once the main market square of Eardisley, one of the places where hiring fairs were annually held. Farmworkers for hire wore a token to identify their trade: for example house-maids sometimes wore a mop, hence the Mop Fair known of elsewhere. Eardisley was served by a tramway from Brecon from which the black and white Tram Inn, part of it 14th-century, takes its name. The route, in fact, lies a few hundred yards to the east and the pub is so named only because the horses were stabled there. It stands opposite the more modern New Strand, which was rebuilt in 1902 after a fire and now features not just a licenced bar but also a coffee house and a second-hand book shop that also sells local books.

If not visiting either of the hostelries, the best place to park is alongside the Church of St. Mary Magdalene towards the far end of the village.

---

2. Eardisley and the font

As expected, there are many black and white buildings in Eardisley, one fine example being a 14th-century cruck structure made of massive curved timbers enclosing three bays, near the village hall. The church was begun in the 12th century and received a number of additions until the tower at the north west-corner was built in 1707. Its most famous and widely documented treasure is the font. Dating it at *c*.1150, Pevsner described it as 'the most exciting piece of the Norman School of Herefordshire Carvers, for composition and even more for preservation'. There is more about these exceptional medieval craftsmen at p.226. Down the narrow road, just to the west of the church, the early motte and bailey Eardisley Castle is now a heavily treed moated enclosure. It has a mound in the south-west corner of about $33\frac{1}{2}$ yards in diameter and is 14ft. high. It is mentioned in Domesday as the likely site of Roger de Lacy's *domus defensibilis* and in subsequent years it belonged to the Baskervilles, perhaps the most ruthless of the Norman Marcher families.

The font at Eardisley Church

Continuing along the A4111, the route soon leaves the Black and White Village Trail and at Willersley turn right onto the A438. The road passes through Winforton, and at the approach to Whitney-on-Wye and closer contact with the Wye the eye catches sight of a large neo-Tudor building on the hillside to the right. This is Whitney Court, built just before 1900 for the Hope family, who now share it as a superb setting for wedding receptions and ceremonies, business functions and other special occasions. The route runs close to the river and shortly reaches a left turn for Whitney Toll Bridge, which carries the B4350 towards Clifford and Hay-on-Wye, though our route carries straight on. On the border, the Rhydspence inn is on the right hand side in England, close to the former Cabalva Arms in Wales.

---

3.   An important collecting point

The Rhydspence Inn

The original Rhydspence Inn was built in *c.*1350 and was one of two on either side of the Cwmygfwr stream which here marks the Welsh border. It was an important collecting point on the drovers' route leading from the Painscastle cattle shoeing centre, over Clyro Hill and to a crossing point on the Wye and into England. As the first pub in England in that area, it was also an important collecting point each week-end during the terrible time when Wales was 'dry' on Sundays!

The village of Clyro is reached a few miles beyond the Rhydspence.

---

4.   Clyro and Francis Kilvert

Close to the river to the left of the B4351, near Boatside Farm, there was a ten-hectare Roman fort, The Gaer. It is within sight of another military station, still called Heol y Gaer (Fort upon the Roadway), on the spur of a hill at Glasbury. Near the village centre, alongside and close to the road junction with the road to Hay are the remains of Clyro Castle, in the form of a particularly large ring-work on a wooded knoll. It is thought to have been one of the earliest Norman castles, constructed with that at Hay-on-Wye, and forming part of the chain protecting the border with Wales—rather like the previous Roman fort.

Well over a century after his death, a former curate of St. Michael's Church, Clyro, continues to captivate a devoted, worldwide, congregation. The surviving diaries of the Reverend Francis Kilvert have become established as a minor classic since their first appearance in 1938, describing as they do this border country and its people of the 1870s. Although Clyro has now altered, Ashbrook House, his home, is still there and it is now an art gallery from Easter until the end of October. As well as displaying the room where the diaries were written, its seven rooms containing contemporary works of art are still authentically furnished as they were in 1851 and have barely changed since Kilvert moved. It is next to the Post Office and nearly opposite The Baskerville Arms Hotel.

Still within Clyro, further along the A438, a drive on the right leads to Clyro Court now The Baskerville Hall Hotel, once described as 'a florid and grandly proportioned pile', built for Thomas Mynors-Baskerville in the 1840s. Sir Arthur Conan Doyle was a family friend and, having learned the local legend of the ghostly hound of Hergest, was inspired to write *The Hound of the Baskervilles*—

---

probably the most famous case of Sherlock Holmes. He initially based it at nearby Hergest Ridge but moved the setting to Devon, to deflect the tourists, so it is said! Equally at home with the great and the good, as well as with the poorest of his flock, Francis Kilvert was also a well documented guest there. In 1946 the place was sold for a school to Radnorshire County Council, was extended, then resold in 1972 for conversion as an hotel. In 1984 it acquired the present owners and they have since incorporated many modern features into the hotel.

Clyro Court

Carrying on westwards, with the Wye and the Black Mountains to the left, the A438 reaches Llowes, where the Kilvert Society erected a sundial in 1954, in memory of the diarist's many visits to the church of St. Meilig. (About one mile to the south-west there are the remains of a castle, a medium sized motte so close to the Wye that before long all signs will probably have been washed away).

5. St. Meilig's Cross

The church dates back over 1300 years, still distinguished by its round churchyard (historically meant to keep the Devil out), but amidst great tribulation was rebuilt by the Victorians in 1853-5. At the rear of the nave there is a Cross slab, a scheduled ancient monument weighing $3^{1}/_{2}$ tons. This is St. Meilig's Cross and it once stood on the mountainside at a spot called Croesfeilig (or St. Meilig's Cross). It was moved in the 12th century to the graveyard in the centre of Llowes—and in 1956 finally into the church to protect it from further weathering.

The upper part of St. Meilig's Cross in Llowes Church

A mile or so beyond Llowes a road leads up a steep hill to the right—signposted to Maesyronnen (Ash field) Chapel.

The main route continues on the A438, and a little further along there is a Lodge and drive serving Maesllwch Castle, visible though a gap in the hedge alongside the A438.

The countryside as seen from near Maesyronnen Chapel

6.   Maesyronnen Chapel and early dissenters

Maesyronnen Chapel

Founded in 1696, this is a rare example of the early dissenters' conventicle, a small meeting house for religious assembly—legalised by the Act of Toleration of 1689. The first Independent, now Congregational, chapel was built in Rhayader and four years later a 16th-century farm building was consecrated and rebuilt as a place of worship at Maes yr Onnen. Just four walls and a roof, and with furniture preserved from the 18th and 19th centuries, it is still in use in 2010 and Communion is taken around a table, the minister seated at the head, and not standing at an altar rail. Visitors are invited to join local families at the 10.30am or 3pm Sunday services, whilst at other times the entrance key may be borrowed—see the notice at the chapel for details.

7.   Maesllwch Castle

Maesllwch is not a castle in the warlike sense, although it is in a commanding position overlooking the Wye valley towards the Black Mountains. The first recorded hall house appeared in the 16th century, replaced by something larger in 1729 for the Howarths, when the castellated part was built. There were considerable additions for the Wilkins (afterwards de Winton) family in 1830 and 1872 but much of it was demolished in 1951.

Soon afterwards the road reaches a sharp left curve and speed limit sign to reach Glasbury. It once had a castle, possibly from before 1088, but more likely from nearer 1144. This only had a comparatively short life, being destroyed during the Welsh wars. There were still some signs of a surviving motte in the 1960s, but later development has all but removed it. One of a succession of timber and stone bridges placed here since the reign of Queen Elizabeth I, the present Glasbury Bridge was built in 1923 and has since been widened twice.

Across the bridge, turn right to Three Cocks (Aberllyfni), which was an important place not only in former coaching days but also as a rail junction for the Cambrian (Mid-Wales) and the Hereford, Hay and Brecon Railways. On a north bank of the River Llyfni and visible from footpaths to the north-west and south-east there is a 3m high earthwork motte, forming the remains of the 12th-century Aberllyfni Castle.

Turn right in Three Cocks on to the A4079, signposted to Builth Wells, to join the A479 at Llyswen. Somewhere here is the legendary site of a palace built at the command of Prince Rhodri Mawr (844-878), hence the name Llyswen: 'white court or palace'. Few borderland communities were without a motte during the Middle Ages, and as well as an earlier fort, there are remains of a possible 'castle' south-west of the village. Local accounts refer to a Second World War command post being set up on the mound, once again to control the valley and the road from Glasbury and Bronllys.

Beyond Llyswen the A470 continues towards Builth Wells, and on the right hand side not far along, is Llangoed Hall. The house is a largely Jacobean mansion, transformed into a great Edwardian country house by the celebrated architect Sir Clough Williams-Ellis (of Portmerion fame). Bought by Sir Bernard and Laura Ashley, it opened in 1990 as a hotel. Sir Bernard has since spent a small fortune on renovations and, of course, on distinctive furnishing and fabrics.

Further along, at Erwood (*y rhyd*, 'the ford') the former ford was used by drovers who watered and rested cattle brought from the Welsh hills—before climbing again to Painscastle for the animals to be shod before moving down to Rhydspence. The present day traveller may also stop for refreshment, at the Erwood Inn, or instead, drive across the bridge to the Radnorshire side, to the Craft Centre, Gallery, Tea and Coffee shop at Erwood's discontinued railway station from mid February onwards.

The road, river and dismantled Cambrian Railway line enter the winding gorge carved through Mynydd Eppynt on one side and The Begwns and Aberedw Hill on the other. There are convenient stopping places overlooking the river, which drops for miles between the woods through massive rocks, projecting craggy ledges and stony-bottomed rapids.

---

8. 'The finest piece of scenery south of the Lakes'

Many words have been written about the Wye between Hay and Builth, described by one writer as 'more beautiful than in any part of its course'. Francis Kilvert was told of a conversation with William Wordsworth when the poet judged 'the Wye above Hay to be the finest piece of scenery south of the Lakes'. Kilvert himself, shortly to be presented to the remote living of St. Harmon a dozen stations up the line, travelled in September 1874, on the 10.16am train from Hay to Builth and beyond and wrote

> I never had a lovelier journey up the lovely valley of the Wye. A tender beautiful haze veiled the distant hills and woods with a gauze of blue and silver and pearl. It was a dream of intoxicating beauty. I saw all the old familiar sights, the broad river reach at Boughrood flashing round the great curve in the sunlight over its hundred steps and rock ledges, the luxuriant woods which fringe the gleaming river lit up here and there by the golden flame of a solitary ash, the castled rock towers and battlements and bastions of the Rocks of Aberedw, the famous rocky wooded gorge through the depths of which the narrow stream of the Edw rushed foaming to its Aber to meet the Wye ... and to the sudden bend of the river below Builth.

Kilvert's train would have halted at Erwood station, and on the present journey, instead of following the A470 to Builth, cross the river on the B4567 signposted Aberedw and follow Kilvert's route, This is often close to the track of the old railway passing below the terraced mile-long Aberedw Rocks. This way offers a scenic roller coaster run to the A481 and A483, on which you turn left on each occasion. At the approach to Builth it will be seen that the landscape at Llanelwedd has been badly scarred since Kilvert's day. Extensive quarries have been blasted, in no small measure between 1893 and 1904 in order to provide masonry to build the Elan dams and water works. Turn left again at the roundabout at the entrance to the Royal Welsh Showground to head into Builth Wells. There is a large car park close to the river bank reached by turning right immediately after crossing the bridge.

---

9. Aberedw, last refuge of Llywelyn

There have been two castles at Aberedw—Hen Castell, a ditched motte built to protect the entrance to the Edw valley, probably the castle which was visited by Llywelyn ap Gruffudd (1246-1282), the grandson of Llywelyn the Great, just before he was killed. It is said that he took refuge in what is now known as Llywelyn's Cave, on higher ground to the south-east. Now overgrown by trees, a square second castle was built of stone soon after his death, one of the last to be built in Wales. Much later, part of what remained was crossed by the Cambrian Railway, broken up and used for its construction. The church of St. Cewydd stands beside the River Edw, its gate not far from the Seven Stars Inn.

10.   Builth Wells / *Llanfair-ym-Muallt*

The bridge over the Wye at Builth Wells

At the major crossroads of the A470/483, the Wye bridge at Builth Wells was built in 1779 and has six three-centred masonry arches. It was widened in 1925 and received further structural attention in 1975. There was a town here in the 11th and 12th centuries but as the farthest Norman/English outpost in the wilds of central Wales it frequently suffered from attacks by the Welsh. In 1282, after failing to muster support, Llywelyn ap Gruffudd was killed in a chance encounter with some English soldiers. They sent his head to Edward I as a special trophy, for his death removed a large threat to the king's ambitions. The headless body is thought to have been buried at the abbey church of Cwmhir (see below) and in 1956 a jagged 15ft. high granite memorial was erected close to where he died at Cilmery, 2 miles west of Builth. The town's succession of castles commanding the river crossing is now marked only by some earthworks and foundations behind the Lion Hotel. Builth was also almost completely destroyed by fire in 1691, but recovered to become a fashionable spa town during the 19th century, but for little longer. It now flourishes as a market centre for a considerable rural hinterland, and across the river the Showground at Llanelwedd is the scene every July of the Royal Welsh Agricultural Show. Although blighted recently by Foot and Mouth Disease, this is very popular and offers a wide range of exhibitions, crafts, entertainments and displays. However, anyone not that interested should steer well clear of Builth whilst the Show is running—unless they can face severe traffic congestion, extending for miles in every direction, or are making a special study of 'road rage' as delivered in Welsh!

A Builth Wells market

Return to the roundabout at the entrance to the Royal Welsh showground and turn left onto the A470 towards Rhayader, but part company with the Wye for a few miles.

Just below Cwmbach the river begins a turbulent half-mile of rapids, known as Builth Rocks. Here also, in the depths of mid Wales, the road runs close to a country railway line which, amazingly, is still operating. There is a small station nearby at Builth Road, on the 120 miles long Heart of Wales Line from Shrewsbury and Craven Arms to Llanelli and Swansea.

At Newbridge-on-Wye, well before the railway was built, there was a road from Shropshire and north-east Wales to south Wales and several new timber bridges have succeeded the former ford. In 1911, near the beginning of the car age, the last such bridge was replaced by, for then, a revolutionary new one, designed of reinforced concrete. It was the first to be built spanning the Wye anywhere and, with its masonry piers, had an elegance which went well with its surroundings. But by 1972 it showed signs of failure, put down to inadequate reinforcement. In 1981 it was replaced with a most unlovely bridge and supporting structure, all constructed of austere reinforced concrete.

As an antidote for such a sight, it would be worth making a short detour on the B4358 towards Llandrindod, breaking off right at the signpost for Disserth to see the tiny 13th-century, mainly white-washed church of St. Cewydd.

11. Disserth, and laying an evil spirit

Disserth Church

The charm of St. Cewydd's embraces its setting close to the River Ithon, despite a recently arrived caravan site neighbour. It is one of a number of churches which have been placed in a circular churchyard, which points to the ground having been regarded as sacred for well over 1,000 years. One of the bells calling the faithful to worship dates from about 1300 and inside, the 17th-century high-backed box pews are painted with names of owners and their dates from between 1666 and 1714. And they also identify some more recent proprietors, who include James Watt, the Scottish engineer, (see below) a member of the congregation in the early 19th century. From 1687, the congregation would have faced the distinctive three level pulpit, which was installed that year, and were perhaps able to make something of the wall-paintings, which may still be recognised in their fragmented state.

It has not always been serene and peaceful at Disserth, for according to local folklore, there was an evil spirit about, requiring for its subjugation an assembly of parsons at the church, complete with books and candles. During his lifetime, Charles Lewis had been a tanner from nearby Henllys and had earned a reputation as a dishonest scoundrel for the way in which he juggled his weights—according to whether he was buying or selling. After his death he was buried in the churchyard at Disserth, but his spirit was said to persist in accosting anyone passing Henllys at night. So the evil tormentor was summoned to appear before the spirit-laying assembly, and by prayer, solemn anathema, and with no small difficulty, was reduced to the size of a bluebottle fly, popped into a snuff box and dropped into a well, or other safe place, from where it could never emerge.

After crossing the Ithon, the A470 converges with the Wye below Newbridge and they remain close all the way to Rhayader and beyond, parting slightly at Doldowlod. This is where the dismantled Cambrian railway station and yard have been laid out as an unobtrusive riverside Caravan Club site.

Rightly said to enjoy 'glorious views of the surrounding hills', it is on part of the estate created by the son of James Watt. His work in the improvement of the steam engine played a crucial part during the Industrial Revolution and his descendants have continued to live at Doldowlod House.

12.   Land of the red kite

The whole area contains a variety of unfamiliar wildlife, and at Dyffryn Wood, three-quarters of a mile short of Rhayader, the Royal Society for the Protection of Birds has a nature reserve and lay-by parking alongside the A470. This is true red kite country, so do not be surprised to see the distinctive forked tail of at least one of these agile, beautifully coloured, rusty-red birds of prey. They are one of the rarest raptors among the most threatened birds in Europe. Persecution by farmers, gamekeepers and egg-collectors had reduced numbers in Wales by the early 1930s to two breeding pairs, and despite subsequent protection there were still only 50 pairs by 1987. The main threats continue to be illegal poisoning and egg collecting but after firmer legislation and much effort, numbers in mid Wales are now extending past 600 pairs.

One place where they are free from persecution is Gigrin Farm, South Street, just 300 yards south of Rhayader town centre. Here the farmer has provided five bird hides, suitable for wheelchair access, where it is possible to 'watch breathtaking feats of aerial piracy as 60 red or more kites swoop down to feed to within 25 yards, competing with opportunist buzzards and ravens for choice pickings!'. In ways which do not disturb or endanger them (except perhaps to make them too reliant on handouts), the birds are fed each day at 2pm from October to March and at 3pm during the summer, the birds being unable to cope with the changes in the hour. The farm also contains an interpretive centre, nature trail, bird reserve, picnic site, children's play area and badger viewing via C.C.T.V. It is a 198-acre working farm and these are ways in which this farmer is making ends meet in the dire circumstances often facing farmers in the rural west.

As they also do at Gigrin, a more usual way of supplementing often meagre, hard won farm income is by providing bed and break-fast. Farmhouses can date back to the 15th century, are often 'listed', and offer an insight into life on a working dairy, sheep or beef farm, special walking facilities with stunning unspoilt views, fishing at some, traditional home-produced fare and modernised rooms and equipment graded by the National tourist boards. Full details and booking arrangements are available at local Tourist Information Centres.

The outline of a kite in flight—with the prominent forked tail

The road at Rhayader becomes South Street and passes the former Victorian Workhouse, now the Brynavon Country House Hotel and Workhouse Restaurant and arrives at the War Memorial Town Clock Tower at the main crossroads. Turn left into West Street and the B4518 towards the Elan Valley, passing the old Cwmdauddur Arms. The clock is the starting, or finishing, point for the official Wye Valley Walk between here and Chepstow, 112 miles or 181 kilometres downstream.

---

13. Rhayader / *Rhaeadr Gwy*

The town's earliest days date from the 5th century and it has known much warfare and lawlessness. A castle was built by the Welsh in *c.*1177; a much mutilated motte which is mainly on private property and can be seen from the Elan Valley road near the church. There is another, south of the church on part of a public playground, which followed in around 1200. Years later a sitting Assize judge was murdered by bandits, and in the 1840s the Rebecca rioters—farmers dressed as women and with blackened faces—violently assaulted the toll-gates and gatherers at the town approaches. The town's name is a curiously Anglicised version of *Rhaeadr Gwy*, Welsh for 'Waterfall on the Wye'.

The road to the 'Lakeland' of mid-Wales passes over the river bridge of 1780 not far from the clock tower. Before the channel widening at that time there is said to have been a truly spectacular cataract, especially in times of flood, and even the present waterfall can be quite impressive (but do not even think of joining local youth who delight in jumping from the bridge parapet into the pool below!).

The road soon shadows the River Elan to its left, and this passes by Elan Village down below, originally built for the first Elan Estate employees.

---

14. Elan valley reservoirs

Before going any further it is well worth calling at the Visitor Centre, open each day from Easter to the end of October. It has an information office and offers a wide range of maps, books, fact-sheets as well as mounting exhibitions and audio-visual presentations. Countryside Rangers encourage nature conservation and help the public to enjoy the area—leading more than 100 free events each year, including guided walks and birdwatching trips on the 70 square miles estate. The Elan Valley Dams were built after Birmingham Corporation compulsorily acquired the land in

The Claerwen Dam

1892 in order to provide clean water for its ever-growing population 73 miles away. In the process houses, farms, meadows, woods and other features were submerged under 100 feet of water, a community of some 400 people dispersed with little or no recompense. The epic work of James Mansergh, which had begun with his search for a site as far back as 1861, the three Elan dams were commissioned in 1904.

Looking down the Elan valley

It is usual to tour the dams in a clockwise direction and the first, Caban Coch, looms to a height of 122 feet just above the Visitor Centre. It contains a submerged dam at Garreg ddu, where there is sufficient head for the aqueduct at the Foel Tower to carry water by gravity for the 73 miles to the Frankley Reservoir in Birmingham. Just visible above the reservoir are remains of the redundant Nant-y-Gro dam, used for underwater explosion tests during planning of the Dambuster raid of May, 1943. The Claerwen, the largest of the present reservoirs, reached on a detour to the left, was constructed between 1946 and 1952 and, with 10,626 million gallons, impounds almost more water than all the others put together. It was opened by Queen Elizabeth II at one of her earliest ceremonies as sovereign—just under half a century after her great-grandfather, King Edward VII, fulfilled a similar role at Elan. Pen-y-Garreg has an island and, as at the others, there is a small parking area for soaking in the view. The top dam is Craig Coch and is some 120 feet high. In a catchment area receiving an average rainfall of 65 inches a year, the Water Supply Scheme supplies enough water to keep the River Elan and Wye flowing, sufficient to serve Birmingham and parts of Staffordshire and Radnorshire and, in times of drought, areas of South Wales through a downstream transfer from the Wye to the Usk.

Proposals have recently been announced for a new dam at Craig Coch which, at 320 feet, will be three times the height of the present dam. If it proceeds it will contain 55 billion gallons, becoming Europe's largest man-made reservoir. For future days of climate change and major water shortages it is being seen as the centrepiece of a new national water grid which will convey water from Wales to taps in London or Suffolk. There will be many years of planning, involving land incorporating 12 Sites of Special Scientific Interest, ranging from ancient pasture and meadows to woodland and rare upland marshes—and with special protection under the EC directive on wild birds. The Welsh community, not least dispossessed long serving farmers who were unhappy about aspects of the Elan scheme, might also have much to say.

Our road continues through vast open moorland to connect with the old mountain road to Aberystwyth at Pont ar Elen, which may eventually be submerged, and we turn right to return to Rhayader, turning left at the junction at the edge of the town to return to the Town Clock.

The quickest way back to Kington is straight ahead at the clock-tower along East Street, perhaps allowing time for a call at the Welsh Royal Crystal Visitor Centre on the Brynberth Industrial Estate on the far edge of town, and then eastwards down the A44.

But time permitting, there is a highly rewarding alternative which climbs another 650 feet up into the Radnorshire hills, before descending to 'The abbey of the long valley'—and then rejoining the A44 at Crossgates. To follow this route, take the left-hand turn off the A44 at the direction sign 'Abbeycwmhir' at the edge of town. The road quickly becomes single track but it has no shortage of passing places, rather of fellow motorists, and you could drive the 6 miles to the abbey ruins without seeing anyone else. Watch out for the signposts though, for some tend to get lost in the hedges. About 3½ miles from Rhayader, look out for the sharp right turn over the Dulas Brook, signposted for Abbey Cwmhir, a further 2½ miles on. After already marvelling at the views and the sheer beauty and solitude all around, and facing some further sharp inclines, you will reach the highest point by the Cwm yr og forestry plantation at about 1,340ft. above sea level. This is one of those lonely unfrequented places high up in Radnorshire where you can imagine yourself on top of the world, and really 'getting away from it all'. From here it is a steady drop, through a valley of hills densely planted with fir trees, to a car park and picnic spot at Lower Cwmhir. Then on to join an equally exciting and wider road which has come from Bwlch-y-Sarnau, and enter the small hamlet of Abbey Cwmhir.

15. Abbey Cwmhir

At first it is something of a surprise to meet typically Victorian buildings whose Gothic spiky style seems so out of keeping with this wild and remote setting. Dating from the 1850/60s, St. Mary's Church (which followed an earlier church of 1680) and the Hall, were designed by the same architects—Poundley and Walker—and with a former red brick school and the Happy Union Inn and Post Office stores are grouped by

The remains of Abbey Cwmhir

the road. It also seems strange that there have been two schools for such a small community. Locally the reason is alleged to be that an autocratic former Mistress at the manor was not over fond of school-children, especially at playtime, and so a second school was built about a quarter of a mile away, out of her imperious earshot. It would be interesting to know now how the design of her 'gaily detailed' ashlar Hall of 1867 would compare with that of the earlier house on its site, reputedly built in *c.*1656 for a member of the prominent Fowler family. The Fowlers are said to have acquired part of the abbey lands in *c.*1536, after the Reformation, making them the richest family in Radnorshire. Using material from the abbey, nearby Dyfaenor was built in 1670 for Richard Fowler, who is mentioned in a familiar jingle about Radnorshire's dearth of rich estates and prosperous squires:

The stone marking Llywelyn's grave

> Radnorsheer, poor Radnorsheer,
> Never a park and never a deer.
> Never a squire of five hundred a year,
> But Richard Fowler of Abbey Cwmhir.

Just beyond the Hall, in a meadow below the right-hand side of the road are the ruins of Cwmhir Abbey. The strict Cistercian Order (the White Monks) chose remote valleys for its houses, believing that manual labour should be woven into a timetable of prayer and spiritual reading. Cwmhir is disputedly said to have been founded in 1143 and, joined by the monks of Whitland, refounded in 1176. Although typically simple and unadorned, at 242ft. the nave of the church was enormous, quite the longest in Wales and even in England said to be exceeded only by those at Durham, York and Winchester. It was

Early English arches in Llanidloes Church, re-used from Abbey Cwmhir in 1542

designed for a community of an abbot and 60 choir monks, but their chancel was never built and buildings which were started in the 13th century were also not finished. To register a major claim to fame, a stone tablet now marks the place where the headless body of Prince Llywelyn, the last native Prince of Wales, is thought to have been buried in 1282 after his fatal encounter near Builth. In 1402 the abbey was sacked by Owain Glyndwr and life there never really recovered, to the stage when eventually only three monks remained. Dissolution followed in 1536 and, like many other monastic buildings, as well as defunct castles and town walls, its fabric soon became a useful quarry for other building projects. Little more than remnants of wall now remain at Cwmhir, but part of its former architecture may still be seen at Llanidloes, some 10 miles away. Of its 14 bays, a five-bay nave arcade was somehow dismantled, moved by cart across the hills and rebuilt at the church of St. Idloes in 1542. The hammerbeam roof at the church, which replaced the stone vaulting destroyed by Glyndwr, may also have come from Cwmhir.

After the abbey, the road gradually emerges from below the wooded hills and there is then a twisting but much flatter run to join the A483 road from Newtown. Turn right, and in just over a mile meet the A44 at Crossgates, where you turn left to return to Kington. But there is a further optional visit three miles away. This is to Llandrindod Wells, sometimes locally called 'Llandod'.

16. Llandrindod Wells

This is the county town and administrative centre of Powys, geographically the largest county in Wales, which since 1973 has comprised Radnorshire, Breconshire and Montgomeryshire. Little more than 200 years ago the area consisted of a few scattered farms, an inn, a chapel and two churches. This was before the healing qualities of its waters became generally known, but by the 1730s things had started to change. Farmers began to sell their well water to travellers and its healing reputation spread. Lower Bach-y-Graig Farm became known as the Pump House, and later on as the famous Pump House Hotel. In 1749 a local entrepreneur built a hotel, complete with gaming and other leisure facilities, to hold hundreds of guests—but after 40 years the gambling and other 'debauched goings-on' had got out of hand, interest in the medicinal and health-giving waters ebbed, and the building was demolished. Llandrindod again became a rural backwater until 1865, with the coming of the Central Wales Railway. From then on easy rail access to all parts of the kingdom quickly produced rapid growth, and this

Evidence of the Victorian Spa in the former Y Gwalia Hotel, now council offices

coincided with a Victorian passion for 'taking the waters'. Visitors to Wild Wales, who would previously have stayed at farmhouses around the common, could soon put up at smartly named hotels—such as The Montpelier, Commodore, Glen Usk, and Metropole (which was first called the Bridge Hotel—until its then prudent owner, having bought at a sale a great deal of crockery and cutlery monogrammed with an 'M', had to make a vital decision!). A pump room and bath house were erected amongst attractive gardens, all becoming the Rock Park and a focus of hotels, boarding houses, grand private houses, shops, a new church, indeed everything needed to meet the needs of the health-seeking Victorian visitors and residents.

'The Cure' at the Pump Room between April and November could involve a regime lasting at least three weeks, with over 30 treatments. Saline helped to ease constipation and the mineral waters were often used to treat scurvy, ulcers, eye problems, asthma—and for 'generally washing out' the system. Sulphur water was certainly a reliable purgative and it was also used in reclining baths and alone, or with the iron and other salts of chalybeate, was good for anaemia and general debility, skin complaints, kidney and bladder problems, gout and rheumatism. Despite the taste, some people waited in queues to be served—although a high proportion of the clientele, often accompanied by their servants, were much too refined for this. An idea of what the chalybeate taste is actually like was bequeathed in 1879 for all in perpetuity by J.W. Gibson-Watt of Doldowlod, lord of the manor, at a marble spout near the pump room. Wine-tasters might say that it has 'a complex palate of

underlying salty character with strong hints of rust and stagnant pond on the finish'. It is certainly not for quaffing—a small egg-cupful might be more than enough. By the 1880s Llandrindod was receiving 80,000 visitors a year and its population had increased tenfold by the turn of the century. Its heyday extended into the 20th century, but went into decline with the outbreak of the First World War, the 1930s Depression and as people started to prefer holidays by the seaside.

The Spa closed in 1971, and in 1974 Llandrindod instead gained new

Llandrindod Victoriana

economic benefits as the administrative centre for Powys. With better roads in central Wales and survival of the Shrewsbury to Swansea Heart of Wales Railway, its legacy of big old hotels and other accommodation and its stunning location, it is also gaining new ground as a conference, meeting and holiday centre. Adding to its interest, it mounts the National Cycling Exhibition of over 200 machines at the Tom Norton Automobile Palace and, for nine days towards the end of each August, former times are re-enacted when people don their great-grandparents' attire for a Victorian Festival of over 200 events. And it is still possible to sample the health-giving properties of chalybeate and other waters at the Rock Park Spa, or to seek relief from aches and pains through remedial massage, manual lymphatic drainage and many other complementary therapies, re-established at the Park at the Centre for Complementary Medicine.

The A44 route to Kington was formerly the old Great Road, the 18th-century coaching road from London to Aberystwyth, and some of the coaching inns still survive, notably the Severn Arms at Penybont. It was known as The Fleece until 1814, and along the road just beyond the village and a cattle-grid, meandering sheep support the connection—and now require full attention. There was once another coaching inn at Llandegley, the next village. This was the Burton Arms and from the second half of the 17th century up to the 1850s was a favourite stopping place for stagecoach passengers attracted by the sulphur and chalybeate spring waters available there. With relatively easy road access, Llandegley Wells was just as popular as Llandrindod, but no entrepreneur appeared and the spa fell into disuse in the 1930s. There is now nothing left to see but an old wooden shack and a ditch showing signs of sulphur. Beyond the village the road begins to rise and then twist amid the slopes of Radnor Forest. After a tight right turning bend and a steepening curve to the left it is difficult to miss a prominent, obviously man-made mound over to the right, Castell Crugerydd.

17.   Castell Crugerydd

The outline of Castell Crugerydd

This is a very fine relic of a motte and bailey, dating from *c*.1150, but there is some argument about whether it was first built by the Welsh or the Normans. It is thought to have been taken by the invading Marchers in *c*.1195, by which time it had been visited for two nights by the colourful churchman, Giraldus Cambrensis, or Gerald of Wales, who called it Cruker's Castle. This was near the beginning of the difficult six-week mission to Wales, carried out in March 1188, by Baldwin, archbishop of Canterbury, to gain support in Wales for the Third Crusade against Saladin, who had seized the kingdom of Jerusalem. They began at Hereford and eventually returned there after signing up 3,000 men. The resulting travel diary by the formidable Giraldus, *The Journey through Wales, and The Description of Wale*s, has provided a detailed and highly perceptive account of Welsh life at that time (rather like the diaries of Defoe in the 1720s and Kilvert in the 1870s). As it happened, the Crusade took so long to organise that none of those who had been 'signed with the Cross' by the archbishop left the country, there being quite enough fighting to satisfy them at home.

Views from near Castell Crugerydd

Water-Break-its-Neck

There is a large parking bay a little further up the hill on the left, and this provides an opportunity to ease legs into action for a very careful walk, close to the side of the road, for a little way down the hill to a gated track. This runs alongside Crug Eryr (the eagle's mound) or *Castrum Crukeri*, two of the feature's other names. From here it is possible to survey the Edw valley far beneath to the south-west and Llandegley Rocks to the north-west. It is not the sort of scene faced very often.

The A44 continues onwards for another mile to the junction with the A481, which has come through Hundred House from Builth Wells, another exhilarating roller-coaster main road through the hills, which maybe deserves a visit on another day. The Forest Inn, right at the junction, is also a former coaching inn. Within sight from the opposite side of the road is another large motte, Tomen Castle. This is close to the base of Mynd Hill, which rises to 1,570ft. directly above the village of Llanfihangel-nant-Melan, about ³/₄ mile further along the A44. The Red Lion here bears a name which is common hereabouts, the emblem being that of the early Welsh rulers of Radnorshire.

On the same side of the road, just a mile further on, there is a car parking area and Information Point indicated by signs. About a mile's walk up the adjacent forestry track (barred to unauthorised motor vehicles and motorcycles) lies Water-Break-its-Neck. Where the track crosses Black Brook there is a recently laid footpath to the left just above the rocky stream, leading through a deep ravine lush with the foliage of overhanging trees and ferns. Then suddenly, around a corner, the path ends at the foot of the spectacular 70ft. high cataract—best visited after a downpour of rain a day or so beforehand, otherwise it may be rather disappointing.

The A44 continues past New Radnor (p.154) and Walton before re-entering England just after the B4594 road to Burlingjobb and Gladestry. It soon arrives in Kington and its road connections with other parts of Herefordshire.

Hereford

Hereford stands on the banks of the River Wye, nearly at the centre of the county to which it gave its name. Most Herefordshire countryside is within a 15 mile radius of High Town, and only beyond Mortimer Forest to the north are there short stretches which lie more than 20 miles away. Once very isolated from the rest of the kingdom because of poor communications, the city is now at the meeting place of ten trunk and other main roads to and from England, south Wales and the West, and also within 10 miles of the M50. And whilst in 1853 it was the last city or town of its size to enter the Railway Age, and despite subsequent Beeching cuts, it still has a rail service provided by four train companies. It is one of Britain's smaller cities and early in the 21st century had a population of about 54,850 within the county total of just over 178,400. It is the only town of any size in Herefordshire, the next largest being Leominster which, together with the smaller satellite market towns provide for a total population of around 39,000. They are spaced out with what has been described as 'still almost medieval regularity', the only gap in the pattern being in the south-west, where Ewyas Harold has failed to develop beyond village size. The remaining 84,560 inhabitants of the county are spread over villages, hamlets, farms and other isolated dwellings. This distribution makes Hereford very much the social, economic, commercial and cultural capital of the area, a hinterland which extends also into parts of east Wales and adjoining counties. Likewise the new County Hospital at Hereford, opened in 2002, provided for between 200,000 and 220,000 residents of Herefordshire, a significant area of Powys and neighbouring parts of Gwent/Monmouthshire, Gloucestershire, Worcestershire and Shropshire. As to the Church, tradition maintains that the first Saxon bishop was created in 676, even before Hereford got its name, and that the present diocese of Hereford was carved out of the Mercian diocese of Lichfield. The present bishop is the 104th and his *cathedra*, from the Latin meaning throne, and his palace and offices are at Hereford Cathedral. This serves as the mother-church of the diocese, which extends from south Shropshire, across the Welsh border as far as Worcestershire and Gloucestershire to the east and Monmouthshire in the south.

First visitors to Hereford often head straight for the cathedral, usually through the north porch. Once inside and standing beneath the massive Norman piers, they do not need to be especially pious to sense the measure of faith which has been practised and witnessed here since the present building was started in about 1080. There have been visits by 13th-century pilgrims from afar at the shrine of St. Thomas of Hereford, gallant stands against violent aggression by 17th-century Roundheads and noteworthy events of all periods. Sometimes these have been grave and solemn, but there has also been joy and celebration — as when the cathedral has been packed for

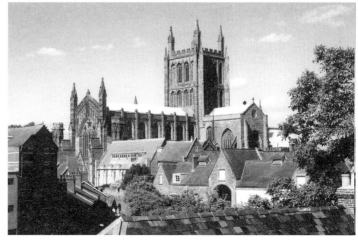
Hereford Cathedral

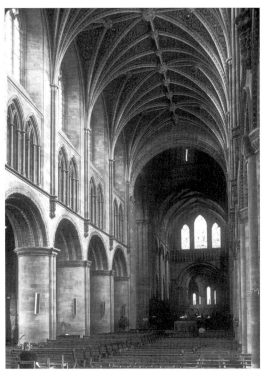

The nave of Hereford Cathedral

the Festival of Nine Lessons and Carols, the Distribution of the Royal Maundy by the Queen, and the music meetings of the Three Choirs Festival. In a rare revival of ancient traditions for the feast day of St. Nicholas, the patron saint of children, a teenager is elected as Boy Bishop. Dressed as a bishop, with mitre, ring and the Lord Bishop's pastoral staff, he occupies the throne, preaches a sermon and gives a blessing—so reminding everyone, bishops included, of the biblical injunction about humility and youthful innocence.

Always, the main role of the cathedral continues daily through the three acts of morning prayer, Holy Communion and evening prayer, when there may be no congregation at all. The tradition of sung services, particularly evensong, is maintained during the Cathedral School term most weekdays and on Sundays by a choir of 18 choristers and up to eight lay clerks (men who sing the alto, tenor and bass parts). As well as singing in the annual Three Choirs Festival and at visits to parish churches in the diocese, this very fine choir sometimes broadcasts and has performed at the Barbican concert hall in London and given concerts from 1989 in Germany, Holland, Ireland and in the USA.

When things have perhaps become too hectic for someone, it is not unusual for there to be a quiet figure sitting alone in the peace and tranquillity reserved in the Lady chapel or crypt. Help is provided

The Stanbury Chapel

or arranged at the Welcome Area and Information Desk, and between April and October this is the base for guided tours. On the south side, the cathedral shop supplies a range of books, music recordings and other items, whilst beyond there is a way to the Cloister Café and the toilets by the Chapter House Garden.

An authoritative and well illustrated guide-book proclaims the role of the cathedral as a place for worship and prayer, but extends it also to those who come to learn more about its history and savour its unique atmosphere. For as well as being a centre of Christian mission and the seat of the bishop, it is recognised as a major museum. Although relatively small, few other cathedrals can surpass its early Norman architecture or subsequent contributions from the Middle Ages. They are to be seen in each of the four later styles of English Gothic and have always been carried out in the style of the day, regardless of the original structure. But the visitor should also look out for other treasures and works of art. The oldest are probably the Norman font in the nave, dating from c.1150 and the chair near the high altar, which was made for the visit of King Stephen in 1138 and since used twice by Queen Elizabeth II. The shrine of St. Thomas Cantilupe of Hereford in the North Transept is that of the last Englishman to become a saint before the Reformation. Close by is the Bishop Stanbury chantry chapel, built with exquisite fan vaulting between 1480 and 1496, and beyond that is the Lady chapel, a beautiful example of Early English work from about 1220, intended for the celebration of services in honour of the Virgin Mary. It is raised above the level of the cathedral floor because, unusually, a crypt has been placed below it. Entered from the Lady chapel beyond a painted and panelled stone screen, the two-storey Audley Chantry was erected by Bishop Edmund Audley in 1500 for his planned burial near the then site of the Cantilupe shrine. But he misjudged his timing and in 1502 was translated to Salisbury and had to start again there, where he was eventually buried. At the foot of the steps in the Lady chapel vestibule there is an example of medieval humour and fun in the shape of the tomb thought to be that of John Swinfield. He was the cathedral precentor from 1294 until 1311 and a pun on his name is carved on the tomb arch of pigs, bearing the arms of the cathedral and feeding on acorns. His feet rest on a wild boar to complete the rebus. The steps on the opposite side of the vestibule descend to the crypt chapel. A tomb immediately on the right is that of

The crypt at Hereford Cathedral

Andrew Jones (d.1497) and his wife, and it serves as a reminder of how long cider has been produced in Hereford, for he was a 'reputed cider maker' and his incised effigy includes a barrel of cider at his feet. And just as in the 1970s the munificence of Hereford cider makers, H.P. Bulmer, made possible the restoration of the superb 'Father' Willis organ of 1892 (marked by a carved motif of a woodpecker, a reference to their chief product, in the centre of the case), one act of Andrew Jones was to transform

The 'swine' decoration on John Swinfield's tomb at the entrance to the Lady chapel

the unique 13th-century crypt from a charnel house to a place of peace for quiet prayer.

But not all the treasures are of that era, and the three John Piper tapestries in the South Transept, representing the Tree of Life, were woven in Namibia in 1976. As a central focus for worship, the Corona at the Tower Crossing was commissioned in 1992 from Simon Beer in memory of John Eastaugh, who was bishop from 1974 until he died in office in 1990.

In 1996 the now world-famous Mappa Mundi and the Chained Library were moved to what has been termed a 'high tech. medieval building'. It was designed by Sir William Whitfield and Partners, substantially funded by Sir Paul Getty and is reached at the west end of the cathedral, beyond the café and through an interpretive exhibition in the 15th-century West Cloister. Here the stories of the Library, which is probably the largest of its kind in the world, and the Mappa Mundi are told with the aid of models, original artefacts and the latest interactive computer technology. After nearly a quarter of a century of intensive use since its restoration in 1979, the Willis organ was again in need of conservation work and with the help of considerable Heritage lottery funds these were completed in 2004.

The River Wye is always a popular attraction and it could once have been reached from the west end of the cathedral by following the line of Broad Street southwards to one of the fords via the subsequent position of the 15th-century bishop's palace gate house. The Palace Ford was the 'ford of the army', because it had long been a place where a marching column could cross the river in close order. In Old English language it was 'the hereford' and this accounts for the present name of the city. It is thought that it is where Watling Street West, the Roman Road from Wroxeter to Caerleon, crossed the Wye, and the Saxons adopted a similar road line within the grid system of their 8th to 11th-century city.

It became Broad Street, where the Green Dragon Hotel is the sole survivor of a number of coaching inns along its length. In 2002 it showed

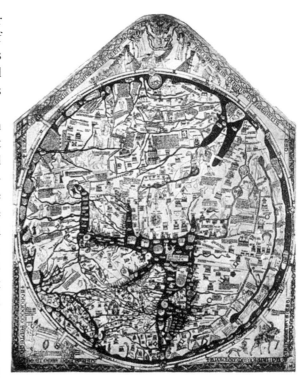

The Mappa Mundi

outward signs of refurbishment under new ownership and almost opposite, the structurally compromised Roman Catholic church of St. Francis Xavier, dating from 1838 with a giant portico and 13ft. diameter fluted columns, had recently been rescued by English Heritage and the Heritage Lottery Fund from the threat of demolition. During a year-long programme of internal restoration the clergy and congregation were invited to hold services at All Saints Church, St. John's Methodist Church and, for the first time since the Reformation, at Hereford Cathedral. The stark 1960s buildings on the opposite side of the road to it are here 'passed over in silence', but the tall library, museum and art gallery cannot be so readily dismissed. It was designed by local architect F.R. Kempson and opened in 1874, and, as with John Oldrid Scott's 1904/08 replacement cathedral west front nearly opposite, people either like it or, at the very least, are not too sure. Classed in what has been termed 'Anglicised Venetian Gothic', it has been called both 'a thing of beauty', and also 'high above its station and pretentious in its architecture'! Until 1856 Broad Street was used for animal sales, linked with the market in King Street and Aubrey Street round the corner. And not just animals, for early in the 19th century there are accounts of wives being quite openly and legitimately auctioned. One went for a shilling, with her consent—the rope around her neck included.

The library, art gallery and museum building

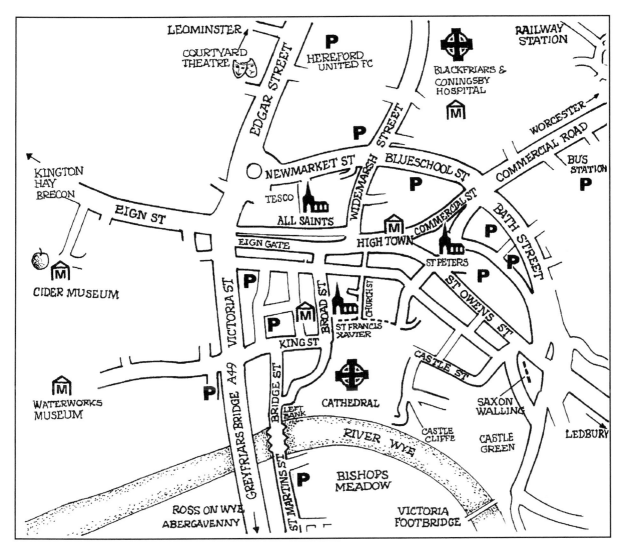

Map of central Hereford

King Street also forms part of the Saxon plan and once ran across the north front of the cathedral eastwards to Castle Street. Westwards, it continued to St. Nicholas Street and a massive turf and timber rampart running north to south—along the line of the subsequent 13th-century masonry walls and bastions. St. Nicholas' Church was first mentioned in 1155 and was the only one within the Saxon defence boundary until it was taken down from its place in front of today's Orange Tree pub in 1841.

It was replaced by a new building outside the walls at the end of Barton Road, on a route which leads to Broomy Hill and to the Waterworks Museum, the home of magnificent and awesome Victorian and other working steam, gas and diesel engines. There are often rides on the nearby miniature steam railway. A more scenic way to get there is along the riverside footpath, starting by the rowing club at the end of Greyfriars Avenue just beyond the ring road bridge. This way produces some of the reasons why the River Wye has been classified as a Site of Special Scientific Importance (SSSI) throughout its course. Access to the museum is to the right, shortly after the rugby club and Cathedral School sports fields, but it is also rewarding to walk further upstream as far as Breinton.

Although the river level may once have been lower, the fords were probably impassable for periods during the winter—as they would be now when the level of the Wye at Hereford can rise almost an extra

131

The Wye Bridge with the Left Bank Village just beyond and the cathedral on the skyline. Note the repaired third arch dating from the Civil War siege

20ft. When in pre-Conquest times it was decided to build a wooden bridge, it must often have suffered the force and velocity of the water coming from the Welsh mountains. Charters of Richard II in 1383 allowed tolls to be levied towards repair costs, and for the use of 30 oaks and quarry stone from the King's Forest of the Haye to assist with the work. The present six-bay bridge, now a Grade I listed building, is thought to have been constructed in around 1490 and it is the oldest surviving crossing over the Wye. During the siege of 1645 the third bay from the north was demolished (as can be detected from the repair work to the arch) as a defensive measure, and the bridge has since been repaired and improved many times. Bridge Street, which was also part of the Saxon road grid, superseded the southern extension of Broad Street towards the ford, and took over as a main connection with the south and west. On its right hand side, the Black Lion is one of the city's longest surviving inns. Although much altered, its main part dates from the middle or second half of the 16th century and it is famed for some carefully preserved 17th-century wall-paintings in the middle room on the first floor—depicting people who are breaking the Ten Commandments.

Directly opposite the inn, but built some 400 years afterwards, is the Left Bank Village, a totally contrasting row of modern shops, a restaurant and a banqueting suite which are all sited at the northern end of the bridge. In 1966, not many yards upstream, the Greyfriars Bridge was built to carry most of the heavy A49 cross-river motor traffic—whilst beyond, the rebuilt and superannuated Hunderton GWR bridge of 1853 now carries a much reduced loading, made up simply of pedestrians and cyclists passing along Great Western Way.

Ten miles further to the west, the sometimes sinister-looking escarpment of the Black Mountains is a reminder of the unmarked Welsh frontier where enemies once ranged. Until 1782 Wye Bridge Gate stood protectively at the other end of the old bridge—looking rather like that still to be seen at Monmouth. Close by, The Saracen's Head is another very old pub, mentioned in documents dating from 1359. It was near wharves and warehouses which were used well into the 19th century in connection with a trade employing barges of from 18 to 30 tons. These brought coal and other goods up river, hauled by teams of men for some 60 miles. Another pub, The Bell, once served the bargees as their headquarters at a quay on the opposite bank but the site is now occupied by the Left Bank Village. In 1809 it was reported that 'the quay walls were thronged with barges', but when the railway arrived the river was soon abandoned, and apart from canoes and rowing-club boats it is unusual to see anything but one or two small pleasure boats. The Palace Ford crossed just downstream of these moorings, and opposite Old Ford House its surviving stony bed has served intermittently to support water crowfoot and the white flowers which have pinpointed its actual position after so many centuries. Nearby is a former warehouse, which until recently was marked 'Dorset Ale Stores, Bridport', at one time occupied by St. Martin's Schools, then used for net-making before becoming a private home.

The riverside footpath alongside the Saracen's Head and the converted quayside buildings, and that upstream to the railway bridge and past the Waterworks Museum, forms part of the long distance Wye

Valley Walk which extends from Chepstow to Rhayader. Just before it reaches Queen Elizabeth Avenue and the playing fields, there is a stone memorial, placed in 1996 by the Wye Drown Campaign in memory of Scott Trout and all others who have been drowned in the Wye. And a short distance downstream there is a wooden carving of Dan, a bulldog. Just under 100 years before, he managed to survive a fall into this often boisterous river when out on a walk with his master, Dr. Sinclair—the cathedral organist, and Edward Elgar—composer of the *Enigma Variations*. Variation XI (G.R.S.) sets the episode to music: falling down the steep bank (bar 1); paddling to find a landing place (bars 2 and 3); and Dan's triumphant bark on landing (2nd

Castle Cliffe on the left, the sole surviving building from Hereford Castle, here seen from the riverside walk on the other bank

half of bar 5). (This is the dog which invariably accompanied Sinclair to choir practices, and is said to have whined when the choristers sang out of tune).

Presenting a medley of styles in red brick on the opposite bank, the Bishop's Palace has been the official episcopal residence for about 800 years. It encases the substantial timber frame remains of a 12th-century aisled hall which has been described as 'one of the grandest and most important of the surviving 12th-century timber buildings in England'. To its right is the College of Vicars Choral of 1473, and College Hall—built later in 1660 with stone taken from the nearby castle. From the early 1700s, barges moored just downstream at the Corporation, or Castle, wharf and warehouses, close to Castle Cliffe. This stone building embodies the water gate and governor's lodge as the only portion of Hereford Castle which is still visible above ground. It abuts the early 19th-century canoe centre building at the beginning of the bank which, surmounted by a stone wall, once formed the southern extent of the castle outer bailey. Queen Elizabeth Avenue leads through the trees to the Victoria Suspension Footbridge, built by public subscription in 1898, and on the north bank, the greensward alongside Mill Street now occupies a refilled part of the water-filled ditch which, fed by the Eign Brook, once ran around the west, north and east sides of the castle. Until the 1860s this discharged into the river at the Castle Mill, roughly on the site of the present converted hospital lodge on the right as you cross the bridge, and close to the Castle Ford. This second important crossing is thought to have been in use by British forces passing to and from Wales through the great forest of Haywood—so accounting for Britons Street as a former name for Mill Street (and also providing another explanation for Hereford's present name). The first buildings of Hereford's former General Hospital of 1783 are poised above the river here and from 2002 these were converted into an enviably situated part of a Laing Homes housing development.

The first Norman castle at Hereford was intended to be of major strategic importance at the approach to central Wales and is thought to have been built before 1052, but it was destroyed by the Welsh three years later. After prompt rebuilding in stone in 1063 by Harold Godwineson, earl of Hereford, it changed hands several times before a rebellion by a later earl led to it being taken over in 1155 by King Henry II (1154-1189). It accordingly became a royal castle and during the following century was greatly enlarged by his successors, not least to accommodate their considerable retinues of nobles, court officials and troops. King John (1199-1216) was a frequent visitor during his campaigns against the Welsh and in his time the defences were strengthened with stone and a small tower was built on the gravel mound to the west. His son, Henry III (1216-1272), followed with a walled court around the tower and other improvements. The castle eventually comprised a walled outer, or eastern, bailey (now Castle Green) strengthened by a wet moat, an impressive entrance on the north-east side, flanked by towers, approached across a bridge of stone arches and a drawbridge and the massive stone keep to the west was elevated on a lofty mound and surrounded by its own wall and deep moat. These features appear on John Speede's map of 1610, are contained in an account by the Tudor antiquarian, John Leland, and so far they combine to provide the best available impression of what the castle used to be like. In the early 16th century it was described by Leland as 'one of the fayrest, largest and strongest castels in England', being 'in circuit nearly as large as that at Windsor', but by then he also thought it 'tendithe toward ruine'. Yet, well within range of Parliament's forces using the supposed Saxon defences alongside St. Martin's Avenue on the other side of the river, it remained strong enough to withstand a siege during the Civil War. But not long afterwards most of the structure was sold for £600 and then demolished. There is now little to see, except during very dry weather when outlines of a county hall, prisons, troops' quarters, stables, stores and other buildings may be picked out in the parched grass of Castle Green, the former outer bailey. This may be reached from steps or a ramp on the left of Mill Street, close to Victoria Bridge, where substantial earthworks along the east and north edges of the bailey rise to Hogg's Mount at the north-east corner, where there are further steps.

Castle Green has additionally been the site of a monastic settlement, dedicated to the Mercian St. Guthlac. This was there until 1143, when it was transferred to the site of the present County Hospital, because of symbolic pollution of the castle ground from the gory outcome of a siege. For 500 years the southern part of the bailey also served as the city cemetery, and archaeological research shows that between 7,000 and 15,000 burials took place from the foundation of the city until the 12th century—when they ended and continued at the cathedral. John Speede's map places a garrison chapel there, and excavations in 1960 and 1973 exposed a stone church which had been about the same size as that at Kilpeck (p.225). Dedicated to St. Martin, it is thought to have survived until the end of the 17th century.

Fronting the former castle watergate and governor's lodge to the west, Redcliffe Gardens is a pleasant public greensward laid out over the site of the great 13th-century keep which had once been described as 'high and very stronge', having 'one great towre' encircled by ten semi-circular towers. Beneath the grassy surface there is not a single piece of masonry from the keep or a pebble remaining from the motte. On the north side of the gardens is the supposed site where the body of St. Ethelbert was temporarily brought after his murder (p.143). A drinking fountain has been installed in the nearby wall, but it no longer delivers the once health-enhancing water. The road there is called Castle Hill and it leads eastwards towards Castle Pool, which was part of the castle ditch. This accounts for the naming of the house facing its western end—The Fosse, meaning a ditch or moat dug as a fortification. It may seem to be a strange design for a position such as this. In its Grade II Listing, it has been described as 'an irregular composition' and was designed to be built in 'Tudor' stucco in 1825 by Sir Robert Smirke, who had been responsible for the Shire Hall on St. Peter's Square ten years earlier. It appeared a few years after Nelson's Column was erected on Castle Green, minus the intended figure of Nelson and crowned only by an urn because of 'an erosion of funds'. Within sight on the south side of Castle Street, St. Ethelbert's Hospital had existed from 1225 but it was entirely rebuilt in 1805—use being made of stone from the destroyed cathedral chapter house. Castle Street has not always been as attractive as it is now, for with King Street it was part of the east/west through road during the 8th to 11th centuries giving access to the castle and catering for a corn market and many shops. Nowadays it is a peaceful cul-de-sac, the only lively time being when the afternoon bell goes at the cathedral schools. The first grammar school appeared in this locality no later than 1384, and over more recent years many of the fine Georgian and other houses in the street have gradually assumed scholastic uses—from the 14th-century former hall of the cathedral vicars choral behind the Georgian façade of no. 29, to the striking new Viscount Portman Centre for Art and Technology on the north side. The mid 19th-century Castle House hotel at the junction with St. Ethelbert Street has recently been thoroughly 'made over' by the owners of the Left Bank Village and is proclaimed as 'The most elegant Hotel in Herefordshire' and 'the perfect place to enjoy unashamed luxury and personal attention''. Holder of recent Hotel of the Year and Heart of Britain awards, its restaurant has been one of only a dozen in Britain and Ireland with four AA rosettes.

The rebuilt Saxon timber wall and part of the later stone wall, as seen (when plant free) at the rear of St. Owen's Court

St. Ethelbert Street connects with St. Owen's Street to the north and a right turn leads to St. Owen's Gate and the eastern end of the City Walls Relief Road. A good section of the old wall is visible at the back of St. Owen's Court, by going through the entrance arch on the right at the traffic lights. Looking left along St. Owen's Street, it is easy to understand why Nikolaus Pevsner has described it as the most consistent Georgian brick street in Hereford. Many of the buildings have been refronted and include much early 17th-century oak panelling, fine staircases, fluted friezes, carved and arcaded panels and medieval cellars.

The front of the early 17th-century no.14 is modern, but timber framing is visible at the rear, and inside there are paintings on plaster against a landscape background of the muses Euturpe, Urania and another. Most of these buildings are not usually open to the public, but private viewing arrangements have been welcomed. Soon after the Town Hall was opened in 1904, its massive, commanding brown terracotta front was regarded as 'probably a little out of harmony with its surroundings'! 'All very gay and busy' wrote Pevsner in 1963, and charitably the Grade II listing note accepted it to be 'characteristic of its date'. And so is the Shirehall, built to face St. Peter's Square just under a century earlier, with a portico of giant Greek Doric columns to a design by Sir Robert Smirke. The 30ft.-high memorial in the square was erected in 1922 in the form of an Eleanor Cross and it commemorates some 2,000 Herefordshire men and women who gave their lives in the 1914-1918 War, and many others who have since died on active service.

The Church of St. Peter was founded in 1085 by Walter de Lacy, who was afterwards accidentally killed by falling off it. It is the civic church, the oldest in the city, and is of great historic interest. No part of the original building now exists and most of the main structure dates from the 13th century. Parts of it have often been rebuilt and it suffered badly from Victorian 'restoration' between 1874 and 1885 from the heavy hand of diocesan architect, Thomas Nicholson.

The Old House has stood at the other end of St. Peter's Street since 1621 as the sole survivor of a block of shops and dwellings which once filled much of High Town. Typical of Herefordshire buildings of the early 17th century it was, from its lavish use of expensive oak and rich decoration, built for a well-to-do tradesman. This was quite probably John Jones, a butcher and certainly the arms of the butchers' guild still appear over the porch and crossed slaughtermens' poleaxes are carved under the eaves. Other uses have occurred since 1822, including saddlers, china, glass and hardware and wet fish shops. In 1882 the house was bought and renovated by the Worcester City and County Banking Company, which was later taken over by Lloyds Bank. In 1928, after outgrowing it, the bank presented the Old House to the city and moved next door to the market hall in High Town. The new museum opened the following year and as far as possible exhibits rooms of 17th-century character, set out with English oak furniture and typical Jacobean furnishings and other objects.

High Town has been the commercial hub of the city for well over 900 years, ever since the Norman conquerors set up a huge new market place between St. Peter's and All Saints churches and Commercial Square. Over the centuries the pitches and stalls were replaced with timber and brick buildings and many of these have developed into today's shops, banks and offices. The area has also provided the setting for many significant events, such as the beheading of Owen Tudor (great-grand-father of Henry VIII) in 1461, the building of a superb 3-storey Elizabethan market-hall and guild-hall (sadly demolished in 1862) and a visit by King Charles 1 in 1645. More recently the entire city centre had become choked by through traffic, but after completion of a relief road this eased after 1969 with the introduction of pedestrianisation. Next came 48 modern shops, 21 first-floor flats, a restaurant and an underground car park. Connecting with the Tesco supermarket and car park to the west, the Maylord Orchards Centre was designed to integrate with the traditional shopping axis passing through Widemarsh Street, Maylord Street, the Market Hall, Gomond Street and Brewers Passage. There are two links with Commercial Street, which extends north-eastwards and ends at The Kerry pub. The remains of Bye Street Gate here are buried below Commercial Square and the relief road, and Commercial Road continues to the north-east towards the Odeon cinema, country bus station, County Hospital, two supermarkets and Barrs Court railway station.

At the west end of High Town, Widemarsh Street extends northwards towards Widemarsh Gate, passing the Mansion House and the site of the birthplace in 1716 of David Garrick at the Maylord Street

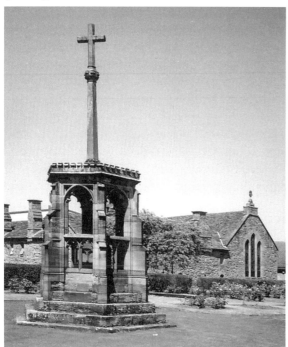

junction. Across Blueschool Street and Newmarket Street, Garrick House multi-storey and surface car parks are on the left and beyond the next junction on the right are the Coningsby Hospital of 1614, ruins of the Monastery of Black Friars and, dating from c.1350, the only surviving example in England of a friars' preaching cross.

High Street leads due west from High Town and this is where it is possible to see the outcome of a strange exercise—whereby part of a 350-year-old timber framed house was rolled into High Town during the 1960s, afterwards rolled back and then lifted to adorn the first floor front of the then new Littlewoods store! Something equally 'different', but far more sensible, opened in July 1997 at All Saints Church, High Street, at the top of Broad Street. Surrounded by streets on three sides and hemmed in by buildings on the fourth, it is a true 'city' church—dating from the late 13th and 14th centuries. The church guide-book tells of the impact of its strongly medieval interior, one which also

The preaching cross at Blackfriars, with the old   serves as an inspired meeting place of the sacred
Coningsby Hospital, now almshouses, beyond

*Looking through remains of Blackfriars monastery
to the almshouses*

and the secular. For upon entering from High Street, the view seen to the right is of a 'High' Church of England place of worship. However in the nave to the left, and on a new gallery above, is the Café @ All Saints, forming part of a centre for music, drama, exhibitions and other events. At some weekday lunchtimes, the café tables may be fully occupied by customers—whilst a Holy Communion service is taking place in the Lady chapel. Trading profits gathered in by the PCC help greatly in maintaining the role of the church in all its aspects. There is perhaps a lesson here for other struggling parishes in a similar situation.

In late 1969 Eign Gate was nearly the first shopping street in Britain to be 'pedestrianised' and afterwards a footway connection was thrust into Bewell Street to provide a link to Tesco supermarket, car park, taxi rank and city bus station. The actual position of the old Eign Gate was by the pedestrian subway which runs beneath the relief road at the western end. Eign Street then continues westwards, past two supermarkets, Pomona Place and the access to the Cider Museum and King Offa Distillery, which are to the left. Then the A438 becomes Whitecross Road as far as Whitecross Roundabout and the A4110 junction for Knighton. Straight ahead, King's Acre Road continues towards the 'flag ship' centre of Wyevale Nurseries and the A480 road for Credenhill and Kington.

Back in High Town, the monthly Farmers' Market (for which all produce has to be grown, reared, caught, brewed, pickled, baked, smoked or processed within a range of 30 miles) has revived the 11th century practice when meat, dairy products, and other country fare were obtained direct from the producers. Later, other thoroughfares came to be associated with particular merchandise—and thus the passage leading south from High Town, across the old Saxon ditch and present East Street towards the cathedral, came to be known as Cabbage Lane. It has also been called Capuchin Lane, but nobody knows why, and it is now Church Street. One shop there still sells cabbages, as well as other vegetables and fruit, whilst this now rare street of small independent stores offers a wide variety of useful and attractive wares. A wall plaque at Leicester Place marks the birthplace in 1721 of Roger Kemble, founder of a theatrical dynasty which included the great 18th-century actress Sarah Siddons, and almost opposite, just before the entrance to the cathedral close there is the gated garden of 20 Church Street. This exceptional 2-storey private house of stone, timber framing and brick has recently revealed many of its internal secrets, particularly a main wing built in the 15th century. It must also hold many special memories of the days when it was the home of cathedral organists Dr. G.R. Sinclair and then Sir Percy Hull. And of when it became a regular haunt of Edward Elgar and a host of other great artists and composers of the 19th and 20th centuries (as well as 'Dan', Sinclair's bulldog with perfect pitch, who is now buried in the garden).

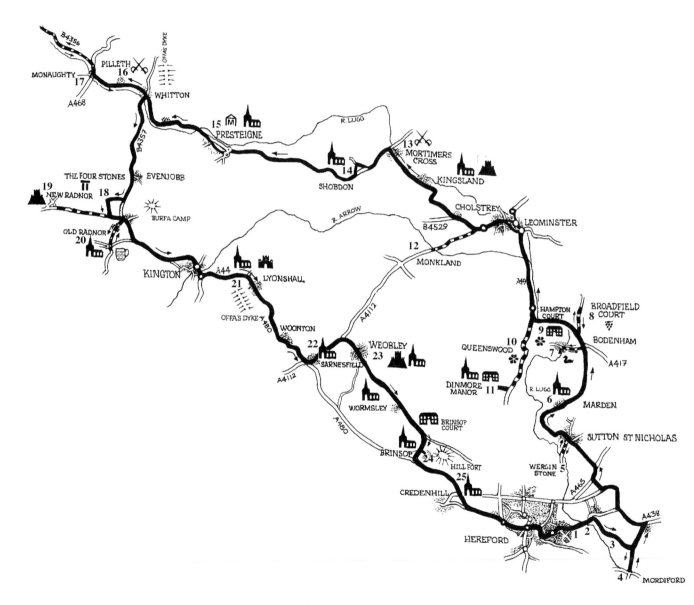

Outline map for Tour 6
The numbers 1 to 25 relate to the boxed information given within the tour

Tour 6   The Arrow and Lugg Valleys, North Herefordshire and Radnorshire

A largely scenic tour, but with several churches and places of interest *en route*, it starts from Hereford and first heads for the outfall of the Lugg where it enters the Wye at Mordiford. Backtracking for a short distance, the journey then follows the course of the river to its source in the Radnorshire hills beyond Llangunllo. The Lugg is often within sight northwards through Marden, Bodenham and Dinmore Hill as far as Leominster. River and roads then tend towards a north-westerly direction, passing close to the Wars of the Roses battlefield at Mortimer's Cross. After Shobdon and its very pretty church, there is a change in the landscape upon entering the characteristic valleys and hills of Radnorshire at the approach to Presteigne. Beyond this town the tour crosses Offa's Dyke to reach Pilleth, the site of another bloody 15th-century battle. Beyond Monaughty the Lugg valley narrows at the approach of the road to the initial signs of the river. Then there is an optional extension which climbs higher into unfrequented mountain and moorland scenery of rare beauty.

There is a variety of return choices from the junction of the B4356 and A488 at Monaughty. The one suggested here crosses the infant Lugg before climbing from the river valley to enter the Walton Basin, another valley of great pre-historic and historic interest. It is an area of Bronze Age and Iron Age activity, there are motte and bailey works, the site of a Roman fort, good surviving sections of Offa's Dyke—all overlooked from Old and New Radnor. The route then heads for the valley of the River Arrow at Kington and from there the journey heads generally south-eastwards back to Hereford. It takes in a further number of 'black and white' villages on the way, such as Lyonshall and Weobley. Without detours, the distance as far as Llangunllo is 48 miles, and complete extent 80 miles. (OS Landranger 148 and 149)

The route is largely on quiet A and B roads.

The River Lugg

The Lugg is the lesser known and documented of Herefordshire's two main rivers—and yet at one time it was much weightier than the Wye, which was then one of its tributaries. At the end of the Ice Age it had combined with the River Teme, swollen with meltwater, to create a wide valley, and a catchment which still covers about half of today's county. After the ice receded, deposits of moraine debris diverted the Teme eastwards to the Severn and only the Lugg and its smaller tributaries remained in this wide river valley.

Since then the scenic qualities of the now mightier Wye have moved great poets, not least William Wordsworth. But so also have those of the Lugg. For a while Lord Byron set up home not far from its source, and he is said to have worked on *Childe Harold's Pilgrimage* there. But long before most other writers set pen to paper, Michael Drayton (1563-1631) had produced his *Odes and pastorals on the topography of England*; and about 'that more lovely Lugg' he wrote:

> For Hereford, although her Wye she hold so dear
> Yet Lugg (whose longer course doth grace the goodly Sheere [Shire],
> And with his plenteous stream so many brooks doth bring)
> Of all hers that be North is absolutely King.

For 60 miles below its source in the hills of Radnorshire the Lugg takes many forms before losing itself in the Wye. Rising at 1,600 feet on Pool Hill, north-west of Llangunllo, in Wales it is known as *Afon Llugwy*. During its first 10 miles, through Monaughty, Pilleth, and almost to Presteigne, it falls 1,000ft. Then the gradient gradually flattens to take another 50 miles to descend a further 450ft. over the remainder of its course through Aymestrey, Leominster, Bodenham and Tupsley to Mordiford. The differing water velocities produce a gradual change to the river bed—from stones and pebbles deposited near the source, to the sand and silt which are carried along in the water over rock and boulders and dropped lower down, on the river bed or, depending upon the time of year, the adjoining floodlands. This process produces a wide range of waterside plantlife and landscape, from mosses among the rocks and boulders in the hills to a variety of species seen in the nutritious clay, silt and sand. The aquatic and bankside habitats support many rare and threatened species which have disappeared from most other British rivers. There have been otters (always a good indicator of the state of health of any river), water voles, grayling, brown trout, crayfish, lampreys (like eels—do not eat a surfeit as Henry I fatally did!), dippers, kingfishers, and much more. In November 1995 the river was confirmed as a Site of Special Scientific Interest (SSSI), giving it national status. It also has wider status as a candidate under the European Special Area of Conservation Habitats and Species Directive.

There are, however, worries about its future state because of increased silting and levels of nitrates and phosphates from agricultural sources which are acting as excessive nutrients. These enrich the water, causing changes in the communities of plants and animals. Attempts are being made to create 'buffer strips' alongside the river to 'comb out' all the chemicals now used for agricultural crops, particularly potatoes, which are grown on previous pasture land—one consequence of falling meat prices, at least that paid to farmers.

Starting from Hereford, take the A438 towards Ledbury. At the edge of the city on the right is The Cock of Tupsley, whilst towards the bottom of the old road on the left hand side is Lower House Farm, now the headquarters of Herefordshire Nature Trust.

1. The Cock of Tupsley—Horses or roosters?

This is a 1960s pub, replacing a much older establishment across the road at Tupsley House. It too was known as The Cock and stood on the former 'Cock-road', which is now the steep narrow road to the left, connecting again with the main road at the bottom of the hill. As at Three Cocks, west of Hay, there has been speculation about the origin of the pub name, but the strongest theory is that it concerns the heavy 'cock horse' which was harnessed to provide extra horse-power for wagons tackling a rise like that at Tupsley. According to

The sign for the Cock of Tupsley, and the road leading down to the old Lammas Meadows

their fine sign, the present owners appear to think that this is the answer, whereas in Breconshire they opt for poultry.

2.   Lammas Meadows and wildlife conservation

Until recently Lower House Farm was a working farm, but after the farmer died, the Jacobean house of 1614, with the fields and woodland, were purchased by Herefordshire Nature Trust, helped by a substantial grant from the Heritage Lottery Fund and donations from many groups and individuals. The work of the Trust covers all aspects of wildlife and nature conservation within the county and much of this is performed through the acquisition of nature reserves as areas of wildlife interest. The farmhouse stands above the Upper Lugg Meadow, one of over 50 reserves managed by the Trust. It has paths and a bridleway which are open for public enjoyment and forms part of a very extensive area of the Lugg Valley which is liable to flood during the winter. Each season, thin layers of silt are deposited, producing a high level of fertility which has been highly valued since medieval times. Since then a system of Lammas or Dole Meadows has evolved, whereby from Candlemas (2 February) to Lammas (1 August) the meadow is 'shut for hay' and no animals may be grazed. Despite initial appearance, the meadow has been divided into strips and plots which are bought and sold, the boundaries being marked by dole stones rather than hedges and fences—which would only become damaged in times of flood. After Lammas Day the meadow is thrown open for grazing to those with 'commoners rights'. This long history of management as a hay meadow, using no artificial fertilizers or herbicides, has resulted in a range of plants no longer seen elsewhere—where well over 90% of meadows have been lost to other uses. Every April rare snakeshead fritilleries appear and it is said that the narrow-leaved water-dropwort is hardly to be found anywhere else in Britain. Part of the meadow is designated as a Site of Special Scientific Interest. There is a leaflet and a lot more about the work of the Trust to be found at Lower House Farm—and walkers will greatly appreciate the booklets: *Six Walks exploring the landscape history of the Lower Lugg Valley* and *The History and Natural History of Lugg Meadow*.

The A438 causeway separates the Upper from the Lower Lugg Meadow as it approaches Lugwardine Bridge. After crossing the river, turn right and head for Tidnor.

3.   Ancient mills

The Lugg has always provided a good source of power and at one time there were at least ten mills on the lower reaches of the river. Today there are signs of only two, one at Tidnor and the other at Lugg Bridge, near the northern end of the Upper Lugg Meadow. This is close to the A465/A4103 Bromyard/ Worcester road and it has been greatly enhanced by a recent conversion into modern riverside dwellings. Near the mill site at Tidnor a footpath leads to Hampton Meadow, another of the 16 surviving Lammas Meadows in the country. It continues to Hampton Bridge, which gave the inhabitants of Hampton Bishop access to their common meadow, and to the site of the former Hampton Mill—probably that recorded in Domesday Book. Before *c*.1698 the bridge and its supports were built entirely of stone, but the arches were then broken and rebuilt in brick—and with greater clearance to allow the passage of barges or trows.

Our route crosses the River Frome at the far end of the straight at Longworth Bridge on the approach to Larport. Turn right here on the minor road for Mordiford, and in the village right again on the B4224 to the bridge. This was probably built in the 14th century and is one of the oldest on the river. It is usually possible to park near its Hereford end, whence a footpath leads to the point where, after flowing for 60 miles from its birthplace close to Radnor Forest, high in the hills, the Lugg is lost in the River Wye.

4. Mordiford and The Navigation

At one time, both rivers were used for navigation, when commercial traffic was undertaken with trows or barges, pulled along by teams of 'bow-hauliers'. These were named after the bow placed around the men's shoulders for their gruelling task. This operation required a system of locks, and in the 18th century there was one of these on the Lugg at the confluence. Nothing shows there now, but some of the material may still be buried in the river bed. There is more to see at the next lock, also below the bridge. Navigation of the Lugg operated as far as Leominster and many of the existing bridges on the way, including Mordiford Bridge (p.232), were adapted to allow the passage of boats at times of flood.

Mordiford

Back in the car, look for a safe turning space and retrace your route into Mordiford and thence turn left back onto the unclassified road, this time heading along it until you reach the A438 at Dormington. Turn left for Bartestree where you are now plainly in hop country, and in the Spring among fields of daffodils. At the approach to Bartestree turn right at a crossroads for Whitestone, and then after about half a mile left on the A4103, back towards Hereford. After about half a mile turn right just before the railway bridge seen ahead signposted Withington to reach the A465 road on which you turn right through Nunnington. At Sutton Marsh half a mile along the road take the first left turn onto Ridgeway Road to follow the Sutton St. Nicholas sign. Make for the village, coming to the early 13th-century church of St. Nicholas on the left at the approach to the main crossroads and the Golden Cross Inn.

The route goes straight ahead at the crossroads, but for a short detour, you could take the road to the left, which leads back towards Hereford. Nearly opposite the fourth walled culvert on the left, counting from the village and across Wergin's Bridge over the Lugg, is the 5ft. high Wergin Stone. You will need to park with care on this fast road and peer through the hedgerow to see it in the meadow, surrounded by a fence.

Retrace your steps to the crossroads and turn left.

From the crossroads Sutton continues to straggle north-westwards, past the small church of St. Michael. It dates from Norman times and gives its name to this outer part of the village: only local people know where the dividing line is! Continue along the road and pass the left hand turning, signposted Moreton-on-Lugg, and follow the next sign down the narrower minor no through road to the church at Marden.

Marden is where a Holy Well is said to have sprung up where St. Ethelbert (see box) was first buried, and this may still be visited within the church, when it is not locked up. St. Mary's stands less than 20ft. from the Lugg, and sometimes during the winter suffers as a result.

5.   Wergin Stone—Work of the Devil?

In fact one stone on top of another, the Wergin Stone attracted the attention of Daniel Defoe as long ago as the 1720s and there are stories about its purpose extending even further back to 1650. The strongest received wisdom is that it is a depth marker for when the floods are out: during the winter, when parts of this road are sometimes well under water. Or perhaps it was a boundary marker? More fanciful accounts tell of this, and another large stone, having once been moved, no-one knows how or why, some 240 paces from their former positions. Nine yoke of oxen were said to have been required to return the stone to its present position. Some put it all down to a supernatural agency, and called it The Devil's Stone. A further mystery is that in the base there is a cavity, about 4ins. deep, sloping inwards. Was it to hold money? No-one can really say.

Wergin Stone

6.   Marden and St. Ethelbert—Foul murder

Marden Church

About a quarter of a mile north of Marden church is Sutton Walls, an Iron Age hillfort now covered by trees. Occupants of this 30-acre encampment, successively Celts, Romans and Saxons, once looked out over the Lugg Valley. It has had a gruesome history. Roman invaders are suspected of being responsible for a massacre there, leaving many skeletons—several with wounds and decapitations which show that they did not die naturally. Then in Saxon times, when traditionally this was thought to be the site of the palace of King Offa of the Mercians, more murder was done. Following recent archaeological excavation at Freen's Court, below the hillfort, doubt has, however, been cast upon the long-held belief about this being the precise location of the palace.

Expecting to be married to Offa's daughter, the teenage King Ethelbert of East Anglia, was instead treacherously killed for dynastic reasons in King Offa's name and his decapitated body disposed of in a Lugg-side marsh. King Offa soon came to regret the treachery and as a penance he is thought to have founded a church over the place where the body was first buried. Ethelbert was afterwards taken to Hereford to a splendid shrine, erected at Offa's behest. The then timber cathedral was dedicated to the Blessed Virgin and later to King Ethelbert, who was canonised as

143

a saint. Miracles were said to have been performed there and these attracted many pilgrims, and revenues which in no small way helped to enrich the fabric fund, as well as the economy of the city. Much more recently the hill at Sutton Walls Camp was excavated for gravel extraction and outrage of a different order was done. Against local advice, the authorities allowed the resulting pit to be used for the dumping of toxic waste from the Midlands. After great disturbance for miles around caused by lorries heading to and from the site, all the signs of leaching of chemicals were discovered on the hillside—and there were patches where nothing would grow. This discovery brought the disgraceful arrangement to an end and the tip was capped with inert material.

Return to the 'main' minor road and turn left. This leads on through Bodenham Moor towards the A417 on which you turn left and head towards Leominster. But there are two detours you may wish to take, one to the pleasant village of Bodenham and its church; and one to a local vineyard.

To reach Bodenham, before you reach the A417 you turn left at the England's Gate inn, near Brockington 9-hole golfcourse. Meantime the River Lugg is half way along its serpentine diversion round Dinmore Hill, which stands high above the village, as seen from John Gethin's graceful old Bodenham Bridge. Once across the bridge, the left turn for St. Michael's Church, which stands close to the Lugg and a steel footbridge, soon follows.

7. Bodenham's new lake and birdlife

Bodenham village and church

In recent times Bodenham has acquired the largest man-made area of standing water in the county. A 20-hectare disused sand and gravel pit, its mixed shingle and mud shorelines, surrounding woodland and meadows had by 2000 become a breeding ground, it is said, for 71 species of bird and a wintering site for a further 28. It was bought by the local authority in 1994 and the eastern end is now open to the public, whilst there is a sailing centre for the Youth Service on the north bank.

Here there is the opportunity for not just drinking in the views, but also calling at Broadfield Court to taste and buy Bodenham wine (see opposite). This estate was mentioned in the Domesday Book of 1086, and in the summer, visitors are invited to enjoy the peaceful charm of this truly historic English house, its six south facing gables displaying some 600 years of history. There are also 300-year-old barns and extensive gardens.

To reach the vineyard, turn left just past England's Gate inn onto the A 417 and then right at the crossroads by the garage and passing through Bowley, about a mile along the road.

---

8.   Wine Making at Broadfield Court

After much research into grape varieties suitable for the English climate, some 379 vineyards had been established in Britain by the end of the 20th century. They were then capable of producing more than 3 million bottles a year and Broadfield must be one of the most northerly and challenging of them all. After a modest start in 1971, Keith James now reports an extraordinary ability to produce fully ripened grapes on his land, even in poor summers. Success with his original 50 vines has led to a 14-acre vineyard and the earlier Mueller Thurgau and Seyve Villard grapes have been joined by Reichensteiner, Huxelrebe and Madeline Angevine. These are used both singly and in blends to produce the six wines on the present Bodenham list.

The main route continues on the A417 to Hampton Court, and access is through an imposing gateway on the left, built as recently as 2000. The drive leads to the gardens, orangery (by Joseph Paxton), restaurant and river and woodland walks—which are open between the ends of March and October.

---

9.   Hampton Court and the Van Kampens

The new gateway to Hampton Court (above) and the house itself (below)

The manor is said to have been founded in 1430, as a reward by Henry V, together with a knighthood, in recognition of the role of Rowland Leinthall, his Yeoman of the Robes, for services rendered in 1415 at Agincourt. He had contributed 8 mounted men and 33 bowmen to the force, but also secured many French prisoners. Sir Rowland is said to have ransomed these in exchange for funds to build a stately new home, predating its namesake on the River Thames by several years. After the Leinthalls, it was the home of the Coningsbys for 300 years and the Arkwrights, descendants of Sir Richard Arkwright (1732-1792), inventor of the Spinning Jenny, between 1810 and 1912. During their time the house was further remodelled after major work by Lord Coningsby in 1700. There were another six owners before 1994, by which time it had become half derelict. Then that year an American family who had fallen in love with the Herefordshire countryside struck a deal through Sola Scriptura. This is a US non-profit making organisation funded and overseen by the Van Kampen family—with the primary purpose of 'affirming the authenticity, accuracy and authority of God's word, the Bible'. Since then about £12 million has been spent in returning the Grade 1 listed building to first-rate condition. Work on the 8 acres of gardens of the house was started in 1996, with designs involving a Gothic tower within a 1,000 yew tree maze, octagonal pavilions overlooking formal borders, canals and water steps, a restored Victorian sunken garden and a Dutch garden. Robert Van Kampen, a reclusive Christian fundamentalist and multi-millionaire, died at just 60 awaiting a heart transplant. Under new owner-ship what is now titled Hampton Court Castle and Gardens is available for private parties, licenced for weddings and open for tours and visits at times available from local TICs.

The main route bears right at the junction with the A49 shortly beyond Hampton Court Castle, but a detour can be made by turning left and heading on the A49 to Queenswood Park and Arboretum, off to the right at the top of the hill. Here, some 170 acres of woodland within the Hampton Park estate were purchased in 1935 by Herefordshire County Council to mark the Silver Jubilee of King George V.

The detour can be extended by continuing on the A49 over the hill towards Hereford, turning right shortly after the road flattens out at the foot of the hill to Dinmore Manor.

10. Queenswood Country Park and Arboretum

This is now one of the most popular leisure attractions of Herefordshire and far beyond.

Before it was moved, most of the café at the entrance had been the half-timbered 17th-century Essex Arms at the Widemarsh Street toll-gate in Hereford. The Tourist Information Centre and shop, where there are useful guides and maps and an upstairs display and meetings room, used to be a tannery building beside the Lugg at Leominster (called there the Kenwater).

Because of its 170 acres there is never an impression of crowds at Queenswood. Grown ups, children and dogs are quickly assimilated within the woods, along the Deer Trail, Fox Trail, Badger Trail and other waymarked paths and trails. Individual trees have been planted from the 1930s at the Arboretum, the heart of the park, and you are invited to enjoy the scarlets and yellows of Japanese maples or wander through a natural cathedral of California Redwoods. All the trees are numbered and there is a catalogue to help with identification. Leave time to visit the Viewpoint at the southern end, beyond Queen Elizabeth Grove and a quarry. With the aid of a Toposcope erected in 1977 to commemorate the Silver Jubilee of Queen Elizabeth II, it is possible to identify landmarks extending from the Malvern Hills, Ledbury, Haugh Wood, Hereford, Skirrid, the Black Mountains, the Sugar Loaf and Credenhill across a stunning pastoral landscape far below.

11. Dinmore Manor and Knights Hospitaller

Hidden beyond trees to the right is a place not known to have been involved in any of the many battles fought in the county and Marches, but it is closely associated with the Crusades.

Two knights in niches at the entrance to the park of Dinmore Manor provide a hint to what lies beyond the woods at the fine old manor house, and an ancient church flying the flag of St John. A Commandery of the Knights Hospitaller of St. John of Jerusalem was founded here in 1189. The tiny church

Dinmore Manor

retains traces of 12th century work, but is mainly of the 14th century. Dinmore was one of a number of conventual buildings giving help and lodging to travellers and the needy, even sanctuary, and also acted as a resting place for the knights who had returned from, or were on their way to, the Holy Land. The community absorbed Broadfield Estate (see above) in the 14th century and in 1614, Sir Thomas Coningsby built a hospital, now almshouses, in Widemarsh Street, Hereford. Very little else of the original buildings remain at Dinmore, but reconstruction over the centuries has been imaginatively carried out in accordance with medieval principles. And the Knights Hospitaller were disbanded—as words on a panel in the church aver:

> The knights are dust
> Their swords are rust:
> Their souls are with
> The saints, we trust.

N.B.: In early 2004 the buildings were closed for restoration under new ownership and are now not open to the public.

The main route follows the A49 towards Leominster, passing the subtly toned Cadbury's factory buildings and plant on the right. It is not exactly a lovable design for such surroundings, but is regarded as important for the economy of the considerable dairy industry of the county and region, producing a high proportion of the company's chocolate crumb and other primary needs. At the roundabout take the Leominster by-pass straight ahead, the Lugg returning to sight on the right, soon to receive the waters of the River Arrow. The only bridge across the by-pass serves Wharton Court, the tall, stone-built building also on the right. Except for its 2-storey porch, which was added in 1659, it dates from 1604. A distinctive interior includes a staircase which is reputed to be the finest in Herefordshire. After it was built for Richard Whitehall, it passed to the Hakluyts and then the Hampton Court estate and is still in private use as a farmhouse. From this point the A49 by-pass, the main railway line and the Lugg run close together along the flood-prone river corridor, said to be rich in rarely-seen wildlife, such as hares, kingfishers and possibly otters. At the next roundabout turn left into Leominster (see p.49), shortly crossing the railway line on a dog leg.

The Navigation, and recasting Leominster's bells

Upstream, not far beyond the A44 Eaton Bridge, the river reaches the site of the former quay at the Navigation terminus. The barges were never a great success, and despite some effort in building up to a dozen locks and much adjustment of bridge clearances, the Navigation was probably abandoned before the end of the 18th century. This was not before the bells of Leominster Priory Church had famously been sent down river by barge to Chepstow in the mid 1750s for recasting, and then returned for rehanging. Generally, apart from the physical difficulties, there seems to have been apprehension about competition from imports among local manufacturers. Yet others may have wondered whether Leominster's famous wool, Lemster Ore, (compared by Drayton with 'a silk worm's web'), and good sources of water power, might have enabled them to rival many mill towns in prosperity, were it not for the 'lack of transportation'. By the time the railway arrived in 1853 it was in any case too late. Now part of that has also gone, but some of the route of the former Leominster to Kington Railway, opened in 1857 via Kingsland, Pembridge and Titley, has been put to good use for building an effective flood relief channel for Leominster.

Follow the road round a left hand bend and up to a T junction at the end, where you turn left, then almost immediately right at the mini-roundabout, swing right at the next roundabout and turn left at the lights, on the A44, until Morrisons appears on the left.

Across the roundabout at Morrisons entrance, you come to the Barons Cross Inn on the left, and a choice as to whether to take a slight detour to the left to see Monkland Church and cheese making in the village, for the main route swings to the right at the inn. To take this detour turn left on the A44 towards Brecon and Monkland is reached after a couple of miles, the church on the left and the cheese-making signposted off to the right a little further along.

---

12. Cheese making and hymns at Monkland

Monkland has given its name to a cheese, and also a well known tune set for two popular hymns.

The cheese is one of a number produced at Pleck Farm from the milk of cows that graze the lush grasses of Herefordshire. Because the cheeses are unpasteurised, it is interesting that their flavours are not only very good but can also vary slightly with the seasons to reflect the changing nature of the pastures. As well as being able to buy English and Welsh farmhouses cheeses at the farm shop and café, on certain days and times visitors may watch the processes and learn about the history of Little Hereford cheese, one of the favourites revived by Karen and Mark Hindle from a hundred years ago.

Some while before the days of Ellen Yeld, who originally made this cheese, the vicar of Monkland from 1851-1877, Sir Henry W. Baker, heir to a baronetcy, brought different fame to the village through the great number of published hymns he wrote or translated. Many are still in current use in *The New English Hymnal* and *Hymns Ancient and Modern Revised*, and one tune is called *Monkland*. Few people who switch on the BBC Sunday Songs of Praise will not recognise *The King of love my Shepherd is*, written by him in 1868 for the debut of Monkland's new village school.

The main route continues to the right at the fork near the Barons Cross inn following the B4529 and, about 1 mile further on, just beyond Cholstrey, turn right on to the B4360 and follow the road to Kingsland. The road through the village stretches out for almost a mile, past many black and white cottages, and others of them which have been brick-fronted. Behind the large 13th- / 14th-century St. Michael's Church, where there is a small car park, are earthworks of a substantial Norman motte and bailey castle, the former about 17ft. high and 180ft. in diameter. The large church is particularly noted for the mysterious Volka Chapel, which opens out from the north porch. Locally it is believed that this was built as a chantry in which masses were said for the soul of an early benefactor, and for those killed at the Battle of Mortimer's Cross. The grave of John Gethin (b.1757), builder of many fine bridges in Herefordshire, is to be found in the churchyard. Almost opposite the turn to the church and its car park is the 17th-century Angel Inn, next to the much older Angel House. There is also the Corners Inn and, half a mile further on, at the junction with the A4110, the Monument Inn. The monument concerned is right at the road junction and was erected by subscription in 1799 to perpetuate the memory of the Battle of Mortimer's Cross, fought on St. Blaise's Day, 3 February, 1461.

The Monument to the Battle of Mortimer's Cross

At the Monument Inn turn right and soon the A4110 passes through the battle site as it approaches the crossroads with the B4362 at Mortimer's Cross, where the tour turns left. Just to the right, over a bridge across the Lugg, there is a working 18th-century water-mill, one of the few survivors of at least 50 which once operated along the river, some until after the

Second World War. There is a display which includes information about the battle. This road continues towards Lucton and Croft Castle (p.65).

Follow the B4362 from the crossroads towards Shobdon, turning right after just over a mile at a brown sign for a rather exceptional church, making a left turn at the next brown sign up an avenue of limes to the car park.

---

13.   The Battle of Mortimer's Cross

This was the last major battle in Herefordshire, and is partly remembered because of three 'mock' suns seen in the mist (a phenomenon now known as a parhelion). Superstitious Yorkists regarded this as an omen of victory. The Lancastrians, led by Jasper Tudor, half brother of Henry VI, faced the Yorkists in the flat meadows between Kingsland and Mortimer's Cross, Edward Mortimer setting up a command post on his home territory under an oak tree by the present Blue Mantle Cottage at the approach to the crossroads. This name relates to the title of Edward's pursuivant or herald, who may, as was then customary, have passed between the armies in order to try and reach a peaceful settlement. (It is also thought that he may have been treacherously taken and slaughtered by the Lancastrians). The bloody battle lasted from sunrise to sunset and although details are obscure, figures of up to 4,000 dead have been mooted, and disputed, by historians. Many Lancastrians were captured, including Owen Tudor, Jasper's father and grandfather of the future Henry VII, who, with other Welshmen, was taken at Kingsland and beheaded in Hereford. The victorious 19-year-old duke of York was proclaimed king on 3 March (not the 5th shown on the monument) and on 29 June 1461 was crowned King Edward IV. He later included the Sun in Splendour in his Arms, as a portent of his victory. Jasper Tudor became a fugitive, and then exile, and it would be 24 years before he reappeared from France, via Dale in Pembrokeshire, in the company of his nephew and an army. Owen's grandson, Henry Tudor, was to win back the crown for the Lancastrians from Richard III at Bosworth Field on 22 August 1485, and became the first Tudor monarch, King Henry VII.

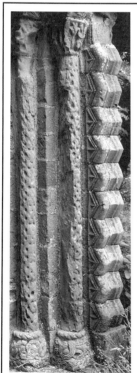

14.   Shobdon church and Strawberry Hill Gothic

For some people, St. John the Evangelist, Shobdon, borders on the sickly, except perhaps for those brides who, unyielding, have guarded the right to hold a 'white' wedding. For although the outside of the church is unexceptional, the

Shobdon Arches (above) and detail (left)

149

interior—right down to the kneelers—is like a white and sky-blue confection. Yet this 18th-century building, possibly by architect Richard Bentley, has gained much approval from many, including the late John Betjeman. It is ranked by Simon Jenkins alongside Abbey Dore, Kilpeck, Ledbury

and Leominster among the top 100 in his recent book: *England's Thousand Best Churches*. But this has been at a heavy cost, for in order to build it, the 2nd. Viscount Bateman demolished a major part of a Norman church, consecrated in *c*.1143, which must have rivalled, if not surpassed, Kilpeck. Amidst faint praise, he re-erected the chancel arch and two doorways, with their tympana, as a vista on the skyline of his park. Over 200 years of exposure have blunted the detail of the intricate carving of the Shobdon Arches. Except during a few years' service as a garden ornament, the rugged Norman stone font has not been affected by the weather, and this stands uneasily within the Strawberry Hill Gothic church interior.

The west entrance to the present
Strawberry Hill Gothic church

Continue on the B4762 through Shobdon, on the far edge of which you pass the Pearl Lake Caravan Park on the right, and the lake itself. This is the largest natural area of water in Herefordshire and a habitat for birds such as great crested grebes and tufted ducks. The B road continues to Presteigne, until 1971 the county town of Radnorshire. In 1867, George Borrow, the author of *Wild Wales*, considered it to be 'Neither in Wales nor England, but simply in Radnorshire'. These days the town centre is relieved by a by-pass—reached by turning left at the first roundabout and right at the next. This provides easy access to a car park on the right hand side whence a lane joins the main street.

15.   Presteigne, and the sad story of Mary Morgan

From the 16th century until 1970 the town had been the venue for the county assizes and one lord chief justice on Circuit described it as 'A sort of Paradise'. Little wonder, in view of the special comforts of its Judges Lodging. Formerly the Shire Hall, and on the site of the old County Gaol, this opened in 1829. In 1855 his lordship was to call it: 'the most commodious and elegant apartments for a judge in all England and Wales'. Situated in Broad Street, it is now a museum, linked to the TIC, and has gained Britain's Local Museum of the Year award to add to other plaudits. However not all of his majesty's judges enjoyed such a relaxed time in Presteigne, especially Mr. Justice Hardinge.

For one of the town's saddest stories concerns Mary Morgan, a 16-year-old undercook at Maesllwch Castle near Glasbury, who knifed her illegitimate baby girl soon after giving birth and was quickly found out. She was held in gaol at Presteigne from early October until the start of the Grand

The Library, Presteigne

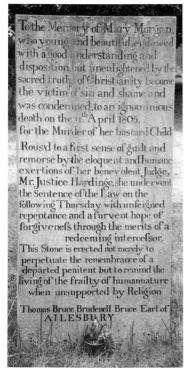

Left: Mary Morgan's gravestone; above: The Radnorshire Arms

Sessions the following April, when the grand jury returned a true bill of murder against her. In delivering his sentence, Hardinge's words were 'full of nauseating preachments explaining why he refused to take too merciful an attitude', which in a case of infanticide, even in those harsh days, would usually have resulted in his death sentence being commuted. Two days after sentencing (and two hours before arrival of a reprieve, so it is said), Mary Morgan was trundled over rough cobbles to Gallows Lane and, mercifully unconscious, was hanged on 13 April 1805. Local outrage against Hardinge, and perhaps a measure of remorse from him, led to a crude gravestone being erected on his behalf. Packed with awful cant, it may still be seen in the churchyard of St. Andrew's, further down Broad Street. The present church, from which the town obtains its Welsh name—*Llanandras*—dates mainly from the 14th/early 16th centuries. After well over 400 years, the clock tower has a curfew bell which, except on Sundays, is still rung each evening. The original church was granted to St. Guthlac's Priory, Hereford, in 1145 and the parish has always been in that

The Duke's Arms

diocese, parishioners declining the opportunity in 1920 to become part of the Church in Wales. At Lugg Bridge, further down the road, the river marks the boundary between Herefordshire and Radnorshire, England and Wales. Presteigne is often said to have an 'Englishness' and is also unique as the only town in Wales lying to the east of Offa's Dyke. Certainly its importance in the 18th century brought many travellers along the road from England, calling for some 30 inns. The railway followed in 1875, and among the many remaining fine timbered buildings there are still the Radnorshire Arms of 1616, the even older Duke's Arms—which is probably medieval and was embroiled in a skirmish in the Civil War, and the Bull Hotel.

151

Continue westwards on the B4356 by-pass, turning sharp right over the river after a mile and crossing Offa's Dyke at Dolley Green, drive with the Lugg in sight down in the valley to the left, through Whitton towards Pilleth. Facing you, high up on the steep hillside of Bryn Glas overlooking the upper Lugg Valley towards Offa's Dyke, there is an enclosure containing four tall wellingtonia trees and, up a fine arts and crafts style stepped approach, the quiet and lonely 13th- /14th-century church of St. Mary our Lady of Pilleth. In the valley below there is a Norman motte and bailey—Castell Foel-allt.

16. The Battle of Pilleth or Bryn Glas

The site of the Battle of Pilleth, with the church centre right and the wellingtonias marking the site of men buried after the battle on the hillside to the left

Just over 600 hundred years ago, on 22 June 1402, the bitter and bloody Battle of Pilleth took place between Owain Glyndwr, seeking to establish Welsh independence (and now regarded as the Father of Welsh nationalism), and Sir Edmund Mortimer, in command of an army raised on the borders. After numbers of men of Welsh origin changed sides to join Shakespeare's 'irregular and wild Glendower', up to a thousand of the remaining English army were butchered by the archers of his lieutenant, Rhys Gethin (the Terrible) and their bodies allegedly mutilated with knives 'with beastly shamelessness' by Welshwomen who swarmed onto the battlefield. Sir Edmund was captured in this, the last most complete Welsh victory over the English and, regarding him, as a Mortimer, a rival for his throne, the usurper Henry IV did not rush to deliver the ransom demanded. Mortimer consequently formed an alliance with Glyndwr, marrying one of his daughters to clinch it. Secretly, at the Archdeacon's house in Bangor, the former combatants joined with Henry Percy, Earl of Northumberland in the Tripartite Indenture of 1405 which would have split the country into three parts: 'All Westward, Wales beyond the Severn shore and all the fertile land within that bound to Owen Glendower', with Mortimer to have southern England. Glyndwr held his first Welsh Parliament as Prince of Wales at Machynlleth, but his support soon faded and little over five years after Pilleth, he was a fugitive. No-one really knows where he ended up, although there are credible theories about Monnington Straddel in the Golden Valley in Herefordshire,

Pilleth Church before restoration works

having a link with the Scudamore marriage to Alice, his daughter, and less convincing ones about Monnington-on-Wye, also in Herefordshire. Many human bones have been turned up on the hillside and the prominent wellingtonia trees were planted there in a grove—as a memorial to all those killed, and perhaps also to unrealised Welsh dreams.

The little church suffered badly in the battle and it was again gutted by fire in 1894. A restoration of 1911 was not completed and by 2002 the whole building, especially the dreadful 90-year-old 'temporary' roof and the propped north wall, were in a very sorry and unsafe state. However a restoration project, estimated to cost £225,000, involved a new traditional roof covered by Welsh slates over a barrel-vault ceiling, and repairs to the walls, tower with holy well by the north wall.

17.   Monaughty—The monks' house

Monaughty

A former name, *Mynachdy*, translates as 'the monks house', and it was associated with a grange of Radnorshire's only abbey at Cwm Hir, further to the west. Owain Glyndwr is thought to have put up there in 1402, before the Battle of Pilleth, and it was rebuilt in stone to an unsymmetrical H-plan towards the end of the 16th century. The interior was lavishly equipped and furnished, but by the 1960s it had become dilapidated and too costly to maintain. Left empty it rapidly disintegrated over the following 30 years. Then Douglas Blain, a new owner, started upon a gradual restoration programme and by the beginning of the 21st century there were signs that the care and funds applied to the buildings and gardens, which are not open to the public, were having a good effect.

The B4356 meets the A488 at Monaughty (locally pronounced 'Munawtee'), and below the junction is the gaunt Late Elizabethan stone-built house and a range of other domestic and farm buildings. Once the largest house in Radnorshire, as befitted the prominent Price family of that time, it is in a striking position at the narrowing of the upper reaches of the Lugg valley.

To get to the source of the Lugg, turn right on the A488 and then left to rejoin the B4356. Beyond Llangunllo, turn sharp right under the railway. The road then bends to the right and left past some houses and on the next major bend left, park where you see a track off to the right, and another off to the left leading to a collection of farm buildings. The river springs from the slopes of Pool Hill about an hour's walk away. Should there be time left, a hugely rewarding extension here heads further up the B4356, high into the Radnorshire moors and hills, before dropping sharply down to Llanbister for a left turn to join A483 and, from Crossgates, A44 to Kington.

Otherwise, for the return journey, first get back to Monaughty and the A488, on which you turn right and left to stay on the B4356 to pass Pilleth and reach the hamlet of Whitton. Here turn right onto the B4357. This crosses the Lugg and then sharply turns left to face a steep climb out of the Lugg valley to enter the Walton Basin. Evenjobb has a number of medieval half-timbered buildings and the area was another favourite haunt of the poet Wordsworth, whose sister lived nearby at Hindwell Farm. About half a mile beyond Evenjobb, turn right onto an unsigned minor road. Opposite the T junction with another road lie the Four Stones. The route turns left at the junction and heads down to the A44.

---

18. The Four Stones and the Prehistoric Era

In the late Neolithic or early Bronze Age, some 4,000 years ago, a former climate change brought the first settlers to this part of Radnorshire who cleared away trees, planted crops and grazed their animals. And for reasons which are not completely obvious, as their lasting contribution to the landscape they erected stone circles and standing stones. Perhaps these were for ceremonial or meeting purposes, perhaps boundary or route markers—or even rubbing posts for the animals. But inevitably they were also the source of myth and folk legend and these Four Stones

The Four Stones with the Whimble, left, and Radnor Forest in the background

are no exception. Like The Whetstone on nearby Hergest Ridge (p.109) and The Wergin Stone at Sutton St. Nicholas (p.143), they are reckoned to move about—in their case resuming human form as four local chiefs—to go off to drink at the pool at Hindwell Farm (alongside the B4357) whenever they hear the bells of Old Radnor church, still well in sight to the south. Evidence of a large cursus, or processional route, marked by wooden posts has been found at nearby Walton.

When you reach the A44 you have the choice of turning right for a short detour to New Radnor with its enormous castle mound, or left to follow the main tour route. If you turn right, New Radnor will be reached in about 2 miles, signposted off to the right, the A44 now acting as a by-pass.

---

19. New Radnor's famous son

The big local landowners since the 16th century were the Lewis family of Harpton Court, whose most illustrious son was George Cornewall Lewis (1806-1863). A formidable scholar and popular politician, the bells rang all day for him in 1855 when he became M.P. for the Radnor Boroughs, and until his early death he held several offices of State under Lord Palmerston, not least as Chancellor of the Exchequer. As a kindly Harpton squire he is credited with doing much good for local people—and nobody is likely to forget

The castle mound looming above New Radnor

The memorial to George Cornewall Lewis

it. For at the entrance to the village is his huge 71ft. high neo-Gothic memorial, bringing immediately to mind the Albert Memorial in London, although at tiny Radnor far more at odds with its setting. (As he had previously been Herefordshire's M.P. and chief steward of the city, Sir George's newly repaired and bronzed likeness also stands before the Shirehall, up to 2003 Hereford's sole free-standing statue).

New Radnor (*Maesyfed*) is not really new, for it was laid out as a planned settlement on a grid pattern in the 13th-century. Its castle, now a mound at the top of the High Street, was probably begun as a Saxon wooden keep before 1070 and its stone successors were frequently destroyed in Border conflict. After leaving Hereford in 1188 at the start of their recruiting journey through Wales, Archbishop Baldwin and the voluble Giraldus Cambrensis made the castle their first stop prior to moving on to Castell Crugerydd (p.125). It commanded a strategically important valley on the boundary between Normans and Welsh and, not unusually, the supporting settlement gradually formed below it, laid out on the still recognisable grid pattern and defensive ramparts and ditches. Under the 1536 Act of Union it became the New Radnor county town, but despite market privileges and other advantages it did not flourish economically. Presteigne became county town after the Civil War, succeeded by Llandrindod Wells in 1889, whereas New Radnor did not advance much beyond its medieval scale, except that the railway belatedly arrived in 1875 and lasted until 1951.

Return past the Eagle hotel (which is on the former prison site), and the Lewis monument, to face The Smatcher, a singular rounded hill. Then make a left turn back on to the A44 to drive along the level valley of the Summerhill Brook to Walton.

It is worth making a small detour to visit Old Radnor, either just to see its church or to take in the views from between the church and inn, or even simply to visit the inn itself—the Harp—as it was once owned by the Landmark Trust who restored the 15th-century former farmer's longhouse, and it still retains a lovely atmosphere. To take this diversion, turn right at the Crown inn some 2¹/₂ miles from New Radnor in the village of Walton onto the minor road which leads up the hillside, turning left again in Old Radnor to the car park between the church and inn. The first thing to do is marvel at the immense view over Radnor Forest—you can identify the area's many topographical features from a 'lookout' next to the churchyard entrance.

The Harp Inn at Old Radnor

155

20.   Old Radnor Church

The church has been built on the slopes of Old Radnor Hill at 840ft. above sea level and visibly occupies Bronze Age earthworks within a large round churchyard. There is very little else at Old Radnor (*Pen-y-graig*), yet surprisingly this is the biggest church in all Radnorshire, and justifiably regarded as one of the finest in Wales (although it has chosen to remain in Hereford diocese). Because of the outcome of earlier Welsh wars, not least the familiar wanton destructiveness of Owain Glyndwr in 1401, it dates chiefly from the 15th-century.

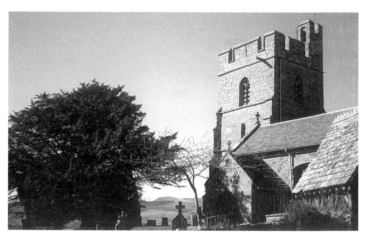

Old Radnor Church

Visitors should look out especially for the late 15th-century screen spanning the whole width of the church across the nave and aisles, the relaid medieval glazed floor tiles in different parts of the church and the early 16th-century organ case. This is the earliest in the British Isles, and so probably is the large font. Shaped from a doleritic erratic boulder, it is roughly rounded and flat-topped and is thought possibly to have been associated with Christianity from the 6th or 7th centuries. There is also a theory that it is connected with the line of standing stones on the plain to the north, perhaps that it is even the stone that left the gap among the Four Stones just a mile away?

Leave the car park and rejoin the 'main' minor road by turning left. Continue along the road for half a mile, turn left at the T junction, go over the bridge across the Burlingjobb limestone quarry entrance and turn left again on to the B4594 to rejoin A44 opposite Stanner Rocks. Turn right on the A44 for Kington (p.107), cross the first roundabout and turn left at the second to follow the signpost for Leominster. The A44 climbs from the Arrow valley past 14th-century Penrhos Court, now a hotel on the right. If you wish to stop to see Lyonshall's 13th-century church and the remains of the castle nearby, then once you pass a garden centre on the left, drive slowly, for the signposted lane to the left to the church will suddenly appear amongst the trees in about 200 yards.

21.   Lyonshall Church, Castle and Offa's Dyke

Lyonshall appears in the Domesday survey as Lenehalle, the first element now being spelt 'land' and said to relate to Kingsland, Monkland and Eardisland. Despite the fact that Lyonshall is just outside the catchments, these others all share the same second element because they lie in the 'land' between the rivers Lugg and Arrow. Lyonshall's second element derives from the Old English *halh*, meaning nook or hollow. When, at a time of hostilities against the Welsh, the original village of Lyonshall was set up close to its castle and church, Offa's Dyke had already been built in the 8th century, just $^{1}/_{4}$ mile to the south-west. Rare in Herefordshire, substantial traces of the bank are still to be seen some 12 centuries later. (Hereabouts the designated National Footpath follows a different line heading south-east from Kington).

The form and extent of the castle may partly be judged from the recently cleared bailey and moat, which may be seen from the churchyard path to the north-east of the church, but the rectangular outer bailey, a third enclosure and their moats are less easy to discern. The castle passed through many hands, but after damage by the Welsh it ceased to be occupied as a residence after the early 15th century. It is ironic that the church, expected to be under its protection, has greatly outlived the fortress. Although mostly from the 13th century, it retains the surviving window of a former Norman tower. Very much later, in 1820, the horsedrawn tramroad came this way, and opposite the church there is still a row of

Lyonshall Church, with the castle in the trees to the right

cottages known as The Wharf, partly also the Weymouth Arms, with which it is associated as a depot. After 40 years, some of the trackbed was used by the GWR and just down the road the A480 passes between rail bridge abutments, past the converted Lyonshall station building on the Titley to Eardisley line, which was closed in 1940. After devastating losses from the Black Death in the 14th century, the present village had grown in this direction from the church and at one time supported eight pubs and

Offa's Dyke at Lyonshall

other amenities. Unhappily, and typically, the village shop closed in the 1990s, but after a worrying gap there is again a post office and the 16th-century Royal George continues as the surviving pub.

This is a good place from which to reach the well defined length of Offa's Dyke, by following the minor road opposite the Royal George in a south-westerly direction for about half a mile when the Dyke is reached. Another is from the church car park partly via the footpath leading towards Lynhales nursing home.

The tour turns right off the A44 opposite the church to join the A480 and passes through the village and Burgoynes long-established marquee and tent hire establishment on the right. Like Kington, Lyonshall is one of 14 villages and places of interest along the 50 miles-long Black and White Village Trail and the A480 leads towards another, Sarnesfield, at the A4112 crossroads, on which you turn left. The main point of interest in this village is the church, reached after a couple of hundred yards along the A4112 on the left, but parking is difficult as it is on a bend of a busy road.

Not always open, the 13th-century church of St. Mary has two points of interest that can be seen from the outside. The west tower, built in *c*.1300, was specially designed to provide a fresh supply of protein for the rector from more than 100 nesting-holes, whilst the final resting place of John Abel (see below) is a tomb chest just outside the entrance porch.

22.   Sarnesfield Church and John Abel—The King's Carpenter

John Abel (1577-1674) designed his own plain tomb chest in the churchyard, and the fading epitaph he composed tells that he was an architect—or, as he preferred, 'architector':

> His line and rule, so death concludes, are lock'd up in store;
> Build they who list, or they who wist, for he can build no more.

As well as small effigies of himself and his two wives, there is a panel depicting the instruments of his art, his square, rule and compasses. During 97 years of a largely unknown career he must have built many fine domestic buildings in and around Herefordshire, although little now remains. He designed and built timber-framed market halls at Kington, Brecon and Church Stretton and these have gone, but still to be seen are his buildings arguably at Ledbury, and Leominster (although the latter is no longer where he put it (pp.52-3). His most enduring church restoration work is at Abbey Dore (p.219) and possibly Vowchurch and there are still parts of the first Grammar School which he built of stone at Kington. For something completely different he devised a hand-operated mill for gun-powder and suitable for grain which aided the beleaguered Royalist garrison at Hereford during the 1645 siege—earning him at 68 his honorary title of The King's Carpenter from King Charles I.

The A4112 continues towards Leominster, but on the second part of a double bend about 1½ miles beyond Sarnesfield and which has a garage on the left, turn right onto the B4350 for Weobley (pronounced 'Webbly'). The brick workhouse of 1837 appears on the left within a couple of hundred yards at Whitehill. Early in the 20th-century, the village was a mecca for tramps, for attached to the workhouse it boasted a 'Spike'. Vagrants unable to afford the few coppers for a lodging house bed were first ordered to bath in a horse-trough contraption (legally the water had to be changed after every sixth bather) before spending the night on straw in a cell. A rude early call was grudgingly followed by the reduction of about 2 hundredweight of stone to sizes suitable to fill potholes, before their threadbare clothes were returned to them. The buildings have since been used as council offices and are now private flats. After another ½ mile turn left into Bell Square, once called The Docks when a stream ran across.

Here is the 14th-century Manor House, thought to be the oldest surviving house in Weobley and for contrast, look out on the left for a late 20th-century half-timbered example of Herefordshire domestic architecture and craftsmanship. Then right at the Red Lion inn to reach the centre of the village for more of the finest 'magpie' architecture of the country.

23.   Weobley

Old as they are, the various buildings did not always look as they do now, for in the 19th-century, many, including the Red Lion, were covered with plaster and pebbles. And before the invention of 'Brilliant White' paint, for routine maintenance of oak frames and wattle and daub panels it was more usual and effective to apply a periodic limewash covering. Until 1943 there were more black and white houses in what is now the open space in the village centre, when a baker's oven caught fire and they were burnt down. On Market Pitch, immediately to the south opposite the Olde Salutation inn there had also been a market hall—but this had gone by 1860. In 1999 Weobley won the National Village of the Year Award, and to mark the occasion local artist Walenty Pytel produced his striking metal sculpture of a magpie. The commanding spire of the Church of St. Peter and St. Paul is regarded as one of the finest in England and can be seen from many directions, sometimes appearing like a stone moon rocket set for take off, whilst the architecture of the church dates from Norman, Early English and Late English and subsequent periods. It contains some interesting tombs, one of them with the alabaster effigy of Sir William Devereux who was killed in 1402 at the Battle of Pilleth (see p.152) and, controversially in the chancel an erect white marble statue of the Parliamentary commander, Colonel John Birch of Garnstone.

The Ley, a large private farmhouse built in 1589, was once described as the most perfect example of the Elizabethan Manor House type in England. Long the seat of the Brydges, it can be found by walking along the B4230 towards Hereford and turning right into a narrow cul-de-sac road. The sight of its intricate silver-grey (not painted black) timber framing and the play of the eight front gables should make the stroll very rewarding.

Walk up the hill from the Salutation Inn, pass the Unicorn on your left, then turn right (signed The Pyons and Wormsley) onto the Hereford Road. On the left is The Throne which, as the former Unicorn Inn, then the Crowne Inn, provided King Charles I with half-board in September 1645, following his part in raising the siege of Hereford. This was not long before the tiny

Weobley Church

Old Grammar School, 'a very good example of Renaissance timber-framing', was built almost opposite. Now private, it is said to retain a large whipping post from the good old days! Some time afterwards, the stone-built Castle House appeared next door, and until her death in 1928 was the home of Ella Mary Leather. In 1912 she compiled and published *The Folk Lore of Herefordshire*, the epic 300 page book of superstitions, customs and traditional carols, ballads and songs, and in 1920 the ever popular *Twelve Traditional Carols of Herefordshire*, in collaboration with Ralph Vaughan Williams and his wife.

The castle site behind these houses can be reached by returning towards the Salutation Inn, but before descending the slope, turning left onto the path between the houses to enter the site of the former oval shaped bailey. Parts of the enclosure measure up to 20ft. high and the large mounds ahead outline the walls, keep, moat and even a cockpit of Weobley Castle. It has existed from *c.*1138 and was almost immediately seized by King Stephen (1135-1154) in person during the civil war following his usurpation of the throne. Walter de Lacy became lord by early in the 13th century, and his father-in-law, William de Braose, based himself there during his rebellion against King John, engaging in a savage attack against the town of Leominster in *c.*1208/9. It was soon after then that de Lacy is thought to have rebuilt the castle in stone, but by the 16th century it had badly deteriorated and not long afterwards all the masonry above ground level had been redeployed to other uses in and around Weobley.

Leave Weobley on the Hereford road (passing the Unicorn, and then bearing right at the bend). Beyond Weobley the road climbs a steep hill then descends down Ravens Causeway. This is at Wormsley and since 1933 it has been the address of Herefordshire Golf Club, on the left of the road. It is not known for the absence of contours, a possible reason for a cardiac defibrillator kit at the clubhouse entrance! Continue downhill until the first right-hand junction, signposted Brinsop. A short distance down the road, on the left, is a drive leading to Brinsop Court. This is one of a very small number of surviving ancient moated houses, dating from the 14th-century. Further down the road, again to the left, is the short bumpy lane leading to St. George's Church.

24. Brinsop Court, Church and the Wordsworths

Entered in the Domesday Book as Hope—'and on the slope of a hill', Brinsop derived its earlier name *Brunshope* from a local family named Brun and the slopes of Merryhill and Credenhill. Dating from the 12th century and growing steadily from the 14th, 16th and 17th centuries, Brinsop Court is one of very few remaining moated manor houses. During the early 20th century much of it was carefully restored and rebuilt by Delavel Astley, 'felicitously preserved' as Pevsner put it in 1963. It was leased from 1824 by Thomas Hutchinson, brother of William Wordsworth's wife, Mary, and delighting in 'the romance of the house and its lovely woodland and pastoral surroundings', they visited many times between 1827 and 1845. So did members of their family and many are either commemorated by stained-glass windows at St. George's Church, or in the churchyard. The property has recently changed hands and, in a most

Top right: Brinsop Court; middle right: stained glass in memory of members of the Wordsworth family in the church; lower left: interior of the church; right: tympanum of St. George

160

enviable setting, the house seems likely to be divided into separate dwellings and nearby sturdy stone outbuildings converted into a further five units.

Half-a-mile down the road, the little church of St. George has traces of 12th-century work, but it dates mainly from the 13th and 14th centuries and is regarded as one of the most beautifully appointed in the diocese. Now removed to the north wall, a tympanum featuring St. George is just one example of work by the Herefordshire School of Romanesque Sculpture (p.226) to look for, the chancel screen dates from the late 14th/early 15th centuries and below the 14th-century glass of the east window, the altar reredos is of alabaster sculpted by an Italian artist. A north vestry, south porch and west bell-tower were added in 1866, when much of the old church was sensitively restored and refurnished to preserve the best of the ancient features—and for £1,000 to save this gem of a church from certain ruin. Earthworks covering some 4 acres around the church and surrounding buildings are thought to indicate a deserted medieval village and to the north-east of the church there is an interesting rhomboidal-shaped feature, surrounded by a moat.

Returning to the road, turn left and shortly afterwards left again onto the A480 for Hereford and head for Credenhill, past an abandoned snail farm on the right. Opposite the small green, set beneath a spreading chestnut tree at the entrance to the main village street, and some attractive black and white houses, turn left up the drive towards the church car park. Beyond is the red brick Credenhill Court. Built in 1760 for the Ecroyd family, it was the home of Polish refugees during and after the Second World War and many ended their days there and are buried at nearby St. Mary's churchyard. It sits on the lower slopes beneath Credenhill Park Wood and high above, hidden within a dense cover of trees, was the capital hillfort occupied by a Celtic tribe some 2,400 years ago.

25.   Credenhill

During the Iron Age, Herefordshire, especially the west of the county, contained several hillforts. One of the largest was Credenhill, covering nearly 50 acres, and huge ramparts were formed at 600ft. above sea level. They are still visible along a 1¼ miles long footpath circuit, but unfortunately ill-judged conifer planting in the 1960s and dense vegetation have mantled much of the earthwork. (In 2002 a successful appeal enabled the hillfort and Park Wood to be purchased and managed sensitively for greater public access). It has been suggested that Credenhill camp may have been the capital of a territory broadly corresponding to modern Herefordshire—and that before the arrival of the Romans up to 4,000 people could have dwelt there. (This is equal to the 2001 population of Bromyard and 70% more than that of Kington). They will have left much for future archaeologists to find.

Credenhill was the first of the three 'capital' settlements in the vicinity, the second followed about a century after the expeditions of Julius Caesar to Britain in 55-54 BC, when the conquest was consolidated by military centres. In the face of tough opposition by the resident tribesmen, as noted by Tacitus, *Magnis* (now Kenchester)

On the rampart of Credenhill hillfort

161

was built late in the 1st century AD in the shadow of Credenhill and at the point of contact of connecting roads leading through Herefordshire. One came from Stretton Grandison and continued westwards to Clyro, whilst Watling Street West, ran from Chester in the north, past Leintwardine, through the centre of Credenhill and on to Abergavenny and Caerleon. An irregular-shaped bastion-walled town of 20 acres, *Magnis* comprised houses, shops and good amenities. An artist's impression of *Magnis*, an example of its mosaic paving and other relics may be seen in Hereford city museum. The town of some 500 residents lasted until early in the 5th century and it was then abandoned. Apart from a slight rise in the ground, there is little left to be seen of the buried remains, or of any suburban extensions, and again there is still a great deal more to be discovered.

The third settlement in the neighbourhood appeared during the Saxon period just over 4 miles to the south-east of Credenhill, at Hereford, close to the two already established fording-places.

Glass depicting Sts. Thomas Becket and Thomas Cantilupe in Credenhill Church

St. Mary's, Credenhill—and the cider industry

The city and its cathedral can clearly be seen from the hill, and from the churchyard on its lower slopes. St. Mary's Church dates from the 13th-century and has a distinctive triple chancel arch, leading in the chancel to a stained glass window of *c.*1310 representing the saintly archbishop Thomas Becket of Canterbury and bishop Thomas Cantilupe of Hereford, their hands raised in blessing. At the cathedral, the shrine of St. Thomas of Hereford, who was canonised in 1310, attracted many pilgrims, and hence wealth, which played a large part in the fortunes of medieval Hereford.

A quite different source of wealth for the county came from fruit culture and the production of cider and pectin. H.P. Bulmer Limited, signs of which may be seen on the western outskirts of the city, was founded in 1887 by the younger son of the rector of Credenhill after firstly achieving successes with apples from the rectory orchard and secondly following up his mother's advice that 'neither food nor drink ever goes out of fashion'. Eventually the company produced almost 60% of UK cider, whilst after the last war pectin production was instrumental in sustaining the nation's vital jam ration. One of Percy Bulmer's descendents still lives in the Old Rectory.

Thomas Traherne—'in the pursuance of felicity'

In St. Mary's Church every Trinity Sunday the works of the Reverend Thomas Traherne (1637-1674) are remembered. The son of a shoemaker, he was born in Hereford but soon lost his parents and was brought up by Philip Traherne, an innkeeper who was twice mayor of the city. After taking his BA at Oxford he was presented to the living of Credenhill in 1657, was ordained following the Restoration and remained rector for the rest of his life, although finally not in residence. He was a writer of metaphysical works which classed him with Henry Vaughan (p.173) and George Herbert (p.12) and was initially known for his *Centuries of Meditations*. The 3rd Century is regarded as autobiographical and has famously been set to music by Gerald Finzi as *Dies Natalis*. Much of his poetry written at Credenhill was lost until discovered on a London bookstall in 1896, only to be first attributed to Henry Vaughan before further scholarship revealed the true origin.

One poem, *Bells*, clearly relates to the sound of bells chiming from the area of Credenhill and one verse mentions 'The Minster', presumably Hereford Cathedral which was, and is, visible from his church. The whole scene is thought to evoke Christmas morning in either 1660 or 1661, and in 1976 the words (here in original spelling, punctuation and capitalisation) were set by Paul Drayton in a Three Choirs Festival commission and called: *Canticle of Bells*:

> Hark how remoter Parishes do sound!
> Far off they ring
> For thee, my King
> Ev'n round about the Town:
> The Churches scattered over all the Ground
> Serv for thy Prais, who art with Glory crowned.
> This City is an Engin great
> That makes my pleasure more compleat
> The Sword, the Mace, the Magistrate,
> To honor Thee attend in State;
> The whole Assembly sings;
> The Minster rings.

Certainly the 595th mayor of Hereford was so attended at the cathedral for the Opening of the 249th annual Three Choirs Festival in 1976.

Return down the drive and turn left onto the A480. After the departure of the Romans and Saxons, Credenhill was not to see the last of a military presence, for in 1940 a new force arrived. The Royal Air Force was not occupied in flying duties there, but in technical training, torpedo maintenance, aircrew officers' school, administration, accountancy, catering, trade training and apprenticeship. The A480 runs right through the Station, the part on the left being mostly married quarters. The RAF moved at the end of the 20th century and their place was quickly taken by 22nd Special Air Services Regiment—making a short move from their former base at Bradbury Lines in Hereford. It would probably be wise not to linger along this section of road, but continue towards Stretton Sugwas, crossing the east/west Roman Road, where early in 2004 archaeologists unearthed a preserved Roman cobbled roadway underneath the existing road together with other 2000-year-old artefacts. Joining the A438 at King's Acre for the final run into the city along Whitecross Road, past the entrances to the huge Bulmers cider works.

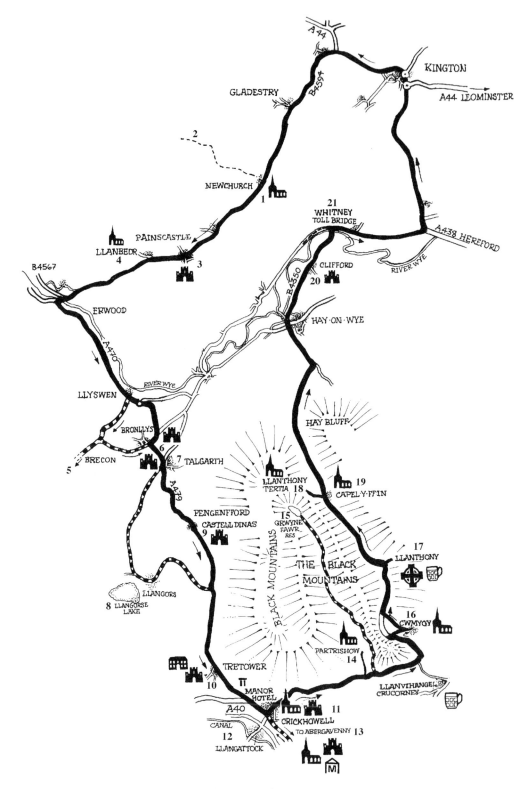

Outline map for Tour 7
The numbers 1 to 21 relate to the boxed information given within the tour

Tour 7   Radnorshire and into the Black Mountains

This tour starts at Kington and begins by visiting places connected with the diarist Francis Kilvert before taking in castles in the area of the Brecon Beacons National Park around the flanks of the Black Mountains. After visiting Crickhowell the route visits a couple of intriguing churches before heading up the Vale of Ewyas (see Note below). It passes through Llanthony with its ruined priory (in the cellars of which is a pub) and Capel-y-ffin, rising to 1765ft. below Lord Hereford's Knob at Gospel Pass with its extensive views northwards. It then follows a winding descent through about 1,400ft to Hay-on-Wye, where it leaves the Park as it heads for Clifford and Whitney toll-bridge and thence returns to Kington. The total distance is about 75 miles. Apart from wide views at several points along the route, there are villages and small towns which can be visited, and several churches, castles and other places of interest. There's endless scope to leave the vehicle and gain some fresh air in the hills.

Along the way there are opportunities to branch off to various places of further interest, including: at Newchurch to the source of the River Arrow at Glascwm (just over 4 miles, plus a walk of just over 1 mile); at Talgarth to Llangorse Lake (an extra 3 miles for the loop); at Crickhowell to continue on to Abergavenny (6 miles); at Partrishow to drive up the Lower Grwyne Fawr Vale through Mynydd Ddu Forest to the Grwyne Fawr Reservoir (6 miles by vehicle and 2 miles on foot); and at Stanton to turn right for Llanvihangel Crucorney and the ancient Skirrid Inn, where you could order a hangman's lunch (1 mile).

The journey is on a great mixture of roads: some wide A roads, some B roads, one of which varies constantly in width, and several country lanes, some of which are very narrow—see Note below.

NOTE: The route up the Vale of Ewyas and through Gospel Pass to Hay-on-Wye is very narrow—especially from Llanthony—and there are not many motor vehicle passing places. It is best therefore to avoid Sundays, Bank Holidays and other busy periods. Even then, consideration for other road users calls for care, courtesy and a fair share of reversing skills.

Head towards Rhayader on the A44 from Kington, and the Welcome to Wales/Powys (Radnorshire) border sign appears about 2 miles along, quickly followed by a sign pointing to the left for Painscastle on the B4594 road, onto which you turn left. This leads through Burlingjobb, close to quarries on the right, and then starts the climb below rounded Hanter Hill and alongside Hergest Ridge to Gladestry. This scattered village stands at the foot of the ridge and that of Yewtree Bank—from which it takes its name of 'Gladestree'. It is very good walking territory and the refuelling provided at the Royal Oak inn is much appreciated. The climb continues to a high point about 2 miles further on, near a place shown as Blaencerde on the OS map. This is about 1,200ft. above sea level and some 650ft. above the starting point of this tour at Kington by-pass in Herefordshire. Already there are sweeping views over the mountains which encapsulate the wildness and beauty of Radnorshire, and you can certainly tell that you are no longer in England.

After a steep drop for half a mile and past the old Congregational chapel on the right, a small bridge leads over the infant River Arrow and the road reaches the bottom of a deep valley at Newchurch.

Should there be time for a detour, it is possible to visit the source of the River Arrow by following signpost directions to Glascwm along a minor road for about $3^1/_2$ miles to the tiny hamlet. There is then a walk of about one mile to the actual spot between Little Hill and Cwm Kesty. This is another part of the countryside well known to Kilvert during the idyllic days of his curacy at Clyro between 1865-72.

The B4594 climbs out of Newchurch and there are again hills all around, making not only for energetic walking but also ideal horse riding. This caters for most of the family and is widely avail-

1. Newchurch, and Emmeline Vaughan

Opposite St. Mary's church there is the old Rectory, where Kilvert's friend, the Reverend David Vaughan (1819-1903) held his school, at a time when it was not a defrocking offence for the young curate from Clyro to kiss a pupil in class for getting her sums right! At their father's farm he once surprised the Vaughan girls castrating lambs, so that on 6 May 1870 Kilvert was to write: 'Glad however that Emmeline was not present'. Tragically his most favoured of the rector's daughters died when only 14, and much later, in 1876, he wrote: 'The mountain was full of the memories of sweet Emmeline Vaughan'. These words appear on her gravestone in the churchyard opposite the rectory. South of the church, and built over many years between *c.*1490 and the late 18th century, the Great House is still there. It is famed for a two-bay cruck hall, with a span of 28ft.—the widest known in Wales, and all forms a side of the farmyard sited next to the Michaelchurch-on-Arrow road. The blacksmith's forge has gone and so has the Royal Oak inn, and there are no shops or cafés. Yet it is still possible for a parched hiker to find a refreshing tea or coffee, for at the rear of the church the hospitable congregation has provided an electric kettle of water, instant coffee and tea bags—as well as some biscuits. Close by, the font dates from the 10th/11th centuries and a roughly circular cemetery is said to indicate pre-Christian origins—although the church itself was rebuilt in 1856-7. When the great yew tree

Emmeline Vaughan's grave and Newchurch Church

high above Emmeline's grave fell in the great storm of 1991, it had reached the age of 1,100 years, and some of its wood still lives on, crafted into the church offertory plate and a handrail.

2. The rivers of the area—a 'fairy land'

An important tributary of the Lugg, the river Arrow is important in its own right and supports a wide range of wildlife. After issuing near Glascwm it is soon joined by the Glasnant, lyrically described by Kilvert after a visit on 13th October, 1871:

> The beautiful Glasnant came leaping and rushing down its lovely dingle, a flood of molten silver and crystal fringed by groups of silver birches and alders, and here and there a solitary tree rising from the bright green sward along the banks of the brook and drooping over the stream which seemed to come out of a fairy land of blue valley depths and distances and tufted wood of green and gold and crimson and russet brown.

The combined waters, with those of other un-named streams and springs, soon reach Newchurch, flowing on then through Michaelchurch-on-Arrow, Kington, Eardisland, Monkland and Leominster—where they join the River Lugg.

able, including here at the Bryngwyn Riding Centre. This is signposted to the right about a mile out of Newchurch and offers hacking, lessons and accommodation. The road then passes through Rhosgoch to reach Painscastle. There is not much happening here now, but it was not always so tranquil.

3.   Troubled times at Painscastle

There is something of a clue about the past on private land just outside the village. High up in a field to the left above the B4594 road to Erwood there are large grass-covered mounds and deep ditches. They are all that remain of a substantial motte and bailey established as part of Norman efforts to control the border country early in the 12th century. It seems likely that a castle was built there by Pain fitz John and that this is how the village came to be named. Painscastle was subsequently the scene of much conflict between Norman and Welsh forces, coming into the possession of the Braoses in 1195 with great loss of Welsh life. The warrior poet, Prince Gwenwynwyn of Powys led a fruitless attack on the castle in 1198 and after a number of subsequent exchanges it was taken in 1231 by Henry III, who rebuilt it in stone (during his months of residence also, it is said, commanding the local people to 'bestir themselves' to destroy the exceptional number of wolves in the area). Later, in the 13th century it was to be destroyed and rebuilt again, and was effective as a garrison for the Earl of Warwick against Owain Glyndwr as late as 1401.

The views along this drive are richly varied, but for something really exceptional there is a detour to the Begwns by turning left in Painscastle down the road signposted to Clyro. After half a mile, just over a bridge, turn right and then sharp left—ignoring the sign to Llanddewi-fach church. Be careful, for the lane is narrow and steep and you must be prepared to give way to farm traffic. After half a mile and a cattle grid you emerge on the open hillside and in less than another half-mile it is possible to park, and walk up to the summit on the right, to enjoy the really breathtaking panorama as far as Hay Bluff, the Black Mountains and Brecon Beacons. Then about turn, and drive back up the lane to Painscastle.

There is still a United Reformed chapel in Painscastle, but the nearest Anglican church is 1½ miles further along the B4594 at Llanbedr, signposted to the right if you wish to visit it. It is the 14th-/15th- centuries church of St. Peter's, Llanbedr Painscastle.

4.   Llanbedr and 'The Solitary'

Llanbedr Church

Being well within Kilvert's walking range from Clyro, the diarist was able to write of a visit to meet the vicar in 1872. Ordained in 1834 after graduating at Cambridge, the Reverend John Price had moved to the parish in 1859. There was no vicarage, a meagre stipend and he quickly became a recluse, living 'as a common labourer' in three old bathing huts which served as study, bedroom and kitchen. After they had accidentally burnt down, he moved to a small stone hut at the foot of Llanbedr Hill, where he passed the rest of his lonesome days in a state of utter squalor and disorder until shortly before he died in 1895, having to pay tramps and vagabonds to attend the church services. Yet among his published temporal achievements were two successful methods of shorthand. Today there is a special sign near the memorial cross and grave of Kilvert's lonely host, who he called 'The Solitary of Llanbedr'. Not far from the church there is now a fine vicarage to the right of the road for Erwood.

The drovers, and shoes for the oxen

For more than six centuries, great herds of Welsh black cattle had been driven from farms further west, across the Wye and along different trails on their way to the fattening grounds and butchers of England. Many crossed the river near Erwood and were then taken to shoeing forges at Painscastle to be fitted for the long journey over Clyro Hill to Rhydspence and on to Hereford—and often as far as London and Kent. Being cloven-hoofed, they required eight shoes, or 'cues', which were twin arcs of narrow metal. As a main clearing house, Painscastle must have provided grazing and water for herds of 300 to 400 at a time and sometimes far more, and also overnight accommodation for the drovers. There were six inns in the village up to the 1860s, including the Maesllwch—an inn and forge combined, and one aptly named the Black Ox. Then came the railways and, with them, the rapid eclipse of the drovers. Now there is little to show for all the former commerce—except for sturdy old houses with names such as The Old Post Office and The Old Shop and telling evidence of the drover trails through the mountains.

From Llanbedr the B4594 first descends gently—until just before a cattle grid past the right turn for Llandeilo Graban. Then, after dodging the first of many slow-witted, jay-walking sheep it is necessary for motorists to prepare nerves, gears and brakes for a challenging zig-zag drop of about 400ft. to the road junction below, over what seems to be little more than the same distance.

To help restore some colour to the cheeks for the next leg of the journey, tea and coffee are often served at the Craft Centre based in Erwood's former Cambrian railway station. This is on the left, a short distance along the Aberedw road to the right and open from mid February onwards.

Otherwise, after reaching the B4567 at the bottom of the hill, the route leads to Erwood Bridge and the A470 on which you turn left. Follow this to Llyswen—you can read about places along this stretch in boxes 8 and 9 on page 116—where you continue straight through the village on the A479 and climb to its junction with the A438 at Penmaes, where the northern foothills of the Black Mountains can be seen straight ahead. Turn right on the A438 towards Brecon and the National Park.

5. Brecon and the National Park

Left: Brecon street scene; above: the remains of the castle's hall adjoins the Castle Hotel

Set between the Brecon Beacons and Mynydd Eppynt, the historic cathedral town of Brecon straddles the River Usk at its confluence with the Honddu—which accounts for its Welsh name of Aberhonddu. With much of interest extending back to Roman times, it was the county town until 1974 and is still the main market, shopping and social centre of the Park. Its central streets keep essentially to the medieval pattern, whilst some of the castle ruins now form part of an hotel. High above the town, the mainly 13th- to 14th-century church is described as 'the most splendid and dignified church in mid-Wales' and was once the centrepiece of the Benedictine priory of St. John the Evangelist, becoming Brecon Cathedral when the diocese was formed in 1923. Other attractions include the Brecknock Museum and Gallery, Royal Regiment of Wales Museum and the red brick Theatr Brycheiniog—a modern 436 seat theatre and arts centre well sited at the new Basin of the Monmouthshire and Brecon Canal. By contrast, the fine seven-arched stone Usk bridge of 1535 has been shamefully widened by the use of a grossly insensitive modern concrete and steel parapet. On the west bank, just beyond it on the left, is Christ College, a public school which was founded on a directive from King Henry VIII in 1541. It has a striking collegiate chapel and had been the Dominican friary of St. Nicholas. The National Park and tourist information centre is served by a large car park at the former cattle market in the town centre, but anyone visiting the Brecon Beacons should also make an early call at the highly regarded National Park Visitor Centre, Libanus. A short distance off the A470, 5 miles south-west of Brecon, it has been fittingly designed on Mynydd Illtud common, where it commands outstanding mountain views, taking in Pen y fan (2,900ft.), the highest peak in south Wales.

Less than half a mile from Penmaes along the A479, turn left along a narrow one-way road, signposted Abergavenny (*Y Fenni*), at Bronllys. This village suffers from being split by a busy trunk road and another main road from the south.

6.   Bronllys

Bronllys Castle

St. Mary's, Bronllys is unusual for Wales in that it has a detached tower and as in Herefordshire, which has seven of the few other such churches in Britain, it is of medieval origin. Like many during times of border assaults, it served as a refuge for women, children and even animals. In 1887, the 12th-/13th-century nave and chancel suffered disruptive visitations of the Victorian architect 'restorers', but there are still interesting old features in the church. They include the ancient font and a 16th-century Tudor screen, typically between nave and sanctuary depicting a green man, his foliate head sprouting leaves from the mouth.

Served by a convenient layby opposite the pathway entrance, Bronllys Castle is signposted to the left just beyond the village and is cared for by CADW—Welsh Historic Monuments. It is on high ground above the junction of the Llynfi with its tributaries Ennig and Dulas and consists of a 16m. high 13th- century round tower with a vaulted basement and a high level entrance. It is thought to be on the site of a late 12th-century motte, established by Richard fitz Pons of Clifford, Herefordshire, and was often modified until 1521, when it became 'beyond repair'.

169

Just beyond Bronllys the tour route enters the Brecon Beacons National Park, where it will remain until leaving Hay-on-Wye. Comprising 520 square miles of remote mountains, rolling moorlands and deep river valleys, the Park offers many recreational opportunities such as walking, cycling, pony-trekking, pot-holing and caving.

7. Talgarth

A tower twinned with that at Bronllys has not survived, but there is still a 13th-century, 9.5m.-high pele tower and former look-out post at the Ennig bridge, now the home of the Tourist Information Centre. Dedicated to a local saint, shared locally with Llyswen, the 15th-century church of St. Gwendoline is large and with the churchyard is believed to occupy the enclosure which once contained the earliest inhabitants of Talgarth. It has a famous connection with the Methodist Revival from 1735 through the charismatic Hywel Harris, with one of his celebrated converts, William Williams Pantycelyn, arguably Wales's greatest hymn-writer, responsible for 'Guide me, O thou great Redeemer' among more than 900 works of inspirational prose, and with the present conference and retreat centre in the parish at Trefeca. Harris (d.1773) is buried, along with his wife Ann, within the church in front of the altar rails. In 1873 the church interior was over-restored by the architect, not for his first time by Thomas Nicholson. Lower down, much of the village dates from the 19th century and at one time it contained some 65 shops and many chapels and pubs. Built in 1900, the large Talgarth Sanatorium used to provide employ-

Pele tower at Talgarth

ment for much of the population and the local economy also enjoyed the advantages of a tramroad route, then a rail service as well as the important road between the Wye and Usk valleys. Now Talgarth is much quieter, although it still operates a market, serves as an important centre for the local farming community and acts as a tourist base at the north-western end of the Black Mountains.

8. Llangorse Lake

Llangorse Lake with the Brecon Beacons beyond

For water sport enthusiasts the main local centre is at Llangorse, the largest natural lake in south Wales. It is $1\frac{1}{2}$ miles long and has a shoreline of about 4 miles, providing for sailing, rowing, canoeing, water-ski-ing, wind-surfing and other such activities, mostly originating from the northern shore. The lake also supports rich wildlife, especially birds, and conservationists are concerned about disturbance and the other adverse effects caused by so many activities.

From Talgarth there is a chance to take a detour to Llangorse Lake. If you wish to do this, take the B4560 to Llangorse passing Trefeca, and from Llangorse take a minor road through Cwm Sorgwin, between Mynydd Llangorse (1,661ft.) and Mynydd Froed (1,997ft.) to rejoin the 'main' tour once you reach the A470, on which you turn right.

The main route itself turns right at the T junction in Talgarth, crosses a bridge and then bears left to take on the serpentine climb to reach 1,059ft. at Pengenffordd. On the way up and to the left there are signs to Talgarth's Black Mountains Gliding Club, and yet another recreational opportunity which claims to be the UK's premier ridge, wave and thermal soaring site. Because of the favourable position and climatic conditions it is able to offer training flight times of at least 45 minutes for much of the year.

---

9. Castell Dinas

Plainly visible above the road summit at Pengenffordd are the remains of what must have been the highest Norman castle in Britain, certainly in Wales and England. Those prepared to tackle a 400ft. climb from the convenient road-side layby to the site at 1,475ft. above sea level will discover more signs of walling and stone fragments and see the whole involved layout of the 12th-century Castell Dinas, surrounded by a deep dry moat. It has the rare distinction of being one of the few castles, as

Castell Dinas

well as churches and other major buildings within the borders, which have not been badly 'knocked about' by the ruthlessly destructive Owain Glyndwr—for it is said that it served as one of his operational bases. During the Iron Age the whole eminence was occupied as a large hillfort and vantage point, whereas nowadays in the 21st century it can be regularly overlooked from the soaring gliders of Talgarth.

From Pengenffordd and the Castle Inn, the A479 makes a long and steady descent of over 800ft. down the Rhiangoll valley to Crickhowell, starting between the peak of Mynydd Troed on the right and Allt-mawr (great cliff), the western-most of the four principal ridges of the Black Mountains, on the left. Passing another riding school it soon confronts Pen Tir, another huge mountain, before skirting to the left.

The Black Mountains

The Black Mountains rise abruptly to over 2,200ft. from the level of the Wye valley at their north-western extremity. Above, an extensive plateau connects to seven ridges, the chief four of which run parallel for about ten miles towards the south. Geologically they are composed of Old Red Sandstone, aged about 400 million years, except for the most westerly, the Pen-allt-mawr ridge, which overlooks the Rhiangoll valley and A479. As the name of the peak at its southern end suggests, Pen-cerrig-calch is capped with limestone and it is sometimes known as Chalkstones Head. The next ridge is called after Pen-y-gader fawr (2624ft.), starting from Pen-y-Mallwyd—the highest part of the escarpment. Between the two ridges runs the secluded Grwyne Fechan valley, whilst the eastern side of this 'Head

---

171

of the great chair' ridge descends to the Grwyne Fawr valley. The third, Ffwddog ridge, rises to over 2,200ft. to the east, and descends to the Ewyas, or Llanthony, valley. This in turn is separated from the Olchon and part of the Monnow valley by the Hatterall ridge, most easterly of the four, which at its northern end slopes abruptly at Hay Bluff. The frequent dark appearance from the Herefordshire direction of the steep eastern face of this long hogsback is said to account for the title of the range, The Black Mountains.

After a drive of about four miles between the mountains, and soon after the village of Cwmdu and The Farmers Arms, the scene begins to change and the vista to the right gradually opens out across the Usk valley. Six hundred years ago a drive by any hostile Welsh military force down the same Rhiangoll Pass would quickly have been faced by a formidable obstacle. For a major castle, with a great stone tower, had been placed to guard the Usk valley and control the strategic route through the mountains to Talgarth and the Wye valley. Certainly in 1404 it thwarted Owain Glyndwr, who could have been operating from Castell Dinas. The village of Tretower (Tretwr to the Welsh) obtained its curiously bi-lingual name from the same round tower, and this prominent feature can still be seen from the A479, to the right of the approach to this old coaching stop.

10.   Tretower Castle and Court, and Henry Vaughan, 'Silurist'

Tretower Castle (above) and Court (right)

A Norman earth and timber castle was first built towards the end of the 11th century and strengthened in stone as a shell keep in the middle of the 12th. This was not a tower but a circular stone enclosure containing domestic apartments and built to replace wooden palisades. Today's large round three-storey tower was placed within what was left, along with added walls to the castle bailey, after it was largely demolished by the Welsh in the early 13th century. However as tension eased over the following century the cramped conditions within the rugged stronghold became less suffered and early in the 14th century a more comfortable and expansive defended house was under construction nearby. This coincided after 215 years with the ending of the Norman Picard control and there was then a succession of other owners until the 1450s, when Sir William Herbert presented Tretower to Roger Vaughan. The Vaughans were prominent local landowners and although Roger Vaughan, knighted in 1464, came to be beheaded at Chepstow in 1471, the family was to retain the seat for more than 330 years. Starting with the north range, they made many additions and refinements to create 'one of the most complete and interesting great houses of the medieval period in Wales that time has spared'.

In the 17th-century, the illustrious Tretower Vaughans produced one of the greatest of Welsh poets. After Oxford, Henry Vaughan (1622-1695) had read law and medicine before returning to Breconshire, quietly to practise medicine for the rest of his life. On his rounds close to the River Usk around Scethrog he found inspiration there to write poetry which, after John Donne, came to rank him with Richard Crashaw, Thomas Traherne (see p.162) and George Herbert (a distant relative) (see p.12) as one of a select group of four 17th-century Metaphysical poets. In literary circles known as Silurist after the Celtic Silures tribe of the region, he was regarded as a mystic of nature—'each element conveying to him some aspect of the divine spirit'. Invoking the Usk he loved so well, he once wrote:

Tretower Court

> In all thy journey to the mayne
> No nitrous clay or brimstone veyne,
> Mix with thy stream, but may they pass
> Free as the air and clear as glass.

When he died, Henry Vaughan was buried not far from Tretower at Llansantffraed churchyard where his brother was rector, within sound of his beloved River Usk. In 1783, just under 80 years later, the Vaughan line died out and Tretower was sold and became a farm. Afterwards it had several successive owners and was eventually bought in very poor condition by the Brecknock Society. After much repair work, which still continues, it is now protected by CADW. There are usually special events there between March and October, when it is open to the public.

The A479 continues downwards for another mile, until it joins the A40, on which you turn left towards Crickhowell and Abergavenny. At the junction to the left is the Nantyffin Cider Mill Inn, converted from a 16th-century cider mill and once a drovers' hostelry—whilst further down the road on the same side at the head of a drive is The Manor Hotel. The hotel is on a site which has been continuously occupied for 800 years. Excavations in 1978 at the hotel

The Manor Hotel

entrance from the A40 revealed an elaborate Stone Age chamber tomb dating from 4000-3000BC. It had already been robbed and there is now little left to see but some upright slabs and a rough outline in small blocks. Apart from an awful looking extension block, the house assumed its present appearance towards the end of the 18th century. It was the reputed birthplace of Sir George Everest

The burial chamber at the entrance to the Manor Hotel

(1790-1866) who, after service with the East India Company until 1830 became Surveyor General of India. During his time the world's highest mountain was surveyed and measured, and afterwards named Mount Everest in his honour.

Head through Crickhowell to the car park at the far end of the town centre, signposted off to the left on the road to Llanbedr.

Aspects of Crickhowell
Top left: The Bear Hotel with Crug Hywel in the distance; above: the remains of the castle; left: Bridge Street

12. Crickhowell

In 1804, George Everest had just entered his teens when Richard Fenton, a well-travelled poet and topographer, was quoted as saying that Crickhowell was 'the most cheerful looking town I ever saw'. This opinion could still hold good today, for despite the relentless impact of traffic on the London to Fishguard trunk road through High Street, its townscape has suffered relatively little when compared with many other places. On the opposite side of the main road from the car park are the ruins of *Alisby's* or Crickhowell Castle, the scene of many attacks by the Welsh until the 15th-century. They are on a public recreation and children's playground which was presented by a grieving father to perpetuate the memory of a son who fell in a much later conflict—at Cambrai in November 1917. St. Edmund's Church dates from the 14th-century and contains much of interest, not least the huge tablet of stone filling one side of the porch. To all who are about to enter it carries a pointed reminder about a whole string of relatives, close and distant, whom they must not marry!

The bridge across the Usk

Anyone disenchanted with shopping streets almost universally filled with the same national stores and logos, will find a refreshing change at Crickhowell. For it is quite difficult to find any multiples, and many of the town's wide selection of 18th- and 19th-century buildings are occupied by an attractive range of independent shops and businesses and there is fine Georgian architecture which is worth exploring. The Bear on High Street is a widely renowned coaching inn, dating back to 1432, and as well as brimming with historic character, it has shone in Great Britain and Wales Pub of the Year awards. Below the town the longest stone bridge in Wales was first mentioned in 1558 and has been rebuilt oddly, with 12 arches on one side and 13 on the other. It may be reached on foot down the steep, largely 18th-century, Bridge Street ending at the 16th-century Bridge End Inn, once a toll house. Another way is via New Road, just to the west of the town centre.

From Crickhowell the canal, river Usk and A40 all head south-eastwards for Abergavenny—which can be visited as a side excursion to the main route.

The canal at Llangattock

12.   Llangattock

Rising to the west above the river, rivalling the southern slopes of the Black Mountains on the far side of the Usk valley, is the Llangattock Escarpment. Scars of intensive 19th-century limestone quarrying are now fading and, with the geologically and botanically important Craig y Cilau National Nature Reserve of 1959 and its many cave systems, it creates an imposing skyline overlooking the village and Monmouthshire and Brecon Canal. Lime from the quarries was burnt in multiple kilns at the canal wharf until *c.*1920 and for a century, with the stone, was widely distributed along the canal and by connecting tramroads as far as Hereford and Kington for use in building, agriculture and steelmaking. The village and canal may be reached by making an immediate right turn off the A4077.

175

The main route itself continues by turning left at the exit from the car park at Crickhowell and winding up the narrow road above the Grwyne Fawr. The varied views of the receding Usk Valley are epic and so, towering above to the left, is the sight of Table Mountain. At 1481ft. above sea level—just 5ft. higher than the pre-Norman fort at Castell Dinas—the Iron Age rampart and ditch stronghold of Crug Hywel there has produced the English name for the Usk-side town below.

13. Abergavenny

Abergavenny Castle

Four large hills stand around the town—the Sugar Loaf (contrary to some opinions not an extinct volcano like Mount Fuji, but an outlier of the red sandstone Black Mountains, like Mynydd Troed seen earlier), Ysgyryd Fawr, Ysgyryd Fach and Blorenge and these are constantly in sight for many miles by anyone heading for the life and bustle of this busy market centre. Abergavenny (*Y Fenni*) has a long history from when the Romans established their fort of *Gobannium*. Its Norman record includes Camden's view that the castle 'has been oftner stain'd with the infamy of treachery than any other castle in Wales'. This doubtless has largely to do with an event in 1175 when William de Braose, a powerful member of the famous Marcher family, invited some 70 Welsh chieftains to a Christmas banquet, persuaded them to disarm as an act of good faith—and then had them all murdered at the tables! Fairly substantial remains of the castle still overlook the Usk and the later hunting lodge built at the high point in the castle grounds has been converted into a museum.

St. Mary's Priory Church was the former Benedictine church and has seen many sackings, Puritan cleansings and Victorian and subsequent 'modernisations'. But it continues to play an active part in the life of the town and is renowned for a Norman font, 24 choir stalls dating from the end of the 14th century and a fine collection of ancient treasures and medieval monuments. The most impressive of these are the 15th-century carved figure of Jesse, father of King David, and the tombs in the Lewis and Herbert chapels. The two earliest are those of Eva de Braose (1246), and of Christian Herbert (1307), one of the large family of the 14th and 15th century who lie in the nearby chapel in carved splendour. In

One of the tombs in St. Mary's Church, Abergavenny

complete contrast there is a wooden effigy of a warrior, clad in mail, who has been thought to be a George de Cantelupe, who died at the age of 20 in 1273.

Abergavenny is not best known for its architecture, the most prominent other feature there being the green copper-clad tower of its Town Hall of 1870. Good use is made of the theatre and the covered market hall below, which displays a wide range of local products—greatly augmented outside on each Tuesday, the main market day. This is when the town car parks and difficult one way street system, carrying the A40, are most under strain, and when it pays to get there early. The centre is well blessed with the shops expected in an important county market town and there is no shortage of eating-places and pubs—famously The Angel and The King's Head.

As is to be expected, the church at Llanbedr is dedicated to St. Peter (Bedr being Welsh for Peter) and its foundation is thought to date back to 1060. The village is at the foot of the Grwyne Fechan Valley, once described as 'a delightful epitome of the various perfections of moorland and upland dale and

wooded gorge'. The narrow road beyond, ending in a cul de sac, is not however suitable for motorists but there is much to be enjoyed by experienced hill walkers. A favourite route leads upwards below Pen Cerrig-calch and Pen Allt-mawr, across Cwm Banw and past the aptly named Hermitage to climb over the escarpment at Bwlch Trumau at 2023ft. before the steep drop down to Pengenffordd pass.

The Sugar Loaf, seen on this part of the tour

14.   The Church of Merthyr Issui at Partrishow

Partrishow Church, a wall-painting of 'Time' and a modern figure cast in aluminium

The rood screen

This mainly Tudor church is on a commanding but secluded hillside at the bottom of Grwyne Fawr and it managed to defy searches by Puritan iconoclasts, despite the proximity of a former main route from Abergavenny to Talgarth. This escape has preserved its greatest treasure, a splendid late 15th-century rood screen and loft of carved Irish oak. Wall paintings and texts include the figure of 'Time', a skeleton with scythe, hourglass and spade on the west nave wall, and a faint version of the Royal Arms on the north wall. There is a small chapel built onto the west wall which may mark the site of an earlier 11th-century church. Latin wording on the huge ancient font in the church suggests a link with that era. The old building alongside the path had a fireplace which helped to dry the priest's clothes during the service and probably acted as a stable for his horse.

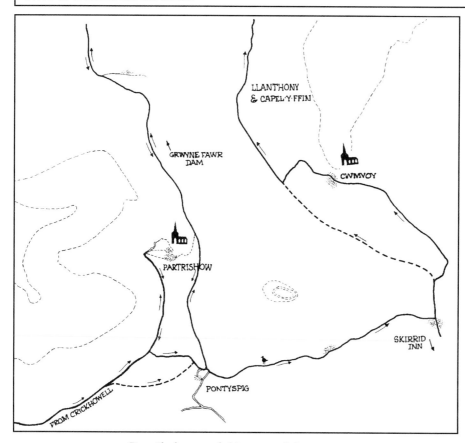

Detailed map of this part of the route

There is actually no record of any hermit in this valley (see box no. 17), but before the tour reaches Hay-on-Wye there will be lasting evidence of no less than three. The first of them appeared in the Dark Ages, when tradition claims that a holy man named Issui had a cell near Partrishow. This is where the road signs point as the route progresses eastwards below Sugar Loaf mountain, looking as impressive here as it does from every direction. It was named after the former conical shape of sugar loaves and, at 1,955ft., is said to be 'just the height for an afternoon's scramble'. Usually climbed from the south, there are several car parks part of the way up and many well-trodden trails to the summit, where the views on a clear day are well worth all the effort.

Nearer Partrishow, there are two roads signposted to the left and they combine to meet at a dingle. A Holy Well is still to be seen just below the road at the sharp bend and Issui is said to have had his cell close by. A steep climb leads to a small car park by the modern stone lych gate at Partrishow Church.

Back down the hill at Pontyspig, near Pont Escob Mill, is the foot of the Grwyne Valley road. There is a connection here (unsurprisingly one of several during these tours) with Archbishop Baldwin and Giraldus Cambrensis who were on their recruiting journey for the Third Crusade and coming from Talgarth to Abergavenny in 1188. For not only is the archbishop said to have preached at Partrishow Church, but the Welsh name of the bridge and mill significantly translates as 'bishop'. Their way down the narrow Grwyne Fawr trackway probably remained in much the same state until the early 20th-century, and until Abertillery's pressing need for a lot of water.

---

15. The Grwyne Fawr Dam and Reservoir

Grwyne Fawr Dam

The first survey for a potential dam started in 1906 and by 1912 a new access road had driven into the heart of the Black Mountains for 10 miles to service what would then be the highest masonry reservoir in Britain. Late the following year a 3ft. gauge railway was laid along its route and by 1925 there was a community of over 400 people, including 49 schoolchildren, in the timber and corrugated iron village at Blaen y cwm below the reservoir site. Self-contained, it had a shop, school, hospital, police station, labourers' hostel, bath house and railway engine sheds. Some workmen from places such as Talgarth and Hay left home each day at 4am to climb over 1,000ft. and walk more than 3 miles over the mountains to the quarry—and face a 3 hours trudge back at the end of the day, all for 9d. per hour (say 4p. or about £2.50!). There was a Navvy Missioner to look after religious and social life and medical needs were served once or twice a week by Dr. Tom Hincks of Hay-on-Wye. He acted as panel doctor from early 1913 and thought nothing of riding his cob 10 miles over the Gospel Pass, down to Capel-y-ffin, over the Ffwddog ridge to tend his patients. But after the war he went by car via Talgarth, Crickhowell, Pont Esgob and the footplate of the steam engine. (In 1922 he was in the national news—after his suspicions about the mysterious condition of the wife of a Hay solicitor (see p.190). These led to the murder conviction of Major Herbert Rowse Armstrong at Hereford Assizes and his execution that May—all a source of great excitement at Blaen y cwm, where some had come to meet the murderer professionally!). About 15 years late, the dam was officially opened in 1928 and the railway and construction village soon removed. Building foundations are still visible from the Forestry Common car park and picnic site just beyond the forest at Blaen y cwm, whilst the reservoir may be reached after a reasonably gentle 2 hours return walk of just over 4 miles. When at the dam, do not emulate Princes William and Harry in attempts to abseil down the face.

Except when a large timber lorry looms, dam engineer Latham's 1912 construction road is still adequate for motorists driving back down, past Coed Dias, scene of an ambush and massacre in 1135 recorded by Giraldus Cambrensis.

Richard de Clare, a member of one of the most powerful Marcher families, was returning home through the mountains with an escort provided by his host at Abergavenny when he rashly decided to manage without protection and continue on his way with just a few attendants. But upon entering the thickly wooded Grwyne Fawr valley, he was ambushed by Welsh partisans led by Iorwerth ap Owain of Caerleon, and he and his party were all killed. To commemorate the event, the Welsh later erected a cairn on the mountain above, calling it Crug Dial, the Cairn of Revenge.

The beech forests of that time have now been replaced with conifers all the way down towards Lower Cwmyoy. Near Pontyspig, Forest Coal Pit has no record of any coal mining but rather of charcoal burning. And whereas since 1919 when the Forestry Commission was set up, extensive slopes of the Grwyne and Llanthony valleys have been smothered by blocks of conifers, ancient trees still reach out across the road to form a magical green tunnel. At Cwm Coed-y-cerrig (vale of trees and rocks) there are National and Local Nature Reserves protecting a variety of woodland communities—ranging from wet alder wood in the valley bottom, to coppiced ash and wych elm on lower slopes and high forest of beech and oak on the upper slopes.

There is an opportunity to turn right at the next junction at Stanton and visit the Skirrid Inn, the undisputed oldest pub in Wales at Llanvihangel Crucorney. According to court records it certainly goes back to 1110 when it was also used as a place of judgement—when miscreants stood before a very different bar. The wickedest, as then judged, were promptly despatched to their Maker beneath a stairway beam. The beam is still there, and although this dark practice has now ceased, it has been possible to order a hangman's lunch from the bar menu. Outside there is an ancient horse-mounting stone, which doubtless has its own stories to tell, but the old road has been replaced by an adjacent new section of the A465 to Hereford and, below Ysgyryd (Skirrid) Fawr—a setting of ancient legends, to Abergavenny.

The main route turns left at the T junction in Stanton, and just beyond there is another chance for refreshment at the 300-year-old Queens Head, a place well regarded by generations of wiry brown-legged hill-walkers. Here is the easternmost of the three U-shaped glacial valleys, the only one with a through road. Lower down, the flow of its river has been obstructed by a large moraine and because of this the Honddu has diverted eastwards to join the Wye, rather than join the Grwynes to enter the Usk. Another huge glacial deposit halted to the east of the valley, at present-day Cwmyoy. This hamlet may be reached by making a right turn just beyond the pub and going across the Afon Honddu bridge, the narrow road afterwards looping back to rejoin the through road further up the valley.

16. The leaning tower of Cwmyoy

Cwmyoy is on the hillside below the Hatterall ridge, on a rocky hillock detached by glacial action in c.10,000 BC and swept down from the red sandstone cliff face higher up the valley. The church masons of 700 years ago were not to know that this was not right for placing their new St. Martin's Church—and the outcome chimes with the biblical warning against building on sand. After many years the ground instability weakened foundations and so, heavily buttressed, the tower now leans eastwards towards the hill, there is a distinct slope in the floor within the gloomy nave and the chancel leans westwards. In the nave there is a 13th-century cross, strangely with a mitre on the head of Christ, which was discovered in 1871 at a nearby farm. It is thought to have once stood on the Pilgrim Way to St. David's. According to the wall plaques, costs of buttressing and other rescue operations have been a great source of worry for successive vicars and it is to be hoped that donations from the many camera-toting tourists will provide some cheer.

The road leaves the small parking area in the lane near the church and continues onwards to rejoin the route towards Llanthony, to the once wild and secluded place where the second hermit to be met on this tour is said to have come in the 6th century to live in prayer and solitude.

17.   Llanthony Priory

Llanthony Priory

Support for the early presence of the future patron saint of Wales lies in the full name of the district, of which Llanthony is a corruption. *Llan-ddewi-nant-honddu* translates as the church of David (*Dewi* in Welsh) on the river Honddu. There are over 50 such ancient dedications and place names, mostly in south Wales—but also at Much Dewchurch and Little Dewchurch, Herefordshire. In 1188 Giraldus Cambrensis, who often visited Llanthony as a place 'truly fitted for contemplation, a happy and delightful spot', attested to a tradition that, living only on wild leeks and river water, David built a cell there. After five centuries the Norman William de Lacy came across the ruins whilst hunting—and was immediately inspired to change his ways by its secluded charm and live there as a hermit—later to be joined by others in building a small church. A hostile local atmosphere caused delays in plans to follow with a priory but in 1118 a house of Augustinian Canons was formed. The eastern part of the present church, aptly dedicated to St. John Baptist, patron saint of hermits, was started in *c*.1175 and the nave and buildings around the cloisters and the prior's lodging in the west range followed by 1230. The contemporary 13th-century church of St. David still remains in use, but by 1538 and the Dissolution the priory, comprising various Norman, Early English and Transitional styles of architecture, was becoming ruinous and it was sold off privately. It remained in seclusion and mostly unvisited well into the 19th-century. Once, in April 1870, the Reverend Francis Kilvert called there after walking over the ridge from Clyro and, after encountering two other visitors, exploded into his Diary: 'Of all the noxious animals, the most noxious is a tourist. And of all the tourists the most vulgar, ill-bred, offensive and loathsome is the British tourist'! Usually the most charitable of people, he had perhaps forgotten that he was something of a tourist himself. How would he have written up a visit to Llanthony in the 21st century, when the spacious CADW car park sometimes overflows with visitors to this most popular tourist attraction of the Black Mountains. And also what would the prior have made of the hotel created from his former lodging, complete with its 12th-century bar? Or, up the 62 narrow steps of the Norman spiral stone staircase, the romantic four-poster bedroom with floor-set lancet window overlooking the moonlit ruins and mountains. To the peaceful sounds of stomping horses' hooves and distant calls of ewes and lambs, the only trace of monastic penance these days is the twisting flight of 42 steps back down to the bathroom!

Long favoured by anglers, grouse-shooters and hill-walkers, the Llanthony Abbey hotel menu usually includes the Welsh lamb, whilst horses may be rented from Court Farm, to the left before returning to the road for Hay-on-Wye. Turn right up the narrowing road and past the original priory gatehouse (private) on the right and the Half Moon inn on the left, and head 4 miles further up the valley for the hamlet of Capel-y-ffin (meaning chapel of the boundary)—where the three counties of Hereford, Brecon (Powys) and Monmouth meet. Up another narrow road to the left is where, in 1869, this journey's third religious ascetic came to the Black Mountains 'to serve the Lord in solitude'.

18. Father Ignatius and his abbey

Joseph Leycester Lyne was born in 1837, ordained a deacon of the Church of England in 1860 and arrived in the valley in 1869. He had an ambition to re-establish monasticism in the Anglican church, and chose Llanthony, which he had hoped to restore. Failing to agree terms with the owner (heir of Walter Savage Landor, the poet), he discovered a beautiful secluded 34 acres site at 1,150ft. above sea level, but on

The remains of Llanthony Tertia

the shaded, damper and colder side of the vale, along a cart track above Capel-y-ffin. Describing himself as Father Ignatius, Evangelist Monk of the British Church, he was joined sporadically by other eccentrics of like mind—or as unkind critics described them 'various cranks and off-beats'. With financial gifts from friends and proceeds from preaching tours (from June 1890 over 12 months in the Mid-States of America), he built a monastery and convent for a mixed Anglican community with its own rituals and interpretation of the Rule of St. Benedict, calling it Llanthony Tertia (Secunda was at Gloucester). In August 1880 the vision of a woman with veiled face and upraised hand, regarded as an apparition of the Virgin Mary, was observed by choir-boys and repeated on several occasions. About a central garth and quadrangle, the monastery is in typical Gothic revival style to designs by Charles Buckeridge. The church he started to build, with a large and impressive choir styled after that at Llanthony, was never completed and work ceased in 1882. Ordained as a priest in 1898 by a wandering American prelate in the monastery church, Ignatius died very suddenly ten years later. He is buried in the choir, a slab marking his lonely tomb—'Here lies Ignatius of Jesus, O.S.B., Founder and First Abbot of this House, R.I.P. He died on October 16th, 1908'. Not only the first but the last unelected abbot, his abbey, which is usually a major monastic establishment superior to a priory, remains a regular source of confusion with William de Lacy's much older foundation four miles down the valley. Apart from the ruins, his most tangible memorials are the elaborate church reredos, rescued in the 1920s for St. Julian's Church, Newport, and a wayside Calvary provided by his two nieces and dedicated near the monastery in 1936 at a pilgrimage of some 1,500 people.

Our Lady of Llanthony

Closer to the monastery stands a statue of Our Lady of Llanthony, a focus of regular events marking the 1880 Apparitions, and across the valley is Vision Farm. This is where the author, Bruce Chatwin, stayed when he researched his well-received book and subsequent film *On the Black Hill.*

Eric Gill and his companions

There was no-one to follow Ignatius so his community dispersed and from 1916 to 1924 the monastery was empty and deteriorating. Then the property was acquired by Eric Gill (d.1940), a man of ideas and personality to compare with his predecessor there. He was a talented engraver and designer of classic typefaces such as Perpetua and Gill Sans Serif (as this entry uses). As a master stone carver he is best remembered for work at Westminster Cathedral, the Prospero and Ariel sculpture at Broadcasting House, the Geneva League of Nations building and a celebrated black marble monument at King's School in Canterbury. He and his wife were joined in their remote isolation by a community of craft and literary workers, who 'led a life of intense creative activity'. But after four years all went their separate ways and the monastery has since had a range of private uses.

St. Mary's Church stands by the side of this tour route at Capel-y-ffin, where in 1870 Francis Kilvert described it as 'squatting like a stout grey owl among its seven great black yews'.

Capel-y-ffin is the highest settlement in the valley, and over the next 1¹/₂ miles the scenery from the 'main road' gradually changes to open mountainside as it reaches the col 500ft. below Twmpa and Hay Bluff. This is known as the Gospel Pass, or Bwlch-yr-Efengyl to the Welsh, and is the watershed at 1,778ft. above sea level. If you want to stop to take in the view, you need to do this before it bursts upon you, but stopping in the small car park just before the crest. The sight is dramatic as the pass is finally crested to reveal the Wye ribboning its way 1,000ft. below in a great loop from Builth to

19. Church in miniature

Originally built of local sandstone in the 15th century, St. Mary's is whitewashed to help it cope with the weather and is roofed with thick sandstone tiles. Like many churches on the Welsh border it has a small wooden bell tower—with a lean that rivals that at Cwmyoy. Inside it is just a hall, measuring *c*.25ft. by 13ft., but on the west wall there is a long gallery which nearly doubles the tiny seating capacity. By its side, across the river footbridge, is a very similar, equally small, white Baptist chapel of 1762, differing outwardly only in having a chimney instead of a belfry.

Whitney. The contrast between the narrow wooded seclusion of the Llanthony valley and the sweeping view laid out to the distant backcloth of the long Radnor Forest ridges is complete. There are another 3 miles of road through open moorland past wild ponies and more sheep, with stopping places to admire the spectacular scenery. For anyone who has the appetite and energy to ease the legs into action, the car park just before the crest is a good starting point for a hugely rewarding, moderately steep walk to the top of Hay Bluff —to Offa's Dyke Path and the chance of seeing six counties all at once.

Ahead the road soon descends once more into woodland and rapidly reaches Hay (see p.187). (see p.187) Turn right at the bottom of the hill and follow the road through the town, leaving the National Park just beyond the town's edge. Continue on the B4350 alongside the Wye. About a mile out there is a last chance to collect some reading matter, at The Children's Bookshop at Pontvaen. Just beyond Toll Cottage the railway once branched off to run down to Pontrilas through the Golden Valley, whilst from 1864, 25 years earlier, the Hereford line headed for the Wye crossing, passing far beneath Clifford Castle, in ruins but still standing sentinel over the village.

20. Clifford Castle and Fair Rosamund

The bold eminence rising 150 feet from the banks of the Wye has served as a border stronghold on many occasions, quite possibly back to Roman times. Soon after the Conquest, William fitz Osbern, earl of Hereford, founded a borough at Clifford. In 1089 this was registered in the Domesday Book with 16 burgesses, 13 smallholders, 5 Welshmen and—common in society then—6 male and 4 female slaves. In view of the military importance of the site in the Wye valley, close to Wales, it is

Clifford Castle viewed from the road from Hay

quite likely that a motte and bailey castle was built, as were others in the neighbourhood. Also, by 1130, monks from Cluny Monastery in Burgundy founded a priory less than half a mile away—where they remained until the Dissolution in the early 16th-century. The Cluniacs were venerated by the Norman kings and are said to be responsible for instituting All Souls Day (2 November) as an

Clifford Castle as seen from the no through road that leads towards the Wye, with the gateway to the bailey on the left

Priory Farm on the site of the old priory

appropriate sequel to All Saints Day (1 November). Except for stony fragments, there is little sign of them now, but Priory Farm remains productive on the site and there are indications on the OS sheet of the monks' original fish ponds. The farmhouse is solidly built of stone, partly with 14th- and early 18th-century ranges, and according to his accounts it was busy in Kilvert's day. The castle passed to the Clifford family in the 12th century and in the 13th Walter de Clifford is credited with building the present structure, then covering $3\frac{1}{2}$ acres. Generally reckoned to have been born there, his grand-daughter, Jane Clifford—known as Fair Rosamund—(*c*.1134-76), subsequently caught the eye of Henry II during a visit and become his 'favourite', with dire consequences—immortalised by Tennyson in *Dream of Fair Women*. The castle later passed to the Mortimers and received a pounding by Owain Glyndwr in 1402. After 1485 it ceased to be of importance and what little was left is still visible from the road, high among trees on the crag above the Wye, its gatehouse and barbican remains in the field below.

Like most other villages in the Marches, Clifford has lost many of its former prime attributes—its own vicar, policeman, nurse, village shop and post office (recently even its cherished, rare Victorian letterbox), whilst the two remaining pubs are out on the fringes. But close to the road there are still some very solid stone farm buildings, partly built from 'architectural salvage' which could well have served a more warlike purpose nearby in former times!

Continue along the B road to reach the toll bridge across the Wye.

21.   Whitney toll bridge

During the summer, part of the role of the castle was to guard the river ford down below, although there are signs that it was ineffective in 1402 when, leading his Welsh forces, Owain Glyndwr captured Clifford. During wetter months there was a ferry, whilst freight barges could be towed up to Hay. Then in 1774, Parliament gave authority for a stone bridge to be built, as well as a toll house and a scale of charges. It was the first to be swept away by the turbulent Wye, the third being in the winter of 1796 when the bridges at Glasbury and Hay were also lost. Then a hybrid approach was tried by introducing three timber spans on braced wooden piers between stone arch survivors of one of the previous structures. Yet despite Pevsner's disdainful comment as 'Rough Work', it has greatly outlasted more stylish predecessors, with the help of constant maintenance. This is paid for through

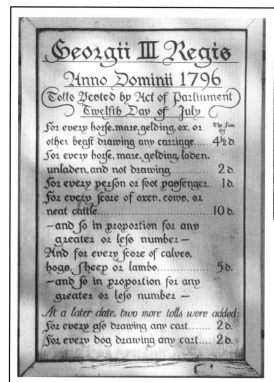

Georgii III Regis
Anno Dominii 1796
Tolls Vested by Act of Parliament
Twelfth Day of July

For every horse, mare, gelding, ox, or
other beast drawing any carriage.....4½d.
For every horse, mare, gelding, laden,
unladen, and not drawing............. 2d.
For every person or foot passenger... 1d.
For every score of oxen, cows, or
neat cattle.................................10d.
—and so in proportion for any
greater or less number—
And for every score of calves,
hogs, sheep or lambs................ 5d.
—and so in proportion for any
greater or less number —

At a later date, two more tolls were added:
For every ass drawing any cart....... 2d.
For every dog drawing any cart.... 2d.

The old charges for the toll bridge

Whitney Toll Bridge

government approved tolls, charged by the private owners of the exclusive rights of crossing (80p. for a car in 2010), and helped by a reassuring weight restriction of 7.5 tonnes. Such were the rights of the owners that from 1818 the Hay-Eardisley horse-drawn tramroad company was made to lay its 3ft. 6in. gauge track across the bridge, and pay up. And when in 1863 the Hereford, Hay and Brecon Railway finally obtained Parliamentary authority to build its own bridge until it closed in 1962, it also had to guarantee the tolls on the present bridge up to £345 a year.

After a brief pause to enjoy an ice-cream, available at the toll-house (not a commodity offered at most booths), turn right to join A438 and travel Route 5 in the opposite direction back to Kington, turning right at Willersley for Hereford and, just short of Eardisley, along A4112 towards Leominster.

Hay-on-Wye—a Meeting Place

The word March or Marches signifies a border region, especially one between two countries such as England and Wales. In origin it is related to the Middle English *marche*, Old French *marche* itself of Germanic origin, and *mearc* from Saxon days.

Hay is a true border town of the Welsh Marches, its name derived from the Norman *haie*, which means 'a fenced or hedged enclosure' or *haie-taillee*—'the cropped hedge'. In Welsh these have become *Y Gelli* or *Y Gelli Gandrill* and are shown on modern road signs and Ordnance Survey maps. During Norman times there was an English Hay, which was the town, and Welsh Hay, which covered the countryside to the south and west, and for comparative administrative purposes there have recently been the Hay Urban and Hay Rural Districts. The town is situated at the meeting place of three counties: Breconshire to the south and west, Herefordshire to the east, and northwards, immediately across the River Wye, Radnorshire. With Breconshire and Montgomery-shire, Radnorshire now forms the county of Powys, created in 1974.

The Brecon Beacons National Park embraces Hay on three sides at its north eastern boundary and Offa's Dyke Path, which began at Prestatyn in Clwyd, passes through the town to continue along much of the Park's eastern limit, rising to Hay Bluff and the eastern ridge above the Vale of Ewyas. It meets the Wye Valley Walk from Rhayader near the town centre, whence they and the River Wye depart on their separate ways towards Chepstow and the Bristol Channel.

At a strategic gateway position between the lowlands of the broad English Wye valley into the Welsh highland region, Hay suffered more than a fair share of unwelcome visitors and upheavals originating from

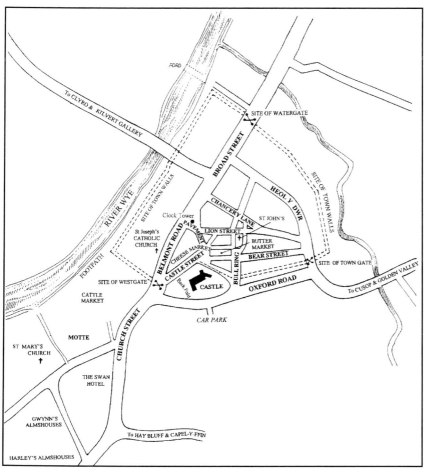

Hay-on-Wye

Hay-on-Wye castle—the wing of c.1649 with evidence of The Town of Books in the foreground

both sides of the border during the Middle Ages. Little is known of the place before Norman times, although from their earliest days of occupation the Romans established a large camp at Boatside farm on the Radnorshire bank of the Wye. By the late 11th century the Normans had a firm presence after their conquest of Brycheiniog (Breconshire) and William Revel, lord of the Manor, built a strong point to the east of the Login brook in *c*.1100. The mound can still be seen from the road between St. Mary's Church and the cattle market and this motte and bailey served to house the garrison until the stone castle was built close to the centre of the current town by William de Braose II (d.1211) and his wife, Maud or Matilda. This became the nucleus of the walled town early in the 13th century. (This William was not named The Ogre of Abergavenny for nothing, for the treachery which is referred to at page 176 is only a sample of his cruel and perfidious behaviour. Eventually he was driven into impoverished exile after his wife crossed King John, and she and their eldest son, William de Braose III, were starved to death at Corfe Castle). As was then customary the church, which was dedicated early in the 12th century, was built close to the motte and bailey castle. But the town wall was not built until 1237, after the major castle was completed and so both St. Mary's and the old castle were left outside the defences. It extended from the Westgate, across today's Belmont Road, down towards the river and then alongside and above it as far as Wyeford Street (the site of a ford), before turning at right angles for the Watergate across Broad Street. From there it continued around the town, west of Dulas Brook to turn at the Town Gate, continuing alongside Oxford Street to the castle walls and back to Westgate. The gates have all gone and there is now next to nothing left of the town walls. After a long history of assaults by Welsh patriots, English lords and reigning monarchs, there is also very little remaining of the Norman castle, except for the ruins of the keep and the adjoining gateway, which are not open to visitors. These can be seen from below in Castle Street and to their right, high above more open-air book-stalls, is the mansion which was built in part of the castle site during the first half of the 17th century. After an eventful life of its own, during which it was leased to the vicars of Hay between 1825 and 1902,

The 'standard' Victorian clock tower of many a border town hereabouts with narrow streets leading towards the castle beyond

and after experiencing a disastrous fire in 1939, it is now owned by Richard Booth, 'King of Hay', suffering another fire in 1977.

As a true border town Hay enjoyed the privileges and commercial advantages of a chartered weekly market which brought in people and trade from a wide rural hinterland as far back as 1233. In addition two annual fairs attracted business from even further away, and most took place in a large area of the town which is thought to have been bounded by Castle Lane, Bull Ring, St. John's Place and High Town. Market and fairs have continued ever since and sales of cattle, sheep and pigs extended into pens at the sides of Broad Street, Oxford Road, Chancery Lane and outside St. John's chapel. Before the introduction of employment exchanges, hiring fairs took place twice a year, when men and women paraded with appropriate symbols of their trades or duties to be engaged for the year as farm hands or domestic servants. Then, immediately after the First World War, the council purchased the old coalyard and tramway wharf above the river and laid the area out as the cattle market. This is still in use today, mainly for sheep sales. The weekly street market still continues each Thursday, close to the former Cheese Market on the site of the original Town Hall and the open colonnaded Market House in Market Street. This was erected on the site of the old Butter Market in 1833. Throughout the shopping week, the range of food retailers, antique and arts shops, boutiques, bistros, cafés, pubs and inns to be found within the climbing, characterful jumble of streets and back lanes of Hay surpasses anything found in most towns and villages of comparable size.

And nowhere else within such a small space can there be 39 second-hand book retailers.

King of Hay

The years immediately following the end of the Second World War were very difficult throughout Britain, but nowhere more so than in rural communities such as Hay. Its Border remoteness became even more pronounced between 1941 and 1963, when a succession of rail-service reductions shut the station at Newport Street. The Golden Valley line via Dorstone closed first, followed by the lines from Hereford city, Presteigne and Kington and on to Brecon and South Wales. From Three Cocks Junction station, just to the west, the old Cambrian Railway links with Builth Wells, Llanidloes and its connections in mid Wales were also dismantled. So the town was at a very low ebb in 1962 when the 23-year-old Richard Booth bought one of the several available and cheaply-priced shops with the intention of selling not traditional commodities, but great quantities of second-hand books. It was a brave undertaking in those hard times, but he pressed ahead in his one-time Fire Station premises in Church Street, buying up large volumes (in every sense) of books wherever he could afford them. By 1965 he was in a position to purchase the town's redundant Plaza Cinema, and filled it with shelves and books. Now in other hands, it is said to contain up to 200,000 volumes, their subjects ranging from Art to Zoology and selling from 50p. to £5,000. There is also a large open-air bookshop in the garden in front of the cinema building, for those who would like to browse for 'a lot of books for their money'.

Hay-on-Wye

Richard Booth bought Hay Castle for his home in 1963 and from there, early in 1977, declaring Hay to be an independent State, he pronounced himself King Richard of Hay. He re-named his horse Caligula to make him Foreign Secretary, or was it Prime Minister, just as that evil Roman emperor had done! It seems that this 'revolution' quite unsettled the town clerk, who was ever watchful over his council's authority. He must have become even less happy when 'King' Richard was joined for a while by the gorgeous and eccentric April Ashley—previously George Jameson, merchant seaman—as his consort and 'Countess of Offa's Dyke'. Of course the media went wild! Ever since, the high profile of Hay, which was renamed Hay-on-Wye in 1947 (partly, it was said, because of some postal confusion with Hoy in the Orkneys, but also further to promote its image) has attracted new streams of tourists towards its many other natural virtues.

Newly gained repute was followed in 1988 by a further local phenomenon, with the founding by Norman Florence and his son, Peter, of the annual Hay Festival of Literature.

'The most prestigious Festival in the English speaking World'

The *New York Times* was not alone among prominent and influential national and international sources with such plaudits as that above, and the reputation and attendances at what has become recognised as one of the premier events on the literary calendar have grown year by year. 'In my mind it has replaced Christmas'—enthused Anthony Wedgewood-Benn, the veteran parliamentarian, diarist and festival regular. Visitors have attended from all over the world to enjoy the Festival, and have been drawn into the surrounding hills and valleys in and around the Brecon Beacons National Park. The event is presented as 'a spectacular holiday party', where there are opportunities 'to indulge tastes for the finest books, food, music, comedy, gardening, art, argument, conversation and literature'. The most innovative and exciting writers and thinkers have appeared from Wales, England, Europe and beyond (ex-President Clinton from the USA came upon publication of his biography). In May and early June, 2003, voices from across the Arab world included Queen Noor of Jordan, and the finest American novelists of three generations were among a widely varied list of almost 400 participants during the 10 day event. According to reports, during that short period the 1,500 people of this small town were joined by some 85,000 festivalgoers, the highest number to date!

At a discussion of a new book concerning her father at a previous festival, a surprise stage appearance was made by Margaret, the daughter of Major H.R. Armstrong. His actions and the consequent events of over 70 years before, when she was only six, had drawn very different visitors to Hay.

Herbert Rouse Armstrong—The Hay Poisoner'

After serving in the First World War and achieving the field rank of major, Herbert Rowse Armstrong returned to Hay in 1919 as one of only two solicitors practising in the town, at offices opposite each other in Broad Street. He also held the appointments of clerk to the magistrates of Hay, Clyro and Bredwardine and was held in very high esteem by the townspeople and others in the surrounding countryside. It therefore came as a great shock when he, a true pillar of the community, in late 1921 appeared in the dock of his own court at Hay charged with attempted murder—of all things by administering arsenic to his brother solicitor.

Katharine, Armstrong's ailing wife had died in February that year and, suspicions roused, an exhumation order was granted and large amounts of arsenic were found in her body. At the magistrates court, Armstrong was committed for trial to Hereford Assizes charged with the murder of his wife and also of the attempted murder of the solicitor, Oswald Martin. Several books have since been written about the trial and its other participants, who included Mr. Justice Darling, the reputed 'hanging judge', the attorney-general and other advocates, and expert and other witnesses. Real doubts remain to this day about its fairness, and the validity of the verdict and judgement. Some of these were voiced during the discussion at the Literary Festival of *Dead Not Buried* (later *The Hay Poisoner*) by Martin Beales after its publication in 1995. But after being found guilty at a sensational trial, which started in April, 1922 at Hereford Shirehall, and losing on Appeal in London, Herbert Rouse Armstrong was executed at Gloucester Gaol at the end of that May, the only solicitor ever to have been hanged.

Eglwys Ifan, the guild chapel of St. John

At the junction with Chancery Lane, the office premises of Armstrong and Martin still house solicitors on opposite sides of Broad Street, not far from properties once occupied by other leading participants at the trial. All now form part of interesting stretches of buildings which range from the timber-framed 16th-century Three Tuns, the oldest pub in town, to 18th- and 19th-century houses and the Crown Hotel. Where Broad Street reaches The Pavement, the Town Clock, built in 1884, has been disparagingly described as 'in off-the-peg Gothic' style, and is typical of others in Welsh towns, such as that seen at Knighton on one of these tours. One intriguing old building of uncertain age within the town is the little chapel and former parish church in Lion Street. St. John-within-the-walls was once a chantry chapel, associated with a guild of town tradesmen, and—until recently—the last religious services cannot have been held there any later than the mid-16th century. Since then it has had many secular uses, first as a school house before becoming ruinous for about a hundred years from about 1700. Then it was rebuilt and used as a lock-up and gaoler's quarters until 1875 and afterwards served as various forms of shop and as a hairdresser's into the 20th century. It was then further renovated and 'made over' for holding meetings and functions and part has been restored as a place of worship.

Walking around Hay

Much of Hay was officially designated as a Conservation Area in 1969, but in essence its 'character' and its 'atmosphere' have not really changed much since at least as far back as the beginning of that century. A happy time can be spent strolling below the castle, going up, down or along the jumble of tiny, narrow streets and alleyways, or into the shops—where the interior floor layout and levels of some older ones are equally rambling. Descending to flatter ground, there is the opportunity to walk through trees above the River Wye along Bailey Walk. This follows the track-bed of the former railway line and earlier horse-drawn tramway, and it may serve as a reminder that there is more to Hay-on-Wye than just castles, book-shops and accounts of terrible murder. For it sits among some of the finest landscapes to be found anywhere in Britain and makes a good centre for exploring the Black Mountains and other parts of the Brecon Beacons Park, the upper Wye valley and Herefordshire, which John Masefield once called the Land of Beauty and Bounty.

The Wye from the bridge into Hay

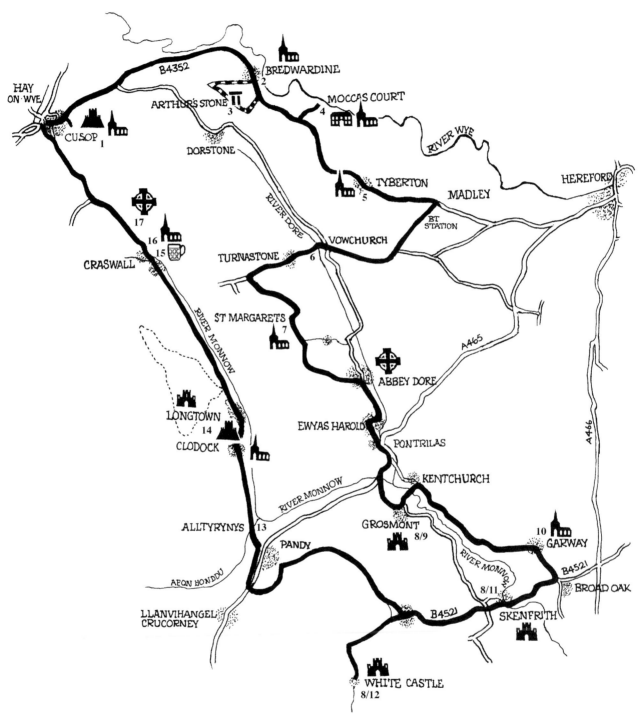

Outline map for Tour 8
The numbers 1 to 17 relate to the boxed information given within the tour

Tour 8   Western Herefordshire's Hills and Valleys

This tour is set in the valleys to the east of the Black Mountains and in the countryside of west Herefordshire. It includes a prehistoric burial chamber, an ornately carved church screen and a Cistercian abbey converted to a parish church amongst a few churches visited *en route*, but is most particularly a castle tour, taking in the remains of the three stone castles of The Trilateral as well as that of Longtown on the flanks of the Black Mountains. It commences at the border town of books—Hay-on-Wye. There are extensive views to be had, and the opportunity for countless strolls or longer walks, often in parts of countryside served by the Reverend Francis Kilvert, known for his classic Victorian diary of country life.

The journey is made largely on minor roads, with some stretches of B road in the first half of the tour. The total distance, without any detours, is about 68 miles. (OS Landranger 148 and 161)

From the car park in Hay, turn right onto the B4348 in the direction of Cusop, and immediately after crossing the Dulas Brook (and so entering England and Herefordshire), turn right to reach this suburb of Hay and then left to follow the sign for St. Mary's Church.

---

1. Cusop Dingle and waterfalls

Cusop has ancient origins and its name is thought to come from St. Cewydd, and *hop*, in Old English meaning 'enclosed valley'. The church was probably founded by the monks of Llanthony Abbey during the 11th century and there are some very fine yew trees in the church-yard which are old enough to have been there in 1086 at the time of the Domesday Survey. They would have been noticed by Francis Kilvert when visiting his friend the curate, perhaps on one occasion commis-erating with him after he had been mistakenly Confirmed by a tetchy bishop of Hereford as he presented

Cusop Church

his real candidate! By those days the church had been heavily restored, but it has managed to retain some original Norman work in the nave and at the blocked north door.

Across the road from the church car parking area is Cusop Castle, a ringwork, or circular embankment, amounting to about an acre in extent and left with a negligible amount of its former stonework. With the castle at Hay, and that of Clyro to the north-west, it formed a defensive line which straddled the broad Wye valley, protecting areas to the east against Welsh marauders. These three fortresses have been compared with the more formidable Trilateral of Skenfrith, Grosmont and White

193

Castle which once blocked a southern routeway out of Wales (which are to be visited at the furthest extreme of this tour).

It would be best not to depart in too great a hurry without attempting a hugely rewarding stroll beyond to drink in the romantic scenery of Cusop Dingle. Here the Dulas, dividing England and Wales, tumbles down a series of waterfalls from its source, high in the Black Mountains.

On returning to the B4348, turn right and follow the signs for Bredwardine and Madley, changing to the B4352 to continue straight on at Hardwicke. The road runs along on the eastern side of the wide valley and there is a temptation to stop to admire the expansive view to the left. Down there the Wye lazily weaves its way between hedged fields past Clifford, Rhydspence and beneath Whitney toll bridge, to be met again at the handsome red brick Bredwardine bridge, built as a toll bridge in 1769. (Now privately occupied, the toll house on the Bredwardine side is still there). High up on the right, and rising to 1,043 ft., is the densely wooded Merbach Hill. At the top, the same views become positively cosmic and breathtaking (provided there is much breath left after tackling the steep paths).

Before you reach Bredwardine you'll need to decide whether you want to make a very short detour to Bredwardine Church to see some carvings, an old 'knightly' tomb and the burial place of Francis Kilvert, and/or tackle the steep ascent to the outstanding chambered tomb called Arthur's Stone with its fine views to the Black Mountains, or carry on along the B road, the two routes rejoining after a short while.

You'll need to have made your choice by the time you reach the Red Lion at the crossroads in Bredwardine: left leads after a short distance to a lane off to the right to Bredwardine church; right to Arthur's Stone; the B road straight ahead.

2. Bredwardine Church and a faithful country clergyman

By 1872, the Reverend Francis Kilvert had served seven of his happiest years a few miles up the Wye as curate at Clyro where, in January 1870, he had chosen to open a systematic diary of his work among the people and countryside of the borders. He then served a curacy with his father in Wiltshire, before becoming vicar of St. Harmon in north Radnorshire in 1876. Then he was presented to the living of vicar of Bredwardine and rector of Brobury in 1877 and was to continue with his diary until March 1879, never dreaming that extracts would later be edited and published to become a minor classic

Possible Saxon doorway and walling at Bredwardine Church

which would be sold and avidly read throughout the world! Or that a Kilvert Society, formed in 1948 'to foster an interest in him, his work, his diary and the countryside he loved' would, just over 50 years later, have a worldwide membership of more than 600. His new ministry was the pinnacle of his ambition, and he quickly earned the respect and affection of a widely dispersed new flock. The three volumes of *Kilvert's Diary* have since been classified as 'an important social document, providing a rare record of rural life in the 1870s in the heady mid-Victorian days'. They describe happy moments, as when in January 1879 he heard of the games and sports, the fights and merriments, that went on in old times upon Bredwardine Knap. 'What kind of games?' he asked. 'I wouldn't suggest,' said William Davies a parishioner and probably a farmer, 'that they were of any spiritual good'. And there were also the most harrowing of times, as when, just a month beforehand, during the bitter cold of a winter when the temperature fell to below 2 degrees to produce the coldest night for 100 years, he was to place on record one of the most poignant of all his experiences. A young parishioner, David Davies aged 8, a shepherd's son, had died just before Christmas and the funeral was to be held on Christmas Day, 1878. In his Diary he wrote: 'Immediately after dinner I had to go back to the church, for the funeral of little Davie of the Old Weston who died on Monday was fixed for 2.15. The weather was dreadful, the snow driving in blinding clouds and the walking tiresome. Yet the funeral was only 20 minutes late. The Welcome Home, as it chimed softly and slowly to greet the little pilgrim coming to his rest, sounded bleared and muffled through the thick snowy air. The snow fell thickly all through the funeral service and at the service by the grave a kind woman offered her umbrella which a kind young fellow came and held over my head.'

Although Kilvert had by then been unwell for some weeks, no-one expected that this would be not just his second but also his last Christmas Day at Bredwardine, or that in less than a year he too would be buried in the churchyard, to the north side of the church tower close to David's grave. After years of struggle on a curate's very modest stipend he had become at last sufficiently well-off to wed, and on 20 August 1879 he married Elizabeth Rowland. They returned from their honeymoon on the 13th September, when he was taken ill, and on the 23rd died from peritonitis at the age of 38 years.

On the marble cross marking his grave are aptly prophetic words taken from the *Epistle to the Hebrews* which read: 'He being dead yet speaketh'. Elizabeth Kilvert lived until 1911, by which time insufficient room had been left for her to be buried next to her husband. Her grave, beneath a very similar white marble cross to his, is sadly at the furthest corner of the overflow churchyard, which is alongside the bridleway leading to the old vicarage where she lived for such a very short while. Beyond what since 1959 has been a private house, and also enviably poised above the Wye, are earthworks and buried foundations of what is generally thought to have been Bredwardine Castle.

In 1952 the Kilvert Society went to restore and reletter Davie's neglected grave, which is close to those of his parents, and they added the words: 'In memory of Francis Kilvert's love of little children'—a love which he was destined never to have for his own.

Kilvert's Grave

To visit Arthur's Stone, take the minor road to the right of the inn. This book endorses the advice signposted at the bottom against taking a caravan up, for at 25%, or 1 in 4, the gradient is the steepest encountered at any of these tours and the road is quite narrow and not over-blessed with passing places. After about a strenuous mile, the Wye Valley Path departs to the right as it heads for the humpy green summit of Merbach Hill and staggering aerial views, across hundreds of miles. (Anyone feeling energetic, and having a sensible regard for their level of fitness, should be able to make it to the top). The road continues on upwards, rising above striking views of its own, to reach Crafta Webb, which is close to the top of Bredwardine Hill. This is now a 'lost village', but during the 19th century it was a squatters' hamlet of people wishing to claim resident status in order to benefit from a local charity. It had its own grocer, tailor and shoemaker and Kilvert often visited to hold 'Cottage Lectures' on themes taken from the Scriptures. Still climbing, the road turns sharp left and left again to level off on Arthur's Stone Lane. The barrow is highly visible on the right hand side of the road with its surrounding wooden fence; there is a parking area just beyond it.

3. Arthur's Stone long barrow

This is the most northerly of the Severn-Cotswold Group of Neolithic (New Stone Age) multi-chambered tombs of between 3700 and 2700 BC. The people usually lived in communities of no more than from 25 to 100 and such tombs might have been used over several generations, perhaps for just one or two, or maybe between 10 and 100 individuals—accompanied with simple grave goods such as pots, stone beads and flint arrowheads. The Herefordshire Woolhope Club Archaeological Research Section observed that above Dorstone, 'the mound was oval, measuring 26 by 17 metres with a height of about 2

Arthur's Stone, looking along the entrance passage to the tomb's main chamber with its partially surviving capstone

metres. The western half, however, appears to have been removed, leaving the polygonal chamber, passage and false portal exposed. The six-sided capstone, weighing an estimated 40 tonnes, is 0.5 metre thick, has maximum dimensions of 5.8 by 3 metres and stands 2 metres above ground level at its highest point. Three of the nine vertical stones which supported it have fallen, and the capstone itself has broken in half, the lower half having split longitudinally. Two sections of passages at right angles to one another are formed by nine vertical stones. The "false portal" stone, a few yards from the south-east side of the chamber, is set vertically and is about 0.25 metre thick, 1.5 metre high and a metre wide'. The burial chamber is high above the one-time medieval village of Dorstone, the source of the River Dore and the head of the Golden Valley and once again, from this height of over 900 ft. above sea level, it is a strain not to wax lyrical over the views.

The view across the Golden Valley to the Black Mountains

From the car parking area by Arthur's Stone, continue down in the direction of Dorstone for just over a mile, and at the T junction turn left for a shorter, somewhat wider but still quite steep descent to the B4352 on which you turn right to rejoin the main route.

Continue along the B4352 past the medieval 300-acre Moccas Deer Park on the right, noting the special fencing with wooden palings, cut to irregular lengths to prevent the fallow deer from judging the height and clearing it. Moccas is a small hamlet at a cross roads and the road to the left, signposted for Preston-on-Wye, leads after a few hundred yards to a gateway and private drive across the parkland to Moccas Court and St. Michael and All Angels' Church.

4.   Moccas Court and Church

Legend has it that the first church was founded in the 6th century by St. Dubricius after a dream involving pigs. Enjoying all the acorns, these were common in the oak forest and this explains the place name, which comes from *mochyn* and *rhos*, meaning pigs' moor. Dubricius's move from Hentland (p.241) was short lived because of attacks by marauders and yellow plague. It was not until the 12th century that the present Romanesque village church was built. St. Michael and All Angels is much simpler, but in some ways similar to St. Davids,

Moccas Church

Kilpeck, with three cells comprising nave, chancel and apse beneath a sequence of descending roofs. Except for the Norman doorways of red sandstone, it was almost entirely built of tufa, or travertine, a locally quarried delicate pink material, formed by limestone-rich springs which produce spongy, porous but hard and durable rock. There are 14th-century windows and a musician's gallery and organ at the west end, but otherwise the church is still almost as the Normans left it.

The rector in Kilvert's time was the Reverend Sir George Cornewall, who lived at the family seat at Moccas. This has been owned since the 13th century by only four families—the de Fresnes, Vaughans, Cornewalls and, from 1962, the Chester-Masters. Two and a half storeys high, the present house stands with commanding views on the bank of the Wye after being built from 1775 with red brick, made on the estate, to designs from Robert Adam and Gloucestershire architect, Anthony Keck. It is set in gardens and parkland which were laid out at different times with the aid of G.S. Repton, Capability Brown and Humphrey Repton. From 1869, until devastating flooding of the Wye during 1960-61, there was also a decorative three-span toll bridge on masonry piers and abutments a short distance downstream from the house, which the Cornewalls had provided to replace a ferry to part of their then estate at Monnington. The elegant structure would have been familiar to Kilvert, who often visited Moccas Court and Park and Thermuthis (Thersie), his sister, who was married to William Smith, the vicar of Monnington. After enjoying the deer park in 1876, he was to write of 'the vast ruin of the king oak ... that may be 2,000 years old, measuring 33 feet round by arm stretched', and the 'grey old men of Moccas, those grey, gnarled, low-browed, knock-kneed, bent, huge, strange, long armed, deformed, hunchbacked misshapen oak men', which were there. These are now protected within a National Nature Reserve, managed by English Nature, and can only be visited by special arrangement.

Back at the crossroads, continue along the B4352 to twist through the small hamlet of Blakemere towards Tyberton. It is typical of a great many settlements throughout the Marches, where there has been great change during relatively recent years. Villagers have contrasted the present culture, in which a great many of the inhabitants commute to work, with that of the 18th century when Tyberton consisted of a manor house, a church, and three farms and cottages belonging to the lord of the manor. There were blacksmiths, carpenters, woodmen, gardeners and servants who, with their families, were all dependent on the manor, forming part of a completely self-sufficient community. The manor house, reputedly built in 1728 by John Wood, the elder, of Bath (d.1754) who was responsible for the Crescent and other fine buildings there, was demolished in 1950-51. Now the farms have been amalgamated to employ just three people and only five properties are occupied by farming folk. Yet after almost 300 years, the church still survives as the nucleus of the village—but maybe even its future could one day change. For vicars and churchwardens are agonising over most of their 417 churches in the diocese. Hardly any are not facing pressing repair costs while regular churchgoing, and giving, memberships are mostly in steep decline.

If you choose to visit the church the best place to park is on the opposite side of the road by the gate.

---

5. St. Mary's Church, Tyberton

Poised high up on the right, a most unusual pink brick exterior is almost the first thing to be noticed of the church when entering the village from the direction of Hay-on-Wye. A Restoration period piece from 1720, with most of its furniture and fittings contemporary with the structure including the box pews and ornate curved wooden reredos, it was built by William Brydges on the site of an older church and incorporates its doorway. Except noticeably for the unapt Victorian plate glass windows the likely architect was John Wood, as for Tyberton Court. This house was

The unusual red brick Tyberton Church

later to pass to the Lee Warners and before it was demolished, it stood behind the church. To enhance the present setting some of the parkland has been left, with parts of the former ornamental pools which are said to be the home of kingfishers, dippers, mallards and water-rails.

Only museums for architecture students and tourists?

Roughly 95% of the church buildings in the diocese are regarded as part of the heritage of the Marches and listed as of historic or architectural importance. As places to visit, their appeal is still very strong for in many villages they are a notable feature of the landscape, too often the only interesting one remaining. But reports indicate that there are just 7,830 regular churchgoers attending the 417 churches of the diocese, which averages at about 19 per church. Other figures show that fewer than 4% of the adult population now regularly attend church and as one result, most are grouped within multi-parish benefices. For example, that which includes Kilpeck and Abbey Dore embraces another 11 parishes. Inevitably a strain is placed on an already diminished number of parish clergy, deflecting them from their ministry and mission and further weakening the fundamental role of churches as places of worship. Inevitably consideration is being given to emergency measures, such as further amalgamations, closure or 'mothballing' of churches, further adoptions by the Churches Conservation Trust, deconsecration and conversion to housing or other uses, or even demolition. There would be great distress, even among many 'non-believers' of a community, if some of these steps were taken, for each church building is quite unique—an intrinsic part of their community. This has certainly been so for nearly 300 years at Tyberton.

The B4342 continues past the pool in Tyberton, and on to Madley. Turn right just before the church (for which see page 217), and after passing the entrance to the BT worldwide communications earth station that offers a glimpse of several huge global satellite dishes on the wartime airfield site on the left, after 2 miles this unclassified road reaches the B4348 on which you turn right. Leaving behind the great expanse of the Wye Valley to head towards Vowchurch, Peterchurch and Hay-on-Wye, the route now enters the Golden Valley and a first sight of the Black Mountains escarpment and Hay Bluff ahead in the distance. Enjoy the great scenery along this road until reaching a rather sudden and almost concealed third turning to the left, signed Vowchurch and Michaelchurch Escley. This minor road descends towards the first of two churches which were once said to be 'a bow-shot asunder' they were so close.

6.   I *Vow* I will build my *church*, before you *Turn a stone* of yours

The churches at Vowchurch and Turnastone, on either side of the River Dore, are only about 500 yards apart. An oft-quoted tradition holds that many centuries ago, two pious ladies decided to build a church to serve the respective parishes—but could not decide upon the best site. Eventually one exclaimed: 'I *Vow* I will build my *church*, before you *Turn a stone* of yours!' Other theories, to do with 'a thorn thicket by the stone' are hardly more convincing. At St. Bartholomew's, Vowchurch, the weight of the queen-post roof is carried, not on the walls but unusually on hefty oak supports inside the church. John Abel, the King's Carpenter improbably in the past has been associated with some of the furnishings. The rustic Jacobean screen from 1613, the communion rails and other work certainly help to furnish what is otherwise a plain interior, but they do not measure up to any of his proven work.

St. Mary Magdalene   in Turnastone is another pretty small building, with a Norman doorway, a handsome waggon-roof and Jacobean pulpit. One well known

The church and bridge at Vowchurch

incised slab monument of 1552 inside remembers Thomas Aparri (Ap-Harry?) and his wife, which amusingly shows a satyr with a large hat, playing a pipe.

The Golden Valley Railway line ran between the two churches until 1941, when Vowchurch station closed, and after crossing its route and the old stone bridge across the Dore (a stream reputedly excellent for trout), there is the village sign for Turnastone. The second parish church is straight ahead.

On the left after a sharp left turn past the church there is a true relic of the past, the old village shop and petrol filling station, a firm attraction for vintage car owners. Quite recently it became a source of concern for the fire authority which, because of the age and proximity to the road of the pre-war pumps, wished to shut them down. There was inevitable resistance, but eventually appeals and petitions and fevered media involvement extending to worldwide CNN television, resulted in a stay. Beyond the ancient pumps (which can still only understand part and whole gallons),

The old filling station at Turnastone

there is a sharp right and then a left bend through Turnastone, beyond which the road heads up to the ridge. Near the crest, take the first left turn signposted to St. Margarets and its church. Follow this narrow road for 2 miles high above the Dore and the Dulas valleys, past Gilfach. It is as well to notice the rare passing places, for it may be necessary to reverse into one, accepting graciously that most motorists or tractor-drivers from the opposite direction work and live here—and have to do it all the time. However it is usually blissfully quiet, and in no time St. Margarets and the church car park appear, next to a farm, on the right.

7.   St. Margarets—'A screen and loft all delicately carved and textured pale grey with time'

St. Margaret's Church and part of the rood screen

On arrival, at nearly 800 feet above sea level, to view the Herefordshire plain far below and look towards distant Dinedor, Aconbury and Garway hills, and westward to the Black Mountains, it is easy to appreciate the reaction of John Betjeman to the same scene many years ago. He wrote: 'My own memory of the perfect Herefordshire is a Spring day in the foothills of the Black Mountains and finding among the winding hilltop lanes the remote little church of St. Margaret's where there was no sound but a farm dog's distant barking. Opening the church door I saw across the whole width of the little chancel a screen and loft all delicately carved and textured pale grey with time'. It was completed just before the reformation in 1520—and might have been promptly torn down again as adulatory by Henry VIII's men, had they managed to find St. Margaret's. Pevsner later considered the 'deliciously carved' rood screen to be 'one of the wonders of Herefordshire'. But actually it has close Welsh origins, for the simple Grade I listed two-cell church readily compares with others in the Welsh Hundred of *Ewias*, and until 1852 was in St. Davids diocese. With a present congregation of about two dozen, the parish is linked with that of nearby Newton, and each in the past probably had teams for the game of fives, or handball, which used to be played outside against the north side of the nave wall (after attending church no doubt feeling exempt from the stern injunction up on the wall inside the south doorway: 'Go and sin no more'!). There are still signs of the 'fives court' plaster on the wall, and also the hinges for the shutters to protect the windows. In the churchyard, many of the inscriptions on the soft local sandstone have badly weathered and scaled, but interestingly above the grave of Harriet Powell (d.1910 aged 77, well before the NHS) there are the words: 'She was District Nurse. Attended 526 births, and never lost a Mother'.

Looking towards the flank of the Black Mountains in the countryside of Western Herefordshire

To press on, turn right out of the car park, turn right again and continue past the former inn, The Sun, now a private house, and down the steep narrow lane to Newton. At the crossroads take the road ahead, signposted for Bacton and Pontrilas, and continue ahead through Bacton to join the B4347 Vowchurch to Pontrilas road. Turn right there to pass through Abbey Dore (p.219) and Ewyas Harold (p.220) to arrive at the junction with the A465 Hereford to Abergavenny road. Turn right to join it for a mile, running alongside the River Dore, winding beneath the main railway line following the same route, and continue as far as the sharp turn across the bridge crossing the River Monnow at the National and County boundary. This is close to the confluence of the two rivers, at what has become known as Monmouth Cap. Like the village and former railway station at Three Cocks, west of Hay-on-Wye at the start of this trip, the place owes its name to a coaching inn. Now privately occupied, this stood in the angle between the two roads ahead and its survival after the inn closed is mainly thanks to William Shakespeare! For it relates to once popular local headgear which entered into lines spoken on the battlefield before the castle at Agincourt, when in Act IV of the play Fluellen referred King Henry V to the Welshmen who did good service—'wearing leeks in their Monmouth caps'. As a teenage Welsh prince, born at Monmouth Castle in 1387, Henry would have been familiar with such wear, and had also been no stranger to this part of Wales, particularly Grosmont in 1405 (below).

Leave the Abergavenny road immediately after the bridge by bearing left and then proceed up the valley after Llangua, turning left onto a minor road, signposted for Grosmont and the Castle, after half a mile turning right on the B4347 to reach the village and the tall ruins of Grosmont Castle.

---

8. The Three Castles: Grosmont Castle, Skenfrith Castle and White Castle

A heritage of deep hostility by the Welsh against the hated presence of the Saxons produced regular conflict along the border between England and Wales, and nowhere was this more savage that at Hereford in 1055, when the city, cathedral and surrounding areas were sacked and burnt with great loss of life. During the years that followed, Harold Godwineson, made earl of Hereford from that time, so excelled as a military leader in driving back the Welsh and mounting retaliatory measures that he became the inevitable successor to the throne in 1066. But he was destined to be the last of the Old English Kings, for within the year he was defeated and killed by the Normans at the Battle of Hastings. They were no more welcomed by the Welsh than the Saxons, and William the Conqueror was not able to extend his newly won territory any further into Wales than it had been before. He quickly appointed a valued supporter as earl of Hereford to secure and control the southernmost of three divisions of the border, extending from Chepstow to beyond Hereford. By the time he was killed in Flanders in 1071, Earl William fitz Osbern had completed the first castles at each end of the river cliffs of the lower Wye, at Chepstow and Monmouth, whilst attention was being paid to securing the pastoral lower Monnow valley, immediately to their north. This extended as far as the Welsh hills, close to Abergavenny, and formed one of the major gateways between Herefordshire and south Wales. Starting with earth and timber construction, the Normans built in this area a set of three further castles, two being added to that at Monmouth. These were also on the River Monnow, at Grosmont and Skenfrith, with a third to control the high divide between the Monnow and the Usk near Llantilio Crosseny. First called Llantilio Castle, and then White Castle, it completed a 'triangle of power' which is sometimes referred to as The Trilateral. Garrisoned by various lords for the Crown over many centuries, and then in separate ownerships, all three former strongholds are now protected, conserved and managed by Cadw: Welsh Historic Monuments.

---

9. Grosmont

Although situated on a lofty ridge in upper Gwent, the name has a Gallic ring and is derived from Old French for 'big hill', which is thought to refer to nearby Graig Syfyrddin. The Welsh form, *Y Grysmwnt*, known from the late 12th century, is shown on OS maps and appears on some road signs. It is likely that Grosmont Castle continued as a wooden fortification until towards the end of the 12th century before it was rebuilt in the present red sandstone masonry, quarried in the locality. Strategic importance on the England/Wales border coincided with the creation of a borough and market town under its protection during the 13th century and the phased building between 1180 and *c.*1300 of a large and handsome church.

Grosmont lasted as a town of considerable size and importance until as recently as the 19th century, was a borough until 1860, having a mayor, corporation, an official ale-taster and even 'ducking-stool' operatives at the pond in Poorscript Lane. There was a large Town Hall near the Angel inn in the centre, and the scale of the duke of Beaufort's replacement for it in 1831 is symbolic of the relatively recent significance of Grosmont and its market. The size of the cruciform St. Nicholas' Church and its octagonal tower and spire attest to its former importance, while high quality Gothic Revival designs in 1858 by J.P. Seddon (the Newport architect also responsible for the unusual Italianate Hoarwithy church) have helped to adapt the building to a more modern scale of use. The character of the huge nave is still preserved by the removal of all furniture from the floor, now flagged with old gravestone paving, whilst the interior from the crossing eastwards has been separated by a glass partition to make it warmer and more intimate for services for the smaller congregation of current times.

Grosmont Castle

Grosmont Castle, perched imposingly on a bluff overlooking the Monnow and surrounded by a deep grass-grown moat, can be reached up the lane opposite the post office. The ruins date mainly from the 13th and 14th centuries, during which period Henry III suffered acute embarrassment when taken by surprise by disaffected Border barons, in league with Llywelyn the Great. It is said that, early one morning in November 1233, they fell so suddenly upon the king's sleeping troops and his hapless foreign associates when camping around the town and castle, that they had to flee in their night gear—abandoning money, baggage, provisions and 500 horses. There was a much graver event here in 1405, when forces of Owain Glyndwr besieged Grosmont and its small garrison. The Welsh born Prince Hal of Monmouth, future victor of Agincourt, despatched such a strong relief force that some 1,000 foot soldiers out of the 8,000 in the Welsh force were killed. Critics of Glyndwr's approach to patriotism might still regard them as another example of the way his countrymen were used as 'arrow fodder'. Looking now from the high castle walls over the quiet village and countryside it is hard to grasp how so much blood could once have been spilled here, but soon afterwards a yet greater disaster, at Usk, led effectively to the end of Owain Glyndwr's revolt (1399-1406) and he vanished from sight with no further place in the history books. The military role of Grosmont Castle had finally reached an end, although the previous conclusion of the Wars of Welsh Independence (1277-83), with the death of Llywelyn ap Gruffudd, the first and last Welsh prince of Wales, had already removed its strategic importance. It became a favourite residence of the earls of Lancaster, with the addition of a new range of rooms forming the North Block early in the 14th century which is still dominated by a tall octagonal, coronetted chimney. The castle remained with the Duchy until 1825 and was once traditionally spoken of as The Castle of the Red Rose and named Rosslyn Castle—a corruption of the Celtic *Ros llwyn*, reflecting the badge of the Lancastrians.

Whilst it is possible to reach Skenfrith Castle by continuing along the B4347 down the west side of the Monnow valley below Graig Syfyrddin hill, an even more scenic route (and the additional bonus of taking in Garway—and what Pevsner called 'an uncommonly interesting church') begins by first returning back along the B4347, but continuing on it to descend steeply to river level, the Monnow bridge and National boundary at Kentchurch. Immediately across the bridge, turn right towards Kentchurch village on a minor road and after about half a mile sharp right again, avoiding Bannut Tree Lane ahead, to pass St. Mary's on the right and the private drive to Kentchurch Court on the left. Beginning alongside the winding river down to the right, the narrow road starts to rise under trees and below huge Garway Hill on the left, opposite the even loftier ridge of Syfyrddin, rising across magical valley scenes to the right. After the sign for Garway there is a another to St. Margaret's Church, pointing to the right just short of the Baptist chapel, at what the locals call The Turning.

10. Garway and the Crusaders

The manor of Garway was owned between the 12th and 16th centuries first by the Knights Templar, and then the Knights Hospitaller, and the first church was designed by the former with a round nave, adopting the shape of the church raised over the supposed site of Christ's sepulchre in Jerusalem, as was their usual practice. After military service in the crusades, the Templars resorted to avaricious and other unfavoured ways and were suppressed in 1308, their resources taken over by the Hospitallers, the Knights of St. John (to whom the St. John's Ambulance service can trace its origins). Dependent on the commandery at Dinmore (p.146), they rebuilt the Garway nave to a more customary rectangular design. They kept the earlier richly carved chancel arch, once described as 'rather Saracenic in appearance' and raised on shafts with typical Norman water-leaf capitals. Just beyond it on the north side are blocked heavy stone steps which led to a rood loft. The chancel roof structure above exhibits sturdy ancient beams, collar beams and wind braces—which contrast with the recently restored barrel vaulting over the nave. The huge,

Garway Church

roughly formed 16th- or 17th-century oak pews stand out firmly among the furnishings, whilst on the wall at the west end there is a framed diagram of the building which explains why it is so oddly laid out. For the square, loopholed 13th-century tower at the west end is quite out of line with the body of the church, and was in the past one of Herefordshire's completely detached bell towers, before it was later linked to the nave with used tufa blocks. The present Church Farm next door is on the site of the knights' commandery and incorporates a circular dovecot with a dome-like roof and circular opening. Designed to provide meat for the community, it contains tiers of 666 nesting holes in 19 rows and has been there at least since the date on its Latin inscription, which translates: 'In the year 1326 this Dovecot was built by brother Richard'.

Although there were at one time shops, a post office and a forge, Garway now has no obvious centre and is made up of scattered small hamlets and several farms. Continuing from The Turning at the Baptist chapel, the road reaches The Garway Moon inn on the left, opposite Garway Common where the villagers have established a well tended cricket and sports field. The route then curves to the right to head for the B4521 at the Broad Oak crossroads—so named from a very broad old tree standing in front of a former inn. Turn right here, following the Skenfrith and Abergavenny sign to follow a winding descent of what used to form part of the main stagecoach route from London to Milford Haven, and spare a thought for the horses which once struggled up in the opposite direction from the Monnow Bridge and the Bell inn (which much later was to become AA Pub of the Year for Wales and gained further awards).

Skenfrith Castle

11. Skenfrith

Skenfrith is a small secluded hamlet on the River Monnow, in a valley surrounded by steep sloping fields and woods and principally centred on a single street which winds past its early 13th-century castle and church. Skenfrith Castle is thought to date from *c*.1228-1232 and comprises a four-sided curtain wall, still almost to its original height, with drum towers at each angle and an additional semi circular tower in the middle of the west wall. Within there is a distinctive round keep of 21ft. internal diameter, deemed, when it was built, to have clear advantages over square-sided structures. The curvature certainly made for a superior field of fire, leaving no 'dead ground' and no corners vulnerable to ramming. (Three other such castles of the same period featured in this book, are at Bronllys, Tretower and Longtown). In each case, the top of the keep and the corner towers would originally have been capped by strong timber 'hourds' or fighting galleries with arrow loops, and these could

in time of war also be suspended below wall-walk level around the outer walls. Unlike Grosmont Castle and White Castle, there is now no obvious sign of a moat, but during the 1950s archaeologists were able to show that the curtain wall was at one time surrounded by 9 feet of water, 46 feet wide and separated from the wall by a 7ft. berm on the south, west and north. The Monnow completed the water defences on the east side.

Once Border hostilities ended, the castle continued in use as an administrative centre and repairs and

Skenfrith Church

remodelling were undertaken during the mid-15th century to equip it for domestic purposes. But by 1538 it had become disused and abandoned and a 16th-century survey showed that it had become roofless and derelict. At one stage, cottages were built against the outer walls and an orchard was planted around the keep. In 1825 a long connection with the Duchy of Lancaster came to an end with a private sale and more recently it passed to the National Trust, and the guardianship of Cadw.

Typically during the Middle Ages, the parish church was sited not far away from the castle, and there are good reasons for choosing 1207 as the date of the older parts of the present building, which are the tower, nave and chancel. The tower closely resembles that at Garway, and its five feet thick walls would likewise have served to protect villagers during Welsh raids: otherwise the chief difference is the open lantern or 'dovecote' cap here.

After its foundation, the growth of Skenfrith, with castle and church and possibly as a borough, surprisingly did not come up to expectation, despite being in a promising Monnow valley location, right on the border and on a major main route between England and Wales.

The tour continues westward on the B4521, to head for White Castle, passing a sign to the right for Dawn of Day and then through Cross Ash, before making a left hand turn signposted Brynderi and Llantilio Crossenny. Continue straight on at the sign pointing left for Brynderi and turn right opposite a tall boundary wall and built-in letter box at the sign pointing back to Cross Ash. Turn left after The Old School and left at Newordden Farm leading to the drive for White Castle on the right. It is the only castle of the three where there are admission charges and standard hours of opening, and where detailed official handbooks about the three castles are available.

12.   White Castle

Although there is now little showing, like Skenfrith there might at one time have been a small borough under the protection of White Castle, but the usual closely associated church is here over a mile away at Llantilio Crosseny. Standing by itself on the summit of a commanding hill, the castle strategically formed the forward centre within the wide region enclosed by the northward bend of the River Monnow. Because of this remoteness, stone robbers

White Castle

have always been put off and consequently it still looks almost as it must have done during the mid-13th century, when this hotly disputed area was under ever growing threat from Llywelyn ap Gruffudd. But it has been roofless since the 16th century and at first sight the other main difference is that the plastered rendering, which prompted its name, has also gone, except for remnants in sheltered crannies. Visitors first enter a grassy outer ward, part of a one-time larger enclosure, protected by a stone curtain, flanking towers and a gatehouse, defended by a shallow ditch which is believed always to have been dry. This area could be used as a defended camp and base for the royal army and hopefully prevent surprise attacks, such as that at Grosmont in 1233 (above). Ahead, a modern wooden bridge crosses the deep steep-sided moat to allow entry to the main defences of the castle. These comprise a central pear-shaped inner ward defended with a stone curtain of 1184-86 with later circular flanking towers. The entrance of the 12th-century masonry castle was on the south side of the ward, where further protection was provided by a crescent-shaped outlier or hornwork, but in the 13th century there was a 180 degrees reorientation of the castle. The present gatehouse with two further round towers were built on the north side and the strong flanking towers added along the circuit of the older curtain. A postern, or small gate, was retained at the position of the original entrance and it was at this time that the palisaded outer ward was also refortified with its stone curtain. White Castle thus became the first of many great fortresses to be built in Wales by the Lord Edward, responsible for many more when he became King Edward I. Unlike Grosmont and Skenfrith, all his work was for military and not domestic reasons, and after it lost its primary strategic purpose, White Castle was left with only administrative roles—and by the 16th century had become derelict, like the others of the Trilateral.

Turn left after leaving White Castle and continue straight ahead as far as the T-junction with the B4521 where you turn right, but at Cross Ash turn left to join the road initially signposted for Grosmont, driving below the south-western flank of Graig Syfyrddin. Keep on this road, but head for Llanvihangel Crucorney, making a gradual turn south-westwards until the impressive mass of Ysgyryd Fawr, or the Skirrid, appears in sight directly ahead. Then descend to join the A465 Hereford to Abergavenny road, on which you turn right towards Hereford. After about a mile turn left at Pandy, just before the Pandy Inn, to pass beneath the main line railway, with the Caravan Club site afterwards on the left. The River Monnow, soon appears on the right—much slenderer than when met with earlier on the tour. After descending from its source in the hills, it makes a sharp right-angle turn around Alltyrynys in Walterstone, to flow gently eastwards towards Monmouth Cap before resuming its former bearing towards Grosmont and Skenfrith.

13.   Alltyrynys—A cradle of the Cecils

Alltyrynys has been freely translated as 'the island steep' or 'the height of the island', because of its position on a neck of almost encircled land at the confluence of the Honddu and Monnow rivers, and parts of a Tudor house here have been incorporated in the present Country Hotel and Restaurant. This is signposted to the right, and at one time it was part of an estate of the Cecils. Originally of Welsh origins and bearing the Celtic name of *Sitsyllt*, probably their most famous son was William Cecil, Lord Burghley (1520-98), chief Secretary of State, later Lord High Treasurer and a well trusted counsellor of Queen Elizabeth I. This is perhaps one place where good Queen Bess may rightly be claimed to have slept, for she is known to have visited the Cecils—and would have been familiar with many of the fine buildings which have long since been lost or ill-used. The hotel still retains traces of these glorious days in some of the oak panelling, beams, a moulded ceiling of *c*.1600—and a four-poster bed.

The road moves northward on a parallel course below the long Black Mountains ridge, carrying at close range the Offa's Dyke Path some 1,350ft. above to the left, and the River Monnow down to the right, soon to arrive at Clodock, followed almost imperceptibly by Longtown. In between the two hamlets, the Olchon, Monnow and Escley valleys merge as their waters combine not far upstream from Clodock church, the Cornewall Arms, a weir, masonry bridge and disused Victorian water mill.

Clodock Bridge

14. Clodock and Longtown

The village of Clodock grew around its parish church, which was founded in *c.*520 AD and dedicated to *Sant Clydawg* (Saint Clodock). A King of Ewias, he was murdered during a love quarrel, buried on the bank of the Monnow and afterwards elevated to sainthood as a martyr. *Ewias* was then in Wales and the settlement was called *Llan* (an enclosure) *y Merthyr Clydawg*, but after boundary changes introduced by Henry VIII it became part of Herefordshire and England and the National boundary now runs along the ridgeline, high above. The church was enlarged during the 12th century and restored in 1919 after being found in a ruinous state, but as local people thankfully put it, it is 'a church the Victorians forgot'! The broad, aisleless nave has been dated as late 12th century, the chancel (probably the site of the original building) a century later

Clodock Church, with the Black Mountains beyond

The interior of Clodock Church, with its three-decker pulpit on the right

and the tower as early 15th century. The woodwork furnishings are very fine, especially a three-decker pulpit from *c*.1650-80, box pews of the same period and the raked west choir gallery which was built not very long afterwards. The Clodock and Longtown parish served by St. Clydawg's is part of a united benefice which also includes the Craswall, Llanveynoe, St. Margaret's, Michaelchurch Escley and Newton parishes.

Later on during those troublesome times it would have been usual for the church to be under the protection of a castle, but this did not appear until after the Norman Conquest. The de Lacys held the Lordship of the area, embracing more than a dozen modern parishes, and from *c*.1190, as part of a chain of border fortresses, they built a castle on a ridge top site at the top end of the village of Longtown. It was then known as *Longa Villa*, within what became the Hundred, or district, of Ewyas Lacy. The circular keep still crowns a battered plinth and steep sided motte and below it there is an inner bailey which retains remnants of the east and southern curtain walls. A gateway passage separates this from an outer western bailey to the south and across the road there is an east bailey within a high rampart. This has become the village green, used as a sports field and playground, whilst below the western bailey the 13th century castle chapel was largely rebuilt in 1868. As St. Peter's it became a chapel of ease to Clodock parish church, but has more recently been closed and is now converted to a private dwelling. It overlooks the triangular ancient market place and site

of the one-time village well, whence the short medieval borough street ran directly down hill to the south. Despite early expectations, Longtown was destined to become no more than a small village and, left with abandoned burgage plots of former residents, is now regarded by landscape historians as yet another Marches 'failed town'.

The keep at Longtown Castle (left) and the walls to the bailey (right)

Continuing on from Clodock, past what is probably the original motte and bailey fortification at Pont Hendre at the end of the Olchon Brook, not far from the Crown inn and junction for Ewyas Harold and Michaelchurch Escley, today's Longtown has long qualified in the lexicon of modern town planners as a bad case of disapproved 'ribbon development'! Among the strung out stone cottages along the steep long undulating way up the Monnow valley, there are newer houses, a village store and post office, and at the former New Inn, where an old sign reminds of 'spiritous liquors once sold by Thomas Penry', there is the Longtown Outdoor Education Centre of Northampton County Council, and the Mountain Rescue Post. For although this is an acknowledged good starting point for many great walks, it is as well to be reminded that dangers and nasty surprises can exist along the towering and daunting escarpment which is to be a formidable companion on the way up towards Craswall. A plaque just beyond the centre marks the site of the old village pound, once kept for stray animals, and next, at Llanwonog Lane, there is a restored old sheep dipwell, perhaps fittingly on the way to Salem Baptist Church. Just across the road by the castle entrance there are old Church School Rooms, built by subscription in 1816 and in 2003 displaying a 'Sold' sign, suggesting another likely change of use. There was a subsequent village school from 1868 and further up the road during the 1970s Longtown gained a new Primary School.

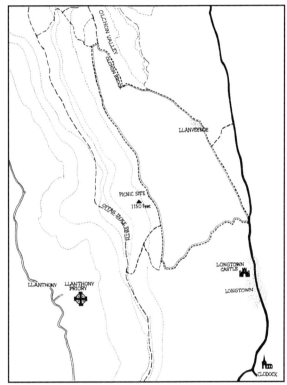

Map showing the details of the detour to the picnic site

Just beyond Longtown it is possible to make a circular detour off to the left for a picnic site stop if you wish (see map to the left). To make this, take the first turning to the left past Longtown Castle, descending to the Olchon Brook and then climbing steeply up again to a single track mountain road leading to what is an idyllic picnic spot. It is at *c.*1150ft. from where the panorama laid out below is generally classed as among the most spectacular scenery in England. You are normally unlikely to meet much traffic up there but wandering sheep have to be watched out for. Follow the road and then down to almost where you started the detour, turning left to the rejoin the 'main' route.

As the main route carrying straight on from Longtown approaches the end of the escarpment towards Hay Bluff, the steep-sided spur of *Crib-y-Garth*, the most northerly ridge of the Black Mountains also shown on the map as Black Hill, looms ever higher above the road. The village sign for Craswall soon appears, but again there is no actual centre but only groups of cottages, some substantial houses, the village hall (the former Victorian school, bought by the parishioners for a village hall with the proceeds of a lamb sale in 1975), a pub and, further up on the right, at a sharp left hand bend in the Hay-on-Wye road is St. Mary's Church.

15. Craswall: The Black Hill and The Bull's Head

In 1982 the author Bruce Chatwin chose a fictional outlying hill farm of 120 acres, with grazing rights on the Black Hill, for his novel *On the Black Hill*. Called The Vision, the property was farmed throughout their working lives by the twins Amos and Benjamin Jones and their parents, and it portrayed, as *The Times* critic put it, 'a sense of the delicate balance between nature, people and animals', The book and later film covered many recognisable places, from Radnorshire as far as Hereford, but they did not bring in the Bull's Head inn at Craswall. Once used by the drovers, this was there throughout the period of the story and had already earned its high reputation long before. It might easily also have been closely studied over the years by pub architects and designers working on some of the range of 'Olde Worlde' pubs, those which sprout low oak beams, flagstone steps and undulating floors where there were none before, plus cosy open log fires and intriguing copper and other antique exhibits around the walls and woodwork. For all of these features have long existed, largely in their authentic form, in the free house public areas of the Bull's Head during the 125 years ownership until 1998 of the Gane family. There is the original serving hatch, and also not generally found at modern pubs, a paddock and guaranteed grazing for patrons' horses and 'rough camping' in one of the fields. Local people can still

The Bulls Head

recall Beatie Lewis, the last member of the Gane family to live there. She played the organ at St. Mary's Church at every service for over 50 years, probably first walking alongside the pub and down to the bottom of the hill to cross the tiny River Monnow as it started the way from its source at Red Dingle, eventually to join the Wye at Monmouth.

16.   Craswall: Sport at St. Mary's Church

The squat little building is set back on the right and has been compared in appearance and construction with others in the border area, notably Capel-y-Ffin, St. Margarets (both met on these tours), and Rhulen, a mile and a half south-east of Cregrina. These others may not, however, have had a cockpit in their churchyard, but here at Craswall a depression in the northwest corner is said to have been so used until early in the 19th century, maybe until it became illegal in 1849. In 1938, one parishioner is said to have remembered that his father, when a child, had seen cock fighting

Craswall Church with its outdoor stone seating near the foot of the walls

there—and had also played the game of fives against the north wall after church. Like St. Margarets, visited earlier, there is still an area of plaster above which there is also a significant large square depression in the ground against the wall. Higher up there are the remains of six projecting timbers which are thought possibly to have been part of a stable roof. Also visible on the north wall of the church is a straight vertical joint which defines an added westward extension. This is now the vestry but in the 19th century it was used as a schoolroom, for which the fireplace was probably provided,

211

and maybe later it became a farmers' storeroom for wool waiting to be sent to the wool fairs. On the east and south walls, and the east wall of the church porch, there is outdoor stone seating, such as that seen at Llanveynoe and Partrishow, and this was once probably in use when sermons were preached from the steps of the churchyard cross. But it is perhaps another relic from when the church was also used as an important social centre for the Craswall community.

Despite much effort from the Grandmontine Society, the Woolhope Naturalists' Field Club and many interested enthusiasts, frost and other adverse influences are combining to produce continuing deterioration of the ruins of Craswall Priory and these may now be said to be of interest limited mainly to students of medieval architecture and antiquarians. They may be reached about two miles along the Hay-on-Wye road from the Bull's Head inn, down the bridleway at the Abbey Farm sign which points to the right—opposite a parking space on the left. The ruins are hidden by trees almost until they are reached at the bottom of the steep descent into Fox Dingle. Cross the small stream and there is an entrance gate to the excavated and overgrown remains not far beyond.

17.   Craswall: Monks of the Fox Dingle

Dedication of Craswall Church to St. Mary suggests a link with a monastery (Cistercian and Grandmontine churches were always dedicated to St. Mary), and here there is no doubt in view of the former existence from *c*.1225 of Craswall Priory, further up the valley which had a ruling prior, three priests and ten lay brothers. It was the second of only three 'alien' houses founded in Britain by the French order of Grandmont. The Grandmontines, were a reformed, rigid offshoot of the Benedictines and chose equally

Remains of Craswall Priory

wild and desolate places for their monasteries. 'For the well being of his soul', Walter de Lacy II, lord of the manor, endowed it with some 800 acres of land between Talgarth and Holme Lacy, with tithes, grazing rights and other privileges, and with a monastery site at the head of the valley of *Cwm-y-Camddo* (the Fox Dingle), by a small tributary brook of the Monnow. It was to become the spartan home of a community living in poverty and solitude for more than two centuries, until from 1441 it came to share the fate of all other remaining alien priories dependent on a foreign abbey, and was dissolved and seized by the Crown. The revenues were made over to Christ's College, Cambridge, and the abandoned buildings soon became a confused mass of ruins as nature took over, along with local people 'quarrying' materials for building projects. Some carved stone has been seen at the nearby Abbey Farm and other 'recycled' materials have appeared at least as far away as Michaelchurch Escley. There is a strong feeling that the east window of St. Mary's Church, dated *c*.14th / early 15th century, comes from the priory and perhaps much of its other stone fabric too. There have in the past also been suggestions that the evicted monks actually built the church.

Until the Suppression, most of the local lay population were probably tenants of the monks and worshipped at their priory church, also dedicated to St. Mary, with no need for a separate parish church. This suggests that the present St. Mary's probably dates from the mid 15th century.

Excavations at the deeply overgrown priory site early in the 20th century and in 1962 exposed signs of a long and narrow church with an eastern apse, a small cloister to the south of the nave, a chapter house and domestic buildings, although no refectory because of erosion by flooding from an adjoining stream.

The Hay-on-Wye road continues to climb a further short distance, past a conifer plantation on the right and a good close-up view of Hay Bluff on the left, before reaching its high point at *Parc y Meirch* (the park of the horses). Here the spot level on OS Landranger map 161 registers 442m. (1,450 ft.) above sea level, whilst another at the lower end of Hay, where the tour finishes, is 77m. This is a difference of almost 1,200 feet, and after leaving the Monnow Valley behind, and taking in for the first time the wide prospect across the Wye Valley towards the Radnorshire uplands ahead, it is not difficult to conclude that there will be some steep roads. These also have many awkward turns and hairpin bends requiring close attention from the driver, but passengers can enjoy the view to the right of the thickly wooded Dulas Glen, later to become the Cusop Dingle met at the start of the tour. This road is also rather narrow, but it has a reasonable number of passing places as far as the 'Give Way' line for the road from Capel-y-Ffin, where you turn right, and to Hay-on-Wye a further two and a half miles further down to the right. From then on, and past New Forest Farm, the road is somewhat wider and the bends and swoops are not quite so challenging.

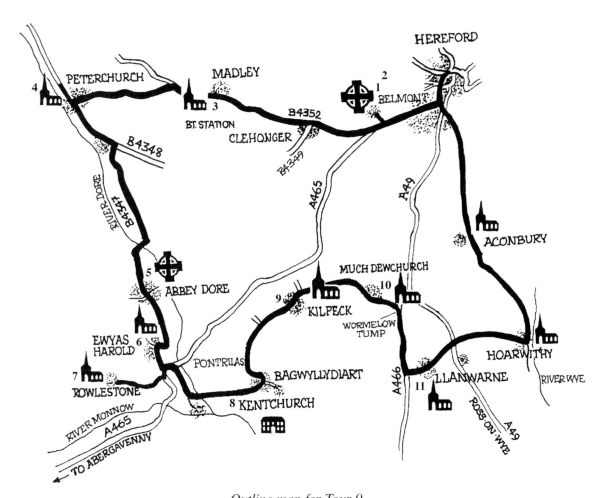

Outline map for Tour 9
The numbers 1 to 11 relate to the boxed information given within the tour
For information on Hoarwithy and Aconbury, see pages 241 and 242 under Tour 10

Tour 9   Churches and Villages to the south-west of Hereford

This tour covers an area to the south-west of Hereford and includes many fine and individual churches as well as pleasant undulating countryside together with the Golden Valley. It follows a mixture of B and minor roads, none of them overly narrow and most with room for two lines of traffic. Without the few small diversions the length of the route amounts to about 45 miles.

The tour leaves Hereford on the A465 heading south towards Abergavenny. After about 2 miles from the city centre, and just beyond the edge of the city, turn right at a sign for Belmont, Ruckhall and Eaton Bishop, turning left after about a quarter of a mile to park at the car park for Belmont Abbey.

---

1   Belmont Abbey

Belmont Abbey

Having recently converted to Roman Catholicism, Francis Wegg-Prosser (*see* Belmont House, box 2) commissioned E.W. Pugin to design a church at Belmont, in consultation with Thomas Brown, a monk of Downside, and thus became founder of what was to be the Abbey Church. Mainly constructed of locally quarried sandstone between 1854 and 1857, it became the provisional cathedral for the newly established diocese of Newport and Menevia (the whole of Wales and Herefordshire) and the seat of its bishop. Built in Victorian Gothic style, it was opened in 1859 and completed during the early 1880s with the addition of a 112ft. high crossing tower and north transept. Thomas Brown was the first bishop and later, in 1916, Belmont became a full cathedral, was declared an independent priory the following year and in 1920 was raised to the rank of an autonomous abbey. At the time it was the only Roman Catholic cathedral to be governed by a bishop, prior and a chapter of monks since before the Reformation. That year the seat of the bishop was transferred to the new cathedral at Newport and the prior, Dom Aelred Kindersley, was elected as the first abbot. For the next 14 years he led the community in the life of the English Benedictine Congregation, of which Belmont forms a part, and observed its educational tradition in 1926 by establishing a boarding and Public School. By the late 20th century a range of 19 subjects was being offered to about 290 boys in 4 boarding Houses and 1 day House, but a changing world was producing rapidly falling numbers of boarders and the school had suddenly to close in 1994. Some school buildings have since been

215

leased to the Primary Care NHS Trust and Benedomus, a house-building company, was set up by the monks to create a small and varied residential community near their own. A building contractor was chosen and work was sub-contracted to be undertaken by members of the community and the result is St. Michael's Court. Close by, a Benedictine tradition of hospitality has been fulfilled with the building of Hedley Lodge, a well appointed monastery guest house for those travelling on business or leisure. There the monk Guestmaster caters for groups and individuals in 17 twin or double bedrooms, all highly rated by the English Tourism Council, there is an elegant restaurant and a choice of conference and seminar suites. An annual programme of retreats and conferences is also arranged and the abbey serves as the church of the large rural parish of Belmont. Outside, the community of about 50 monks serves other parishes in Herefordshire, South Wales and Cumbria. Belmont's monks have acted as chaplains to convents, universities and to H.M. Forces, and a former headmaster and abbot was in 2001 ordained bishop of the diocese of Menevia, South Wales. Also from 1967 a missionary tradition was pursued from the abbey in Uganda and this was followed by pastoral and liturgical work and a new monastery in northern Peru in 1985.

You can turn left out of the car park to take a look at Belmont House making a right turn into well-manicured grounds at the sign for Belmont Golf Club about a further quarter of a mile down the minor road, or turn right to rejoin the main tour by turning right again back onto the A465.

2. Belmont House

The name Belmont means 'beautiful hill', and Old Hill was aptly chosen as the site for Belmont House, originally named and started in late 1788 to the design of James Wyatt. He was the architect responsible for rebuilding much of Hereford Cathedral after the collapse in 1786 of the west front, half the nave, aisles and roofing. Then in 1867 the house was extensively remodelled for F.R. Wegg-Prosser by Edward Welby Pugin, son of the revered architect Augustus Welby Pugin and it is now a Grade II* listed building. Today it contains the bar, restaurant and changing rooms of Belmont Lodge and Golf Club and has been joined by a much later building which provides 30 purpose-built hotel rooms looking over the 18 hole golf course to the River Wye.

Once back on the A465 turn right back onto the Ruckhall road and right again to the A465 Abergavenny road. Pass the abbey almshouses on the right and then turn right onto the B4349, sign-posted to Hay-on-Wye and also Clehonger, Kingstone and Madley, the road becoming the B4352. Past Eaton Bishop the road crosses the course of the Roman road running south from *Magnis* (p.162). Soon the site of BT's Satellite Earth Station is passed on the left. Associated with the station at Goonhilly Down, Cornwall, which in 1965 pioneered the use of Telstar as the first satellite for trans-Atlantic broadcasting, Madley entered service in 1978 with an initial 105ft. diameter dish aerial which provided circuits for telephone, telex, telegram, data and facsimile calls, as well as television, to and from nearly 40 other countries. These were mainly in the Middle East, Africa, India, the Far East and Australasia and came via a satellite which, from Madley, appeared to be just above the horizon—but is out in space 22,300 miles over the Indian Ocean. The development of global satellite communications has greatly progressed with the addition of several more dishes at Madley since those pioneering days.

Keep following signs to Madley, and some distance from the village its church dominates the view, first appearing to be on the right hand side of the road, and then shifting finally to the left. Here, on the opposite side of the road, the fine timber-framed Town House is thought to date from the 16th century.

3.   Madley: Church of the Nativity of the Blessed Virgin Mary

Madley Church

The crypt at Madley Church
before restoration and rededication

It was unusual for this church dedication to survive the Reformation, for generally it was seen as a sign of Popery and discontinued. Parts of the building still in use were built in around 1050-1100 AD and later, in the Middle Ages, Madley drew its pilgrims in large numbers, like a miniature cathedral. For records of 1318 mention the Statue of the Blessed Virgin Mary in the crypt underneath the chancel, which is itself a very rare feature in a parish church and was probably constructed to accommodate the shrine and accessible down steep steps from the north side of the chancel arch and from outside. This was restored and rededicated for meditation and prayer, childrens' and other community uses after years as a general store or coal boiler house. The east window contains examples of the oldest and finest stained glass in England, some of it dating from about 1250. Above the chancel arch there are recently restored wall-paintings from *c*.1300, whilst at the opposite end there is one of the largest fonts in Britain, where countless children and adults have been baptised since Norman times. Well before then, in *c*.550 AD, St. Dubricius, or Dyfrig, (p.241) is thought to have been born at Madley. He probably founded the first Christian community there before he became an important church leader, centred at Hentland and Moccas, and eventually was bishop of Llandaff. It is possible that an earlier church at Madley was dedicated to him and not far away to the south, the church at St. Devereux (a corruption of his name) has this dedication.

Continue along the B4352, ignoring directions to Shenmore. Look instead for a sign pointing to the left for Stockley Hill and Peterchurch, at a sharp right bend in the B road, and turn left onto the minor road. Early parts of the ensuing 3 miles run are along a single track road of capillary width, with few passing places, and some reversing skills may be called for. It is all worthwhile, for the climb up Stockley Hill produces the best of Herefordshire countryside and the extensive views below are all breathtaking. After a while the road begins to widen, especially over the last mile or so, passing Wellbrook Manor, a very special 14th-century base-cruck house on the left. At the junction with the B4348, turn right into Peterchurch. This rather straggling village is at the centre of the Golden Valley and, symbolically pointing heavenwards, the tall spire of St. Peter's Church is visible for many miles in both directions. Only much closer can it be seen that it is made of fibreglass. To reach the church, turn left at the brown direction sign.

4. Peterchurch

*The church at Peterchurch
before refurbishment*

As a rule, churches have three divisions but at St. Peter's there are four, the nave, two chancels and an apse. Consequently there are three Romanesque arches leading to a fine window above the Saxon stone altar with its four incised consecration crosses—another surprising local survival from the Reformation. Local legend has it that, much earlier, St. Peter passed this way on his way to Rome and that he blessed a spring for baptising his converts, and also that a fish with golden neck chains was caught in a nearby pool. There is certainly a plaster panel of a painted fish high on the wall of the nave, and this has been there at least as far back as the 1870s, for it attracted the attention of the Reverend Francis Kilvert. Doubtless he would also have seen the impressive stone church spire, which dated from 1320, long before the top two thirds had to be removed for safety reasons. This happened in the 1940s, and it is impossible to guess what would have been written in his 19th-century *Diary* if he had prophesied what was to happen next. For after much resolute fund-raising for the next 20 years, it became clear that the cost of a new stone spire was steadily outpacing the replacement account. So instead, over £30,000 went on a fibreglass replica and in 1974 (after an initial scare when it did not quite fit) this was raised into position on the 13th-century tower by a 240ft. high crane. More recently the church has been renovated and adapted with floor heating to serve as a Childrens Centre, a volunteer-run public library (in the belltower), all served from a modern kitchen.

St. Peter's Church is on the banks of the River Dore and close to the station site of the Golden Valley Railway, which was closed to passengers in 1941. Back at the car, parked just across the small river bridge and near them both, it is possible to ponder over what is especially 'golden' about the valley and also what the origin is of 'Dore'. Although there are several opinions, local received wisdom is that Welsh people in the valley probably told the newly arriving Normans that the river was *dwr*, which is Welsh for 'water'. However this was taken to be *d'or*, French for 'of gold'.

The tour now returns down the B4348, passing the junction on which you joined it, following signs for Hereford and Ross-on-Wye and runs close to the River Dore to proceed down the Golden Valley. There is nothing especially golden to see, but in this wide, tranquil and unspoilt valley of gentle wooded slopes and soft landscape, there is much else of rare beauty along with the stone and stained-glass wonders of its historic churches (realised in the recent choice of setting for *Shadowlands*, the play and film and TV biopic of C.S. Lewis, Cambridge professor and, *inter alia*, writer of children's stories of the land of *Narnia*).

At Vowchurch (p.199) the tour route turns right onto the B4347 for Abbey Dore, remaining quite close to the river and crossing to its west side just before reaching Bacton and Bacton Stud. The hamlet of Abbey Dore appears just a mile further along, and you can park alongside the church on the B road.

5.   Abbey Dore, Church of St. Mary

Dore Abbey through the lychgate

Soon after 1066, various orders of monks began to cross from France to seek out isolated places where they could withdraw from worldly affairs and follow a monastic life. The Cistercians, or white monks, opted for places well away from towns or villages and it is not surprising therefore that some were attracted to Tintern (p.284), Cwmhir (p.122) and Dore in the remote and wild river valleys of the Borderland. And so, under the patronage of Robert of Ewyas (see below): 'In 1147 was begun the abbey of Dore'. In common with all other Cistercian foundations it was dedicated to St. Mary by a community from Morimund, a daughter house of the abbey of Citeaux in Burgundy, the origin of their name. Centuries before, Saint Benedict had not barred manual labour, and as well as offering prayers and spiritual devotions, the Cistercians were to place particular emphasis on farming, employing lay brothers (*conversi*) to undertake much of the heavy work. The magnitude of the resulting monastery reveals the measure of their success in obtaining income from the numerous estates which they acquired, many of them endowments by Normans wishing to ensure a favourable place in the life of the world to come. There were at least 17 granges, or outlying farms, and as at Leominster (p.49), much of the wealth of the abbey came from sheep and a flourishing wool trade (and, wrote Giraldus Cambrensis, from 'avaricious and grasping ways' matching the means of the lowlier faithful, also seeking the promise of an open door to Paradise).

All traces of the first church have now disappeared and what remains dates from *c*.1180 onwards. When it was eventually completed, the church consisted of a presbytery, crossing, north and south transepts, each with two chapels at their east ends, and a nave of 10 bays about 152ft. long with north and south aisles. On the north side were cloisters, a 12-sided chapter house, monks' quarters and other buildings.

In common with all other monasteries in the kingdom, Dore Abbey was suppressed in 1537 and its endowments were restored to secular use, John Scudamore of Holme Lacy (p.233) being a principal purchaser. The abbot was retired with an annual State pension of £13, and over the ensuing years the nave, choir and most of the monastic buildings were demolished, leaving just the presbytery, with its ambulatory and chapels, the crossing, transepts, the stumps of nave columns and one nave arch. About a hundred years later the Holme Lacy estate was inherited by Scudamore's great-great-grandson, John, the first Viscount Scudamore. Sometimes called 'the Good Lord Scudamore', he did much to improve cider-apple strains in Herefordshire and the breed of its 'white-face' cattle, and in 1632 began to undertake the repair of the church which by that time was being used as a cattle shelter. The great arch leading to the nave and the side arches to the nave aisles were blocked and John Abel of Sarnesfield, later to become the King's Carpenter (p.158), was contracted to rebuild the roof (felling 204 tons of local oak at 5 shillings a ton, which was conveyed to the church by Scudamore's men). Abel also carved a rather hefty and elaborate screen surmounted by the arms of Charles I, flanked

The screen, just one of the highlights inside Dore Abbey

by those of Scudamore and the see of Canterbury (signifying the role of archbishop William Laud) and most of the furniture in the presbytery. The present tower was added in 1633 above the inner south transept chapel (at a cost of £90) to harmonise with the medieval architecture, and among a great many other features of special interest are the 13th-century tiles which have been reset in the floor near the altar and the 17th-century stained glass in the east windows above the original monastic 12ft. stone altar (which was rescued from a local farmyard after being used for salting meat and making cheese on). Re-consecration took place on Palm Sunday in 1634 and St. Mary's has ever since served as the parish church, one of very few in England of Cistercian origin which, up to now, is still used regularly for worship. At other times it has provided a setting for musical events, such as The Abbey Dore Festival, when artists of international fame memorably and aptly included the French singer, Gerard Souzey and cellist, Paul Tortelier performing with his wife, son and daughter. But, as in many churches, major repair work is needed and redundancy has been considered (partly in the hope that the Churches Conservation Trust will take over responsibility for preserving the structure, and still allow occasional use for church purposes). After a public meeting, this prospect for what the bishop has described as 'a church of outstanding beauty, holiness and splendour' has been avoided for the foreseeable future by the formation and work of the Friends of Dore Abbey. A major task involving extensive repairs to tiles and masonry has resulted in the abbey being taken off the English Heritage critical risk register.

The tour continues southwards on the B4347 past the Nevill Arms on the right and through Ewyas Harold, a rural gathering point at the southern outlet of the Golden Valley. If you want to stop and look at its setting by the Dore and its church, follow the signs to the village centre off to the right where the B road bends to the left.

6.   Ewyas Harold

Historically, the land of Ewias lay to the Welsh side of the conjectured line of Offa's Dyke in this area, whilst Harold was the son of Ralph, or Ranulph (d.1057), a favoured nephew of Edward the Confessor. Half French himself, through his mother, the king twice created Ralph the first Norman earl of Hereford (initially to replace earl Sweyn Godwineson, who was banished for 4 years for disgraceful behaviour involving the abbess of Leominster (p.49)). Before 1052, Ralph almost certainly erected, in an unwelcoming city, one of the few pre-Conquest castles in the country and established a French garrison there. In order to strengthen the borderland against raids by the recalcitrant Welsh, further early castles were built at strategically important Richard's Castle (p.72), and at Ewyas Harold. But in 1055, about five years later, a force led by earl Ralph was routed a short distance outside Hereford's defences by a combined body of Welshmen, disaffected English and supportive Vikings and this was followed up in the city and cathedral by great slaughter and destruction—and the coining of the nickname Ralph the Timid for the earl's disastrous performance. Hereford was later refortified and so too, in 1067-71, was Ewyas Harold Castle. This work was undertaken by Ralph's successor, earl William fitz Osbern (d.1071) as part of a major consolidation and extension of his designated border territory, which also included major castles at Clifford, Richard's Castle and Wigmore. During the 1090s, Ralph's son Harold was granted Ewyas Castle by William II and thereafter he made it chief of his many abodes in France and England,

Ewyas Harold Church

giving his name to the parish to this day. After his death, his son Robert founded the priory of Ewyas Harold as a cell and offering to the monastery and church of St. Peter at Gloucester, but there is now no trace of where it is supposed to have been, south-east of the castle site. But above the Dulas Brook, Castle Tump as it is now called, survives on private ground as an earthwork covered with trees on a mound overlooking the village and traces of a defended borough have also been recorded. In 1086, Ewias was one of five boroughs counted within Herefordshire at the time of the Domesday Book and, under the protection of its important border castle, like Kington it might have expanded to complete Hereford's ring of satellite towns. But following the defeat of the aggressive Owain Glyndwr, after c.1410 the fortress became redundant and it started to vanish. After that, and lacking any other major source of employment, the village economy was largely sustained by farming and small businesses. Major buildings were built from locally quarried stone—including the castle—and timber from the woods, whilst smaller dwellings were made of bricks formed from the clay dug from the fields and fired in kilns at Pontrilas and nearby.

Situated just off the A465 Hereford to Abergavenny road, the village now has a population of about 900 and this is gradually increasing with the introduction of new homes and small factories. It has a modern primary school, a small number of local shops and services and two pubs, the Dog inn and the Temple Bar inn which also cater for a substantial part of the surrounding area. The parish church of St. Michael dates back to the 13th century, to the time when its imposing west tower was separate from the main building and was used as a place of refuge by the villagers during Welsh raids.

The tour continues along the B4347 to pass through more of the village to a junction with the A465, where a decision is required about a possible short detour. This is to Rowlestone, sometimes spelt Rowlstone, tucked away in the hills to the south west of Ewyas Harold, where St. Peter's Church is of major significance to all who have an interest in the unique work of the Herefordshire School of Romanesque sculpture (see below). To get there, turn right for a very short distance along A465, and then, short of the garden centre to the right, follow the direction sign for Rowlestone up the fairly steep minor road. The church is on the right, about a mile and a half further on. You will need to return to the A465 after visiting the church.

If you wish to give the church a miss, the main tour turns left on the A465 and almost immediately right to continue along the B4347 for Pontrilas.

7. St. Peter's Church, Rowlestone

Carved tympanum and voussoirs above at Rowlestone Church

The Herefordshire School was capable of undertaking a wide range of decorative work, from the most lavish at Shobdon and Kilpeck to the less ornate, such as that seen earlier on this tour at Peterchurch. Because of mid-18th-century vandalism, and a later fire, regrettably only photographs of plaster casts are now left to show of their first and most spectacular work at Shobdon, apart from a badly weathered and eroded relic forming part of an aristocrat's 'folly'. However the tympanum over the south doorway

at Rowlestone is considered to be a comparable version of that so skilfully carved at Shobdon at the same time in about 1130. The same outstanding standard of craftsmanship shows around the doorway, where incidentally on the west side there is included the face of a pagan 'green man', sprouting foliage from his mouth (p.235)—seen at several other churches and places on these tours. Like the south doorway, the chancel arch has two orders of heavy roll moulding carried on capitals and, in allusions to St. Peter, there are sculptured cocks in pairs, face to face and on adjoining stones two figures, those on the south side upside down, thought to represent his downwards crucifixion. Further special features are to be seen fixed on each side of the chancel. These are a pair of 15th-century iron bracket candelabra, 4.5ft. long, hinged to fold back against the wall. Each has five prickets for candles, one being decorated with cocks and the other with swans. Sadly it is proving difficult to care adequately for all the Rowlestone treasures, for as a note by the door states, the normal churchgoing congregation at St. Peter's is now down to no more than nine.

Chancel arch at Rowlestone Church

Pontrilas, which was *Elwistone* in the Domesday Book and *Heliston* until the late 17th century, when it acquired its Welsh name, is near the north-west corner of a district of Herefordshire known as Archenfield and apart from the final few miles, this tour will continue through what was also called 'Little Wales in England'.

Archenfield—'Little Wales in England'

Archenfield was formed from the small Welsh kingdom of Ergyng, both names possibly derived from *Ariconium*, the Roman industrial settlement which was east of today's Ross-on-Wye. Definition of its boundaries has varied over the centuries, but broadly they form a triangle, extending down the River Monnow to Monmouth and thence up the River Wye to within a few miles of Hereford, before striking back to Pontrilas close by the Worm Brook. It is a distinctive hilly upland area near Pontrilas, rising from 250ft. at Pontrilas itself to 1200ft. on the top of Garway Hill, where place-names and road signs reveal an unmistakable Celtic origin. As an enclave of Welshmen living in England, this was once a culturally native small kingdom with its own customs and laws, becoming something of a 'buffer state' occupied by the Dunsaete, an Anglo-Welsh tribe, between the English east of the Wye and the Welsh. It is thought that they were able to convince King Offa of Mercia (757-796) that they could suffi-ciently guarantee the safety of this section of the border to make it unnecessary for him to construct his dyke in their territory. Ergyng has also been regarded as one of the cradles of Celtic Christianity and a base for the mission of St. Dubricius, grandson of a king of Archenfield, who is thought to have been born at Madley (above). When the Normans over-ran Herefordshire, they allowed the inhabit-ants to retain most of their customs—as they did use of the Welsh language—and as an exception to general practice, many of the Welsh church dedications. Those at Ballingham and Whitchurch are still dedicated to St. Dubricius, as is St Devereux (a corrupted version of his name), and there were previously several others. St. Weonard's uniquely recalls St. Gwainarth, while the churches of Much Dewchurch, Little Dewchurch, Dewsall and Kilpeck are generally thought to commemorate Deui, or Dewi, a local holy man, rather than St. David, the patron saint of Wales. The medieval Welsh name of Hentland derives from Hen llan, meaning the old church, and it is closely associated with Dubricius and the clergy training college which he founded in the 6th century at Llanfrother, before moving away to Moccas.

After crossing the Hereford to Abergavenny railway in Pontrilas, the B4347 makes a right-hand turn and heads towards Kentchurch. By the nature of the territory there are very few hamlets or settle-ments ahead and the route misses most of what little there is at Kentchurch by avoiding another sharp right turn of the B road and turns left just before the bridge to head straight on up a fairly steep and narrow road, turning right after half a mile to avoid heading straight on up Bannut Tree Lane, and towards Kentchurch Court. The entrance to the Court is opposite St. Mary's Church, but this is only open to the public by appointment although it may have been seen by many as it was scrupulously 'time-warped' for its part in a major TV period epic, *The Regency House Party*, shown in early 2004. St. Mary's Church itself was rebuilt in 1859 but contains monuments from its predecessor, the most striking being effigies in alabaster of John Scudamore (d.1616), his wife Amy, in widows weeds, and their 10 children—one in a cradle. It bears the inscription:

> His mournful widow to his worth still debtor
> Built him this tomb, but in her heart a better

8.   Kentchurch Court and the Scudamores

First built as a moated manor in the late 14th century, and home of the Scudamores continuously from then on, Kentchurch Court and subsequent additions and internal arrangements designed by the archi-tect, Anthony Keck, in 1733 were supplemented early in the career of John Nash, who was afterwards appointed architect of Buckingham Palace, Regents Park and Regent Street in London (but before then of Hereford county gaol in 1793). The north-west tower of the original medieval building is associated with Owain Glyndwr, one of whose daughters married into the Scudamore family—only to lose her husband, two brothers-in-law and their father when, Lancastrians all, they were separated from their heads for being on the losing side at the Battle of Mortimers Cross in 1461.

Since those days the tower was retained and also heightened during the progress of improvement works, while among the fine internal furnishings are Grinling Gibbons wood carvings, brought over from the Holme Lacy home of the relations of this conspicuous county family. The battlemented Court stands beneath a steep wooded hill to the north and east and has one of the few deer parks left in Herefordshire.

The minor road continues to climb upwards, past Kentchurch Court on the right, in the direction signposted Bagwyllydiart, which is still in Herefordshire. Over the years there has been much puzzlement about the correct spelling and meaning of this word. In 1754, the respected cartographer, Isaac Taylor, spelt it as Bagalidiott and on 19th-century maps it appeared as Bagwylldiart, Bagylidiart and Bagalide. After consulting local people towards the end of that century, the early Ordnance Survey authorities adopted Bagwy Llydiart. The first word translates from Welsh as 'a cluster or bunch', and the second, Llidiart as 'a gate' (in Wales *Llydiart* sometimes denotes the mouth of a pass). However the modern OS Landranger 161 and the highway authorities have produced yet another version, as above, and, as is generally the practice in Wales, it would be interesting to see an accepted English translation on the road signs!

Turn left at the road junction signposted for Bagwyllydiart to the right, continuing past the direct road back to Pontrilas on the left, to head for Kilpeck, in which village you turn left at the Red Lion to reach the car park on the left at the approach to what in 1963 the architectural historian, Pevsner, wrote of as 'one of the most perfect village churches in England'.

9. Kilpeck

As elsewhere on these borderland tours, it may be difficult to understand why a church as sumptuous as this was so expensively built, nowadays serving little more than a handful of the faithful out of a sparse rural community, partly from scattered country cottages and farmhouses. As usual, the answer lies many centuries ago, quite possibly as far back as when the Britons (Welsh) came to occupy a knoll to the west of the church. Later on, the Saxons took possession and created a mound which, soon after 1066, the Normans adopted and enlarged as part of the process of consolidating and colonising the territory they had conquered. Starting with a simple motte and bailey, they progressed to an impressive fortress with a polygonal shell keep, a system of walls, enclosures and outer baileys. It was close to the important route from Hereford into Wales and in course of time was an administrative centre for much of Archenfield. A borough was established and Kilpeck became what has been described as a classic example of a planned medieval settlement and developed into a thriving community with the advantage of a weekly market and annual fair. This success, nearly amounting to minor urban status, was underwritten by the presence and influence of the castle which, by early in the 13th century, became important enough to receive three visits in four years by King John. But the prosperity was not to last, following changes of ownership and management and the impact of the Black Death in 1349. Despite reports that it was in ruins as early as the reign of Edward I (1272-1309), there was still enough left of the castle in the 1640s for it to be of use to the Royalists during the Civil War, but it was afterwards slighted by the Roundheads—and the miracle is that they did not, as was their usual practice, at the same time violate every image at the richly carved church just next door. There are now only fragments left of the castle masonry among the substantial earthworks still remaining, just to the west of the church, and the independently fortified medieval village has been reduced to the mounds and humps still to be plainly seen on the north side of the road to the east.

But the church still stands complete, much as it would have appeared just over 850 years ago, one of 13 churches in the Ewyas Harold Team Ministry and still in use for services at least once every three weeks.

The Parish Church
of St. Mary and St. David

The Norman Conquest in 1066 was more than just a military victory, for it had been blessed by the Pope on condition that should William succeed, he would take prompt steps to initiate a reform of the established Anglo-Saxon Church, change its archaic liturgy and improve upon the architecture of its buildings. During the following century and a half this mission produced numerous new parishes, churches and cathedrals. Thus between *c*.1140-50, a new church was erected at Kilpeck to

Kilpeck Church

complement the slightly earlier chapel of St. Mary at the castle. The architecture might have turned out to be unremarkable—but for the presence from 1134 of a priory or cell of Benedictine monks nearby. It was linked with St. Peter's Abbey at Gloucester and, along with the church, was seen by the Norman lord, Hugh fitz William (d.1168/69), as a civilising centre among the tenants and serfs. It also ensured a regular supply of chaplains for his churches at Kilpeck, Dewchurch and St. Mary's *de castello*. The priory remained active until *c*.1422-48 but was then dissolved and the monks

The south doorway at Kilpeck Church and a detail of the pillar on its right hand side

withdrawn to the abbey at Gloucester (which itself was dissolved in 1539). All signs have now gone, although the priory was probably near Priory Farm, a quarter of a mile south-east of the castle.

The Herefordshire School of Romanesque Sculpture

As the new Norman rulers set about their hectic programme, the 12th and 13th centuries became busy times for church-builders, especially the stone masons. Since Saxon days they had been pre-eminent in most matters of construction and responsible not just for the stability and technology of the buildings, but also for the ornate motifs and flamboyance specified by their Norman patrons. Such ornamentation became much more attainable once chisels started to appear in masons' toolkits during the 12th century, especially where good quality sandstone or limestone were available to enable crisp and clean sculptural detail to be carved. Most heavy manual labour, from quarrying the stone, transporting and erecting it was undertaken by local builders of Saxon or Celtic origin but the intricate decorative work was performed by highly skilled stone carvers. These operated rather like today's specialist sub-contractors, who appear when commissioned by the building promoter. They brought with them catalogues or pattern-books of designs, often carried in their head and sketched out when on site, drawn from a variety of sources which might have traditional Celtic or Anglo-Saxon origins but which could also be inspired by Scandinavian, Byzantine or other forms of art. These might be discussed and implemented alongside whatever ideas the noble client had in mind.

One major source for this work was inspiration gained from the architecture and sculpture of churches along some of the medieval pilgrim routes, and when Oliver de Merlimond, steward to Hugh de Mortimer, lord of Wigmore, returned from a pilgrimage to Santiago de Compostela through northern Spain and western France in the late 1120s, he resolved at once to try and emulate the great variety and beauty of what he had seen. He had been granted the *vill* of Shobdon by Hugh de Mortimer, but it lacked a church and in rectifying this, it is generally thought that he arranged to bring over master masons from the Continent to assist with the decorative work. This probably led to the founding of what has become known as the Herefordshire School of Romanesque Sculpture.

In fact this was not so much a school as a workshop of highly skilled stone masons, one of several formed in England during the middle of the 12th century, the closest others being at Bromyard and Dymock. (The banker shop of the Herefordshire firm of Capps and Capps, which has been carving on site in the Close at Hereford Cathedral since 1985, is arguably the nearest present-day equivalent. In the first fifteen years, five generations of apprentices passed through the workshops, including the head mason, and masons from the cathedral team have worked on many other historic buildings, extending from Wales to Oxfordshire). The term Romanesque in the title signifies the style of art and architecture found in western and southern Europe from the 9th century until the end of the 12th century and the emergence of the Gothic style. It is characterised by round headed arches, often with richly carved columns and capitals and sculptural figures, and by the use of groin vaults.

These features are well represented in buildings met during the course of this book's journeys in Herefordshire, Shropshire and Worcestershire and they would have been seen at their very best at the old church at Shobdon, had it not been knocked down by the owner in 1752. As it is, Kilpeck parish church, which was built at about the same time and likely to have involved the same skilled team, comes a close second and is now regarded as the finest example of the work of the Herefordshire School. It has continually excited academic art historians and ecclesiologists and astonished countless other admirers from all over the world—as the *Visitor's Book* near the door testifies. The illustrated guide produced for the PCC, usually available close by, sets out a well presented exposition of the origins of the church and proceeds to describe details of the exterior and interior, helped by useful background notes, engravings and colour photographs. The approach up the path from the south-west immediately meets what is described as the 'gem' of the whole church, the south doorway. But extending all the way round the church, upon a corbel table beneath the eaves supporting the roof, most of the 85 grotesque motifs, made up of heads of dragons, monsters, birds and humans (and not a few reminiscent of Walt Disney caricatures) are also worthy of close attention. They were produced at a time when few people could read, and therefore became part of the way of conveying messages of Good and Evil, or others such as belief in the spirits of nature. Sandstone is not always too durable for exposed sculpture, for it can flake and also discolour badly (as can be seen from the severe erosion of the 'green' stone used for the carvings now relegated to the Shobdon Arches). But at Kilpeck all is as crisp and as rich as when it was first carved. The building comprises a nave, square chancel and a semi-circular apse and the carving has been carried on into the interior, where figures on the chancel arch are said to have been inspired by those of the Gate of The Silversmiths in the pilgrim church at Santiago. The apse contains an example of very early Romanesque rib vaulting, whereas the east windows date from as recently as 1849, when they were designed by Augustus Pugin (above). As to the furnishings, the huge font, traditionally near the entrance door, is rather a mystery, for it is not consistent with the rest of the building, or indeed with others produced by the Herefordshire School at Eardisley, Castle Frome and Shobdon. Made from one piece of conglomerate stone, its size compares with those at Madley (above), and Bredwardine (p.194), where they both probably comply with an early baptism rule for infants which stipulated not sprinkling as now, but total immersion.

Returning to the car (which is probably parked on part of the former medieval market site), return to the Red Lion and turn left and after a right-angled bend then turn right at the sign for Much Dewchurch and Ross-on-Wye. When you reach the B4348 turn right onto it and enter Much Dewchurch.

10.   Much Dewchurch

It is thought that an early building at Much Dewhurch was the first Welsh *clas* church of four which were founded in honour of St. David—who was probably a local man and not the prominent abbot-bishop and patron saint of Wales. The first word meaning 'greater', it is so named to distinguish it from Little Dewchurch, 4 miles to the east, which is one of the three others. Much Dewchurch and St. David's Church are near

The church at Much Dewchurch

the Worm Brook, often regarded as marking a northerly boundary of Archenfield. There is a 10ft. high motte and bailey earthwork near to it on a ridge to the east of the village and nobody seems to be too certain about its original purpose, except that perhaps it was part of a line extending westwards to Madley to assist as a defence from Welsh attacks against Hereford city. The present St. David's Church is mainly Norman, apart from its 13th-century tower and Victorian shingle pyramid roof and the north aisle and vestry, added during the 1877 restoration. There are several very old houses in the village and the Black Swan alongside the main road dates from the 14th century, as one of England's oldest inns. Of the two large estates in the parish, local research puts the origin of the Mynde at least as far back as 1300, although many subsequent changes have now given it a Georgian appearance which masks the original Tudor house. Before it was divided up, the estate provided employment for large numbers of the people of the neighbourhood and many of their successors have since become tenant farmers and fruit-growers. The Bryngwyn estate was separated off and from 1868 was the seat of a shipping-owner, Sir James Rankin, MP, whose generous philanthropic works included considerable financial help in providing for Hereford's Broad Street library and museum in 1871, and the founding of Hereford County College in 1880, which is now serving as the National College for the Blind and Partially Sighted.

Continue on the B4348 through the village, and shortly before the junction with the A466 is reached, the Tudor-style Bryngwyn House is seen on the right. Since being the home of Sir James Rankin MP, this has been used as a hotel and an army H.Q., before being adapted for multiple occupation housing, and in part even for light engineering.

Turn right on the A466 and drive through the village of Wormelow Tump. This name comes from an ancient burial mound which is no longer there, its site having been taken up by a 19th-century road widening scheme. Some consider the tump to have been the burial place of King Arthur's son, Anir. Carry on along the A466 road towards Monmouth until taking the third turning to the left, a minor road signposted for Llanwarne. There is a convenient car park near the old church.

11.   Llanwarne—'Church by the alders'

Down in this little Gamber valley hamlet there are two churches, one now a sad and roofless ruin, but still in well tended grounds. These are thought to have been preceded during the 7th century by an even earlier, probably Welsh *clas*, church at Henlennie but now totally gone. The church of St. John the Baptist dated from the 13th century and it was rebuilt during the 14th, when the tower was added. The timber-framed lychgate has miraculously lasted since the 15th century, possibly in part because it has not suffered so badly the great problems of the church. The village-name hints at what these were, for its second part

Llanwarne Church of St. John the Baptist

comes from *gwern*, the Welsh for 'a swamp or moist alder grove'. There is no doubt that both church and churchyard suffered increasingly from dampness and flooding from the adjacent Gamber brook, to the extent that floor levels had gradually to be raised by more than a metre and coffins weighted with heavy stones to keep them down in the graves.

Eventually, in 1864, the new Christ Church was built on higher ground on the opposite side of the road. The 17th-century font and panelled chest were moved across from the old church, and some Flemish glass from the same period and source was incorporated in two windows in the south wall of the nave.

Continuing upwards between the trees, the route rejoins the B4348, on which you turn right and travel for a very short distance before making a left turn back onto a minor road, signposted for Hoarwithy. This leads to the A49 Hereford to Ross-on-Wye trunk road and crosses it, still heading for Hoarwithy, down by the River Wye. Turn left opposite the New Harp inn, pass the South-Italian-Romanesque-style church, which seems to be perched precariously at the rock-face above the river, like many Hoarwithy houses, and join what is a scenic 'back road' from Ross to Hereford. The tour will conclude by weaving and rolling along this reasonably good secondary road, in sight of the stunning local and distant scenery visible from areas of Little Dewchurch, Aconbury and Dinedor Hill and the higher parts of Hereford, all as described in another tour on pages 241-242.

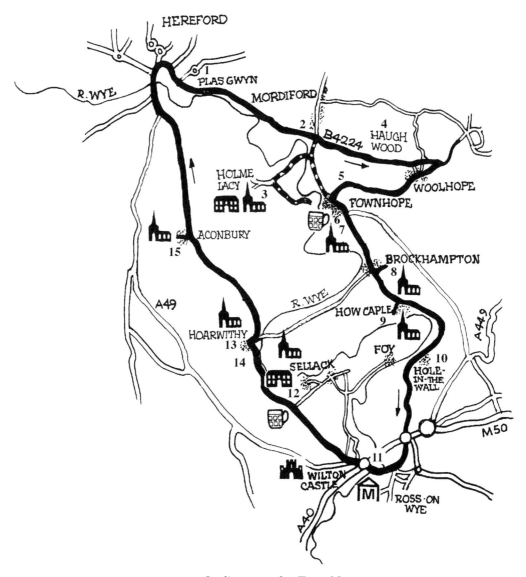

Outline map for Tour 10
The numbers 1 to 15 relate to the boxed information given within the tour

Tour 10   The Wye between Hereford and Ross

This route will enthral you with ever-changing scenery. Its southward course is through villages and on lanes above and beside the eastern bank, and returns on the western side. Apart from scenery, the journey offers the chance to clamber up to a hillfort, visit a few churches (one in the Arts and Crafts style, another in an Italianate), visit some gardens and explore Ross-on-Wye. The total distance is about 30 miles.

Mainly on minor roads, some quite narrow, with short sections of A and B road. (OS Landranger 149 and 162)

From the east of Hereford city centre, Eign Road leads beneath a railway bridge to Hampton Park Road, which quickly reaches Vineyard Road. This comes in from the left, and on the corner of the two roads is Plas Gwyn, a large Victorian house, once the home of Sir Edward Elgar.

1. Plas Gwyn, and The Music Maker

Plas Gwyn

At the beginning of the last century, Plas Gwyn was owned by a prominent High Town grocer and city alderman. In 1904 he rented it to the 47-year-old Edward Elgar, who was by then making his way in the musical world, greatly helped by Alice, his wife. Honours had begun to descend upon him. He was knighted by King Edward VII, and Worcester, because it was close to where he was born and subsequently began his musical career, was about to admit him as an honorary freeman. Not to be outdone, Hereford invited him to accept the position of mayor and chief citizen. He declined and in 1905 the honour went instead to his landlord and grocer friend, Edwin Gurney, an alderman doubtless better suited for endless council and committee meetings. (One can but imagine what Sir Edward, with his lively hobby involving explosive chemistry experiments, would have made of the processes of sewage treatment, public health and all the other exciting local government functions!). Fortunately for everyone he kept to his music, his wife observing to Dora Penny — ''Dorabella' of the *Enigma Variations* — as she looked at his new study: 'I think great music can be written here, dear Dora, don't you?'. And indeed it was, for Elgar, very much a countryman at heart, held a long established affection for Herefordshire — 'That sweet borderland where I have made my home' as he put in a programme note to the newly composed *Introduction and Allegro for string quartet and string orchestra*. Between 1904 and 1911, when he left Hereford, he composed most of the works by which he is known, notably: the oratorio *The Kingdom*, Symphonies 1 and 2, the Violin Concerto, the 3rd *Pomp and Circumstance* March and the *Wand of Youth* suite. Gaining much of his inspiration from the countryside he was heard to remark that: 'music is in the air all around us!'. He walked or cycled for great distances in the neighbourhood and nowadays, driving along Hampton Park Road, it is not too fanciful to imagine Elgar cycling ahead towards Mordiford Bridge, one of his favourite haunts (and the dedication on his manuscript of *The Music Makers*, completed in 1912).

Open country and extensive cider-apple orchards and tree nurseries appear just beyond the city boundary, followed by Hampton Bishop and the Bunch of Carrots. The village is very close to the River Wye and it has suffered a long history of flooding. In Elgar's day there would not have been the flood 'Stank' (or dyke) which can be seen close to the old (modernised) pub these days. Even now, when the river can reach over 15 feet above summer level, there is still disruptive flooding of the area during some winter months.

About a mile further on at Mordiford there is what Pevsner called 'a very handsome group of church, rectory and bridge', with wooded hills for a background. It is still very easy to appreciate why Elgar found this spot such a source of inspiration.

2. Mordiford and the Dragon

Mordiford

Commanding an extensive view a little to the left and north is Sufton Court, a large mansion built for the Hereford family, the lords of the manor. It was designed by Wyatt in Bath stone in the 'classical' style at the end of the 18th century and the grounds were laid out by Repton, the renowned landscape architect. Out of sight a short way beyond, Old Sufton has been in the possession of the same family since the 12th century. The house and lands were held of the Crown by the quaint annual payment of a pair of gilt spurs. Present members of the Hereford family continue to live in both houses.

Mordiford Bridge has nine stone arches in all. Two span the River Lugg, not far from its confluence with the Wye, and the others act as a causeway in times of flood. No account of Mordiford would be complete without mention of The Dragon! One of many legends has it that the serpent lived in Haugh Wood (see box no.4 below) and would come foraging down to the village, even to feed on local people and cause a labour shortage in the fields. And so a condemned man was prevailed upon to hide in a barrel near the beast's drinking place, not far beyond the bridge where the Lugg joins the Wye. Armed presumably with a cross-bow he shot the dragon through a bunghole, but rashly had not allowed for the flames and fumes of its death throes. He did not survive to embroider the stories. But the way down to the river retains the name Serpent's Lane, and until 1811 the image of a large green dragon was painted on the west wall of the Church of the Holy Rood. As is recorded in the porch, on 27 May that year there was an intense storm above the village. The tiny river Pentaloe swelled to 180 ft. wide and 20ft. deep and many buildings were swept away, or damaged. The miller and three others were drowned and afterwards £80 was collected for the relief of those worst affected. The corn mill on the Pentaloe has existed since Saxon times, is mentioned in the Domesday Book, operated until just before the Second World War and still stands solid after recent renovation. During the war, wishing to avoid another calamity along the course of the Pentaloe, the local Home Guard made slits in the walls of the top storey—through which to shoot at any enemy daring enough to approach them that way.

The village pub, The Moon Inn, stands near a junction which presents a number of route choices. The most direct way to Fownhope is along the main road to the right, over the little bridge and past the mill, when there is scope for a detour at Holme Lacy Bridge over the Wye to the right. The main feature in the centre of the village of Holme Lacy is the county's College of Agriculture and National Centre for Blacksmithing, Farriery and Rural Crafts on the right, but you may wish to see Holme Lacy House, now a hotel, and St. Cuthbert's church. Alternatively there is the choice of heading uphill at The Moon and taking in Haugh Wood and Woolhope. To take this option please go to the middle of page 234.

To head for Holme Lacy, follow the B road through Mordiford and turn right onto the B4399 across the bridge over the Wye to Holme Lacy. Holme Lacy House and church are signposted within the village off to he left, opposite the agricultural college. The hotel appears on the right and the church is signposted further along on the left.

3.   Holme Lacy House and the Scudamores

Memorial to James Scudamore in Holme Lacy Church

Approached by the tree-lined drive, Holme Lacy House is an imposing Palladian mansion built by Viscount Scudamore towards the end of the 17th century, replacing a house dating from the reign of Henry III. The family was long prominent in county and country affairs, their seat one of the finest stately homes in Herefordshire. The interior is famed for its range of wood carving and plaster ceilings regarded as amongst the finest in England of their day. But in 1909 the estate changed hands for the first time since the Conquest and afterwards had a number of owners, the house becoming from 1935 a hospital for ladies suffering from nervous or mental breakdown. When this closed there were fears that it would become derelict, but following initial costly attempts to convert it into a hotel, from 1995 Warner Holidays became involved in a further £6 million restoration and extension programme, well befitting its Grade I listing. Now a hugely popular historic hotel, it specialises in 'Just for adults' breaks, offering the use of sports and leisure facilities and entertainments each evening. Themed weekends cover subjects such as tennis, clay-pigeon shooting, wine and cider appreciation, hot-air ballooning and helicopter trips. There is also every opportunity for guests to view the many fine interior features of this historic pile, quite the largest in Herefordshire. Previous guests at Holme Lacy House have included King Charles I, in 1645, William Pitt the Elder, who held Cabinet meetings in the grounds, and Catherine Cookson, who was a voluntary patient when it was a hospital. Less famous visitors may still book there for some meals and look around.

Holme Lacy is one of a number of the county's scattered villages, yet it is still surprising to find the parish church of St. Cuthbert quite so far away from the present village centre, sited with an old red-brick vicarage and noble trees about a mile away in meadows by the Wye. This remoteness is by no means unusual hereabouts, especially among the Celtic churches to the west. Before the church was declared redundant in 1994, the few service-goers found no trouble in driving over by car, but it must have been quite a different matter for the many more devout and regular parishioners who had to rely on their legs during the earlier life of the church. Mainly built from the 14th century, it contains fine carvings in the choir stalls and most splendid monuments, serving as it does as mausoleum for the illustrious Scudamores of Holme Lacy House, a family of Norman descent. Sir James Scudamore was knighted by Queen Elizabeth 1 for his bravery at the siege of Cadiz, and immortalized by Spencer in *The Faerie Queen* as 'the gentle Scudamore'. His son John, the 1st Viscount, Ambassador to France for four years, laid the foundations for Herefordshire's cider industry through his efforts with new varieties of French cider apples. The Lord Scudamore School in Hereford is named after him, but despite his many good works and great generosity he is buried in the church without memorial.

Extensive restoration work has been carried out since St. Cuthbert's became vested in the Churches Conservation Trust and the church is often open for visitors.

The alternative route from Mordiford winds off left uphill and past The Moon in the direction of Woolhope. It narrows through a close avenue of trees to arrive at Poor's Acre and a well laid-out car park, picnic area and a choice of waymarked trails at Haugh Wood. It is easy to see why it is so popular with people from Hereford, but in common with the other features around Woolhope—Backbury Hill, Cherry Hill, Nupend, Broadmoor Common, Little Hill and Seagar Hill—it has also been a source of intense interest to geologists and others concerned with natural history and antiquarian research.

4. Haugh Wood

Silurian rocks have been laid down as sediments in a tropical continental-shelf sea, the limestone beds containing many corals and reef animals. Some 200 million years ago all limestone and shale levels were folded in the Hercynian mountain building period into a domed form. The present landscape has been formed by erosion of this structure. Trimmed, possibly by sea, the land has been eroded to create a level or rolling plain at about 600 to 700 ft. above sea level and at Haugh Wood it accounts for designation as a Site of Special Scientific Interest (SSSI). The Forestry Commission and Forest Enterprise have set up two butterfly trails, relying upon the ability of the woods to sustain colonies of endangered species. The habitat for these is created by a cyclical programme of coppicing and the growth of standards—larger trees left to grow on. Wild flowers grow profusely in the sunshine during the first two years or so after coppicing, hopefully aiding insect feeding from the pollens. As the trees grow, the area beneath becomes more shaded and supports different plants and animals.

Proceeding onwards to Woolhope, it is first worth stopping at Broadmoor Common, a Local Nature Reserve, to look back on the Wye and Lugg valleys.

The village of Woolhope derived its name from Wulviva, sister of the famous Lady Godiva, and 'hope'—Anglo-Saxon for valley. The connection is not lost on visitors to the Norman church of St. George, for an image of Lady Godiva riding her horse through Coventry appears in a window of the north wall. The manor was owned by the sisters in the 11th century and presented by them to Hereford Cathedral.

There is a direct road from Woolhope to Fownhope, passing Wessington Court—a 19th-century mansion was converted to a school, some black and white houses, the prominent TV transmitter to the left on Ridge Hill, and so to Rudge End.

5.   Tom Spring—Heavyweight Champion of England

Rudge End is where, in a now long demolished cottage, Thomas Winter was born in 1795. As a 17-year-old butcher's boy at Mordiford he embarked on a career of pugilism, bare-knuckle fighting. After setting out to seek his fortune in London, adopting the fighting *nom-de-guerre* of Tom Spring, he acquired the title of Heavyweight Champion of England by 1823/4. Before an attendance of 50,000 in January 1824 he fought the Irish champion, John Langan, on the racecourse at the Pitchcroft, Worcester. The 77-round fight lasted for 2 hours and 29 minutes before Langan was finally knocked out. By the following year Spring had become landlord of the Booth Hall in Hereford. Clearly he needed no 'chuckers out', as six sturdy fellows, full of ale and yobbishness, soon discovered in 1825. As the *Hereford Journal* cheerfully reported: 'Right and Left his every blow told on the sconces of his cowardly assailants and on one occasion they were all down on the floor together. In less than 20 minutes they were completely brought to a standstill and the Champion acknowledged victor. They were all stout fellows, at least 13 stone each'.

Tom Spring mural in the Green Man's restaurant

Eventually he returned to London where he died in 1851. Just over 100 years later, in August 1954, a memorial in the form of a slab of stone on a large old cider mill was erected near his birthplace. Using words inscribed on his cherished Hereford Cup, presented in 1823 by admiring 'Countrymen of the land of cider', it was unveiled by J.P.L. Thomas, M.P. for Hereford, then 1st Lord of the Admiralty.

The road carries on down between Cherry Hill hillfort and Fownhope Court to turn left onto the B4224 to the west of Fownhope, where all the routes described rejoin. Soon The Green Man Inn is reached on the right.

6.   The Green Man

The Green Man displays a diversity of architecture and, after first appearing as The Naked Boy in 1485, has known exciting times. In 1645 Colonel John Birch, the prominent Roundhead leader, is said to have lodged there between Civil War sieges at Hereford and Goodrich Castle. It was a coaching-house on what was then the Hereford to Gloucester main road, and in the 18th and 19th centuries it surprisingly served as a petty sessional courthouse. Each May it is at the centre of Fownhope's Oak Apple Day celebrations, commemorating the return of King Charles II to London at the Restoration. Inevitably it is also associated with Tom Spring (above), figured in a mural in the restaurant, who is said to have been a former landlord.

But it is more difficult to associate the name of the pub with the Norman churches of Kilpeck, Rowlestone or others where the Green Man is depicted. He has always been one of the most perplexing images—and not everywhere regarded as friendly. In early days he was sometimes thought to be a demon or devil, the emanation of evil—as carved in the rich south doorway decoration at

Kilpeck, vine leaves and fruit protruding from his mouth (see p.225), and at Pershore Abbey where his tongue pokes out at all from a sneering face. Many other such images may be found in wood, stone or wrought iron at places ranging locally from Tewkesbury Abbey, Worcester Cathedral, Leominster Priory, Much Marcle, Vowchurch, Bronllys and Hereford's Old House porch. Among them, foliage sprouting from his mouth, the stone face of the Green Man on the 12th-century south doorway at St. Peter's, Rowlestone, seems likely to have derived from some pagan forest deity associated with fertility rites. This seems closer to Jack-in-the-Green, the image of Easter and epitome of Spring, as he has been portrayed at Clun, Shropshire, by a festive Green Man in May Day celebrations. It is also closer to the painting on Fownhope's pub sign, and to reasons why so many inns now bear the name (and again why a popular early-flowering primrose, with an unusual ruff of leaves, was so named in Tudor times).

Various house-names in the village recall the tanning industry which was served by barges on the Wye in former years, Tan House and Bark Cottage for example. Further down the main street is the church of St. Mary, its Norman central tower crowned with a 600-year-old broach spire said to be covered with 22,000 shingles, another reminder of Herefordshire's former bounty of oak.

7.   Fownhope, St. Mary

Inside, on the west wall, St. Mary's greatest treasure is a well preserved mid 12th-century tympanum, showing seated figures of a rather masculine-looking Virgin holding the Child, their hands raised in blessing. The remarkably fine detail is a lasting tribute to the artistry and skills of the 12th-century group of travelling masons, who worked in the style that has come to be known as the Herefordshire School of Romanesque Sculpture (p.226). Far less distinct because of weathering at the top four corners of the pre-1130 tower, are contemporary carvings of serpents, a humanoid cat's head, a cowled head and a masked face, for which binoculars are helpful.

In the nearest corner of the churchyard there is a stone mile-post which, since the early days of the motor age in 1907, has asserted that it is $6\frac{1}{4}$ miles and 56 yards from Hereford, and that via the B4224 there are another $8\frac{1}{4}$ miles and 165 yards before getting to Ross. This way passes 'Ye Olde Parish Stocks' against the churchyard wall, railed in 1909 for extra security.

St. Mary's Church, Fownhope

Turn right alongside the west wall of the churchyard where the road soon narrows to single width and is not over-blessed with passing or parking places. The driver will have to miss the spectacular view forming to the right and concentrate on the steep road winding through Capler Wood, hinted by the name of Rise Farm on the way. Just at the top, opposite Capler Lodge, there is a 'Viewpoint' area with provision for parking—there everyone can take a look at the Wye far below. There is spectacle here which is often thought to surpass that further downstream at the more well-known Symonds Yat (p.279). On the other side of the road the Wye Valley Walk rises to Capler Camp, an Iron Age hillfort at the top of the hill, commanding a magnificent strategic position about 600ft. above sea level. There is also a steep path through the woods down to the river, and a little downstream, before the piers of the old railway bridge, there has for some time been a colony of cormorants, birds normally found only by the sea. These, and also a good many mergansers, are not very popular among local anglers.

At the crossroads not far beyond the lookout, it is worth making a short diversion to the left to Brockhampton-by-Ross to visit an Arts and Crafts church.

8.   Brockhampton—Thatched Arts and Crafts church

Brockhampton Church

Brockhampton-by-Ross is a small, neat estate village with a population of about 180. Brockhampton Court is built of dark red sandstone in neo-Tudor style and in the 18th-century was the rectory, restored and rebuilt towards the end of the 19th. The shell of the old parish church of Holy Trinity has recently been converted sensitively into a house and garden. With an estate of some 1,500 acres, house and church were acquired by a rich Bostonian for his daughter, Alice, upon her marriage, and it was she who in 1901-2 built a new church in memory of her parents. In 1963, All Saints Church was described by Nikolaus Pevsner as 'One of the most convincing and most impressive churches of its date in any country', 'Impressive and well composed' had said John Betjeman before him, and most recently it earned high praise from Simon Jenkins in his book *England's Thousand Best Churches*. The architect was William Richard Lethaby (1857-1931). He was a disciple of William Morris, an acknowledged fabric designer, craftsman, writer and poet, and was closely involved with the Central School of Arts and Crafts—a movement of which All Saints, Brockhampton came to be regarded as a temple. Now listed at Grade I, the boldly designed church has been constructed wherever possible of local materials—all the oak is from Herefordshire and the stone comes from Capler quarry, the source used for Hereford Cathedral. The building abounds in good design and attention to detail and furnishings include two tapestries woven by William Morris and Company to a design by Burne-Jones. Opposite the Grade II thatched lychgate stands a Victorian imitation-Jacobean Lodge, which is still serving part-time as a sub- post office and social centre for the small village community. Brockhampton Court eventually became a luxury hotel and venue for wedding receptions, and more recently a gracious and comfortable nursing home run by a local G.P.

237

Return to the crossroads and turn left for How Caple, taking the next road left for a second detour, this time for How Caple Court off the right hand side, sited on the edge of wooded parkland, sloping down towards the Wye.

---

9. How Caple Court and church

Most of this gabled house is relatively modern, but it retains a little of the 17th-century building occupied by Sir William Gregory, one-time Speaker of the House of Commons. The Lees, who are the present owners, are applying much effort to the 11 acres of Edwardian formal and woodland gardens—uncovering terraces, rebuilding walls, refilling ponds and landscaping a narrow valley to the west of the house. These, but not the house, are open to the public and some parts have proved to be well suited for outdoor events—from jazz concerts to Mozart's opera, *The Magic Flute*. In the grounds just below, the Norman church of St. Andrew and St. Mary is well cared for and it is full of interest. Look out especially for its wooden screen, supporting the arms of William III, and the 16th-century diptych on the north wall of the chancel over the choir stalls. In so peaceful an ambience, it is very distressing to face memorials to five members of the owners' family who were killed between 1915 and 1921.

How Caple Court

Back in the car, return to the crossroads, turn left and continue down the single lane road to get much closer to river level (which the road sometimes achieves in places during the winter), passing under Lyndor Wood before arriving at Hole-in-the-Wall.

---

10. Hole-in-the-Wall and Foy

The road to Hole-in-the-Wall near the banks of the Wye

No-one really seems to know why Hole-in-the-Wall has such an odd name, but one thing is certain— there is no point in expecting to find a bank cash dispenser here! Indeed there is initially little sign of any 'civilisation', for many former inhabitants have moved away and there are empty and derelict houses. Yet at Court Farm signs of occupation may turn out to be of the vocal mode, for in 1965 this farm became the original canoeing centre for PGL Adventure UK. The voices might well belong to as many as 150

The footbridge over the Wye near Foy

youngsters who obviously still have spare energy left after canoeing, abseiling, orienteering and the 20 or so other adventures offered for 6- to 18-year-olds by this market leader in activity holidays. This is in East Foy, (previously Eton Tregoes, after John Tregoz who built a castle in 1280). To reach West Foy and the PGL centre at Hillcrest, it is necessary to cross the Wye over a suspension footbridge about half a mile downstream and follow the footpath ahead and then the drive across the road. Foy Bridge was built in 1921, after an earlier one dating from 1876 was swept away, but it only caters for pedestrians, horses and bikes and everything else faces a road journey of 8 miles via Wilton Bridge. West Foy lies within a peninsula created by a vast U of the serpentine Wye. Dating from the 11th and 14th centuries, the little church of St. Mary in Foy is the third church to stand on the same idyllic site overlooking the river. The devotion of local craftsmanship is at once evident in the form of a 600-year old door with strap hinges formed like sickles and there is much of interest inside. A further claim to fame is the tenacity and devotion of its former incumbents. One account names just two parsons serving between 1816 and 1923, whilst another long respected 'Guide' gasps that 'Charles Turner Wilton preached for 61 years'.

Continuing onwards, the road heads for Brampton Abbots, passing over the A40 to reach Ross-on-Wye (p.271).

The way back to Hereford first leads along the B4260 to Wilton Bridge, now having a much easier time than for many centuries, after the A40 trunk road through Ross was diverted in 1985 along the by-pass.

11.   Wilton Bridge, Castle and a sundial which is slow

There are convenient car-parks from which to approach the bridge and castle at the Ross end of the bridge. Linked to a causeway from Ross, the bridge replaced a ferry in around 1600 and it has had quite an eventful time, suffering the indignity, like Hereford's Wye Bridge, of having one of its arches blown away during the Civil War. It has often been badly damaged by floods: by 1914 the river could be seen through cracks in the road surface! However after improvements in 1939 and 1993 it is now much easier and safer to check the time

The remains of Wilton Castle

239

on the unique sundial in the downstream centre refuge (noting however that local historian, Alan Crow, calculates that it is 10-12 minutes slow against GMT!). Just upstream, Wilton Castle was sited at the important Wye crossing, then one of only two in Herefordshire. It was reconstructed in stone at the end of the 13th century and in the late 16th was converted into a grand house for the Brydges family. After adopting a neutral attitude during the Civil War and vanishing to fight other battles in Ireland, Sir John Brydges incurred Royalist pique to the extent that, legend tells, they set fire to the house one day whilst the family was in church. Much later, in the 19th century, another house was built within part of the castle ruins—and this remains in private occupation, but in 2002 was up for sale. Some of the ruins may be seen from Wilton Bridge, and rather more from the footpath starting from its upstream northern end.

The sundial on Wilton Bridge

The Lough Pool

The route leads across Wilton roundabout, where it crosses the A40, and onto the A49 to Hereford at Bridstow, but only for a quarter of a mile, taking the second turning to the right after the roundabout, signposted for Sellack. After a couple of miles, the road to the village church is on the right and the Lough Pool Inn is reached on the left. Almost opposite on the right a drive leads to Caradoc Court, said to occupy the site of a castle once reputed to be the home of the British chief Caradoc Vreich-Vras, or Strong Arm, a knight of King Arthur's Round Table.

12. Caradoc Court and Sellack

Associated with the Scudamore family, the existing mansion was started in the late 16th and extended chiefly in the early 17th and mid-19th centuries. After several owners, the building became derelict for many years following a devastating fire in 1986. An attempt to convert it into separate dwellings failed when the builder went into liquidation but restoration has now included two self-catering units to help ensure a viable future for the grade II* listed building. A footpath leads towards the direction of a single span pedestrian suspension bridge which crosses the Wye to King's Caple, joining another from just to the left of Sellack's church. This is dedicated to St. Tysilio, an early Celtic saint, from whose name that of the village is also derived. It has a graceful 14th-century octagonal spire which soars above the riverside meadows and its fittings include a Jacobean west gallery, pulpit and communion rails.

Often close to the Wye after Sellack, our road continues on towards Hoarwithy.

13. The church of William Poole at Hoarwithy

Hoarwithy Church interior (above) and the 'cloister' approach (left)

Although much has been written about the church of St. Catherine, the most astonishing thing about it is that it was actually built at the expense of its vicar, who was there for 46 years at the end of the 19th century. Such munificence cannot happen much these days, especially when the church style is 'South Italian Romanesque and Semi-Byzantine'. In the words of Simon Jenkins: 'The loggia hangs over the valley of the Wye as an Umbrian church might over the Tiber'. The Reverend William Poole was a wealthy property-owning cleric who became vicar of Hentland and Hoarwithy in 1854. The riverside community had been served by a modest mid-19th-century brick chapel of ease, and, not impressed, he shaped ideas to glorify it with an all-embracing new church and briefed his friend, J.P. Seddon. Making the most of the hillside location, this architect produced a Romanesque campanile, rising at the end of a steep walled flight of steps where it can be seen for miles. On the approach to the interior, another great surprise for an English church is the open mosaic-paved cloister along the south side. Inside there is marble, more mosaic, lapis lazuli, oak said to be from Poole's estate at Homend, and everywhere, extravagant ornamentation. The work was well ahead by 1885, a long-term source of employment for many local craftsmen and also for specialists from Exeter, St. Paul's in London and Italy. Poole lived as a bachelor until his death at the very end of the Victorian era and he also built a vicarage, a school—which he staffed, served as a magistrate and generally devoted himself and his wealth to the needs of his parishioners (although seemingly not gaining overwhelming affection or thanks). Unfortunately, he did not provide for the costly future maintenance of the church structure and finishes, and local accounts from 1971, 1980 and 1988 tell of erosion of the sandstone and of needy restoration works.

14. Saint Dyfrig's college at Llanfrother

On the southern end of the centre of Hoarwithy (back over the rise from the village pub), a footpath leads uphill towards the medieval church of St. Dubricius at Hentland which lies at the heart of ancient

Archenfield. Early in the 6th century a monastery college was established nearby at Llanfrother by Dubricius, or Dyfrig, who was born in Madley, 10 miles to the north-west. One of the most famous of early Welsh saints, who legend claims became 'bishop of Llandaff', he may have crowned 'King' Arthur. The place-name St. Devereux, near Kilpeck, is the Norman-French version of his name. It is said that before his move to Moccas, some 2,000 priests and scholars came to study and worship with him and the college at Llanfrother became one of the major religious establishments in the Border area. Meaning 'Place for the brothers', there is now nothing there to see—although there is still a Llanfrother Farm. As for Dyfrig, he spent his final days on Bardsey—'The Island of 20,000 Saints' just off the Lleyn peninsula in Gwynedd.

The road back to Hereford winds with the Wye between garden banks and overhanging woods, (affording the chance of a right-hand detour from the centre of Hoarwithy of 1$^{1}/_{2}$ miles to Carey and The Cottage of Content Inn), before rising towards Little Dewchurch, and then descending again through Nether Wood, past Aconbury.

15. Aconbury—13th-century nunnery

Aconbury lies below a wooded hill rising to 900ft. above the Wye, with a 17.5 acre Iron Age hillfort on its summit. The small church of St. John Baptist, with its undivided nave and chancel, is well worth a visit when open. Restored with unusual self control by Sir George Gilbert Scott, it is all that remains of a house of the Sisters of the Order of St. John of Jerusalem, women counterparts of the Knights Hospitaller. Founded and endowed in the early 13th century by Margery de Lacy, wife of Walter de Lacy, it was afterwards followed by a community of Augustinian canonesses. Two blocked doorways to the south wall of the church mark their link with the former cloisters when, at the time of the Dissolution there were seven nuns. Surrounded by a moat, the nunnery occupied 5 acres of ground and during the 18th century the remains were converted into a farmhouse, Aconbury Court.

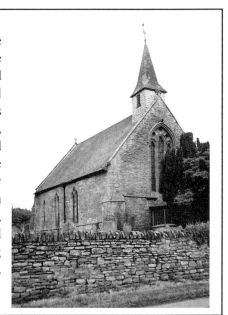

Aconbury Church

Nearer Hereford there is a country road leading right to the 9.5 acre Dinedor Camp, which is another Iron Age hillfort, bought for public recreation.

There are few better places than here to view the expanse of the city, laid out far below. Afterwards continue finally past Bullinghope, Lower Bullingham and the former base of 22 Special Air Services Regiment at Bradbury Lines, turning left at B4399 Holme Lacy Road and right at the A49 traffic lights towards Greyfriars Bridge and the city centre.

Ledbury—a settlement on the River Leadon

Ledbury's Church Lane

As it is so close to the central St. Katherine's car park off Bye Street, visitors to Ledbury quickly come to the special half-timbered Market House. High up on sixteen Spanish chestnut, or maybe oak, pillars, it is regarded as the town's symbol and is at Lower Cross at the north end of High Street near the end of Church Lane. This is where most tourists, as well as calendar and picture postcard producers, reach for their cameras and it has also been much favoured by film location scouts. But no costume saga is ever likely to reach back to its earliest days, for even the Market House, completed in 1668 is a comparative newcomer. When Ledbury was still known as *Liedeberge*, Church Lane, with Church Street and Church Road, formed a triangle surrounding a Saxon village green and market place—just below the minster church of St. Peter. An early church had been founded by the bishop of Hereford possibly as long ago as the 8th century and it was served by a group of priests responsible not only for the parish, but also much of the surrounding region. By 1086, the time of the Domesday Survey, *Liedeberge* had become a thriving market centre and the former timber church was being superseded by a stone structure. Responsible for the spiritual needs of their widely dispersed flocks, bishops of that time were constantly on the move, escorted by large retinues of about 40 staff. They all had to be accommodated and fed during visits within the

diocese, and at *Liedeberge*, the bishop of Hereford and lord of the manor, is thought to have had a mansion and a range of ancillary buildings to the west of High Street. This was on land alongside the main north-south and east-west crossroads, which is now partly occupied by St. Katherine's almshouses, the Master's House and the public car park.

Soon after 1066, the Normans began to exploit the local attributes and as at Hereford, where the old market close to the cathedral was no longer adequate or suitably sited, and also

The Market House

243

like William fitz Osbern there, Bishop Richard de Capella (1121-27) set out a wedge-shaped area as a new market place in a more favourable position. This was just to the west of the Anglo-Saxon market site, but on a north-south alignment, and became known as *Middeltoune*, or Middletown, now the High Street, and was where as part of the process of emancipation from serfdom, burgage tenure was introduced. The new market frontages were divided into narrow strips and freemen could rent these from the lord of the manor and a whole 22 ft. x 198 ft. burgage plot generally cost them about a shilling a year. It was normally laid out by the tenant with a shop and house on the street front and a garden and room for his livestock at the rear, in some instances on part plots. The east (church) side of High Street was divided into 20 plots and the west side with just 6, possibly because of the presence of the bishop's quarters along the remaining frontage. Such was the demand, that a further 78 were soon marked out and rented along The Homend (meaning Ham End or End of the village), 20 at the Southend, 58 in Bye Street and 32 plots along New Street. By 1285, the 283 burgage plots which were entered in the bishop's rent book formed a framework of streets, buildings and land which is still fully recognisable throughout the central streets of Ledbury after more than 800 years. The early burgage holders included mercers, farriers, weavers, bakers, goldsmiths, fullers, skinners and coopers and the diversity of trades and the buoyant trading situation was in marked contrast with that at some of the other towns met on these tours, such as New Radnor and Longtown. These were 'failed boroughs' where there are now only vague outlines of unlet plots. As for Ledbury, far from failure it thrived as the commercial, social and ecclesiastical hub of a considerable area, it returned two members to the Model Parliament of Edward I for a short time and lasted as a borough until 1888. Conventional wisdom has concluded that the name of the town, now with a population of almost 7,500, came from its position as 'a settlement on the River Leadon', but one respected authority has alternatively suggested that the second element, 'bury', could be linked with the presence of a religious house, namely the minster. This is found elsewhere, for example later in the tour at Tewkesbury, and so he thinks Ledbury could mean 'the religious enclosure by the Leadon'.

Whichever is the true answer, the Church has certainly exercised a major local influence, starting at the minster church of St. Peter's and the rural *parochia* of Anglo-Saxon times, and coming now from the mother church of St. Michael and All Angels as it continues to serve parishioners of 16 country churches, covering a comparably large Team Ministry area. Built in Norman, Early English and Decorated styles, the present building at the top of Church Lane is huge, its length only exceeded in the county by that of the cathedral, and it is laid out beneath a separate 202 feet tower and spire raised high up above the roofs of the town. In 1963 Nikolaus Pevsner described with enthusiasm 'the premier parish church of Herefordshire [with] an unusual variety of fine elements, including the detached tower and the splendid north chapel', and in 2000 Simon Jenkins placed it in the 'Top Hundred' list of his critically acclaimed book about *England's Thousand Best Churches*. Typically in Ledbury, all the signs of a high degree of community involvement are present, and it shows in the *Ledbury Parish Church Guidebook*, published by the team rector and The Friends of Ledbury Parish Church.

Since the centre of Ledbury first took shape during the early 12th century there have been considerable changes in the streetscape, arising especially from general rebuilding during the 16th century. There was further expansion and reconstruction in the 19th century, but early in the 21st, many buildings of late 16th and early 17th centuries may still be seen and together they form a major component of the town centre. The future treatment of a high proportion of these is now controlled by their Listing as of Special Architectural or Historic Interest, and also through siting within the Conservation Area boundary which embraces much of the town. But in the past many have been 'modernised' with plasterwork rendering, even the striking 'black and white' Feathers and Talbot inns and the Georgian brickwork which covers the half-timbering of the Royal Oak. Much white paint has been applied to brick front elevations and hardly any of the buildings have not been changed in appearance by the addition at street level of later shop-fronts or other modifications, as is generally the case in historic towns.

Of the few intact remaining Georgian houses, two are close to the church, the more significant of them being the early 18th-century brick-built Old Magistrates House. This was called Rutherglen, then became the police station and magistrates' court, complete with cells, during the late 19th century but by 1973 it was abandoned, vandalised and under threat of demolition. Outraged, the Ledbury and District Society secured support from the Woolhope Naturalists Field Club and other conservationists, and in 1981 forced a Public Inquiry which resulted in a reprieve. However it took several more years, a major exercise by The Hereford and Worcester Buildings Preservation Trust and the expenditure of a large amount of money before the building was restored to the intact state in which it now appears at the top of Church Lane. (The Serjeant's House in Church Road perhaps presents a less rewarding picture for the effort taken, but now it too displays a complete Georgian façade).

Next to the Old Magistrates House in Church Lane is the Elizabethan Old Grammar School, which dates from

The Serjeant's House

1480-1520 and has since had a variety of uses. Its close-set studding on the ground floor and the square studding of the projecting floor above were part of a major restoration scheme just before the building was opened as a Heritage Centre, and for living accommodation, in 1978. The close-studded façade of the 17th-century Church House appears opposite flaunting, as it usually does, the wealth of the original owner, while set back a couple of doors down is what is called Butcher Row House. Much of this building is now on its third site, for not only was the timber-framed property originally in Butcher Row (see below), but after many years it was moved and re-erected in the rear garden of 14 High Street (now a branch of Boots). In 1979 the main timbers were on the move again, this time to the present site and the building now serves as a folk museum. Open since the 15th/16th centuries for rather longer hours on the opposite side of the Lane is the Prince of Wales public house and beyond that a low range of 17th century buildings, including the current public toilets, once used as a fire station, and the Town Council offices at No.1 Church Lane. These are thought to be on the site of continuous human activity for more than 1,000 years, and the present building has been shown to date from *c*.1500. During refurbishment from 1988-90, exceedingly rare 16th-century wall paintings were discovered in the first floor chamber and arrangements have now been made for these to be seen.

This is at the junction with High Street where, following the success of the first phase of development in the 12th century, there was immediate pressure for more trading space. As was the case in Hereford and other flourishing market towns met on these tours, movable street stalls and booths were soon set up within the new market precinct and in course of time these were replaced by permanent buildings. This practice has become widely known as market encroachment and in Ledbury, as at Hereford, it produced a Butcher Row running in three parts down the centre of the street. In addition there was a shorter Shop Row along the eastern side of the precinct and a third encroachment across the former east-west main road from Hereford to Worcester. This was at Nos. 1 and 3 the Homend, as it is now known, and it accounts for the present kink around the building between Church Street and Bye Street. These roads were once on the main Worcester/Malvern/Ledbury/Hereford east to west route where it crossed that from Gloucester on via Bosbury to Bromyard.

At some stage during the early 13th century the bishop is thought to have moved from the west side of High Street to a more favourable site to the south and in 1232 Bishop Hugh Foliot used the vacated land to erect almshouses for six widowers and four widows. His cramped wooden buildings were rebuilt from c.1330, St. Katherine's was refounded in 1580 when the manor passed to Queen Elizabeth, and much later the south wing of the present almshouses was rebuilt in 1822 to a design produced by the celebrated architect, Sir Robert Smirke. Although his projects included the British Museum, Eastnor Castle (see below) and Hereford Shirehall, his work for Ledbury did not impress and the north wing eventually went in 1866 to someone else.

Meanwhile in c.1560 the site of two houses to the south of the site was taken for the Feathers Hotel with a northern addition of the 17th century, which from the early 19th century was an important coaching inn on the main Royal Mail route between Cheltenham, Hereford and Aberystwyth. Then early in the 17th century, Shop Row (above) was cleared to make way for a new Market House. Built as a corn mart with an upstairs meeting room, and

House on stilts near the main junction at the top of Ledbury High Street

originally with a storey below the rafters for storing corn, an open ground floor market area within sixteen pillars also allowed for the posting of official notices—as the numerous tack and nail marks still testify. Completed by voluntary subscription in 1668, it is generally attributed to John Abel, The King's Carpenter (1577-1674) (p.158), but if it was, the look of it suggests that he was perhaps restricted to a tighter budget than those agreed in 1633 for his authenticated work to Leominster's Town Hall and inside Dore Abbey church. However, unlike the Leominster building since ignominiously removed from its site to The Grange, and after extensive repairs in the 1860s and 2005, the Market House has managed to survive on the same site for over 350 years and is still used for public meetings, weddings, itinerant theatre productions and regular open markets. It overlapped for many years with Butcher Row, just to the west, but eventually, after a special Act of Parliament, this was finally demolished in c.1835. After that, for the first time for many centuries, High Street was almost as uncluttered as it had been at the beginning of the early 12th century. Terrified animals were no longer dragged from fasting pens, often to be slaughtered in full view of everyone, and at last there was clear passage for the Royal Mail and other important traffic.

All that remained of the market encroachments were Nos 1 and 2 The Homend, and the building is still there. The TIC is at The Masters House, St. Katherine's, and is well stocked with the usual material, but also with publications about detailed aspects of the town and its history. The nearby Barrett-Browning Institute and clock tower was erected by public subscription in 1895, close to a former tannery site. The building was designed in a Tudor revival style by Brighten Binyon, and although it has to be accepted as a token of its age, in appearance it really does not seem to 'fit' the traditional townscape of Ledbury or 'complement the Market Hall' as the architect intended (Pevsner called it 'Really terrible'!).

It was built as a memorial to the poet Elizabeth Barrett-Browning (1806-1861) who, although not born in Ledbury, spent her early life with her eleven brothers and sisters at Hope End. This is below Oyster Hill at Wellington Heath, 2 miles to the north of Ledbury along a minor road to the right off the B4214. It was here where in 1809 her father Edward Moulton Barrett, who had made his wealth abroad in sugar, had bought the splendid 475-acre estate. At the age of 15, after many idyllic years there, later described in *The Lost Bower*, she suffered a permanently disabling riding accident. This disaster was soon followed in 1831 by the death of her mother, and not long afterwards financial problems caused the family to leave, eventually to settle at Wimpole Street, London. In 1846, Elizabeth eloped from there to marry Robert Browning, the poet, and she spent the rest of her life with him in Italy, never to be forgiven by her unbending father. He died in 1857 and is buried with his wife and infant daughter back at St. Michael's Church, their monument from Elizabeth on the east wall of the north chapel. Eventually there was little left of Edward Barrett's Turkish style mansion, except for the coach house and stable block which became the Hope End Country House Hotel.

The Barrett Browning Institute which houses the library and local memorabilia

The Barrett-Browning Institute was opened by Sir Henry Rider Haggard in 1896 and in the same building in 1938 the public library by the Poet Laureate, John Masefield (1868-1967).

No stranger to Ledbury, he was born a short distance further north along The Homend at The Knapp, opposite the old turnpike and pound, and within sight of barges on the Gloucester to Hereford canal at the bottom of the garden which could have germinated some yearning for a life at sea. After attending the King Edward Grammar School at Warwick, he joined the Merchant Navy Cadet School on the full rigged sailing ship, *HMS Conway*, and as an apprentice sailed round Cape Horn to Chile. Qualified as 6th Officer, he was appointed to the White Star Line but jumped ship at New York and became something of a rolling stone before returning to London in 1897. After three years, and a great deal of reading, he decided to make writing his profession and by the age of 40 was regarded as one of the finest writers of English, bracketed with Thomas Hardy. His output of long narrative poems, novels, sonnets and plays famously included *The Everlasting Mercy* (1911) and *Reynard the Fox* (1919). And although the early call of the sea did not hold him for long, this did not show in a great deal of his verse such as the *Salt Water Ballads*, *Sea Fever*—and *Roadways*, which could well have related to the vision of a young teenager, standing at the side of the future A438 outside The Knapp at Ledbury:-

> One road leads to London
> One road leads to Wales
> My road leads me seawards
> To the white dipping sails

And who is not familiar with *Cargoes*, especially the third verse:-

> Dirty British coaster with a salt-caked smoke stack,
> Butting through the Channel in the mad March days,
> With a cargo of Tyne coal,
> Road-rails, pig-lead,
> Firewood, iron-ware, and cheap tin trays.

John Masefield was appointed Poet Laureate in May 1930, so joining in eminence Edward Elgar, Master of the King's Musick, who too had gained inspiration from his association with the Malverns. In October Masefield was admitted as a freeman of the City of Hereford—the first non-resident to be so honoured since Nelson in 1802. His father was a solicitor in the family firm, started early in the 19th century, and John Masefield's nephews and family continue to run R. and C.B. Masefield at Worcester Road, while his name in Ledbury is further perpetuated by the John Masefield High School for over 800 pupils from the town and surrounding villages.

As the A438, The Homend extends from High Street northwards for about half a mile, past buildings of great architectural age, variety and style, a wide range of independent shops, restaurants, inns and a supermarket, and several of Ledbury's best known alleyways and yards which are associated with former burgage plots. Beyond, the railway station at the edge of the town is one of just four remaining stops in Herefordshire and is still visited by three train companies serving many parts of Britain. At the Hereford approach there is a long viaduct (and Grade II listed building) which must be regarded as much of a wonder as any of Ledbury's other notable historic buildings. The engineer was Stephen Ballard of Colwall, and by the time 31 arches were completed in 1861, each spanning 30 feet and raised about 75 feet high, he had used some 5 million bricks of local clay—moulded and fired near the site. And still spanning the Hereford road nearby and very cleverly designed on a skew, a bridge on the former Ledbury to Gloucester line is an example of another engineer's impressive artistic sense.

The disused track bed of the former line to Gloucester now makes a pleasant traffic-free Town Trail from the station area, over the skew bridge and towards the south. Queen's Walk was created in 1984-85 and joins Bye Street near the Swimming Pool and Leisure Centre, (where until 1959 the ash platform of Ledbury Town Halt helped to attract more rail passengers). Along what was also called Bishop's Street, there is a close link with the town centre. There was once a secondary street market here and this became a permanent row of buildings, similar to those which were in the middle of High Street. Then in 1887 a cattle market was laid out between Bye Street and New Street, and ended animal sales from hurdle pens in the Homend and by St. Katherine's Hospital. This market continued until the end of the 20th century and then closed and now Market Street site contains instead the Ledbury Community Health and Care Centre. This is near The Market Theatre, which opened in January 2000 to follow a superannuated church hall conversion. This literally went out in 'a blaze of glory' in 1994.

After leaving Bye Street and the main road intersection at Lower Cross, the route to Worcester and the return salt trail to Droitwich used to enter Back Lane (Church Street) and then climb up steep Dog Hill. Then in the 17th century, Horse Lane to the south was favoured because of easier gradients and by the 1870s it had become the Worcester Road, connecting with High Street, Southend and New Street at Upper Cross. So this became the new main crossroads, but because of its narrow width and the 17th-century half-timbered House on Stilts which is jettied over the pavement at the south-west corner, New Street enters the junction from the Ross direction as a one way street. It is new in name only, for the street was already so called in 1232 when the final main ground plan of Ledbury became settled. Lower down on the south side, Ye Old Talbot Hotel dates from 1596, has been a coaching inn, and before that was the scene of an encounter between Prince Rupert's men and Cromwellians. This left two visible bullet holes in the dining room and penetrated what is regarded as among the finest examples of old oak panelling to be seen anywhere in the country, coming close to a greatly admired Jacobean overmantel. The mid-18th century Lanark House and The Steppes, a recently restored early 17th-century timber-framed building is opposite, and further down the road, past the Roman Catholic Church of the Most Holy Trinity and another supermarket, was the site of the former New Street Wharf of the Herefordshire and Gloucestershire Canal. This officially opened on 29 March, 1798, enabling best quality coal to be sold there for 13s 6d instead of the previous price of 24 shillings per ton, but subsequent delays meant that nothing would happen about the planned Bye Street Wharf until 1841 and the canal would not reach Hereford until May 1845. By then it was just about too late, for Railway Mania had already set in and before long the route of the canal from Gloucester, and in Ledbury, would be occupied by the Great Western Railway. It would in turn eventually bequeath much of it for the Ledbury Town Trail.

Beyond the Upper Cross towards Gloucester lies Southend, with further alleyways and the Royal Oak inn. This pub partly began as a cider house in 1420, had become a half-timbered coaching inn by 1645, was covered by a brick façade and had its interior work concealed in 1856, and partly restored to its original state in 1998. There are also Georgian and Regency buildings to see before the road reaches the Ledbury by-pass.

The A499 to Worcester passes the eye-catching Ledbury Park at the corner of Upper Cross with the Southend. This is thought to be on the site of the early bishop's palace and subsequent manor house. The present house was originally commenced in *c*.1505 by Edward Skinner, a clothier, became the headquarters of Prince Rupert during the Battle of Ledbury in 1645, received early 17th- to 19th-century additions and from 1688 until 1941 was the home of the Biddulph family. In 1897 the first Lord Biddulph saw to the removal of a covering of yellowish plaster to expose the work of the original fine half-timber building.

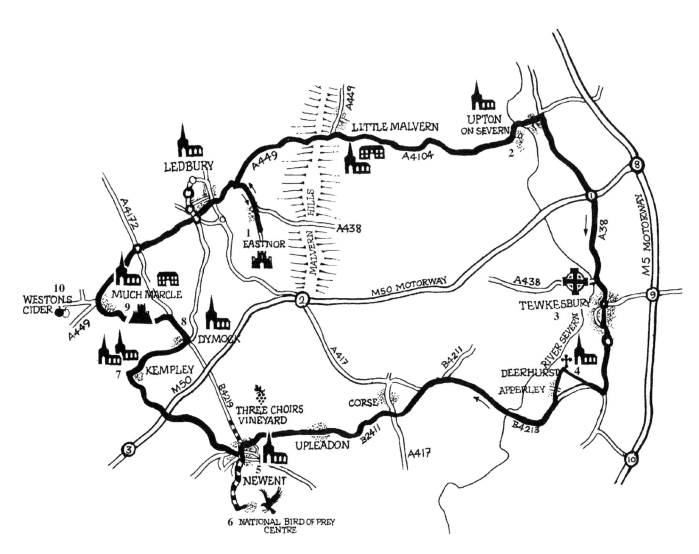

Outline map for Tour 11
The numbers 1 to 10 relate to the boxed information given within the tour

Tour 11   Market Towns and Villages
where The Three Counties meet

The tour includes several historic towns, villages with some notable churches, Eastnor Castle, the Malvern Hills (with the scope for a short walk), and some rolling English countryside along with part of the Severn plain.

Starting from Ledbury, this tour follows a succession of A roads beginning with the A449, to a high pass over the Malverns below Herefordshire Beacon, before descending to the Severn Valley to make for Upton-on-Severn and Tewkesbury. Afterwards, near Deerhurst, it forsakes the A38 and turns westward to follow mostly B roads as it heads for Newent, Kempley, Dymock and Much Marcle before returning to Ledbury, connecting again with the A449 coming from Ross-on-Wye. Without detours the distance is about 55 miles. (OS Landranger 149, 150 and 162)

From the traffic lights at the Upper Cross near the centre of Ledbury, turn uphill on the A499 towards Worcester. The first two miles lead from what was a bishop's 13th-century planned town to an early 19th-century model village, designed around a 'Fairytale Castle', family home and deer park by the 1st Lord Somers. After about a mile, turn carefully half right onto the A438 to follow signs for Eastnor, Tewkesbury and Bromsberrow and in Eastnor turn right as indicated by the brown sign for Eastnor Castle. (As the home of the Hervey-Bathursts, who are direct family descendants, the castle and grounds are usually only open to the public from April until October at certain times. Details of these and admission charges are available at local TICs.)

---

1. Eastnor Castle

Inside Eastnor Castle

Eastnor Castle took nearly ten years to build for John Somers Cocks, 1st Lord Somers, near the beginning of the 19th century and is said to have cost, for then, a massive £85,000. It was one of the early projects of architect Robert Smirke from 1810-20 and, rectangular in plan, it has four embattled towers at the angles and a central keep and over-looks a 22-acre tree-lined lake. A herd of red deer, rather than the more customary fallow deer, can often be seen within the Deer Park on the western slopes of the Malvern Hills. This is designated as a Site of Special Scientific Interest (SSSI) and is within an Area of Outstanding Natural Beauty (AONB) but is much in use by touring caravans and for rallies and a wide range of leisure events. Within the castle, the main showpiece is the 3-storey high, 60-feet-long Norman Great Hall, leading to a series of State Rooms. The High Gothic drawing room was designed by Augustus Welby Pugin for the second earl in 1849 and still contains its original furniture to embellish the civil wedding ceremonies for which the room is licensed. The castle is also filled with paintings, tapestries, sculpture and medieval armour, provides for lakeside and woodland walks and enjoys glorious views. They all add to its appeal not only for individual visitors with children in tow but also for organisers of business meetings, conferences and private parties. And as at Ledbury, Eastnor Castle also appeals to film producers—as those who have seen *The Pallisers* and *Little Lord Fauntleroy* will recall.

The twin summits of Midsummer Hill and Hollybush Hill are much in view, 2 miles to the east, and before the main tour is resumed it is worth carrying on further along the A438 to the Eastnor Estates car park at the top of the pass. For there are opportunities to look 30 miles across the great expanse of the Severn Vale to the Cotswold Hills to the east, and to the west the totally different hilly terrain of Herefordshire and the mountains of mid Wales. The car park also makes a good departure point for a walk on the Malvern Hills, either along the Worcestershire Way, or by climbing to the Iron Age hillfort site on Midsummer Hill (National Trust).

By this stage you should have been able to see a very prominent obelisk, high on a spur of the Malverns to the left. It was erected by John, Lord Somers, while the castle was being built and commemorates his eldest son who was killed at the Battle of Burgos during the Peninsular War, and also Ensign James Cocks of the Guards, who fell in 1758, and other family members. The well chosen site serves as a superb vantage point—only bettered by a lone buzzard which sometimes wheels effortlessly above. A fairly easy way of reaching the memorial and lookout involves a stretch of the legs from the car park and along the Worcestershire Way. Follow the wide and firm track upwards between SSSI woodlands and invading bracken for three-quarters of a mile, and then branch off to the left for a further not-too-challenging short climb.

The tour itself returns to the junction with the A449, on which you turn sharp right, in the Malvern and Worcester direction. The route approaches the Malvern Hills and after climbing Chance's Pitch the A449 arrives at the second of three passes and the car park below British Camp, or Herefordshire Beacon (see p.102 for information if you wish to stop here). Then it enters Worcestershire, and after winding down Black Hill, this route makes another sharp right turn near the bottom onto the A4104, signposted to Upton-upon-Severn. From there it follows the signs for Upton, almost immediately passing the remains of Little Malvern Priory and the Court (see p.102 for information if you wish to stop here), and then zig-zagging across a junction in Welland, to reach Upton. Drive down the main street and turn left at the far end to reach the main car park, signposted to the left just past the roundabout and the bridge over the river.

Obelisk memorial on the Malvern Hills to Edward, the eldest son of Lord Somers, killed in the Peninsular War, and other family members

2. Upton upon Severn

The church seen on the right as you enter Upton is that of St. Peter and St. Paul, built to the design of Sir Arthur Blomfield in 1878-79 in the style of the 1300s, replacing a much older church close to the River Severn. The old spire of the earlier church had been pulled from the red sandstone tower by a team of horses in 1754 and the medieval church was subsequently rebuilt in the classical style, with the addition of a distinctive wooden hexagonal lantern and lead cupola to the tower (later sheathed in copper) designed in 1770 by Anthony Keck. Nicknamed the 'Pepperpot', it has become something of a symbol of the town, but by 1879 the remainder of the church was abandoned and the nave finally demolished in 1937. This was not before many of the monuments, furnishings and most of the bells had been transferred to the new parish church.

Upton is another example of an early planned town, and the route enters one of two parallel early north-south roads and heads towards the River Severn which, unlike the Wye, has been an important transport route since Tudor times. During the 18th century, shallow draught barges, or twin masted trows, often hauled by teams of men, carried cargoes of up to 120 tons between Bristol and Gloucester and as far as Welshpool. Upton served as a port for inland towns, even Hereford and Monmouth, and during its heyday coal and timber from the Forest of Dean, as well as wine, wool and silk and merchandise from upstream such as salt, cider, pottery and brick would be unloaded at the quay. One report in 1849 recorded '200 to 300 vessels at one time in Upton' whose cargoes would be delivered overland by

The 'Pepperpot' at Upton

packhorse and wagon. Commercial traffic has now virtually ceased and the warehouses at the Waterside have assumed many other uses. They are close to the starting point for cruises, and at East Waterside across the river a large marina has been formed from clay pits excavated for the production of bricks and tiles during the 19th and early 20th century. It connects to the river and provides for boat sales, moorings, a slipway, a boat hoist, fuel and a chandlery. Privately owned or hired craft can travel upstream to Worcester, or down towards Tewkesbury and Gloucester, maybe branching off to enter the River Avon to chug past Bredon Hill for Pershore or Evesham. Canal narrow boats are able to enter the extensive Midlands system at Worcester's Diglis basin, while for shorter trips the *Conway Castle*, the largest vessel on the River Severn, can embark up to 200 people from the old quay alongside Upton Bridge. This is the only road crossing between Worcester and Tewkesbury and is the latest in a succession of bridges near this point. It was designed at the start of the Second World War by the county surveyor, B.C. Hammond, and is interestingly one of the last of its kind in England to have a riveted form of construction. Near this point a significant event occurred towards the

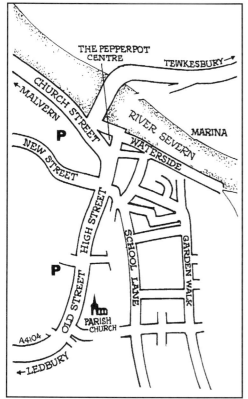

Map of Upton

end of the Civil War and featured a much earlier bridge. This had been substantially demolished to thwart the Cromwellians during the Battle of Upton in August 1651, but a carelessly left plank enabled a small group of 18 soldiers to cross over early one morning and hold Upton until reinforcements could arrive. Some 12,000 men afterwards crossed the river and advanced unexpectedly on the west bank to join in the Battle of Worcester. On 3 September they defeated the Royalist forces of

The waterfront at Upton

Charles II in what became the culminating battle of the Civil War (p.93).

Extending back from the riverside, an exploration of the town might begin at the Old Church, where at the foot of the tower during the summer months there are displays of past and present Upton at the new Heritage Centre. Across the road at 16 Church Street it is possible to visit the Tudor House, one of the oldest half-timbered buildings where there is a seasonal exhibition of memorabilia, and at 4 High Street the TIC has even more to offer about Upton and the surrounding area.

The name meaning 'the settlement up the river', the earliest years of the town were first documented late in Saxon times as part of the manor of Ripple. It was included in the Domesday Survey, had a thriving market and fair as early as 1416 and until 1966, and there was a market house at the end of High Street similar to that at Ledbury until the 18th century. It is likely that the market cross was close by and this has survived to become the War Memorial in the old churchyard in Church Street.

Like most other communities, Upton suffered its vicissitudes during the Middle Ages but had already achieved borough status by the 15th century. The ground plan of the main streets was being decided then and the burgage plots of the period can still be recognised behind buildings such as those in Old Street. The advantages of a prime riverside location generated growth and development until the

Street scene in Upton

18th century as traffic approached its peak, and it was from this prosperous time until the end of the 19th century that the old area of the town obtained its individual character. This came from the juxtaposition of early Tudor houses to Georgian and Victorian commercial and residential premises along Old Street, High Street, New Street, Church Street and others close to the north–south axis. Many were built of brick, but others are timber-framed with the 'smartened up' street frontages of stucco or mellow red brick façades which were then favoured—one special exception being Ye Olde Anchor Inn in High Street, dating from 1601. The Upton Turnpike Trust was established in 1752 in order to improve the standard of local main roads, and for just under 100 years a rail service arrived in 1864 with the opening of the Midland Railway station. Rail transport quickly brought an end to the coach trade on the main route from Gloucester and Cheltenham to Hereford and Worcester, and others, but at the close of the 19th century Upton still boasted 11 taverns and 4 inns. There are not so many now, but still more than in most towns of this size. It has been said that in 1651 the Royalist guard detachment was in the Anchor Inn when the men should have been on duty at the bridge site.

The White Lion, which dominates High Street, has its own, albeit fictional, story to tell—for it is said to have been the setting chosen by Henry Fielding for escapades of his character Tom Jones. The Swan, King's Head and Plough inns close to the river have often been in the news for less agreeable reasons, for although the Severn has historically brought much trade and prosperity to Upton, it is also prone to serious winter flooding. Some roads become impassable and riverside properties, including the pubs, can be swamped, although movable barriers have recently brought promising relief. At other times it is possible to take to The Severn Way, a long distance footpath since 1999 which follows the route of the towpath to Tewkesbury from Upton's Waterside, past two superb Georgian houses, Waterside House and Malt House. Then it reaches the Upton 'ham' meadows, 'unimproved' flood plain meadows which have always been free from all chemicals and soil disturbance. Like Hereford's Lugg Meadows, they have been important permanent pastures since at least Domesday and ownership plots are marked by large stones to register haymaking and aftermath grazing rights. They too attract large numbers of winter birds, especially after flooding. The floods also submerge Fish Meadow further upstream above the bridge on the opposite bank, but not so far in late June. Down by the riverside it provides part of the venue for Upton's annual International Oliver Cromwell Jazz Festival. By the 18th festival in 2003 this was attracting up to 15,000 jazz enthusiasts each August and is followed by the Upton Water Festival, which honours the River Severn to which the town owes so much.

The tour continues by heading through Upton on the road you entered to the mini roundabout by the old church, at which you turn to cross the bridge. It passes the marina on the right and heads to join the A38 on which you turn right. This road passes under the M50 at Junction 1 before proceeding to Tewkesbury. There it is joined from the right by the A438 road from Ledbury and Eastnor just after it has crossed Thomas Telford's 176 ft. Severn bridge, and meets the B4080 Bredon road which enters from the left. Then comes the very busy and often congested High Street and to stop in the town, continue on to the roundabout at the end and turn right round the Cross and War Memorial into Church Street. Then turn left into Gander Lane reached after about 200 yards for the Vineyard long stay pay and display car park.

3. Tewkesbury

The extended shape of the old part of Tewkesbury resulted from the actions of the river, just as at Upton. But here building was constrained not only by the flood plains of the Severn but also those of the Avon, and the amount of suitably dry land was further limited by monastic ownership close to the town, (and until 1808 restrictions at Oldbury common, when it was enclosed and terraced houses could be built around East Street, Chance Street and Oldbury Road). A framework of three main streets accommodated the rapidly increasing population of the end of the 17th and early 18th century and areas in between them were taken up by densely packed dwellings and other buildings, reached by a system of some 90 narrow alleyways. Overcrowded houses extended upwards to three or four storeys and as more were built, the natural light and ventilation suffered. There were

Street scene at the Bell Hotel in Tewkesbury

no piped water supplies, sanitation or any means of refuse removal and by the 19th century every form of disease was rife, including cholera, diptheria and tuberculosis. No relief came before there was a great deal of improved sanitation, demolition and clearance. Today the population has reached 10,000 and only 30 alleyways remain and a selection of the most interesting of these has been described in a leaflet published by the borough council. This is available at the TIC in Church Street. The trail begins at the abbey gate by crossing Church Street, opposite the Bell Hotel, to take in the 16th- and 17th-century buildings of Chandlers Court. They are private, but a short distance along the street, Old Baptist Court houses what is thought to be one of the first Baptist chapels in southern England. Originally a 15th-century timber-framed family home it was adapted as a chapel from the early 17th century until its use for worship ceased in 1805. Restored in 1976 it is now used for exhibitions and events. At the end of the court, the burial ground contains gravestones of the Shakespeare family. Beyond there is a good view of the Mill Avon and ham water meadow.

The fortunes of Tewkesbury declined from the middle of the 19th century, suffering further when its surviving station at Ashchurch, 3 miles from the town centre, was closed from 1971 until 1997. Hardly any significant new building took place until the early 1930s, when some peripheral housing estates were started. During the early post-war years further central area demolition and clearance took place and large modern buildings began to appear. Some of these were greatly out of keeping with the scale and character of the centre and still show the difficulties which were found in assimilating such raw 1960s-style structures into the very distinctive streetscape of a historic town such as Tewkesbury. It was therefore as well that a Tewkesbury Conservation Area was designated in 1967. This has helped to provide the means and backing for protection of over 350 remaining listed buildings of special architectural or historic interest,

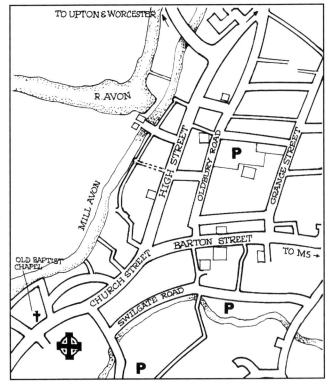

Map of central Tewkesbury

such as Abbey Lawn Cottages, The Cross House and The House of the Nodding Gables, together with other important features of the historic core.

The TIC has booklets and leaflets describing those especially worth looking for, and there is also much to discover about life on, and from, the rivers since the days when Tewkesbury was a thriving inland port. Although navigation of the Severn has presented seasonal difficulties, the lower Avon has had no such problems since 1640 following the placing of locks and

Part of the waterfront at the Abbey Mill

weirs as far as Evesham. These measures produced many transportation advantages for towns and villages close to its banks when the roads were in such a bad state. Wharves and warehouses were established at Tewkesbury near the meeting place with the Severn and many centuries ago a side stream, the Mill Avon, was diverted to provide power for flour mills—as its name suggests. There was originally a mill at Healings Mill in the 13th century where there is now a quayside Victorian factory warehouse. The warehouse was where Samuel Healing's barges once landed American and Canadian grain brought from the Avonmouth or Sharpness docks. Further downstream, the Abbey Mill was probably installed during the late 12th century to provide for the Benedictine monastery but the present building dates from the late 18th century. It was in use until 1933 and has achieved an extra measure of fame since it became Abel Fletcher's mill in *John Halifax, Gentleman*. Although not much read these days, it was once the best known and most popular of many novels, essays and poems written by Dinah Maria Craik (1826-87) and after appearing in 1857 it was translated into several languages. The mill is close to the public Victoria Gardens and also to an entrance to the Severn Ham, a low lying Common which often floods during the winter. Both rivers leave deposits with high nutrient level and because no artificial fertilizers or herbicides are used, apart from whatever leaches from upstream farming land, and as at Upton the ham meadow has become rich in herb and grass species which produce a highly valued hay crop, and also qualify it as an SSSI. After the floods have subsided, earthworms and insect larvae are forced to the surface and these provide rich peckings for wintering lapwings, gulls, starlings and many other birds while the ham is also a breeding ground of redshank and corn bunting. There is now hardly any commercial traffic to be seen from its banks, and instead a wide variety of pleasure boats is available to hire or operate from Tewkesbury Marina at Avon Lock, off the Bredon Road. It offers three directions of cruising and is a popular base from which to use the inland waterways system and the Bristol Channel. Back in the 12th century however a very considerable use of the river included the conveyance of stone which had come by sea to the Bristol Channel from Caen in Normandy for the building of the abbey.

The Abbey

In 1090 building commenced on a site which has been associated with Christianity since the middle of the 7th century and the Norman phase of the Benedictine abbey was consecrated during 1121,

Tewkesbury Abbey

the same year as its sister abbey at Gloucester, which would later become the diocesan cathedral. It is now the second largest parish church in England; 16 cathedrals are said to be smaller. The ground plan dimensions are close to those of Westminster Abbey—although Tewkesbury differs as it has almost completely retained its Norman character. This shows immediately at the west front, which has a recessed arch of six orders, seven until 1661 when the former west window was blown in, and is raised on shafts to the full height of the nave. The lowest parts of the 148ft. high tower which now dominates the town were completed in 1123 (and have prominent inverted V marks marking the pitch of roofs which were lowered in 1614). The upper stages came 20 years later, and only the pinnacles and battlements were left to follow in *c.*1600, and measuring 46ft. square it is the largest surviving Norman tower anywhere in the world. Before entering the nave by the large north porch, it is possible to pause at the consecration crosses, inscribed in October 1121 on the left side of the inner arch. Inside, the view of the nave looking east reveals two main architectural styles. Fourteen huge cylindrical Norman columns, each over 30ft. high and 6ft. in diameter, are surmounted by a Romanesque arch and a lierne vaulted roof which dates from *c.*1340. Central bosses are placed in three groups of five, representing the life of Christ, and bosses on either side mostly show angels with medieval musical instruments. Beyond the ramp which marks the position of the former stone screen dividing the former parish church from the monastic area, the lierne vaulting of the Tower and the stellar vault of the choir appear in colourful and gilded contrast, where circles of decorated 'suns in splendour', emblems of the House of York, (see also p.149), commemorate their victory over the Lancastrians in 1471 (below). The east end of the abbey at gallery level has seven of the finest 14th-century stained glass windows anywhere to be seen, and most if not all were given by Eleanor le Despenser in 1340 to commemorate her first husband, Hugh I, who Roger de Mortimer had ordered to be hung, drawn and quartered at Hereford. As they rise above a group, or chevet, of radiating chapels around the east end of the abbey, some are visible in the first sight of the abbey by anyone leaving the Vineyards car park.

Looking east along the nave, Tewkesbury Abbey

Tewkesbury Abbey has been called 'A treasure house of history', for as well as its austere Romanesque and the more decorative 14th-century architecture, after Westminster Abbey it is thought to have more elegant medieval tombs and chantries than any other church. They commemorate the founder of the abbey, Robert FitzHamon, second cousin of William the Conqueror, and members of the historic de Clares, Beauchamps, Despensers and other prominent dynasties. A brass plaque beneath the tower honours Edward of Lancaster, Prince of Wales, who was buried within the abbey in 1471 after his death at the Battle of Tewkesbury, and the bones of Yorkist George, duke of Clarence, younger brother of the victorious Edward IV, are preserved with those of his wife in a vault behind the high altar (after reputedly being drowned at the Tower in a butt of Malmsey wine). And over the floor of the nave there are more than 200 tomb slabs and monuments of ordinary men, women and children of Tewkesbury. Without the devotion of people such as these, the abbey church might well have been demolished as superfluous in 1540, for at the Dissolution the monastic buildings and the Lady chapel were destroyed, leaving only scars on the south wall of the nave and the ambulatory to the east, the abbot's lodging (now the vicarage) and the monastery gatehouse. To their everlasting credit the townspeople negotiated with the royal commissioners and arrived at a contribution of £453 for the king's coffers in respect of the church bells and all lead on the roofs, which would otherwise have been melted down. And so they gained possession of a superb parish church for future generations, and in 1992 a telling memorial of these events was placed to face the direction of the destroyed Lady chapel. In the form of a sculpture by Anthony Robinson, Our Lady Queen of Peace, an elegant statue of modern stainless steel rises there from a base of rusted scrap metal. This is featured with many of the other treasures of the abbey in literature, postcards and souvenirs on sale at the Abbey Shop in St. James' Chapel. Also there are publications which relate the often turbulent history of the abbey, not least its place in the Battle of Tewkesbury.

The Bloody Meadow

The Wars of the Roses occupied rival descendants of Edward III (reigned 1327-77) in dynastic struggles for power between 1455 and 1485. In 1471, the House of Lancaster, with the red rose as their emblem, and the House of York, who had adopted the white rose, were led respectively by followers of the imprisoned inept Henry VI, and by Edward IV. That spring, Henry's wife, the formidable Margaret of Anjou, landed from France with her son Edward of Lancaster, Prince of Wales, with the object of securing for him the throne of England. With a force of some 6,000 men she moved towards Gloucester in order to cross the River Severn to meet supporters in Wales but was prevented by the Yorkists and so headed for the next suitable crossing place, the ford at Tewkesbury. King Edward got to hear of it and with his smaller force of 5,000 better equipped and armed men he forced battle while the exhausted Lancastrians were vulnerable. In all some 2,000 of Margaret's soldiers were lost as fighting ranged over the countryside south of the town, at what is still called Bloody Meadow, or when heading in the direction of the abbey. Those who were able to seek sanctuary were pursued inside by Yorkists and the slaughter continued until the abbot intervened. (Until it could be reconsecrated after pollution by all the blood, the month which followed was the only time in the long history of the abbey for it to be closed for worship). The most dangerous of King Edward's opponents were removed, tried and promptly executed at Tewkesbury and many of the others who died were buried in the north transept or in graves around the building.

So ended one of the most decisive battles of the Wars of the Roses—from which Queen Margaret managed to escape before being captured, it is thought, at Little Malvern Priory (above). She was conveyed to London just as her husband, King Henry VI, was being put to death in the Tower and

259

was herself imprisoned for several years before a ransom was paid for her release. Edward IV reigned without effective further challenge but died unexpectedly in 1483 and was succeeded as king by his 13-year-old son who was living at Ludlow Castle with his brother Richard, Duke of York. Both were transported to London and, as The Princes in the Tower, disappeared and were presumably murdered. Their uncle, who had fought at Tewkesbury as duke of Gloucester, assumed the throne from 1483 until 1485 as King Richard III, when he was killed at the Battle of Bosworth. There the crown of England was said to have been placed on the head of Henry Tudor, and as the first monarch of the House of Tudor, King Henry VII straightway married Elizabeth of York, so uniting the lines of Lancaster and York and effectively ending the Wars of the Roses.

The presbytery and tower vaults at Tewkesbury Abbey still recall to mind the battle of 1471 with bosses decorated with the Yorkist badges of 'the sun in splendour', adopted by Edward after his ominous experience at the Battle of Mortimer's Cross in 1461, and there are flattened strips of plate armour, gleaned by the monks from the Bloody Meadow, which now reinforce the inner side of the sacristy door. Commemorative services are held at the abbey for the Englishmen who fought other Englishmen and were slaughtered in acts of terrible brutality, and on the second week-end of each July there is a re-enactment of the battle by the Mediaeval Society. And now a Battle Trail has been mapped out for those wishing to picture the scene at different points. It starts at the Vineyards car park, once part of the monastic estate, and an illustrated map has been published with a walk which takes in a memorial plinth on Bloody Meadow and a plantation which bears fitting red and white blossoms.

Assuming you parked in the Vineyard car park, return to Gander Lane and thence turn left to rejoin the A38. Turn right at the roundabout at the end of the main street, following signs for Gloucester and passing the abbey on your left. If you parked elsewhere this is the route you need to rejoin!

The A38 proceeds through parts of the battle site, and after two miles, turn right onto the B4213 and in another half mile, right again following the sign for Ledbury and soon also for Deerhurst, Apperley and Tirley. After half a mile, turn off right at the road sign for Deerhurst and the brown one for Odda's Chapel, where there is a sizeable car park.

So far in Herefordshire, Shropshire and Worcestershire a great amount of exceptionally fine Norman architecture and sculpture has been found during these tours, but surprisingly there has been little Anglo-Saxon work to see above foundation level, other than small areas and fragments such as those at Stanton Lacy near Ludlow. But in Gloucestershire there are about a dozen churches of pre-conquest origin, and remarkably two of them are close to one another at Deerhurst, a small village by the River Severn. Both are well preserved—one was a Saxon minster, the other a chapel which is nearly as old.

4.   St. Mary's Church and Odda's Chapel: Outstanding Saxon survivors at Deerhurst

The church began as a Celtic foundation and the present Priory Church of St. Mary the Virgin has been a continuous place of worship since c.700. The first building was in the form of a rectangular nave and a porch and additions then followed between the 8th and 10th centuries. The impressive 70ft. high rectangular masonry tower was built in several stages and all originate before the Norman conquest. At the opposite eastern end, beyond what is the now blocked chancel arch, there are the exposed footings of a semi-circular apse which was reconstructed as a seven-sided structure during the 9th century. One wall of this has survived to some height to reveal near the top a famous piece of Saxon sculpture, known as The Deerhurst Angel. Also showing both outside and inside are the tell-tale Saxon bands of herringbone work, an early constructional technique in which masonry is laid diagonally to strengthen and level the bed for succeeding roughly coursed rubble. Some of this shows on the tower and more appears where Victorian plaster has been stripped from the Saxon stonework at the east end of the added north aisle. At the north-west corner there is a font carved from a single block of limestone and its Celtic trumpet-spiral decoration must have stood out to Bishop Wilberforce in the 19th century when he discovered it at a local farm, in use as an animal drinking fountain. It is regarded as the finest of all known Saxon fonts and has been reunited with its stem bearing the same pattern.

St. Mary's Church, Deerhurst

A 9th-century expansion of the priory followed a major bequest which made it one of the principal Benedictine monasteries of the ancient Saxon kingdom of the Hwicce, owning 30,000 acres of land which were mostly part of today's Gloucestershire. But in the 11th century its fortunes began to decline when King Edward the Confessor gave Deerhurst to the Abbey of St. Denis in Paris and subsequently it was declared an alien house, the land confiscated and passed to Eton College. In 1440 the monastery became a cell of Tewkesbury Abbey and at the Dissolution the monastic buildings were destroyed. The Priory Farmhouse to the right of the approach drive survived and corbels remain below the eaves which helped to support the cloister roof—the site of the garth, the space bounded by the cloister, which is probably the present lawn of the house. There are more of these stone brackets along the south wall of the church and two arched blocked doorways from the church. Above there is more herringbone work, close to the Perpendicular clerestory and Tudor aisle windows which form part of what Simon Jenkins has called 'a museum of styles and treasures from almost every period of English architecture'. This great variety, and information about the sculptures, the mystery of the blocked doorway 22ft. up above the entrance door, 30 other Saxon doorways and windows, *c.*1330-40 glass depicting St. Catherine with her wheel, puritan chancel pews and much more, is fully covered in a guidebook, the reprints of scholarly annual Deerhurst Lectures, and other literature on sale at the rear.

Odda's Chapel

Odda was lord of the manor of Deerhurst during the mid-11th century, and following the death of his brother, Aelfric, he built a chapel by the Severn to be used for saying mass for the repose of his soul. In course of time the building was absorbed in the 16th- / 17th -century Abbot's Court and only re-emerged from beneath the plaster in the late 19th century during building works at the timber-framed farmhouse. And in a nearby orchard in 1675, irrefutable evidence also surfaced

Odda's Chapel on the left

on an inscribed tablet of stone (now at the Ashmolean Museum at Oxford) which confirmed its date of dedication as April 1056. The tall proportioned construction of the aisle-less nave and rectangular chancel, the double splayed windows and the long and short quoins are certainly consistent with that date and all this is regarded as a valuable gauge of Saxon work for the immediate pre-Conquest period. The chapel is now disused and in the care of English Heritage.

After leaving the church, follow the signs for Apperley and afterwards turn right at a T-junction to rejoin the B4213, crossing the Severn at Haw Bridge to pass through Tirley, turning left after one and a half miles onto the B4211. Drive for just over a mile in a south-westerly direction before turning right on to a minor road signposted to Upleadon, crossing the River Leadon to pass St. Mary's Church on the left hand side close to its banks. Although this was largely a Norman church, its chief glory seen from the road is arguably the Tudor four storey timber-framed tower, built of close-set studs infilled with red brick beneath a pyramidal roof. The village centre is a mile further on, and from there follow the signs ahead for Upleadon and Newent. Turn left at the B4215 and bear right and then left over the by-pass at the lights to enter Newent.

5. Newent: Mellow fruitfulness—and tears

Situated at the north-western corner of Gloucestershire, between the Malvern Hills and the extensive Newent Woods and conspicuous wide slopes of May Hill with its conifer topknot, planted in 1887 to mark Queen Victoria's golden jubilee, Newent is at the heart of fruitful land of deep rich soils where the leading occupations are farming, market gardening, forestry, fruit growing and wine production. From very early days drovers from Wales knew the town and market place well as somewhere worth visiting on their long journeys to the Gloucester cattle market, or far beyond across the ford there towards London and the south-east.

Thought to date back to Roman times and recorded in the Domesday Book as *Noent*, Newent was at that time a manor granted to the abbey of Cormeilles in Normandy and from the 13th century the monks of the small priory secured royal charters to hold fairs and a weekly market. At some later stage a street fair with a difference was introduced, presumably because onions did so well in the area, and after a lapse until 1996, Newent Onion Fayre is again held annually. Each second Saturday in September it attracts over 12,000 visitors to meet in 'an atmosphere of fun, laughter and onion tears', the streets are closed for the day and tonnes of onions are heaped around the 17th-century timber-framed Market House. There is an onion-eating competition among the many forms of entertainment and

*Street scene by the Market House
in Newent*

display, and at a far more serious level, an Onion Growers' Show produces entries from as far away as Devon and Yorkshire in 13 classes under Royal Horticultural Society Rules.

There is a local history of iron smelting, quarrying and lime production, and it was the promise of revenues from the transport of coal from the seams at Boulsdon and to the west and north of the town which produced the 'spin' that helped to convince investors about the profits to be had from a canal via Newent from the Severn at Gloucester to Hereford. After further veins were discovered, the necessary Act was passed in 1791 and in 1796, following the opening of the first section to Oxenhall, two barges laden with Newent coal arrived at Gloucester. But the output of the small Newent coalfield is thought only to have reached about 100,000 tons in all, despite the high hopes. However Ledbury was supplied with cheaper coal on 29 March 1798, following months of great technical problems in building the 2,192-yard-long Oxenhall tunnel, and only on 28 May 1845 could first consignments reach Hereford. By then it was almost too late because of the arrival of Welsh coal by tramway, and the advent of railways. After 1881 the GWR started to close and drain the canal and then build on parts of its route for the line between Ledbury and Over Junction, Gloucester—which opened on 27 July 1885. This in turn is also just a memory after the cessation of passenger traffic in 1959 and of freight in 1964, and part of the trackbed south of Newent was used for the route of the by-pass needed for the Motor Age.

After arriving on the B4215 from Dymock, passing Furnace Lane (named after the Newent Iron Works) and the Tewkesbury/Upleadon Road, it is possible to see beyond the old railway bridge abutments and station approach road a plaque fixed to a rock near the lights. It reads: 'Much of this bypass (1968) marks the site of the Gloucester-Hereford Railway (1885-1964) which in turn replaced the Gloucester-Hereford Canal (1796-1883). Near this spot all three successively occupied the same ground'.

It is hard now to imagine what would have become of the centre of this, the smallest of four towns in the Forest of Dean District, without its relief from heavy through traffic for the past 35 years. As it is, vehicles on High Street, Lewall Street, Broad Street, Church Street and Gloucester Street manage to weave and dog-leg their way through the Conservation Area past a variety of listed timber-framed, refronted and more modern buildings and a fitting preponderance of independent businesses. Its population now at c.4,500, Newent became a borough in 1298 and it is possible to see indications of development as a planned town in the layout of medieval burgage plots, notably on the west side of High Street and the south side of Church Street. Just as at Deerhurst, the priory was dissolved as 'alien' early in the 15th century and now there are only meagre stone remains beneath the early 18th-century Old Court. The ornamental lake and 16 acres of woodland belonging to the former estate is now called Newent Lake and Park and is a most attractive leisure area and wildlife haven at the centre of the town. Parts of St. Mary's Church date back to the 13th century, the Market House on its 12 pillars to 1668 and 1864—serving as a museum of local history during summer months, while The Shambles opposite the 17th-century George Hotel in Church Street is an 18th-century building which has become part of a Museum of Victorian life. The TIC in Church Street has several comprehensive guides to aspects of the town and its environs.

There are a number of short detours available from Newent—to the birthplace of Dick Whittington, to the Three Choirs Vineyard, and to the International Centre for Birds of Prey. If you want to continue with the main tour, then go to page 264, immediately under box no.6.

Richard (Dick) Whittington, mayor of the city of London in the late 14th and early 15th century was born in c.1350 at the small village of Pauntley. This is reached by first striking north from Newent across the by pass traffic lights and onto the B4216 signposted to Dymock, and almost immediately turning right on the road signposted to Upleadon and quickly left on a minor road signposted for Compton Green. After a sharp left hand bend, there is a narrow lane leading to the right at Redlea Farm towards Pauntley Court, itself private. Contrary to legend and pantomime stories, Dick was no orphan boy but came from a wealthy family which lived here until 1545. Return to the traffic light controlled junction of the B4215 and B4216.

To reach the Three Choirs Vineyard, take the same route as for seeing the birthplace of Dick Whittington onto the B4215, but then keep following the signs for Dymock along the B road and the vineyard is reached on the right after two miles. 'It's like being in California or Burgundy' wrote someone in *The Times*, as presumably he made his way along the drive lined with vines, part of the 100 acres of vineyards, open countryside and copses which make up the estate. Single estate wines have been produced since 1975, and during most day times there are opportunities to visit the producing facilities, stroll around the vineyard, follow guided tours which are available all year round, and of course sample or buy some of the wines in the gift shop. There is a restaurant (except on Mondays) and guest rooms for those wishing to stay longer to enjoy the local views. On completing your visit, return once more to the traffic light controlled junction on the Newent by-pass.

The way to the International Centre for Birds of Prey is indicated with brown tourist signs, starting in Newent High Street and then up Watery lane and is reached after travelling south-westwards for about a mile and a half.

---

6.   The International Centre for Birds of Prey

Since a private falconry centre was founded in 1967 with a collection of 12 birds, the present Centre has become one of the largest and most significant collections of birds of prey in the world. Over 110 aviaries house about 85 species, which range from huge eagles, vultures, falcons, hawks, buzzards, kites, caracaras and secretary birds to the tiniest of owls. There are flying demonstrations of different birds selected from the collection each day and the Hawk Walk provides photo opportunities unobstructed by wire netting of birds at close range. The centre plays a leading role in conservation and captive breeding, offers a Falconry Experience Day and runs five-day training courses designed for interested people who are fitted to become involved in keeping and training birds of prey. There is a café, and also provision for picnics around the centre and a children's play area and a range of admission charges.

To continue on the main tour from Newent, return to the traffic light controlled junction on the by-pass and turn left onto the B4221 (or right if returning from Dick Whittington's birthplace or the Three Choirs Vineyard) and then almost immediately right on the minor road signposted for Oxenhall and Kempley. The road crosses over the line of the long defunct Coal Branch of the Gloucester to Hereford canal and then reaches St. Anne's Church, Oxenhall. An interesting rarity inside the church is a late 12th-century font of lead, one of five cast from the same mould, the others are to be found at Gloucester Cathedral and Tidenham, Frampton on Severn and Sandhurst churches. Down the hill just to the north of this church there is a considerable stretch of the disused canal which energetic members of the Herefordshire and Gloucestershire Canal Trust started to unearth in 1991. As part of the exercise the tunnel portal was rebuilt and further restoration work may be seen from the towpath to the south at Lock Cottage and the adjacent lock. After much effort from volunteers, many of retirement age, water flowed over the spillweir there on 20 February 1998 for the first time in over 100 years. Canal work has occurred in the Oxenhall/Newent area with the ambitious aim of restoring navigation as far as the recently restored canal basin at Over near Gloucester. If you wish to see the results of the work, park by the roadside below the church and follow the public footpath.

After a sharp left turn near the church, the road heads towards the woods, descending briefly to the bridge across the dismantled Gloucester-Ledbury Railway before reaching St. Anne's Vineyard on the right. This is a small family enterprise which started in 1979 and went into commercial production in 1984. White and red wines are made and sold as well as varieties of country wines produced from local fruits and berries, and is often open at weekends, along with other days of the week from late Spring to early Autumn, Mondays excepted. From old maps the vineyard appears to lie almost above the seams of the narrow coalfield which extends from Kilcot to the south towards Castle Tump, south-east of Dymock. Oxenhall, The Dymock and Queen's Woods and forest trails of the Forestry Commission extend from here towards Kempley Green, where the road intersects the Daffodil Way, a circular ten-mile path beginning at Dymock (below) which is way-marked through a countryside of wild daffodils.

The village of Kempley gradually shifted its centre of gravity and in 1903 Earl Beauchamp, the lord of the manor, provided a new church for the parishioners on higher ground just over a mile to the south. To reach this now renowned Norman church, it is necessary to leave the Newent/Dymock road as it bends sharply right just beyond St. Edward's (the new church) and instead head straight along a narrower country road, making a sharp left turn at Kempley Court and farm. Turn right at the adjacent T-junction, within sight of the church on the right—where parking is not difficult. Both churches are worth visiting.

The old church at Kempley above and left

7.   Two notable churches at Kempley
The new church was dedicated to St. Edward the Confessor and largely built by local labour and material to the design of the young architect, Randall Wells. The large reticulate west window, the sculpture and range of contemporary fittings all accord with the precepts of the Arts and Craft Movement of that time.

The new church at Kempley

Nearly 800 years beforehand St. Mary's Church was built in memory of Walter de Lacy (d.1085), who had been given the manor of Kempley by William the Conqueror as one of many rewards for his loyalty and support at the Battle of Hastings. He died after falling from the tower of his new church of St. Peter's at Hereford and it is generally thought that his second son, Hugh (d.1121) who had founded Llanthony Abbey in 1108, was responsible for ordering the construction of St. Mary's and the unique wall paintings in the chancel as his memorial. The architecture of the church has many features in the 12th-century style of the Dymock School of Sculpture, such as the south and west doorways and the chancel arch. The structure of the nave roof has been precisely dated by scientific methods to between 1120 and 1150 and is one of the earliest timber roofs in Europe, but the scheme of painting in the chancel is of even wider significance. It depicts the Christ in Majesty from the *Book of the Revelation* and is dated on stylistic grounds to the 1120s. Canon D. Gethyn-Jones, a former vicar, regards the style as 'recognisably Romanesque and has its roots in late Anglo-Saxon as well as Western French painting. Influences also come ultimately from Italy and Byzantium, and from the pilgrim route to Santiago de Compostela'. He also suggests that one of the pilgrim figures appearing in the frescoes is of St. James himself, whose shrine was at Santiago, and not a de Lacy as has been imagined.

Frescoes are work of art where the pigments are applied to damp, fresh plaster and fixed by carbonisation of the lime, and during the reign of Edward VI (1547-83) they all received further lime treatment when they were completely whitewashed over as idolatrous images. They remained covered from the time of the Reformation until 1872 when the vicar noticed some colour showing through. Surfaces of the entire chancel and part of the nave were uncovered and a coat of shellac was applied as a protection. Before long there were signs of 'fading' and by 1955 the surfaces in the chancel appeared as 'a dark mass'. Experts were brought in and they discovered that the darkening was only of the varnish coat and the following year the surfaces of the chancel ceiling and walls were entirely stripped of it. The nave paintings are fragmentary and comprise overlapping images of paintings of different dates from the 12th to the 16th century. They include a Tree of Life, a representation of The Virgin, parts of St. Christopher and the murder of St. Thomas Becket. A different technique, known as tempera work was used for the works in the nave, by which the pigments were ground and used with an emulsion, such as egg yolk and water.

In 1976 the church was declared redundant and was passed to the State. Since 1984 it has been managed by The Friends of Kempley Churches in co-operation with English Heritage and an active conservation programme is continuing. (It is usually open from 1 March - 31 October from 10am to 6pm.)

In order to reach Dymock it is probably best to back-track to Kempley and then turn left at the sign for Dymock, riding always within sight of the distant profile of the Malvern Hills. Further contact is made with the 10 mile Daffodil Way circular walk when passing New Rock before arriving at St. Mary's Church.

8. Dymock: of Daffodils, Poets, Sheep and Romanesque Sculpture

The numbers of daffodils have greatly diminished since visitors used to arrive by train in the spring to admire the fields of these small pale yellow blooms, or see them picked to be sent to market. Yet many remain throughout the area where old fields and orchards have not been recently cultivated or built upon and hark back to the early 20th century, when the poet Lascelles Abercrombie, one of the Dymock Poets, famously wrote in *Ryton Firs*:

From Marcle way,
From Dymock, Kempley, Newent, Bromesberrow,
Redmarley, all the meadowland daffodils seem
Running in golden tides to Ryton Firs . . . .

A thatched cruck-framed cottage in Dymock

Lascelles Abercrombie was one of a group of poets who came to live in and near Dymock between 1911 and 1914, just before the First World War. He and his wife were the first to arrive and they set up home with their family at The Gallows at Ryton, about a mile and a half to the north-east of the village centre. In 1913 they were joined by Rupert Brooke and John Drinkwater and the same year Wilfred Gibson arrived and moved into the Old Nailshop. Edward Thomas and Robert Frost came next in 1914 and this galaxy also attracted special visitors who included W.H. Davies, Ivor Gurney and the children's author, Eleanor Farjeon. It was a creative period in all their lives, and at Ryton the wives of Abercrombie and Gibson organised a 50-60 page periodical which carried much of the poets' work entitled *New Numbers. A Quarterly publication of the Poems of Rupert Brooke, John Drinkwater, Wilfred Gibson, Lascelles Abercrombie. Published at Ryton, Dymock, Gloucester.* Due to the outbreak of the First World War it was short lived, the final issue in December 1914 including the fifth of a number of sonnets by Rupert Brooke, entitled *The Soldier* and probably his best known work, which starts 'If I should die, think only this of me ...'. He died a naval officer and national hero on a hospital ship off a Greek island the following year. And on Easter Monday, 1917, Edward Thomas was killed in Flanders while serving in the Royal Artillery.

There is now a permanent exhibition about the Dymock Poets in the parish church, there has been an association known as the Friends of the Dymock Poets since 1993, and Itineraries and Maps of two circular walks associated with the poets are available at Newent TIC and elsewhere.

The Ryelands

The area of Ryton, and nearby Ketford close to the River Leadon, is thought to have made up a major part of the Ryelands, a breeding place of distinguished native sheep which have been known of at least as far back as 1343. Very sandy and well watered by the Leadon and its small tributaries, the land was ideal sheep country at a time when England was the prime wool country in Europe. There were enormous flocks of Ryeland sheep, their fine quality wool especially favoured by the Cistercian monks, such as those at Dore Abbey and Cwmhir, and it accounted for the great reputation of Lemster Ore, the prosperity of Leominster (p.51) and that of Dymock and other local farming communities. King Edward III (1327-77) is said to have chosen the breed during the 14th century to present to the King of Spain for the improvement of his country's inferior stock, and in Dymock the wool trade was still flourishing in 1608 when four weavers are recorded to have been active.

<hr>

The Dymock School of Sculpture

Wealth created by the wool trade from the 'Golden Fleece' of the Borderlands often went into the building of expensive close-studded timber or dressed stone stately homes, churches and public buildings and skilled craftsmen emerged to undertake the work. For enrichment of the masonry, sculptural 'schools' or workshops were formed within the medieval diocese of Hereford, of which this area of Gloucestershire was then a part, during the 11th and 12th centuries. The Herefordshire School was the best known of these and another has been called the Dymock School, because St. Mary's Church was the largest ecclesiastical building in the centre of a group within a ten mile radius containing related Romanesque work—at Kempley, Preston and Newnham upon Severn.

<hr>

Although in his *Moral Essays* Pope referred to John Kyrle (1637-1711) as the Man of Ross (p.275), he was actually born in Dymock at the White House and would have been baptised at St. Mary's Church, as so many years later was John Masefield of Ledbury (above) at St. John the Baptist, Preston. Dymock is on the site of a substantial Roman settlement on the road from Gloucester to Stretton Grandison and Kenchester (Hereford), and the final leg of this journey follows the Roman Road north-westwards. To do this follow the B4024, the main road through Dymock, towards Hereford (i.e. with the pub and church on your right). Shortly after leaving the village, and a few hundred yards past a golf course on the left, you reach a small crossroads where you turn left, signposted Much Marcle and Ross-on-Wye. Ignore a left turn three quarters of a mile further on for St. Mary's and carry on to Much Marcle, a large parish which is noted for its champion Hereford cattle, cider and perry, and not least the 13th-century architecture of St. Bartholomew Church and its furnishings. Park near the church on the left of the road as you reach the village.

Much Marcle Church

9. Much Marcle

The mid 12th-century Norman tub font is the sole remaining relic of the Norman church and the nave has mid 13th-century north and south arcades of four bays with cylindrical columns. It contains one of only two wooden effigies in Herefordshire (the other is at Clifford) of fewer than a hundred in England and Wales, and remarkably the 6ft. 4in. figure is carved from a solid block of oak. However the effigy which attracts visitors most is on the north side of the chancel. The figure is that of Blanche Mortimer (d.1347), a daughter of Roger Mortimer the first earl of March and the wife of Sir Peter de Grandison, whose tomb is in the Lady chapel of Hereford Cathedral. Like many effigies of women of the time, she is shown at the age of about 30—the supposed age of Christ at the Resurrection. Her head resting on a cushion, a long veil covers a flowered headband above a serene face, eyes closed and lips slightly parted. A fine long left hand holds a rosary, and by the dog at her feet the superbly crafted loose-fitting drapery of her gown falls over the end of the tomb chest. Thoughts inevitably turn to the story of Sleeping Beauty.

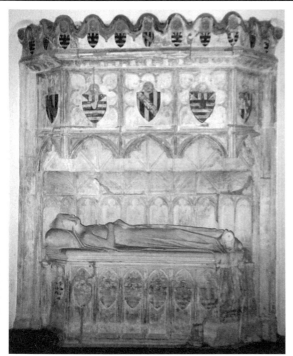

The tomb of Blanche Mortimer

The tomb and effigy of Walter de Helyon,
a rare example in wood

As something quite different, the yew tree by the South Porch is variously said to be between 1,000 and 1,500 years old and it is staggering to realise that it has existed through most of the recorded history of this realm! Understandably it is now in need of some support and redundant gas lamp columns from the streets of Cheltenham have been adapted as crutches for some lower branches and so for further centuries the seat within its 31ft. girth can continue to be used by courting couples! The drive to the west of the churchyard leads to the 16th- to 18th-century Homme House, formerly the seat of the Kyrles, and the north (Kyrle) chapel of the church contains two striking altar tombs and many other memorials to them and to the Money-Kyrle families. Fifty yards north of the church, Mortimer's Castle, which was first recorded in 1153, survives among trees as a motte and bailey earthwork. The central mound has a diameter of *c*.170ft., is 21ft. high and stands above a ditch. It was granted to Edmund Mortimer, the grandfather of Blanche (above) by Edward I, once had a stone shell keep and must have been an impressive fortress.

Begun in 1292, Hellens, Much Marcle, is said to be one of the oldest homes in England, although the present house dates from the 15th, 16th and 17th centuries. It is highly regarded as a living monument to much of England's history and contains a wealth of period furnishings, paintings and decorations. The gardens are in the process of being redeveloped along Tudor and Stuart lines to reflect the luxury of the house and attention is being given to a rare octagonal dovecote of 1641, a walled knot garden, a yew labyrinth and a short woodland and pond walk. Signed access is via Monks Walk opposite the church and details of opening times, admission charges and special events are available at local TICs.

You can make a small detour to visit Westons' Cider by turning left at the crossroads with the A449 just beyond the church, and then almost immediately right just before the local shop and opposite the Walwyn Arms and Westons is reached after three-quarters of a mile, with a car park on the left and the factory, bottle museum and shop on the right. Visitors can join tours to hear how cider and perry are produced, see *c.*200 years old vats and in the autumn the milling and pressing of fruit. There is a museum of old farm machinery, cider-making equipment and a collection of over 700 different cider bottles, a shop retailing over 50 products which provides free samples of ciders, perries and other drinks, and there is a restaurant and bar. Details of opening times, tours, admission charges and Shire Horse Dray Rides through Much Marcle are included in the *Herefordshire Cider Route*, which contains details of a gradually increasing number of other Herefordshire producers and is available from TICs.

---

10. Westons' Cider

A tradition of farm cider-making has existed in Herefordshire for many centuries, well before Viscount Scudamore of Holme Lacy stirred an interest in orchards and cider varieties in the 1660s and introduced the famous Redstreak apple. Cider became the national drink, and farmers used the slack autumn months to produce it for local pubs and merchants and to use it for part payment of their labour force (some of whom managed two gallons in a day!) during the following hay-making and harvest seasons. In the 1870s more august consumers were approached by C.W. Radcliffe-Cooke, the MP for Hereford from 1893 to 1900. Known as The Member for Cider he waged a campaign from his home at Hellens which culminated in Weston's Cider being introduced into the bar of the House of Commons. Henry Weston had founded his business in the village in 1880, a few years before the mother of H.P. (Percy) Bulmer urged him to make a career either in food or drink 'because neither goes out of fashion'. By 1900 no fewer than 12 cider factories had opened around Hereford. Although afterwards the numbers fell, as a family-run business Westons has thrived at the heart of an area which has been called Big Apple Country with little change in its traditional methods of cider-making. After harvesting, milling and pressing, the apple juice is still placed into large casks holding between 60 and 120 gallons where the yeast in the apples begins to work and fermentation begins. After about 6 weeks the barrels are sealed with a wooden bung to exclude the air, and the cider then matures for several months.

To return to Ledbury, keep to the A449 from the crossroads and follow the signs back to the town.

Ross, and the Wye Tour

Whilst early roads were universally in an appalling condition, opportunities for river trade on the Wye, chiefly based at quays, wharves and warehouses near Wilton Bridge, produced significant benefit for the 18th-century economy of Ross and neighbouring areas. Then from about the middle of the century, new business appeared as an early form of tourism. Until then, because of its remoteness there had been little appreciation of the picturesque qualities of the Wye but gradually 'gentlemen of taste and leisure' who included writers, artists and poets began to explore and enjoy what were called 'the wilder aspects of nature'. Clergymen seem to have been well to the fore, headed by John Egerton, rector of Ross from 1745 to 1771 and William Gilpin, a prebendary in the Salisbury diocese. After travelling down the length of the river in a boat he published his *Observations on the River Wye &c*, and by the time the poet William Wordsworth (1770-1850) first arrived on a Wye barge (or trow) at the ivy-clad ruins of the Cistercian abbey at Tintern in 1793, the Wye Tour had become fashionable. He returned after 'five summers and the length of five long winters' had passed to compose his *Lines Written a Few Miles above Tintern Abbey*.

His now familiar poem may have prompted another clergyman, William Coxe, rector of Bemerton and Stourton, to publish his account of *An Historical Tour in Monmouthshire* shortly afterwards but the title covers only part of an excursion which started soon after a summer dawn in 1801. After reading that the 'navigation' to Chepstow would take them down 37 miles and 7 furlongs of serpentine river—compared with a direct line of not more than 15 miles and 4 furlongs, he set off from Ross with a companion in a boat holding eight passengers and the boatmen with a last look at the spire of Ross church towering high up above the trees. The ruins of Wilton Castle were on the right as they were about to pass beneath an arch of the then 200 years-old sandstone bridge, and before long they arrived below the embattled turrets of Goodrich Castle in time to stop at a ferry house for breakfast. After briefly exploring the area they re-embarked, passing the coal mining area of Lidbrook (Lydbrook) and noticing several barges being towed by ten or eleven men on their strenuous two days' upstream struggle from Lidbrook to Hereford. Disembarking again on the opposite shore at Welsh Bicknor they paid a short visit to Courtfield, a seat of the Vaughan family which is reputed to be where a sickly future Henry V was nursed after his birth at Monmouth Castle. Back in the boat they rapidly met a dramatic change in scenery, where rocks clothed with trees formed stupendous cliffs, the most remarkable being Coldwell Rocks and Symond's Gate (or Yat). Visitors usually disembarked there to climb to the giddingly high summit and gaze out at the landscape before descending on the other side, 'following a direct line of not more than 600

Looking up to the Royal Hotel and the church from down by the Wye and 'Swans', one of Walenty Pytel's sculptures

yards instead of the four miles distance by water'. The deep vale in which the river flows is bounded on one side by the Great Doward, a sloping hill which was then sprinkled with lime kilns and cottages, and overhanging iron works at the water's edge, and on the other side a chain of rugged precipices. After further changes of scene and abrupt windings of the river, the boat passed under the Lays (now Wyastone Leys) before entering a long reach to arrive at Monmouth—and bed for the night. The navigation continued at nine the next day and passed below the Kymin, crowned by the pavilion, and the mouth of the Monnow as it fell tranquilly into the Wye. After about two miles the river is also joined by the Redbrook, so named because of staining of the water by the red powdered iron ore or haematite. At the small village the boundary of Gloucestershire and Monmouthshire runs down the centre of the Wye, past the ferry and some iron and tin works. Beyond, there is a sweep and an abyss between two ranges of lofty hills, thickly overspread with woods, and where the banks are less steep there was a distant view of the church and castle of St. Briavel's. Then comes Big's Weir (Bigsweir), before the river winds by 'the beautiful hamlet of Landogo (Llandogo), situated in a small plain tufted with woods and backed by an amphitheatre of lofty hills'. The tidal range of the Wye ended at Book's Weir (Brockweir) and on the left bank there were numerous 80 to 90 ton vessels, mostly from Bristol, anchored near the shore waiting for the tide with cargoes transferred to and from the shallow draughted Wye barges. These drew little more than five or six inches of water, but during the navigation from Ross the boat passed small fishing craft which could operate in even shallower depths. These were called Truckles or Coricles, ribbed with laths or basket work and covered with pitched canvas. They only held one person, who navigated with a paddle in one hand and fished with the other—afterwards shouldering his boat to carry it home with the catch. The party next disembarked at Tintern, disappointed with the celebrated remains of the abbey, which were half concealed by mean buildings, but also glad that their appearance was considerably heightened by the valley and woodland setting. The river, now tidal and discoloured, resumes its serpentile course near Piercefield and the long line of Banagor crags (Ban-y-Gor Rocks) forms a perpendicular rampart on the left bank, opposite narrow slips of pasture and woods on which towers the Wynd Cliff, a perpendicular mass of rock overhung with thickets.

Here, concluded William Coxe, 'the Wye turns abruptly round the fertile peninsula of Lancaut, under the stupendous amphitheatre of Piercefield cliffs.... wholly mantled with wood, there jutting in bold and fantastic projections which appear like enormous buttresses formed by the hand of nature. At the further extremity of this peninsula the river again turns and stretches in a long reach between the

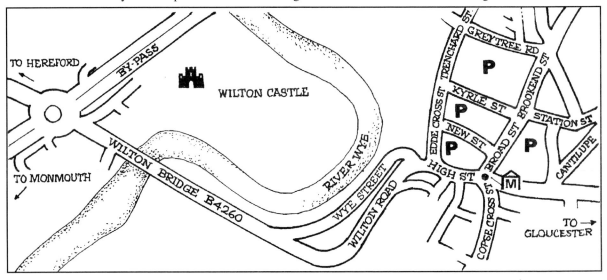

Map of central Ross

white and towering cliffs of Lancaut and the rich acclivities of Piercefield woods. In the midst of these grand and picturesque scenes the embattled turrets of Chepstow Castle burst upon our sight and as we glided under the perpendicular crag we looked up with astonishment to the massive walls impending over the edge of the precipice and appearing like a continuation of the rock itself'.

Many other tourists and families 'did the Wye Tour' from the 1760s and were served by pleasure boat proprietors who hired out boats and provided steady, experienced boatmen for visits to all parts of the River Wye. From 1836 a steamboat, *The Man of Ross*, appeared each summer and for a single fare of ten shillings (and a shilling per dog) ran a twice-weekly tour from Ross to Goodrich, Symond's Yat, Whitchurch, New Weir, Monmouth, Tintern and Chepstow and during the century other river steamers began to arrive from Chepstow or Monmouth.

From the 14th century Ross had been an important market town, serving an extensive rural hinterland, it was a regular stopping place for travellers between England and Wales and gradually became a popular tourist centre which was well equipped with important facilities, not least good inns and hotels. In 1837 the Royal Hotel became a prime example and was built not only to put up the 'right' class of visitor (including royalty) with all the comforts, but also provide views across the river and countryside from a lofty position where it was intended to enhance the skyline. It appeared during a phase when, in order 'further to beautify the townscape', the approach from the Wilton Bridge was elaborately 'medievalised' with mock-Gothic town walling, complete with arrow slits, and a round tower. Other follies included 'a castellated summer house approached by a battlemented terrace' and one enthusiast lavishly concealed his water pump and farm buildings with a castellated wall and towering chimney. In total some 24 hotels, inns and taverns were listed in the town by 1876, many providing not only 'well aired beds, superior post horses and excellent stabling', but from back in 1855 'an Omnibus to meet every train'.

That year, Brunel's broad gauge line opened between Hereford, Ross and Gloucester, and from 1873 it was connected with a branch from Ross to Monmouth. By the autumn of 1876 the Wye Valley Railway was officially opened between Monmouth Troy station, Redbrook, Bigsweir, Tintern, Tidenham and Chepstow. It was followed in 1883 by a branch line from Wyesham Junction (near

A gazebo overlooking the Wye built in the style of a mock castle

Monmouth) to serve the town of Coleford and take advantage of the Forest of Dean's natural resources of coal, ore and timber. Passengers on these new railways of the Wye Valley journeyed through some of the most beautiful countryside in Britain, much of it along the banks of the sinuous Wye, and by the end of the 19th century pleasure boat traffic on the river had been largely displaced. For a while however, the GWR provided excursion packages by operating from Paddington to Hereford, where passengers could join a boat trip down the Wye to any favoured landing place, then be taken on by rail to Chepstow and back to London. When the steam trains were followed by the arrival of the motor car during the 20th century the hiring of boats declined still further. Visitors preferred to undertake their Wye Valley tour by road, and now the way of travelling the whole distance down river to Chepstow is chiefly by canoe (or maybe taking part in the annual charity raft race from Hay-on-Wye).

The new century brought further significant changes at Ross and in an attempt to bolster the tourist trade and overcome confusion with other places, and after great controversy in the town, it was decided in 1931 to add 'on-Wye' to its name—just as Hay was to do for similar reasons in 1947. By then post-war motor traffic had started to create congestion in the centre of both towns and at Ross-on-Wye the character of its historic centre was further blighted by schemes of demolition and a quota of incongruous, unsightly replacements. Although the town has not been best known for buildings of great architectural merit, there are some which stand out. The most famous are the much restored St. Mary's Church dating from 1280, with its prominent graceful 205ft. high floodlit tower and spire, the *c*.1650 red sandstone Market Hall and Rudhall Almshouses in Church Street, founded in 1575. But there are others which hold a special interest, and at an entrance to the churchyard south of the church a sandstone cross bears the stark inscription: *Plague Ano Dom 1637 Burials 315 Libera nos Domine* from one of the town's darkest times.

The Market Hall

To enter the town from the car park, the best way is along Wye Street, and one good reason is to see some outstanding metal sculptures by Walenty Pytel, a Polish refugee and now Herefordshire artist whose work has widely appeared not only locally but at prestigious sites such as Birmingham Airport and near The Houses of Parliament in London. At Ross-on-Wye there are three of his works which were commissioned by the local authority in 1997: *The Mallard in Flight*—a 30ft. high sculpture and the *Swans*, positioned on the riverside walk, and the *Leaping Salmon* at the top of Wye Street—just before it reaches High Street. This is one of the streets where conditions have benefited from recent traffic management schemes and it leads to the Market Place and the Market House Heritage Centre (open all year at given times). Part of the local heritage was its support for the Monarchy during the Civil War, marked by a medallion of Charles II which was fixed on the east side of the Market House. One intensely loyal resident was John Kyrle (1637-1724) whose house was across the narrow High Street where he could not see the figure from his window. Such was his devotion that he arranged for a logogram to go on the south wall of the Market House, consisting of an F and C intertwined with a heart—which has been taken to mean 'Faithful to Charles in Heart'. It still faces the half-timbered house which became his home upon the death of his mother at about the time of the Restoration.

The Man of Ross

John Kyrle was born in Dymock in 1637, and after attending school at Gloucester he entered Balliol College, Oxford, as a gentleman commoner in 1654. There were plans for him to follow his father and be called to the Bar, but this did not happen and instead he devoted much of his energy towards the welfare of the people of Ross, the new home of his parents. Two of his hobbies were landscape gardening and building, and with an aptitude as an amateur town planner combined with exceptional philanthropy, these helped

The Plague Cross

to make their mark on the face of Ross which has lasted for over 350 years. With a reputation for frugality and modesty, he was comfortably off with an inheritance of *c*.£500 p.a. and used his resources to fund or initiate a range of projects for the benefit of the town and its church, for he was also an avid churchgoer. He played a leading part in restoring the causeway over the water meadows to Wilton Bridge (near the present car parks), in bringing a water supply to Ross and initiating ideas for The Prospect, high up near the church, to become a public park. He offered financial aid or loans to those wishing to build their own red brick or timber houses, on condition that he had a say in the designs, and through one of his roles he was able each Saturday to distribute bread baked in his own oven to the needy who were waiting at the steps of the Market Hall. He retained sufficient funds to assist in the upkeep of St. Mary's Church, took a leading part in the rebuilding of the spire in 1721 and provided for the cost of the pinnacles and the new 24cwt. tenor bell. In 1684 he arranged for the planting of an elm tree avenue, not knowing that later a sucker would penetrate the masonry and grow inside the

'The Mallard in Flight',
by Walenty Pytel

church in front of the east window of the north aisle! (The tree was felled as part of an 1878 restoration project, the suckers then died and creepers have been planted to take their place). Exceptionally, when he died at the age of 88 in 1724 his body lay in state for nine days, and everyone from Ross and the neighbourhood attended the funeral. And yet in spite of all that, and of all the time, thought and funds he devoted towards the welfare of his fellow townspeople during most of his lifetime, there was to be no tangible memorial either from the town as a whole, or from any relative, for many years afterwards, and some doubt was even cast on the exact whereabouts of his burial-place. In 1750 a stone inscribed *John Kyrle, Esq., 7 Nov. 1724 aet. 88* was at last arranged for by a cousin, but only in 1776, on the north wall of the sanctuary, did a more elaborate memorial join the assembly of plaques, effigies and statues of the worthy departed of Ross. Later still, in 1924 and 200 years after his death, the municipality at last provided its own timely memorial in the form of the church tower clock.

But long before, Alexander Pope (1688-1744) the leading poet of his day, sought to attract wider notice to John Kyrle's great deeds and generous benefactions in one of his *Moral Essays*, to demonstrate the ways greater and wealthier men ought to use their fortunes. And only then in 1733, through Pope's poetical biography, did the now famous title of The Man of Ross first appear. His work has since been carried on from 1877 by the Kyrle Society and there is also a reminder of his part in instigating The Prospect as a future public park from his monogram above a churchyard entrance gate, there is the John Kyrle Walk and of course a Kyrle Street in Ross, and the title of the High School makes certain that none of the pupils there will ever forget his name.

The churchyard, with the Prospect and the church beyond

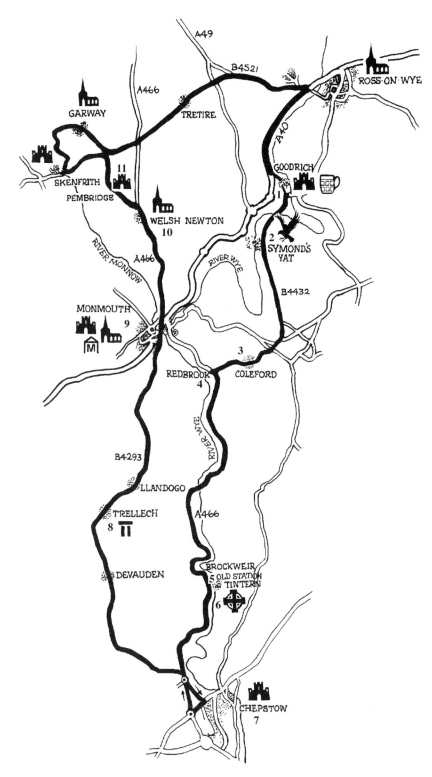

Outline map for Tour 12
The numbers 1 to 10 relate to the boxed information given within the tour
Information on Garway and Skenfrith can be found on pages 204 and 205 under Tour 8

Route 12   The Lower Wye Valley

This tour includes the Lower Wye Valley, taking in the substantial remains of Goodrich Castle, before passing near Symonds Yat East to enter Gloucestershire—and where there is the chance to stop at the famous rock and viewpoint—and the Forest of Dean. The tour passes through Coleford, now the natural centre of West Dean, and after calling at some attractive parts of the Forest the route makes a considerable descent to river level at Redbrook and then follows the Wye downstream, crossing into Monmouthshire to reach Tintern Abbey before arriving at Chepstow with its mighty castle. Then turning about, the tour takes an elevated route to Monmouth, from where the A40 can be taken back to Ross, or a rural route followed taking in more castles and some churches.

The tour is mainly along A and B roads with the exception of the 'rural option' at the end of the tour. Without detours the total distance is approximately 60 miles. (OS Landranger 161 and 162)

It is a good idea to take binoculars if you wish to try and see the birds of prey on the rocks at Symond's Yat.

Appearing in countless calendars, picture post-cards and artistic old railway company posters, the best and most attractive view of Ross-on-Wye is from Bridstow on the opposite side of the river to the north west, or along the A40 extension of the M50 Ross Spur. This road by-passed the centre of the town from 1960, was later followed by a new relief road to the east and the former section of the A49 main road to Gloucester which had brought heavy volumes of traffic thundering and squeezing through the narrow streets, was 'de-trunked'. Now the quieter road from the A40 roundabout crossing the ancient Wilton Bridge and climbing up the hill into the town is re-numbered the B4260, and by the water meadow in between it connects with off-street and kerbside car parks. Down near river level these also make good vantage points for viewing the attractive features of the town above the sandstone cliffs, and they are convenient as starting points for tours, both of the river and the town.

The tour itself starts from Ross-on-Wye by making for the Wilton Roundabout and then turning left on the A40 dual carriageway to follow the sign for South Wales, Abergavenny and Monmouth for just over 3 miles as far as Pencraig. Be ready for a prominent gatehouse on the left (see below), and a fairly sudden turn off to the left along the minor road bearing signs for Goodrich and Goodrich Castle (brown). There are good views across the Wye Valley down to the left before arriving in the village, after about a mile, and after passing Ye Hostelrie inn there are further brown signs to Goodrich Castle which, after two right turns, show the way to a large car park and facilities, including a picnic site, at the beginning of a path up the gentle slope of the hill alongside woodland to the castle itself. This is in the care of English Heritage.

Ye Hostelrie

Ye Hostelrie is unusually replete with tall pinnacles and Gothic lattice windows. A 17th-century coaching inn, it was reshaped in *c.*1830 and is thought to represent the spirit of a much shorter-lived castle which was once prominently high up, half a mile upstream from the ruins of Goodrich Castle.

It too was being built at the end of the 1820s and was in the form of Edward Blore's fantastic castellated house which his client, Sir Samuel Rush Meyrick, named Goodrich Court. Regarded as 'the founding father of the systematic study of arms and armour', he assembled an unsurpassed collection of arms, armour and antiquities in the new mock Gothic castle. The villagers were in no position to say too much about the handiwork of their lord of the manor, or grumble for the horses about an unhelpful diversion of their road onto steeper ground, but William Wordsworth, a frequent visitor to the Wye Valley and admirer of the Picturesque, was not so inhibited and expressed the hope that the building

1. Goodrich Castle

The approach to the castle passes the outer side of the eastern moat towards the south side of the semi-circular barbican, where the dry ditch enclosing this outwork is crossed by a modern wooden bridge. This replaces an original drawbridge and it leads to where admission tickets, the illustrated handbook and the usual souvenirs are available. The purpose of a barbican is to protect the castle Gatehouse and this is now reached across another bridge which crosses the very deep moat cut into solid red sandstone. The Gatehouse has a huge semi-circular tower which houses a chapel, where a window in the west wall commemorates members of the Radar Research Squadron and the loss of 11 personnel on board a Halifax aircraft which crashed near the castle in 1942. The first castle at Goodrich was documented in 1101/2 and was built to guard the ancient Wye ford under the name of Godric's Castle. There is no longer any trace of it, and the oldest visible building now is the 3 storeys- high typically square Norman keep, built of grey conglomerate shipped during the 12th century, it is thought, from the Forest of Dean. It is surrounded by high 13th- and 14th-century curtain walls with round drum towers at the corners and planned out as a fortified

Goodrich Castle

baronial palace. Many of the medieval domestic buildings are fairly intact, apart from roofs and floors, and this is largely because the formidable strength of the castle was not tried in warfare until its use as a home for successive noble families had come to an end. After the 16th century it had become unoccupied, but in 1646 its strength was at last put to the test when it became the final bastion in Herefordshire for the Royalists, there under the leadership of Sir Henry Lingen. After the surrender of King Charles I in the summer of 1646, denial of the water supply, and bombardment with 200 pound missiles from a locally made mortar called Roaring Meg, combined to force the Royalists to surrender. The Parliamentary forces led by Colonel John Birch marked their success by slighting the castle, and it was never inhabited again. It passed through various hands, until in 1920 it was placed under the guardianship of the Commissioners of Works, who were recently succeeded by English Heritage in continuing with the systematic preservation of the ruins.

could be blown up! This did not happen, but after a while it suffered slower disintegration and in 1950 was eventually demolished, leaving only the exotic Gatehouse alongside the A40 Ross-on-Wye to Monmouth road as a token to puzzle passing motorists.

From Goodrich the route continues along the B4229 until you turn left at the sign for Symonds Yat East and Yat Rock, almost immediately crossing over the narrow Huntsham Bridge to climb Huntsham Hill past the cul de sac sign on the right and up beneath the trees into Gloucestershire and the Forest of Dean. If you want to stop to see the view and possibly birds of prey from the rock, the first direction sign to the right at the top, and shortly after you have passed under a wooden footbridge, is towards parking space for disabled people and then comes the entrance to the main Symonds Yat Rock car park.

Since 1949 the lower reaches of the Wye Valley between Hereford and Chepstow have been designated the Wye Valley AONB, consisting of 128 square miles of ancient semi-natural woodlands, 62 miles of pristine 'wild' river, a rich diversity of flora and fauna combined with spectacular landforms, geological and historical features and the entire river is designated a Site of Special Scientific Interest (SSSI).

---

2.   Symonds Yat: The Rock, the Viewpoint and the peregrine falcons

The view from Symond's Yat

Robert Symond, High Sheriff of Herefordshire during the 17th century, was the local landowner and yat is the local name for a gate or pass, where here the Wye enters steep sided wooded valleys from the open farmland of Herefordshire. There is now a Symonds Yat West and a Symonds Yat East, each in a different county. Symonds Yat East, the Rock and Viewpoint are now in Gloucestershire and Symonds Yat West in Herefordshire and there are hotels, guesthouses and various attractions at each, as well as opportunities for walking, rock-climbing, camping, canoeing and 40-minute boat cruises above the rapids. The hand operated cable ferries operated by the 16th-century Saracen's Head (East) and Ye Olde Ferrie Inn (West) cover little more than 100 yards when river conditions allow. Near Symond's Yat East and overlooking the famous views from the rock above the river running some 400 feet below there was then a large promontory hillfort with a developed system of ramparts raised across the neck.

Yat Rock is the most famous of many buttresses of dolomitic limestone outcrops which tower over the huge near-elliptical horseshoe bend of the Wye, here over 60 feet deep in places and in others just a few inches. At short range from the viewing area there is Huntsham Hill and through the gap in the middle distance, Goodrich Church. To help identify places much further away a Toposcope (504 feet above sea level), shows the directions and distances of features ranging from Ross-on-Wye, five and a half miles way, Aconbury Hill, Wormsley Hill and The Kymin, to the Black Mountains 21 miles distant. Beyond the flood plain to the right of the gap is Coppet Hill while well within binocular range are the bare limestone Coldwell Rocks. The cliffs are often at the focus of several bird-watchers' telescopes, for after a long absence they have become breeding grounds for peregrine falcons since 1982.

Although these splendid birds of prey have even been known to adopt urban sites, they usually prefer inaccessible sites like these which are safe from predators and, for the most part, people. The Great Doward Hill rises over to the left from the Viewpoint and on the far horizon are the Black Mountains, while back at short range from the return path to the car park there is a view which acted as Herefordshire's Golden Valley in a poignant closing scene of *Shadowlands*, the film biography of C.S.Lewis, an Oxbridge

The home of peregrine falcons

don, and with several other works, author of children's stories of the land of *Narnia*.

The entire area is well managed by Forest Enterprise with the Forestry Commission and there are also way-marked Forest Trails, an Easy Going Trail, picnic tables, a café and shop, public conveniences and well laid out car parking spaces (pay and display) among the trees.

To leave the car park, follow the exit signs back to the public road and then turn right at the sign pointing to Coleford (2 miles), Monmouth (5 miles), Ross (11 miles) and Gloucester (21 miles). The B4432, which this road becomes, runs alongside Mailscot Wood to emerge from among the trees at Christchurch, where the route bears to the right at the sign for Coleford, Cinderford and Gloucester, following a further sign for Coleford and St. Briavels across the junction with the A4136 at Berry Hill Pike. Turn left at the T-junction in Coleford and then right at traffic lights for the centre. Drive past the church tower on your right and follow the car park signs for a short distance before turning left—where there are also public conveniences, the Railway Museum and a short cut on foot past a supermarket to the centre, passing along the Mushet Walk and beneath the Archway.

3. Coleford, and the Age of steel

The first recorded reference to Coleford was in 1275, when it was called Colevorde, and as the natural centre of West Dean it grew into a busy market town by the 17th century. After the granting of a new market charter in 1662 by a grateful King Charles II, he is said also to have paid towards a new Market Hall after the previous one had been burnt down during the Civil War. After a refurbishment in the 19th century this survived until it was demolished in 1968 to make way for road improvements. From early days Coleford was also a mining and quarrying centre and the industries and communities of the Forest came to be served by horse tramways and then standard gauge railways which approached from two directions, each with a separate terminus.

In the centre of Coleford, noticeable features include the church tower, without the rest of the church. This and the surrounding paving and other features formed the focus of Coleford's Millenium 2000 Project: 'In memory of all persons from Coleford District who gave their lives in the Service of their Country'. Those remembered also include Captain Angus Buchanan of Coleford who rescued two severely wounded men in quick succession whilst under heavy Turkish machine-gun fire in Mesopotamia (now Iraq) in the First World War, an action for which he was awarded the VC to add to his Military Cross. Also completed in 2000, Mushet Walk and a wrought iron archway paid homage to the achievements of David Mushet and his son Robert, who was born in 1811 at what has now become the Forest House Hotel. Father and son were responsible for many advances of the iron and steel industry, and in 1856 Robert Mushet was credited with perfecting the process of converting pig iron into steel. (This was the Bessemer process, named after Sir Henry Bessemer (1813-98) which involved air being blown through

Central Coleford

the molten iron, when the oxygen converted the high carbon content of the ore into carbon dioxide). It was this discovery which made an immense contribution to the inception of the Age of Steel. The dependence of Coleford on the coal, ore and stone bounties of the Forest has now ended and new industries have arrived there, but there are still small reminders such as Coalway and Bessemer Close. Most of all, long abandoned workings, conical spoil heaps, shafts, and quarries remain close to the town, many becoming less obvious as nature reclaims the land, recreational uses are found for the factory ponds and railway trackbeds become walking and cycling routes.

Coleford gave its name to the most important coal seam of the Forest of Dean, the Coleford High Delfh, and during the first half of the 20th century this must have accounted for a good share of the 1 million tons of coal produced annually from the seams in the Forest. Output however declined after the Second World War and the last deep mines had closed by 1965. But that was not the end of production, and in the coal bearing areas there are still small shallow collieries being worked under the Free Miners system in accordance with long-standing Forest traditions. Such matters are conducted at meetings of the Verderers' Court which are generally held four times a year at the Speech House. This was built for Charles II in 1676 as a hunting lodge but later became the administrative centre of the Forest, where people came to talk or make speeches, hence its name. The court had been founded at least as far back as 1338 and is thought to be the oldest functioning court in Britain. Appointed for life, the four verderers are entitled to be paid a doe and a buck a year for protecting the Vert (bearing green leaves) and Venison on behalf of the king, but the word locally is that all the present postholders have yet to claim the salary.

If you wish to visit the court on a detour, return to the 'roundabout' around the church tower from the car park, and go straight across back to the traffic lights. Go across these, and then keep right on the B4226 to Cinderford, the Court Room being on the ground floor of what has now become The Speech House Hotel some three miles along this road. On the left hand side of the road not far before reaching it a brown sign indicates Hopewell Colliery Museum where visitors are taken down an actual drift mine. A short distance further on, down and then up the Cannop Valley, there is another sign pointing left up a drive to the Forest Commission Visitor Centre at Beechenhurst Lodge. Here Forest Enterprise offers 35 square miles of woodland to explore and enjoy along waymarked walking trails or cycle routes, as well as a Sculpture Trail, adventure playground, shop and café at the centre and many picnic spots, car parks and camp sites all around the Forest.

The main tour resumes at Crossways on the B4228, north-west of Coleford town centre. To reach this, from the town car park turn right and take the second exit near the church tower and then turn left after a couple of hundred yards onto the B4228. If returning from the Speech House via the B4226 and B4208, turn right back at the traffic lights in Coleford onto the B4228. In both cases then turn left in Crossways onto Scowles Road. The road then makes a winding descent of over 600 feet past a busy limestone quarry to Redbrook and the A466, close to falling streams and brooks—inexhaustible sources of power which, as elsewhere in the Forest, were once indispensable for its industrial processes. Just before reaching the A466 the tour passes beneath an original steep self-acting Tramway Incline bridge which served the Lower Tinplate Works and the public wharf on the east bank of the Wye, close to some of the cottages and industrial buildings of the Forest's remarkably long heritage of heavy industrial activity.

---

4. Redbrook

The village of Redbrook is in two parts and the first to be reached is Upper Redbrook which lies on the Red Brook, whereas Lower Redbrook is on the Valley Brook. Iron processing with the rich haematite was carried out here from medieval times (for example, use of the ore was observed by Giraldus Cambrensis in 1188) and early industry from the 17th century was powered by both these streams, harnessed at different times for blast furnaces, copper smelting and tinplate works, a paper mill and several corn mills. By 1698 all home consumption of copper and some export orders were being supplied from Redbrook because of its combined advantages of a ready supply of coal and charcoal from the Forest, the water power on the Red and Valley brooks and river access to the sea and to Cornwall for sufficient supplies of high quality ore—by 1697 almost 1,000 tons starting from very little early in that decade. However by 1735 new smelting techniques using Welsh coal favoured Swansea, and Redbrook switched to tinplate production and this lasted until 1961—sometimes along with the making of pig iron, brewing and corn milling. From 1812 the horse-drawn Monmouth Tramroad played a vital part in transporting many materials between the Forest, Monmouth and the river.

At the bottom of the hill, the route turns left along the A466. After just over 3 miles the road crosses the Wye and from England and Gloucestershire to Wales and Monmouthshire at Bigsweir Bridge. Sometimes attributed to Thomas Telford it was actually the work of Charles Hollis (known for Windsor Bridge) and is a single 160ft. span cast-iron former toll bridge of 1828, its spandrils distinctively designed with N-pattern bracing.

The village of Llandogo, reached next, derived its name from the founder of the church, St. Oudoceus, a 6th-century bishop who retired there and founded a monastery in a place which he found 'peaceful and tranquil and abounding in fish and honey'. Many of the dwellings are poised irregularly on the steep hillside to the right, and the names of some which are nearer the valley floor—for example the Sloop Inn (of 1707), Trow Cottage and Ship Inn (now a private house)—show that high tides once brought sea-going vessels this far up-river.

The next place of interest is Brockweir, reached by turning left on the road signposted to the village which you enter across a 3-span lattice-girder bridge on two pairs of cylindrical columns with masonry abutments, built in 1906 and not the handsomest structure spanning the Wye. It is worth finding a spot to park and having a brief wander. The village was at the practical tidal limit of the Wye where vessels as large as 500 tons and over were built, and it was also an important port. Ships from Bristol and beyond anchored there to transfer cargoes to and from the shallow draught river barges and trows which sailed or were hauled up or down river as far as Monmouth, Ross, Hereford, Leominster and even Hay. Not surprisingly at such an important meeting place there were several inns and cider houses in the fascinating tangle of narrow streets at Brockweir when the Reverend Coxe (pp.271-2) was being rowed past in 1801 on his Wye Tour in search of the Picturesque. Just there the nearest approach to this was probably the colourful language of Bristol sailors and equally of the hefty 'bow hauliers', fuelling up before pulling their Wye trows on the long upstream haul!

Return across the bridge, turn left back onto the A466 and after a very short distance there is a sign pointing left to the Old Station, Tintern which offers refreshments, a railway exhibition, displays, books and souvenirs in two railway carriages and the signal box, audio-visual presentations, teaching packs and a regular programme of special events. The station is also well placed for those who wish to explore local lengths of the Wye Valley Walk and Offa's Dyke Path. It tends to close out of season.

---

5. New life for an old station

Despite the superb scenery along-side the line, and its hoped-for appeal to tourists, the Wye Valley Railway never made a profit and by 1958 was said to be losing £20,000 a year. On 4 January 1959, some time before the appearance of Dr. Beeching, the last passenger train ran and five years later so did all goods traffic, and most of the rails were taken up for scrap. There was soon very little to see, save the conspicuously long masonry viaduct, minus its ironwork section, at Monmouth Troy and a steadily deteriorating, overgrown Tintern

Tintern Old Station

station. Opened for passengers in November 1876, this had been the largest railway complex on an otherwise single-line branch, and doubling of the running lines and the inclusion of an additional loop were meant to cater for the many tourists expected to visit the famous abbey. Over 80 years later a rescue exercise was mounted with the co-operation of the then Gwent County Council. After much effort from volunteers, including children from a local school, The Old Station was reopened in 1975, received a Civic Trust Award in 1978 and it has grown in popularity ever since. Now signposted from the left hand side of the A466.

Everyone visiting Tintern reaches it now by road or on foot and it no longer matters as much that the station, once in the timetable as 'Tintern (for Brockweir)', is nearer to Brockweir and about a mile away from the village and abbey.

Beyond The Old Station the A466 soon reaches Tintern and squeezes its way between the Wye and hillside buildings which include a selection of shops, hotels and guest houses. The single way through the village began as a turnpike road in *c*.1820 when it continued onwards without apparent concern to cut through the 27-acre precinct of the abbey. Thus, from what has now become the A466, the access road to the car parks leads off to the left to separate the former Gatehouse, Guest Hall, Guest House, Inner Court and Watergate sites from the heart of the monastery.

6. Tintern

The medieval gateway beside the Anchor Hotel once led to a ferry across the Wye, whilst in 1872 one of Tintern's two railway bridges was built just upstream to provide access to works to the west which for more than 300 years produced strong wire and other metal products. Needed principally for wool carding, wire making had commenced along the Angidy Valley river system during the 1560s, just 30 years after the abbey community had departed following its Dissolution by Henry VIII. It is a little ironic that, whilst aiming to withdraw from wordly affairs in seclusion and tranquillity, with an emphasis on the value of manual labour, the Cistercians should have been occupied not only in their customary farming and sheep rearing but also working with iron ore, unknowingly to lay the foundations for a far from tranquil industrial centre. But as a source of water power, the Angidy Brook was involved not just with the manufacture of iron but also of non-ferrous metals, for in 1568 Tintern became the birthplace of the brass-founding industry through the smelting of copper and zinc to make brass (this was commemorated in 1957 with a plaque on an outer wall of the abbey). There were also many water-powered corn mills and some 20 water wheels were listed in 1821, but towards the end of the century the wireworks went into decline and for a short while tinplate manufacture was attempted instead. But by 1900 both wire making and the tinplate industry had ceased, and after brief use as a horse-drawn tramway, then removal of the rails in 1941 towards the war effort, the Wireworks Bridge has since been adapted as a public access to woodland walks on the Gloucestershire side of the river.

Tintern Abbey

Tintern Abbey

Entrance to the modern abbey is through a newly built gift and ticket shop adjoining the car park close to the river, where there is a well illustrated official *Guide Book*. The abbey was founded in the year 1131 when the Anglo-Norman lord of Chepstow invited an abbot, twelve monks and a number of lay brothers to estab-lish a monastery on one of the few available terraces in the tree-covered slopes of the lower Wye valley. They were Cistercians, of a new Order of monks which took its name from the abbey founded at Citeaux (*Cistercium* in Latin) in Burgundy in 1098 and always favoured sites away from towns and villages 'far from the concourse of men'. Known as White Monks because of their habits of unbleached wool, its priestly members followed very strictly the Rule of St. Benedict, including the injunction to earn a living by manual labour. The ordained choir monks however occupied themselves mostly in worship, study and teaching, while the heavy physical work was undertaken by lay brothers, who cleared and drained land, established sheep farms and corn mills and, here at Tintern, forges for iron making. Their communal life was governed by strict rules, routines and total dedication and the division between the choir monks and the *conversi*, as the lay brothers were called, shows in the architectural arrangement and ground plan of their monasteries. At Tintern the modest early buildings

were largely superseded from the 13th and 14th centuries in a major rebuilding programme and the Abbey Church, built from 1269 to a length of 228 feet and width of 150 feet in the then new Decorated architectural style, replaced the 12th-century Romanesque predecessor church to be consecrated in 1301. After the monastic foundation ended in 1537 the lead was stripped from the roofs and the buildings crumbled until the mid-18th century when the duke of Beaufort, whose forbears had succeeded as owners, tidied the site and turfed parts in recognition of an increasing public and tourist interest. The work of protection, conservation and maintenance has continued with the help of public funds since the abbey was bought by the nation in 1901 and it is now managed by Cadw.

The chief points of interest begin with the nave at the west end where the lay brothers attended services, their altar before a screen between the fourth pair of pillars from the west. The pulpitum, a highly decorative stone screen and a great rarity in a normally austere Cistercian context, formed the west end of the monks' quire, which occupied the first bay of the nave and the crossing, and the presbytery, at least one step higher, took up the three bays from the crossing. At the east end this culminated in the third bay with the high altar, placed one last bay back from the huge, eight-light east window.

The tour then moves into the cloister of four passageways built round a rectangular open court or garth, where one of the rooms to the north is the chapter house. Here the monks gathered each day to hear a chapter of the Rule of the Order and conduct the business of the house, while to the east is the Infirmary group where the sick were tended and aged monks lived out their days. The abbot's lodging and his private apartments were to the north of the infirmary, and to the west, past the novices' lodging or perhaps the monks' day room, the monks' dining hall was entered by them from the centre of the north cloister walk. It was separated by a kitchen from the segregated lay brothers' dining hall and dormitory which formed the usual Cistercians' west range.

From Tintern the route continues along the A466, climbing quite steeply beneath a low tree canopy and after two and a half miles reaches a sign at a car park indicating 'Lower Wyndcliff and 365 Steps' which are high above to the right. You may wish to stop here, or half a mile further on at the Eagles Nest, to walk some paths and take in the views. The Wyndcliff is a steep limestone mass which rises from its base at river level by over 700 feet and provides striking vantage points which can be reached by a gradual woodland path, or up a series of steps. These were constructed in 1829 but the number has reduced somewhat over the years through decay (although not the height to be climbed), and after the Second World War they were repaired by conservation bodies and muscle from the Beachley Army Apprentices School. An easier alternative exists about half a mile up the road, where the first turn to the right leads to another car park and a footpath sign pointing to the 'Eagles Nest, Wye Valley Walk Northbound and 365 Steps'. This section of the Wye Valley Walk is not too demanding, and after only about a hundred yards the initial effort is rewarded, except maybe for vertigo sufferers, with a first spectacular view down below towards the meeting place of the two great rivers of Wye and Severn which first began life on the same Plynlimon mountainside, not very far from the Irish Sea. Higher up the path, the view from the Eagles Nest become even more wide ranging, and as well as providing for an even better look at the Severn Suspension Bridge and the Second Severn Crossing and the M5 viaduct at Avonmouth, on clear days it is possible to pick out seven counties. Much closer, the final reaches of the sinuous Wye curve from the foot of the Ban-y-gor crags round the Lancaut peninsula to make yet another tight U turn at Wintour's Leap. This is a cliff of carboniferous limestone which reaches a height of over 200 feet above river level and, often regarded as a tall story, it is said to have featured in an amazing escape in 1644 by Colonel John Wintour when pursued on his horse by Cromwell's forces.

Continuing on the A466, after more bends the road straightens and there is a good view of Chepstow Racecourse to the left. At the roundabout at the far end of the racecourse, turn left and follow the road into Chepstow. At the T-junction controlled by traffic lights, turn left under the gateway and follow the road down to the bottom the main street, bearing left at the next T-junction and continuing downhill till you reach a car park below the castle on the your left.

---

7. Chepstow

The A48 trunk road from Gloucester (*Glevum*) coincides in places with the course of the Roman road which headed for what is now South Wales, and experts have concluded that at Tutshill, just before reaching Chepstow, it turned almost due west to cross the Wye to proceed through Alcove Wood at a hollow in the cliffs. This was about half a mile upstream from the later castle and it then clipped the site of today's racecourse grandstands before continuing towards Caerwent (*Venta*) and Caerleon (*Isca*). These stations were part of the Roman approach for keeping the land to the west under military control and it is not unlikely that, at a position of such strategic importance at the Wye crossing, there would also have been some form of settlement at Chepstow. No solid evidence has yet appeared, but long after the legions withdrew, and from the days of King Offa, there are traces nearby of the Dyke which he established. From here, at its southernmost extremity where there are sections of dyke or parts of Iron Age earthworks which might be of different origins and purposes, it ran up through the borderlands to the North Wales coast in order to provide a demarcation between Mercia and the ever troublesome Britons. The Anglo Saxon name for Chepstow was *Ceap* (market) and *stow* (place or town) and to the Welsh it is still *Cas Gwent*, meaning castle at a Celtic *venta*, a 'favoured place' or 'market' in the ancient kingdom of Gwent, coinciding largely with later Monmouthshire. The strong trading importance of the town must therefore have been well established when the Normans arrived soon after 1066 to exert feudal control over the border territory. Chepstow came within one of William

the Conqueror's three border earldoms, and William fitz Osbern, earl of Hereford (d.1071), was charged with the duty of defending the Wye basin as far as Ludlow. During the short remaining time before his death in France he organised the building of several castles and within a newly established Norman Lordship of Striguil they included a strong fortification at Chepstow to guard one of the main crossings between England and Wales. Built probably between 1067 and 1070, it was, like Ludlow, one of the

Chepstow Castle

first to be constructed of stone from the start, with no initial timber motte or earthwork, and it has been authoritatively described as 'historically one of the most important castles in the Welsh March'. Opinions differ as to Earl William's precise involvement, except for his fine stone hall, and whereas it has been traditionally thought that he was also responsible for the 3 storey Great Tower, scholarly research now concludes that it is more likely to have been commissioned after his time, possibly by William the Conqueror himself in *c.*1081.

It is one of the most dramatically sited castles in Britain, the later extensions and additions along the ridge to the east and west seeming to merge with the natural limestone high above the bend in the river. One of the best views is from the former main town entrance across John Rastrick's elegant cast iron bridge of 1816. Despite its narrow width, with subsequent strengthening this bridge carried all road traffic into Chepstow from the east until 1987, when a steel and concrete replacement was built downstream following the profile of the adjacent railway bridge built by I.K. Brunel for the South Wales Railway in 1852 (modified in 1962 from his tubular suspension system to Warren truss girders beneath the tracks).

Just across the road from the castle, exhibits at Chepstow Museum explain much of the town's past history as an early borough. In a number of places it is still possible to see sections of the 13th century Port Wall and towers, and there is also evidence of a planned town which extends down the axis formed by High Street, Middle Street and Bridge Street. As a regular part of the process of Normalisation, Earl William founded the Benedictine St. Kynemark's Priory in the lower part of the town, to the south east of the castle, but after the Dissolution this became neglected. The central church tower fell in 1700, was replaced by the present west tower in 1706, and a 'restored' nave and the west front with its richly decorated Norman doorway have remained to serve as the parish church. Displays at the museum also illustrate the role of Chepstow as a trading centre and port and describe industries which have included shipbuilding and repairs, salmon fishing, a considerable wine trade and early tourism, and also the changes and effects brought about by the railways and the strong challenges of the nearby competing ports of Newport and Cardiff.

From the car park by the castle in Chepstow, turn right and follow the road around, bearing left near a church to a set of traffic lights outside a supermarket at which you turn right. Go across the set of lights that follow immediately afterwards and follow the road as it winds uphill to a roundabout. Here you turn right back onto the A466, crossing one set of lights and another roundabout before passing Chepstow racecourse again. At the end of the straight that passes the racecourse turn left onto a secondary road at St. Arvans to climb through Chepstow Park Wood and Fedw Wood towards Devauden, there, by turning right, to join the B4293 road to Monmouth. Much like the Forest of Dean, Symonds Yat and other woodland areas met on these tours, the October colours must compare with those of the famed scenes of New England or Canada in the Fall. And passing through the small scattered communities of Llanishen and Trellech, this ridge-top road always offers striking panoramic views to the west over the Vale of Usk.

8.   Trellech, Town of the stones

Trellech is the only substantial hamlet along this road but it is nevertheless surprising to see the size of the church without knowing its history. For Trellech was a borough plantation by Lords Marcher, the de Clares, and in the late 13th century it had become the largest such settlement in all Gwent. But in 1296 a Welsh attack caused a massive fire, and although St. Nicholas' Church was quickly repaired, the town and market declined, also suffering from a bad outbreak of plague in 1369 so that by the end of the 17th century little else remained but the church. Today it is regarded as one of the finest in Monmouthshire, and also enjoys an unusual distinction for its special stone sundial, dating from 1689. Now kept inside, it is carved with reliefs of the three local antiquities, the first being three large standing stones set up in line in a field off the Llanishen road, the origin of the place name and known as Harold's Stones. Composed of quartz conglomerate, or 'pudding stone', they are 8, 10 and 14 feet high and thought to date from the late Neolithic or early Bronze Ages (c.2600 - 1800 BC) when, 700 feet above sea level, they may have been a very much earlier hill-top focus for the surrounding area. The second local feature is a motte known as Twmp Turett, and the third is the Virtuous Well, formerly St. Anne's Well. It is about 200 yards along the Llandogo road where there are said to be four wells in one, their waters of chalybeate (containing iron). Used by Romans settled in the neighbourhood, the water of one well was taken for healing, of another for eye complaints, a third for 'complaints peculiar to women' and the fourth was neutral and for nothing in particular.

The Three Stones, or Harold's Stones, Trellech

The old motte, or Twmp Turett, Trellech

Soon after leaving Trellech the road begins to drop to river level, exposing half way over to the right a striking aerial view of Monmouth. The B4293 merges with the minor road from Mitchel Troy, entering sharply from the left, then to cross over the River Trothy and the A40 trunk road tunnels to enter Over Monnow, making a left turn into Cinderhill Street. There is a car park on the right-hand side, beyond the new bridge across the River Monnow, and there are others close to the opposite bank within the town centre.

9. Monmouth

Situated outside the defensive walls of Monmouth, the detached suburb of Over Monnow was protected by a ditch, the *Clawdd Du*, and the character and proportions of the Norman church of St. Thomas Beckett of 1186 and the older domestic buildings, some from the 15th century, suggest that it has enjoyed its own measure of success. According to research by Monmouth archaeologists, parts of the area were once occupied by a Roman fort, and other traces have been unearthed across the Monnow in Monnow Street, Chippenham and close to Monmouth School alongside the River Wye. Called *Blestium*, between the middle of the 1st and the 4th centuries AD it was an important station

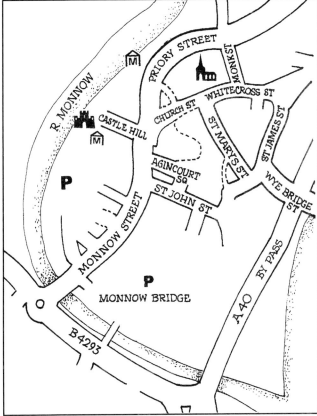

Above: the old bridge, Monmouth;
right: a map of the town centre

in a chain which extended northwards from Caerwent and Caerleon (see Chepstow above) to Chester (*Deva*).

The westernmost of Monmouth's four main entrance roads (but soon to be five) crosses the Monnow Bridge, its fortified stone gatehouse often regarded as a symbol of the town. At one time reinforced with a portcullis, it has certainly fulfilled a major role ever since the late 13th century, not only in defence but at various times as a toll house, store, gaol and even a dwelling. It has undergone several changes, noticeably the piercing of two side doorways for use by pedestrians, but short of total demolition it has never been possible to improve upon the *c.*10 feet available carriageway width. It is difficult today to imagine how, before the A40 by-pass was completed in 1966, this bridge carried through vehicles of all sizes between England and Wales, as well as often handling heavy town traffic and the cattle trucks attending the adjacent livestock market, now resited out of town. Monnow Street rises from the gatehouse to become a wide thoroughfare until it again narrows acutely at St. Stephens Gate on its approach to Agincourt Square. Still a part of the relatively unchanged ancient street system of Monmouth, by 1100 AD Monnow Street was planned for burghal development outside the castle bailey. A deep archaeological dig at one of the properties recently revealed successive layers of occupation, and graphic explanations helped visitors to trace the history of the town from the time when it was one of the earlier Roman garrisons, then a Celtic settlement, and after the Normans began to give the historic core the shape that persists today. The Robin Hood Inn—one of the town's oldest pubs—Chipenham House, Cornwall House and the Lloyds Bank exterior are just some of a number of fine buildings which have attracted particular attention. The street naturally became used for animal sales until the livestock market was built off Blestium Street in 1876 and it has since flourished as

The statues of C.S. Rolls and Henry V in Agincourt Square

an important part of the primary shopping axis as it leads towards the hub of the town centre at Agincourt Square. One of the first features to attract the eye there is a striking statue by Gascombe John of C.S. Rolls (1877-1910), son of Lord and Lady Llangattock of the Hendre. He crossed the English Channel by balloon in 1906, flew with Wilbur Wright in 1908 and in 1910 was the first man to fly non-stop across to France and back, but later that year he established a far less fortunate record as the first British aviator to be killed in a flying accident. Much earlier he had been excited by the emerging new Motor Age and had experimented with early cars during the 1890s. Then in 1904 he met Henry Royce (1863-1933), an engineer who had founded the Manchester firm of Royce Ltd 20 years beforehand and had just produced his first car. The outcome of the meeting and the combination of their talents led to the formation in 1906 of the firm of Rolls-Royce Ltd and that year it produced the first Silver Ghost. It was at once hailed as 'the best car in the world' and was a precursor of a century of Rolls-Royce car and aero engine enterprise and success which would require several more pages to relate.

Trefynwy to the Welsh, Monmouth has a present population of about 8,500 and as a consequence of the Act of Union it became a shire town in 1536 during the reign of Henry VIII. The Shire Hall was built in 1724 in place of a small Elizabethan market house and was later extended, providing two courts and Grand Jury rooms for assizes and quarter sessions as well as a corn, flour, wool and hops market on the ground floor. In 1839, the building witnessed the High Treason trial of John Frost and leaders of the Chartist Uprising and pioneers of modern Trade Unionism as one of its most celebrated cases. They were condemned to death for activities which today are mostly acceptable but because of public outrage they were instead transported to Tasmania, although eventually pardoned. The final assize was held there in 1939. Since then the building has been used by magistrates, the town council and the tourist information centre and weekly markets occur beneath the arches and on the cobbles of Agincourt Square.

Below the clock, there is a niche on the face of the building which has been occupied since 1792 by a prominent, rather grotesque statue of King Henry V. It is very difficult to relate to any accredited

Agincourt Square and the Shire Hall of 1724

representation of his looks, or to his stirring role at Agincourt, but the statue is there, and the square was so named because Henry (1387/1413-1422) is said to have been born at Monmouth Castle. The remaining ruins are to be found up Castle Hill, which leads from the west side of the square.

Like Chepstow Castle, Monmouth was built by William fitz Osbern very soon after the Norman Conquest, and it was to share a strategic role with the castles at Skenfrith and Grosmont, extending control into the heart of southern

Monmouth Castle

Wales along the River Monnow. Sited at the highest point of the town, it was later enlarged, chiefly during the reign of the able and formidable Edward I (1239/1272-1307), when the town wall and fortified Monnow bridge were also constructed. He it was who, following the death near Builth in 1282 of Llywelyn ap Gruffudd, the last native Prince of Wales, took Gwent, alone among the Lords Marcher territories (and later to become Monmouthshire), into England until well into the 20th century. In due course the Lordship passed into the Duchy of Lancaster and the castle became the birthplace of the grandson of John of Gaunt, Duke of Lancaster. Prince Hal spent his early childhood at Courtfield, on the inland peninsula which overlooks the Wye from Coppet Hill, near Welsh Bicknor where, in 1935, the bowl of the font in which he was baptised was found in the churchyard. Prince of Wales by his late teens, was honing his military skills in the Welsh campaigns against the partisan forces of Owain Glyndwr and was crowned king in 1413 at the age of 25. But despite his robust constitution he died in France only seven years later, not from battle wounds but of dysentery, just two months before he would also have succeeded to the French throne.

Monmouth was important during the Civil War because of its strategic position, when it changed hands a number of times until the castle was finally slighted by Cromwell's forces in 1647. Close to the position of the late 14th-century circular Great Tower, the reputed actual birthplace of the prince, masonry was used from the castle ruins in 1673 to build a town house for the marquess of Worcester, whose family had acquired the Lordship. This is known as Great Castle House and it has since been occupied as an assize court, a girls' school and is now the headquarters building of the Royal Monmouthshire Royal Engineers, the senior Reserve Regiment of the British Army. This unit was first raised in Tudor times and there is a Regimental Museum which offers free admission (donations welcomed) and open every afternoon from April to October and at weekends during the winter.

The outer bailey site of the castle is now partly occupied by Agincourt Square, so named in 1830, which during the 18th and 19th centuries contained coaching inns and hotels among several in the town which went with the age of prosperity produced by the considerable river trade and the needs of followers of the fashionable Wye Tour. The King's Head dates from the 17th century and on the opposite side of the Shire Hall was the Beaufort Arms (now Beaufort Arms Court) where Lord Nelson stayed in 1802 in the company of Sir William and Lady Emma Hamilton, when he travelled the Lower Wye in order to report to the Admiralty on the state of ship-building timber in the Forest of Dean. He had received the Honorary Freedom of the town, among many others, and accepted the mayor's offer to visit the Naval Temple, placed in memory of 'the naval heroes who made the name of England famous in the French Wars' (but focuses on the 'noble admirals' involved). It had been erected in 1800 one and a half miles away, 800 feet high up on the Kymin near the Round House which had recently been built in 1792 as a two storey banqueting house for local gentry. Set in 9 acres of woods and pleasure grounds the site still offers extensive view across the Wye and Monnow valleys. (It is in the care of The National Trust). One of Monmouth's remaining 13 pubs, The Punch House, leads round from Agincourt Square towards Church Street. Again it is difficult to imagine how such a narrow main thoroughfare of the county town ever managed to cope until the early 19th century with all the through and local horse-drawn traffic and all the drovers' animals heading for the market place in the square. It has now been 'pedestrianised', and set among the varied range of small independent shops there is the Savoy cinema which dates from the early days of 'talkies' in 1927. Church Street meets St. Mary's Street at the parish church which, except for the tower and spire, was rebuilt in 1736 on the site of the Benedictine priory, founded by William fitz Osbern's successor, the Breton Wihenoc, in 1075-82 to be extensively restored in 1882. Traffic passing though the town now uses Priory Street, which was built in 1837 on a viaduct alongside the Monnow as a valuable early form of inner relief road in order to ease the problems of Church Street. A market hall for local provisions was built at the same time but it was badly damaged by fire in 1963 and instead it now houses the Nelson Museum and Local History Centre, many of the Nelson Collection exhibits and memorabilia donated by Lady Llangattock, the mother of Charles Rolls.

After passing over the former public slaughterhouse, which gruesomely and conveniently operated next to the river below the red sandstone viaduct, Priory Road reaches the traffic signals at Monk Street. Its name comes from the Monks' Gate of the priory and to the right it passes the elegant Georgian houses of Whitecross Street and then St. James' Street to Wyebridge Street, the A40 by-pass and to Wye Bridge. According to a long lost inscription on one of the piers, the original structure dates from 1615 and until 1828 it was the only bridge across the Wye until Chepstow. The old semi-circular arches can still be seen beneath the later five red sandstone segmental arches, built when the bridge was widened on both sides in 1879. Severed from the river with the rest of Monmouth on the opposite side of the trunk road is Monmouth School, which was founded in 1614 by William Jones, a wealthy merchant, who left £9,000 to the Company of Haberdashers 'to ordaine a Preacher, a Free School and Alms Houses in the town of Monmouth'. There has been a great increase in the size of the school since its founding in 1614, the almshouses were rebuilt in 1842 and afterwards incorporated, there were extensions in 1865, 1895 and later and it has become an Independent School. In 1897, the Haberdashers Monmouth School for Girls was opened on a commanding site overlooking the town and reached by turning left from Priory Street and resuming contact with the A466. It heads towards Hereford past attractive Regency houses and the former County Gaol and the building on the left near the top of the hill is the old Union Workhouse of 1871. This has now become part of the Girls' School, joined by a covered footbridge to the main building on the right.

From the town centre car parks, the route follows Monnow Street and Priory Street through the centre of the town and turns left at the Monk Street traffic signals to join the A466 to Hereford. The tour continues for about 3 miles along this road until it reaches Welsh Newton, where the village church holds the rare claim to have the grave of an English martyr and saint in its churchyard, and quite possibly also that of a crusader Knight Templar or Knight Hospitaller.

9.   Welsh Newton and Saint John Kemble

Welsh Newton Church

The Church of St. Mary the Virgin was built during the 13th century, its porch in the 14th, and until 1312 belonged to the Knights Templar and then the Knights Hospitaller, linked with their preceptory at Garway (p.204), four miles away, and Dinmore, near Hereford (p.146). It contains much of interest, especially the Rood Screen, which was erected in 1320 and displays the ball-flower of the Decorated period of architecture and is one of very few existing and early screens built of stone in a parish church. Above it is a contemporary dormer window which was built to give light to the Great Rood, or crucifix, which would have once stood on top of the screen, and now effectively illuminates the chancel and its special 13th-century features. The sandstone font at the west end is Norman, and above it are the early 16th-century ceiled wagon roof and portions of the original structure, which is thought to date from when the roof was made of thatch. The Churchyard Cross has three medieval steps, which usually symbolise faith, hope and charity, and close to the foot is the grave of Saint John Kemble, and next to it another which is thought to be that of a Knight Templar or Knight Hospitaller, discovered in 1979.

'None ever saw one die so like a gentleman and so like a Christian'

John Kemble was born in 1599 at Rhydicar Farm, St. Weonards and was ordained priest in 1625, beginning a greatly respected ministry in the Welsh Newton area that was to last for 54 years. Father

Grave of St. John Kemble
and churchyard cross

Kemble's centre was the chapel at Pembridge Castle, the home of his relations, but during his later years of service during the restored monarchy of Charles II, civil and political anxiety inflamed in 1678 by Titus Oates combined to view Roman Catholicism as treason against the Crown. It was proscribed and priests were forbidden to say Mass. That year, by order of Parliament, Bishop Croft of Hereford dispersed the Jesuit college at The Cwm in the next parish of Llanrothal, when the library of books was moved to Hereford Cathedral, more than 300 years later to become housed in the new library and exhibition centre (opened in 1996 by the Queen). At the same time, Father Kemble became falsely implicated in an imaginary plot and Captain Scudamore of Kentchurch Court was sent by the bishop to arrest him. Urged to flee, but being almost 80 years old by then, he answered: 'According to the course of nature I have but a few years to live. It will be an advantage to suffer for my religion and therefore I will not abscond'. After three months in Hereford county gaol on Castle

Green, and a gruelling journey to and from his arraignment in London, he eventually stood trial before Lord Chief Justice Scroggs at the Guildhall, Hereford and was condemned to death as a recusant priest, who had been ordained overseas in France and was therefore a traitor as the law stood. The morning before he was hanged at Wigmarsh by Hereford (now Widemarsh Common) on 22 August, 1679, he calmly made his usual devotions, drank a cup of sack and smoked a pipe of tobacco with the under-sheriff and the prison governor, starting the old Herefordshire custom of calling a parting drink or smoke a 'Kemble cup' or 'Kemble pipe'. Although his body was afterwards beheaded, public feeling prevented the then customary 'drawing and quartering', and afterwards the martyr's body was buried with dignity in Welsh Newton churchyard and a stone slab over the grave was inscribed: JK / Dyed the 22 / of August Anno Do / 1679 . John Kemble was beatified on 15 December, 1926 , canonised as a saint on 20 October, 1970 and there has been a pilgrimage for many years to his grave beneath the churchyard cross on the Sunday nearest to 22 August.

Turn left off the A466 almost opposite the church in Welsh Newton on the road signposted to Skenfrith and Garway. After about half a mile Pembridge Castle lies on the right hand side, it being easy to miss the castle entrance drive between the tall hedges on the right at the crown of the hill.

10. Pembridge Castle

Pembridge Castle, as seen from the end of the entrance drive

From its elevated position the castle has a magnificent view of the mountains to the west and the valley woodlands and fields far below. It dates chiefly from the 13th century when Ralph de Pembridge (d. *c.*1219) settled at Welsh Newton and gave to his residence the connection with his family name. It passed through many hands, becoming a Royalist outpost and suffering in the process until, after a period of occupation by Parliamentary forces it was slighted in 1646. Bought by a kinsman of John Kemble, the damaged buildings were repaired and made habitable and after further restoration and rebuilding they have continued in private use ever since. Access to the internal courtyard is through the splendid 700 years old gatehouse facing the road between the Norman towers, and tucked away in the north-west corner is the 16th century chapel with a stone altar where John Kemble said Mass, and where he was arrested in 1678. The chapel and courtyard have for some time been open to the public on Thursday afternoons, free of charge.

Continue on down the minor road where there is a fine view back behind you of the western elevation of the castle, this road eventually leading to the B4521, Abergavenny to Ross-on-Wye road at Broad Oak. If there is time, it might be tempting to continue straight head towards Garway, and the Crusaders' church (p.204) higher up about 2 miles away, or turn left and descend the B4521 to Skenfrith Castle, one of The Three Castles (p.205), rather nearer. Otherwise, turn right onto the B4521 and enjoy views to the left and right on the way through Tretire before crossing the A466 and A4137 to join the A49. Then turn right for Peterstow and Bridstow before reaching the A40 roundabout, and the road straight ahead over Wilton Bridge to Ross-on-Wye.

Further Reading

Listed are some other books about the area published by Logaston Press and in print in April 2010:

Ludlow Castle: its History and Buildings *eds*. Ron Shoesmith & Andy Johnson
ISBN 978 1873827 51 2   £14.95
Several different authors provide chapters on different themes of the castle's history and buildings.

The Origins of Ludlow *by* David Lloyd
ISBN 978 1904396 95 6   £10
A study of the form and shape of the early settlement of the town.

The Fitzalans, Earls of Arundel and Surrey, Lords of the Welsh Marches (1267-1415) *by* Michael Burtscher
ISBN 978 1904396 94 9   £12.95
A detailed look at the Fitzalan family history and that of their estates.

English Architecture to 1900: The Shropshire Experience *by* Eric Mercer
ISBN 978 1904396 08 6   £20
An extensive study of Shropshire's architecture and how it compares with the national picture.

The Lead, Copper & Barytes Mines of Shropshire *by* Michael Shaw
ISBN 978 906663 09 4   £12.95
A detailed history of mining in south-west Shropshire.

A History of Presteigne *by* Keith Parker
ISBN 978 1873827 79 6   £12.95
A history of Presteigne, as you would expect!

Castles of Breconshire *by* Paul Remfry
ISBN 978 1873827 80 2   £8.95
A county guide for its castles.

Prehistoric Sites of Breconshire *by* George Children and George Nash
ISBN 978 1873827 57 4   £7.95
A county guide for its prehistoric sites.

The Book of Hay *by* Kate Clarke
ISBN 978 1873827 61 1   £6.95
A brief history of the town of Hay-on-Wye.

The Celtic Christian Sites of the central and southern Marches *by* Sarah & John Zaluckyj
ISBN 978 1 904396 57 4   £12.95
Covers all the early Christian sites along the central and southern Marches.

Merrily's Border: The Marches share their secrets *with* Phil Rickman & photographer John Mason
ISBN 978 1 906663 16 2   Hardback £20   ISBN 978 1 906663 17 9   Paperback £12.95
A look at where novelist Phil Rickman obtains his ideas.

Leominster Minster, Priory and Borough c660-1539 *by* Joe & Caroline Hillaby
ISBN 978 1904 396 55 0   £10
A detailed study of Leominster Minster and its connections with the town.

Leominster Revisited *by* Tim Ward
ISBN 978 1 906663 28 5   £10
A collection of photos and items portraying Leominster over the last 100 years or so.

The Castle Green at Hereford: A Landscape of Ritual, Royalty & Recreation *by* David Whitehead
ISBN: 978 1904396 77 2   £12.95
The history of St. Guthlac's Priory, Hereford Castle and the subsequent park.

Castles & Moated Sites of Herefordshire *by* Ron Shoesmith
ISBN 978 1 906663 30 8   £10
A gazetteer and history of all Herefordshire's castles.

Dore Abbey: A Definitive History *eds.* Ruth Richardson & Ron Shoesmith
ISBN 978 1873827 66 6   £14.95
Several authors provide chapters on different themes of the abbey's history, art and architecture.

Knights Templar & Hospitaller in Herefordshire *by* Audrey Tapper
ISBN 978 1904396 35 6   £4.95
A look at the places associated with and occupied by the Knights of both Orders in Herefordshire.

Herefordshire Churches through Victorian Eyes
ISBN 978 1 904396 59 8   £12.95
Victorian watercolours and descriptions of some of Herefordshire's churches.

Herefordshire Place-Names *by* Bruce Coplestone-Crow
ISBN 978 1 906663 21 6   £12.95
The derivation of Herefordshire place-names, from the city and towns down to individual farms.

Roses round the door? Rural Herefordshire, 1830s-1930s *by* Tim Ward
ISBN 978 1 906663 22 3   £12.95
Rural life in Herefordshire in words and photos between the 1830s and 1930s.

The Changing Face of Ross-on-Wye *by* Tim Ward
ISBN 978 1 904396 42 0   £12.95
A look at Ross in the last 150 or years so using old photographs and postcards.

The Story of Ross *by* Pat Hughes and Heather Hurley
ISBN 978 1 906663 25 45   £12.95
A detailed history of this town in the south of Herefordshire.

Landscapes of the Wye Tour *by* Susan Peterken
ISBN 978 1904396 89 5   £14.95
A study of the art of the Wye Tour, using old and modern works.

Chepstow Castle: its History & Buildings *eds.* Rick Turner & Andy Johnson
ISBN 978 1 904396 52 9   £17.50
Several different authors provide chapters on different themes of the castle's history and buildings.

Tewkesbury Abbey: History, Art and Architecture *eds.* Richard Morris & Ron Shoesmith
ISBN 978 1904396 03 1   £17.50
Some 20 authors provide chapters on different themes of the abbey's history, art and architecture.

Index

Index of Castles and Churches (also included in the main Index)